THE CAMBRIDGE COMPANION TO
LATIN AMERICAN POETRY

The Cambridge Companion to Latin American Poetry provides historical context on the evolution of the Latin American poetic tradition from the sixteenth century to the present day. It is organized into three parts. Part I provides a comprehensive, chronological survey of Latin American poetry and includes separate chapters on Colonial poetry, Romanticism/*modernismo*, the avant-garde, conversational poetry, and contemporary poetry. Part II contains six succinct chapters on the major figures Sor Juana Inés de la Cruz, Gabriela Mistral, César Vallejo, Pablo Neruda, Carlos Drummond de Andrade, and Octavio Paz. Part III analyzes specific and distinctive trends within the poetic canon, including women's, Quechua, Afro-Hispanic, Latino/a, and New Media poetry. This *Companion* also contains a guide to further reading as well as a chapter on the best English translations of Latin American poetry. It will be a key resource for students and instructors of Latin American literature and poetry.

Stephen M. Hart is Professor of Latin American Film, Literature, and Culture at University College London and founder-director of the Centre of César Vallejo Studies. He has been awarded the Order of Merit for Distinguished Services by the Peruvian government for his research on the life and work of Vallejo, made a Miembro Correspondiente by the Academia Peruana de la Lengua, and awarded the Order of Merit from the National University of Trujillo.

A complete list of books in the series is at the back of the book.

THE CAMBRIDGE
COMPANION TO
LATIN AMERICAN POETRY

EDITED BY
STEPHEN M. HART
University College London

CAMBRIDGE
UNIVERSITY PRESS

CAMBRIDGE
UNIVERSITY PRESS

University Printing House, Cambridge CB2 8BS, United Kingdom

One Liberty Plaza, 20th Floor, New York, NY 10006, USA

477 Williamstown Road, Port Melbourne, VIC 3207, Australia

314–321, 3rd Floor, Plot 3, Splendor Forum, Jasola District Centre,
New Delhi – 110025, India

79 Anson Road, #06–04/06, Singapore 079906

Cambridge University Press is part of the University of Cambridge.

It furthers the University's mission by disseminating knowledge in the pursuit of
education, learning, and research at the highest international levels of excellence.

www.cambridge.org
Information on this title: www.cambridge.org/9781107197695
DOI: 10.1017/9781108178648

First published 2018

Printed in the United States of America by Sheridan Books, Inc.

A catalogue record for this publication is available from the British Library.

Library of Congress Cataloging-in-Publication Data
NAMES: Hart, Stephen M. editor.
TITLE: The Cambridge companion to Latin American poetry / edited by
Stephen M. Hart, University College, London.
DESCRIPTION: Cambridge ; New York, NY : Cambridge University Press, [2018]. |
Includes bibliographical references and index.
IDENTIFIERS: LCCN 2017043870 | ISBN 9781107197695
SUBJECTS: LCSH: Latin American poetry – History and criticism. | Poets, Latin
American – Biography.
CLASSIFICATION: LCC PQ7082.P7 C23 2018 | DDC 861.009–dc23
LC record available at https://lccn.loc.gov/2017043870

ISBN 978-1-107-19769-5 Hardback
ISBN 978-1-316-64785-1 Paperback

CONTENTS

CONTENTS

ILLUSTRATIONS

NOTES ON CONTRIBUTORS

KAREN BENAVENTE is Visiting Associate Professor at the University of Texas–Rio Grande Valley. Her present research focuses on poetry and poetics in Luso-Hispanic Studies, primarily on the work of Jorge Luis Borges, María Zambrano, Gabriela Mistral, Cecília Meireles, and Walter Hugo Khouri. Her publications include *Poetry and The Realm of the Public Intellectual: The Alternative Destinies of Gabriela Mistral, Cecília Meireles, and Rosario Castellanos* (2007) and *Gabriela Mistral: Carta para muchos: España, 1933–1935* (2014).

BEN BOLLIG is Professor of Spanish American Literature at St Catherine's College, Oxford. He researches on contemporary literature and film in Latin America, with a particular focus on Argentine poetry. He recently completed a book, with the aid of a Research Fellowship from the Leverhulme Trust, under the title *Politics and Public Space in Contemporary Argentine Poetry. The Lyric and the State* (2016). His other recent books include a translation of Cristian Aliaga's *The Foreign Passion* (2016) and, with Alejandra Crosta, a volume of new British poetry in Spanish translation, *Antropófagos en las islas*, published in Argentina. He is an editor of *Journal of Latin American Cultural Studies* and a member of the advisory board for the Patagonian cultural supplement, *El extremo sur – Confines*.

RODRIGO CACHO CASAL is Reader in Spanish Golden Age and Colonial Studies at Clare College, Cambridge. His research focuses mainly on Renaissance and Baroque cultures and Spanish American colonial literature. His recent writings have been concerned with literary genres, such as burlesque and epic poetry, and the works of Francisco de Quevedo, which are treated in his latest monograph, *La esfera del ingenio: las silvas de Quevedo y la tradición europea* (2012). He also works on Colonial poetry, and has coedited a volume on Golden Age poetry *Los géneros poéticos del Siglo de Oro* (2013). He has recently been awarded a British Academy Mid-Career Fellowship and is currently preparing a monograph on Spanish American Colonial poetry.

SARA CASTRO-KLARÉN is Professor of Latin American Culture and Literature at The Johns Hopkins University. She has been the recipient of several teaching awards and, in 1993, the Foreign Service Institute conferred upon her the title of "Distinguished Visiting Lecturer." She was appointed to the Fulbright Board of Directors by President Clinton in 1999. Her publications include *El mundo mágico de José María Arguedas* (1973), *Understanding Mario Vargas Llosa* (1990), *Escritura, sujeto y transgresión en la literatura latinoamericana* (1989), *Latin American Women Writers* (1991), edited with Sylvia Molloy and Beatriz Sarlo, *A Companion to Latin American Literature and Culture* (2008), and *The Narrow Pass of Our Nerves: Writing Coloniality and Postcolonial Theory* (2011).

MICHAEL DOWDY is Associate Professor in the Department of English Language and Literature at the University of South Carolina. He has published *Broken Souths: Latina/o Poetic Responses to Neoliberalism and Globalization* (2013) and *American Political Poetry in the 21st Century* (2007). His essays have appeared in *American Poetry Review, Appalachian Journal, Aztlán: A Journal of Chicano Studies, Callaloo, College Literature, Hispanic Review, Journal of Modern Literature, MELUS*, and *The Writer's Chronicle*. With Claudia Rankine, he is coediting the forthcoming critical anthology, *American Poets in the 21st Century: Poetics of Social Engagement* (2018). As a poet, he has published a full-length collection, *Urbilly* (2017), and a chapbook, *The Coriolis Effect* (2007).

BRAD EPPS is Head of the Department of Spanish and Portuguese, and Professorial Fellow at King's College, Cambridge. He was previously Professor of Romance Languages and Literatures and Professor and former Chair of the Committee on Degrees in Studies of Women, Gender, and Sexuality at Harvard University for over two decades. His research interests include eighteenth- to twenty-first-century Spanish and Latin American literature, Catalan literature and film, Ibero-American cinema, photography, and art, Hispanophone Africa, theories of visuality, modernity, critical theory, gender and sexuality studies, feminist thought, queer theory, urban cultures, immigration, and postcolonial studies. He has published extensively on modern literature, film, art, architecture, urban culture, queer theory, and immigration from Spain, Latin America, Hispanophone Africa, and Catalonia, and is the author of *Significant Violence: Oppression and Resistance in the Narratives of Juan Goytisolo; Spain Beyond Spain: Modernity, Literary History*, and *National Identity* (with Luis Fernández Cifuentes); *Passing Lines: Immigration and Sexuality* (with Bill Johnson-González and Keja Valens); *All about Almodóvar: A Passion for Cinema* (with Despina Kakoudaki); a special issue of *Catalan Review* on Barcelona and modernity, and a special issue of *GLQ* (with Jonathan Katz) on lesbian theorist Monique Wittig, among other works. He is also Series Editor for the *Routledge Companions to Hispanic and Latin American Studies*. He has taught as visiting professor or scholar in Spain (Galicia, Catalonia, the Basque Country, and Madrid), Germany, France, Chile, Cuba, the Netherlands, Sweden, and the People's Republic of China, and has given public lectures throughout Europe, the Americas, and China.

ADAM FEINSTEIN is an acclaimed author, translator, journalist, and Hispanist. His biography, *Pablo Neruda: a Passion for Life*, was first published in 2004 and reissued in an updated edition in 2013 (Harold Pinter called it "a masterpiece"). Also in 2013, Feinstein launched *Cantalao*, a biannual magazine dedicated to Neruda's life and work. Feinstein's translations of Neruda, Lorca, Benedetti, and others have appeared in many publications, including *Modern Poetry in Translation* and *Agenda*. His book of translations from Neruda's *Canto General*, with color illustrations by the Brazilian artist Ana Maria Pacheco, was published in 2013. He also wrote the introduction to the Folio Edition of Jorge Luis Borges' *Labyrinths*, which appeared in 2007. He has written for *The Guardian*, the *TLS*, and the *New Statesman* and has broadcast for the BBC on Neruda and autism. He is currently writing a novel, as well as preparing a book on Cuban cultural policy since the Revolution.

VALENTINO GIANUZZI is Lecturer in Latin American Cultural Studies at the University of Manchester. His research interests include César Vallejo, Latin American avant-gardes, Latin American poetry, Peruvian literature, Latin American literary magazines and print culture, fin-de-siècle and early twentieth-century intellectual history, journalism and transatlantic literary relations, translation and cultural mediation, and textual scholarship. His publications include "César Vallejo's Journalism in Context: A Quest for Autonomy" (2013); (with C. Fernández), *César Vallejo en Madrid en 1931: Itinerario documental* (2012); (with M. Smith), *César Vallejo: The Complete Poems* (2012); and (with C. Fernández), *César Vallejo, textos rescatados* (2009).

STEPHEN M. HART is Professor of Latin American Film, Literature, and Culture at University College London. His main research specialism is the life and work of the Peruvian poet César Vallejo. He is founder-director of the Centre of César Vallejo Studies at University College London (UCL) and he has published a number of works on Vallejo, including *César Vallejo: A Literatury Biography* (2013; Spanish translation with Cátedra Vallejo, 2014). He has been awarded two Orders of Merit, one from the Peruvian government and the other from the National University of Trujillo as a result of his published research on Peru's national poet. He is currently writing a new biography of Santa Rosa de Lima and producing a critical edition of the Apostolic Process in a research project funded by the British Academy and the Leverhulme Trust.

ALISON KRÖGEL is Associate Professor of Spanish at the University of Denver. Her research includes studies of the roles played by food in colonial and contemporary Spanish American literature and culture, artistic representations of resistance by the Quechua people in colonial and contemporary contexts, as well as Quechua poetry and oral traditions. The recipient of a Fulbright Research Grant to Ecuador (2013–2014), she has published the monograph *Food, Power and Resistance in Quechua Verbal and Visual Narratives* (2011), as well as articles in journals such as *Revista de Crítica Literaria Latinoamericana, Journal of Latin American and Caribbean Anthropology, Food and Foodways, Revista de Estudios Bolivianos*, and *Kipus: Revista Andina de Letras*. Her current book project focuses on contemporary Quechua poetry.

MARTHA OJEDA is Professor of Spanish and French at Transylvania University where she teaches courses on Latin American Culture and Civilization, Latin American Literature, and Afro-Hispanic Literature. Her publications include "Búsqueda y negación del yo en 'Malambo' de Lucía Charún-Illescas" (2004); "Nicomedes Santa Cruz and the Vindication of Afro-Peruvian Culture," in *Contemporary Latin American Cultural Studies*, ed. Stephen Hart and Richard Young (2003); and the monograph, *Nicomedes Santa Cruz: Ecos de África en Perú* (2003).

CHARLES A. PERRONE is Professor of Portuguese and Luso-Brazilian Culture and Literatures at the University of Florida. He has published widely on Brazilian culture and poetry, and his publications include monographs such as *Brazil, Lyric, and the Americas* (2010); *Seven Faces: Brazilian Poetry Since Modernism* (1996); and *Masters of Contemporary Brazilian Song: MPB 1965–1985* (1989; reprint 1993); along with edited volumes such as *First World Third Class and Other Tales of the Global Mix* (2005); *Brazilian Popular Music and Globalization* (2001); and *Crônicas Brasileiras: A Reader* (2014).

THEA PITMAN is Senior Lecturer in Latin American Studies at the University of Leeds. Her research career started with work on travel writing produced by Mexican authors, published in book form as *Mexican Travel Writing* (2007). It has since evolved to focus on the subject of Latin American online, and more broadly digital, cultural production. This work is published in article form as well as in the coedited anthology *Latin American Cyberculture and Cyberliterature* (with Claire Taylor, 2007), and the coauthored monograph *Latin American Identity in Online Cultural Production* (also with Claire Taylor, 2013).

CECILIA ENJUTO RANGEL is Associate Professor of Spanish in the Department of Romance Languages at the University of Oregon. Her research interests include nineteenth- and twentieth-century Spanish and Latin American poetry; transatlantic studies; comparative literature; and literature, cinema, and history. Her publications include the monograph *Cities in Ruins: The Politics of Modern Poetics* (2010) and articles such as "La mirada nostálgica del exilio en *En el balcón vacío* (1962)," in *Exiliados y cosmopolitas en el mundo hispánico*, ed. Araceli Tinajero (2013); "Góngora, Unamuno y el 27 en clave transatlántica," in *Reyes, Borges, Ramón: La vida literaria en Madrid de los años 20*, ed. Julio Ortega (2011); and "Tres generaciones del exilio: la memoria guardada," in *L'exil espagnol dans les Amériques*, ed. Carmen Vásquez (2011).

ADAM JOSEPH SHELLHORSE is Associate Professor of Spanish, Portuguese, and Global Studies at Temple University, where he serves as the advisor of the Portuguese and Brazilian Studies Program. His research examines modern and contemporary Latin American literature and poetics, visual culture, critical theory and women's writing, with particular emphasis on comparative Inter-American studies and the relationship between aesthetics, affect, and politics. His publications include the monograph *Anti-Literature: The Politics and Limits of Representation in Modern Brazil and Argentina* (2017)–which is currently being translated into Portuguese by Editora Perspectiva for its Estudos series; and articles such as "A Poetics of Resistance and Multiplicity: Valle-Inclán, Spanish Theater, and War in the Work of Dru Dougherty. Or Lessons of a Master," (2017); "Subversions of the Sensible: The Poetics of Antropofagia in Brazilian Concrete Poetry," (2015); "Formas de Fome: Anti-Literature and the Politics of Representation in Haroldo de Campos's Galáxias," (2014); and "The Explosion of the Letter: The Crisis of the Poetic and Representation in João Cabral de Melo Neto's Morte e Vida Severina: auto de Natal pernambucano," (2013).

JASON WILSON is Emeritus Professor of University College London. Since his retirement in 2008 he has published *The Andes. A Cultural History* (2009), *Buenos Aires* (2014), and *Living in the Sound of the Wind. A Personal Quest for W. H. Hudson, Naturalist and Writer from the River Plate* (2015), as well as translating *Jorge Luis Borges & Osvaldo Ferrari, Conversations 1* (2014). He remains a judge for the prestigious Valle-Inclán translation prize.

PREFACE

Stephen M. Hart

– "An Aymara poet said to Vicente Huidobro: 'The poet is a
god, don't sing about rain, poet. Make it rain.'"

"Buena lengua nos dio España, pero nos parece que
no puede quejarse de que se la hayamos maltratado."
(Spain gave us a good language, but she can't complain if
we mistreat it.) José Martí

There is a wonderful scene in Pablo Larraín's witty and controversial film
Neruda (2016), in which Pablo Neruda's wife Delia (Mercedes Morán)
meets the detective, Oscar Peluchonneau (Gael García Bernal), who is pursuing her husband and, in a "sharp meta take on the concept of character and
story,"[1] tells him that he is a "secondary character" in Neruda's story, and
that Neruda "created" him. While this may be a sly reference to the possibility that Neruda (Luis Gnecco) is his unacknowledged father – since Neruda
lies hidden among the prostitutes at precisely the time when Peluchonneau
raids the brothel and, believing himself rather grandly to be the son of the
founder of Chile's penal system, instead "discovers" that he may have been
born there in that very brothel – it is also more importantly an allusion to the
mysterious status of the poet-magician who, in earlier phases of humanity as
well as during the Romantic era, was seen to have God-like creative powers
because of his skill with words. This very "Nerudian" film about Latin
America's arguably most important poet[2] shows that the poet is in direct
connection with the world, with men and with women, with nature, with
trees and animals and birds, with words and politics – the true ruler of the
world. This book celebrates and analyzes the special place that the poet
occupies in the field of the arts, and particularly in a part of the globe that
is more well known for its novels and its films than for its poetry.

One of the reasons for Latin America's poetry being less celebrated than
other genres in the subcontinent is the fact that – apart from a few iconic

---

[1] Benjamin Lee, "*Neruda* Review – Unconventional Drama Constructs Rather than Retells
Chilean Poet's Life," *The Guardian* (May 14, 2016).
[2] Larraín described his film as a "Nerudian" take on Neruda's life; see Jay Weissberg, "Film
Review: *Neruda*," *Variety* (May 13, 2016); http://variety.com/2016/film/festivals/cannes-
film-review-neruda-1201773713/.

figures such as Neruda himself, the Mexican Sor Juana Inés de la Cruz, and the Peruvian César Vallejo – there is very little agreement about who the main poets are. As the editors of *The Oxford Book of Latin American Poetry* point out: "Latin America has a complex and prolific poetic tradition that is little known outside its geographic and linguistic boundaries. Although a few poets such as Borges, Neruda and Paz have become emblematic of its richness, many voices remain unheard."[3] The point is well taken, even though, at first flush, the evidence seems stacked up against it. There is, after all, no lack of published anthologies of Latin American poetry, ranging from Antonio R. de la Campa and Raquel Chang-Rodríguez's anthology of colonial poetry (1985) to José Olivio Jiménez's anthology covering the period 1914–1987 (1988). There are even a number of respectable bilingual anthologies produced by Anglo-Saxon publishers; notable examples are Stephen Tapscott's and Ludwig Zeller's anthologies, both of which came out in 1996, as well as Cecilia Vicuña and Ernesto Livon-Grosman's 2009 collection and Ilan Stavans' 2011 poetic gathering.[4] These different anthologies suggest that the public likes to read Latin American poetry. But what these books also highlight is that – if the respective editors were to draw up a list of the "best" Latin American poets – each would come up with a different list. So, for example, of the sixteen poets chosen by Ludwig Zweller to represent "Spanish America," twelve were not included in Stephen Tapscott's bilingual anthology of *Twentieth-Century Latin American Poetry*.[5] Jacobo Sefamí's bibliography of primary and secondary sources for "Contemporary Spanish American Poets" lists poets whose work also does not appear in Tapscott's bilingual anthology. A spot-check based on poets beginning with "A" reveals that of the four listed only one is in Tapscott.[6] At times the lack of coincidence between different publications is striking. Not one single poet

[3] "Preface," in *The Oxford Book of Latin American Poetry: A Bilingual Anthology,* ed. Cecilia Vicuña and Ernesto Livon-Grosman (Oxford: Oxford University Press, 2009), xii.
[4] Antonio R. de la Campa & Raquel Chang-Rodríguez, *Poesía hispanoamericana colonial; antología* (Madrid: Editorial Alhambra, 1985); José Olivio Jiménez, *Antología de la poesía hispanoamericana contemporánea: 1914–1987* (Madrid: Alianza, 1988); Stephen Tapscott, *Twentieth-Century Latin American Poetry* (Austin, TX: University of Texas Press, 1996); Ludwig Zeller, *The Invisible Presence: Sixteen Poets of Spanish America 1925–1995* (Oakville, ON: Mosaic Press, 1996); *The FSG Book of Twentieth-Century Latin American Poetry*, ed. Ilan Stavans (New York: Farrar, Straus and Giroux, 2011).
[5] The poets not included were Rosamel del Valle, César Moro, Enrique Gómez-Correa, Braulio Arenas, Jorge Cáceres, Ludwig Zeller, José María Arguedas, Pablo de Rokha, César Davila Andrade, Aldo Pellegrini, Eduardo Anguita, Humberto Díaz-Casanueva; the four included were Enrique Molina, Alvaro Mutis, Olga Orozco, and Gonzalo Rojas, a coincidence rate of 25%. See Ludwig Zweller, *The Invisible Presence: Sixteen Poets of Spanish America 1925–1995* (Oakville, ON: Mosaic Press, 1996).
[6] Jorge Enrique Adoum, Roberto Appratto, and Braulio Arenas are not in Tapscott but Homero Aridjis is – a coincidence once more of 25%; see Jacobo Sefamí, *Contemporary*

included in Rafael Aráiz Lucca's anthology of twentieth-century Venezuelan poetry, his *Antología: la poesía del siglo XX en Venezuela,* coincides with Tapscott's anthology.[7] One could be forgiven for thinking that the relationship between critics, historians, and anthologists of Latin American poetry is – to borrow Rodríguez Monegal's resonant phrase – a "dialogue between the deaf."[8] The problem is not only that no agreed canon of Latin American poets exists. As Donald Shaw points out, there is a "virtual absence of any critical framework within which we can situate all but the most famous of the individual poets."[9]

There are – it is true – many studies dedicated to the major figures of the poetic canon such as Rubén Darío, César Vallejo, Pablo Neruda, and Octavio Paz, as Shaw suggests, although these only serve to draw attention to a nagging feeling about the ones who missed the bus. There are also significant books on important poetic movements such as Gwen Kirkpatrick's *The Dissonant Legacy of Modernismo* (1989) and on national traditions, especially the Argentine, such as Jill Kuhnheim's *Gender, Politics and Poetry in Twentieth-Century Argentina* (1996) and Ben Bollig's *Politics and Public Space in Contemporary Argentine Poetry* (2016).[10] There are excellent studies of twentieth-century verse – such as Mike Gonzalez and David Treece's wide-ranging and insightful *The Gallery of Voices* (1992), William Rowe's thoughtful *Poets of Contemporary Latin America* (2000), Jill Kuhnheim's comprehensive *Spanish American Poetry at the End of the Twentieth Century* (2004), and Donald Shaw's measured *Beyond the Vanguard* (2008).[11] But there are surprisingly few studies of Latin

---

Spanish American Poets: A Bibliography of Primary and Secondary Sources (New York: Greenwood Press, 1992), 1–8.

[7] Rafael Aráiz Lucca, ed., *Antología: la poesía del siglo XX en Venezuela* (Madrid: La Estafeta del Viento, n. d).

[8] Rodríguez-Monegal used this expression to describe early discussions of the meaning and import of magical realism; see "Realismo mágico versus literatura fantástica: un diálogo de sordos," *Otros mundos, otros fuegos: fantasia y realismo mágico en Iberoamérica* (East Lansing, MI: Latin American Studies Center, Michigan State University, 1975), 25–37.

[9] Donald Shaw, *Beyond the Vanguard: Spanish American Poetry after 1950* (Woodbridge: Tamesis, 2008), 156.

[10] Gwen Kirkpatrick, *The Dissonant Legacy of Modernism: Lugones, Herrera y Reissig, and the Voices of Modern Spanish American Poetry* (Berkeley: University of California Press, 1989); Jill Kuhnheim, *Gender, Politics and Poetry in Twentieth-Century Argentina* (Gainesville: University Press of Florida, 1996); Ben Bollig, *Politics and Public Space in Contemporary Argentine Poetry. The Lyric and the State* (New York: Palgrave Macmillan, 2016).

[11] Mike Gonzalez and David Treece, *The Gallery of Voices: Twentieth-Century Poetry of Latin America* (London: Verso, 1992); William Rowe's *Poets of Contemporary Latin America* (Oxford: Oxford University Press, 2000); Jill Kuhnheim, *Spanish American Poetry at the End of the Twentieth Century: Textual Disruptions* (Austin: University of

American poetry as an evolutionary genre from colonial times to the present day. The notable exception is Gordon Brotherston's classic study *Latin American Poetry: Origins and Presence* (1975), but even this study, which appears to address the whole canon, in fact homes in mainly on the big names (with Rubén Darío, César Vallejo, Pablo Neruda, and Octavio Paz forming the backbone of the book) while marginalizing the poetry of earlier years. The notion that "writing a history of Latin American poetry before Modernism is uninviting because there is little to say"[12] has been superseded by subsequent research on poets such as Sor Juana Inés de la Cruz, Alonso de Ercilla y Zúñiga, Bernardo de Balbuena, Juan del Valle Caviedes, Mariano Melgar, José Joaquín de Olmedo, Andrés Bello, José María Heredia, Gonçalves de Magalhães, Manuel Antônio Alvares de Azevedo, Gertrudis Gómez de Avellaneda, and José Asunción Silva, to name but a few. This book is justified by the fact that no comprehensive and up-to-date history of Latin American poetry is currently available; the most comprehensive study is still Brotherston's monograph, which is now nearly 40 years old.

The emphasis in current research on Latin American poetry on the big figures in the field – who, in our revised version, are Sor Juana Inés de la Cruz, Gabriela Mistral, César Vallejo, Pablo Neruda, Carlos Drummond de Andrade, and Octavio Paz – has had the effect, we believe, of deflecting scholars away from the study of the evolution of Latin American verse from its foundation in the sixteenth century to the present day. And therefore, for example, we lose a sense of that visceral shock which gripped Latin American literary circles when poets – in the first few decades of the twentieth century – turned away from nature, melancholy, and love, and began writing about life in the big city, neon lights, fast cars, and the irrational, and threw all their rhyme schemes into the dustbin of history. But some of the flavor of that jump-cut is present, we hope, in this volume when passing from Chapter 2 to Chapter 3. This focus on the big names of Latin American poetry also had another, perhaps unintended, consequence, namely the marginalization of poetry written in, for example, the Amerindian languages, as well as women's writing, and LGBTQ and Afro-Hispanic poetry. So we decided that the best way to address, on the one hand, the continuity of the Latin American poetic tradition as well as, on the other, its heterogeneity was to divide the book into three parts. Part I, thus, focuses on the historical development of the Latin American lyric, beginning with Colonial poetry, followed by an analysis of Romantic, *modernista*, and avant-garde poetry,

Texas Press, 2004); Donald Shaw, *Beyond the Vanguard: Spanish American Poetry after 1950*.
[12] *Latin American Poetry: Origins and Presence* (Cambridge: Cambridge University Press, 1975), 5.

and concludes with two chapters on conversational poetry (corresponding roughly to the 1950s, 1960s, and 1970s) and contemporary poetry from 1980 onwards. Part II studies the value and impact of the work of the six key figures mentioned above – namely, Sor Juana Inés de la Cruz, Gabriela Mistral, César Vallejo, Pablo Neruda, Carlos Drummond de Andrade, and Octavio Paz. Part III, entitled "Diversity and Heterogeneity," addresses a number of crucial subgenres within Latin American verse, ranging from the "traditional" subaltern genres such as women's, Amerindian, and Afro-Hispanic poetry to "newer" fields such as LGBTQ, Latino, and New Media verse. The aim of this third part is to create new hermeneutic vantage points from which to survey and then dig down into the deeper layers of Latin American poetry, and we hope thereby to offer a more inclusive snap-shot of the richness of the Latin American lyric. In order to address the problem of different groups of poets included in existing anthologies of Latin American verse, we also decided to include a chronology of the main poetic "events" that occurred in Latin America from the sixteenth century until the present day. We also attempted to bridge one of the least acknowl-edged divides that characterizes Latin American studies: Spanish America versus Brazil.[13] So, in each of our separate chapters, we sought to provide a more even coverage of Spanish American *and* Brazilian authors; Chapter 12 is exemplary in this regard. This book also includes a final chapter on Latin American poetry available in English translation which is designed to orient the English-speaking reader interested in finding out more about Latin American poetry.

The aim of the *Cambridge Companion to Latin American Poetry* is to provide the long view (namely, by supplying some historical context on the evolution of the Latin American poetic tradition from the sixteenth century to the present day) as well as the contemporary view (i.e. a balanced and up-to-date evaluation of some of the new voices that are emerging in Latin American poetry of the twenty-first century). Neither an overview nor a casual collection, the *Cambridge Companion to Latin American Poetry*, consists of a set of scholarly meditations on the history and evolution of Latin American poetry from its Amerindian roots until the present day. Each chapter is written by a leading scholar and offers an original contribution to the field. The methodological aim here is to incorporate a variety of theore-tical and critical perspectives in a history that seeks to move beyond the

---

[13] In my study, *A Companion to Latin American Literature* (Woodbridge: Tamesis, 2007), I suggest that analyzing Latin American literature – rather than its poetry specifically – "in its Portuguese- as well as Spanish-language manifestations is often like watching a three-legged race (two individuals more or less moving in the same direction but often tugging against each other)"; p. 288.

limitations of existing literary historical narratives about Latin American poetry. In this sense each of the eighteen chapters can be read as an independent and self-contained unit. All bibliographical references are contained within each individual chapter, and the concluding bibliography is not a works cited, but instead focuses on general and more generic studies of Latin American poetry. Even so, there are a number of ways in which the chapters in this collection bounce off one another: the Mexican, Sor Juana Inés de la Cruz, is mentioned, for example, in Chapter 1 and has a whole chapter dedicated to her work (Chapter 6); the Chilean, Pablo Neruda, is an important reference point in Chapter 4 and has his own chapter later on (Chapter 9); the Peruvian, César Vallejo, is analyzed from different perspectives in Chapters 4 and 10; the Brazilian, Carlos Drummond de Andrade, is mentioned in Chapters 3 and 10; and the Argentine, Alejandra Pizarnik, pops up in different guises in Chapters 3, 5, 12, and 13.

This book is intended for the undergraduate and graduate students who are pursuing the academic study of Latin American poetry in individual courses and formal programs of study at university. The *Cambridge Companion to Latin American Poetry* will also, we hope, appeal to scholars who are not specialists in the field but whose interest is piqued by their awareness of the work of some Latin American authors – such as the Colombian Gabriel García Márquez and the Peruvian Mario Vargas Llosa, both of whom have acquired much notoriety as a result of winning the Nobel Prize in Literature – whose international impact has been widespread. All quotations of the poetry are provided in the original text as well as in English translation. We hope, therefore, that the *Cambridge Companion to Latin American Poetry* will draw on the appetite for, and interest in, Latin American literature stimulated by the successful *Cambridge Companion to the Latin American Novel*. Because the chapters are reflective and speculative, yet grounded in particular texts and literary conventions, we believe that the *Cambridge Companion to Latin American Poetry* will speak to the academy as well as reach out to new readerships further afield.

S.M.H.

CHRONOLOGY

1539	The first printing press was established in the New World in Mexico City
1560	Cervantes de Salazar, *Túmulo imperial a las exequias de Carlos V*
1569–1589	Alonso de Ercilla y Zúñiga, *La Araucana*
1583	A poetical tournament ("certamen poético") was established in Mexico City in which around 300 individuals participated
1584	A printing press was established in the City of Kings (Lima, Peru)
1589	Juan de Castellanos, *Elegías de varones ilustres de Indias*
1596	Pedro de Oña, *Arauco domado*
1598	Fray Luis Jerónimo de Oré, *Símbolo católico indiano*; Mateo Rosas de Oquendo, *Sátira hecha por Mateo Rosas de Oquendo a las cosas que pasan en el Pirú, año de 1598*
1599	Antonio de Saavedra Guzmán, *El peregrino indiano*
1601	Bento Teixeira, *Prosopopéia*
1602	Martín del Barco Centenera, *Argentina y conquista del Río de la Plata*; Diego Dávalos y Figueroa, *Miscelánea austral*
1604	Bernardo de Balbuena, *Grandeza mexicana*
1608	Diego Mexía de Fernangil, *Parnaso antártico*
1609	Luis de Belmonte Bermúdez, *Vida del padre maestro Ignacio de Loyola*
1611	Diego de Hojeda, *La Cristiada*
1613	Martín de León, *Relación de las exequias en la muerte de la reina nuestra señora doña Margarita*
1619	Diego Cano Gutiérrez, *Relación de las fiestas triunfales que la insigne Universidad de Lima hizo a la Inmaculada Concepción de Nuestra Señora*
1624	Bernardo de Balbuena, *El Bernardo o victoria de Roncesvalles*

1875	Antônio de Casto Alves, *Gonzaga ou a revolução de Minas*
1876	José Martí, *Amor con amor se paga*
1878	José Martí, *Guatemala*
1879	José Hernández, *La vuelta de Martín Fierro*, Part II (narrative poetry)
1880	Antônio de Casto Alves, *Voces d'Africa-navío negrerio*
1882	José Martí, *Versos libres; Ismaelillo*
1885	José Martí, *Amistad funesta* (pseudonym); João da Cruz e Sousa, *Tropas e fantasias* (in collaboration with Virgílio Várzea); Rubén Darío, *Epístolas y poemas*
1887	Rubén Darío, *Abrojos; Rimas*
1888	The year when Rubén Darío, with the publication of *Azul...*, was said – in a poetic sense – to have sent Spain's galleons back to Spain
1888	Olavo Bilac, *Poesias*
1891	José Martí, *Versos sencillos*
1893	João da Cruz e Sousa, *Broquéis; Missal* (prose poems); José Santos Chocano, *La selva virgen*
1895	Francisca Júlia, *Mármores*
1895	José Santos Chocano, *En la aldea*
1896	Rubén Darío, *Los raros; Prosas profanas*
1897	Leopoldo Lugones, *Las montañas del oro*
1898	Amado Nervo, *Místicas; Perlas negras*; João da Cruz e Sousa, *Evocações*
1899	Ricardo Jaimes Freyre, *Castalia bárbara*
1900	João da Cruz e Sousa, *Faróis*
1901	José Santos Chocano, *El canto del siglo*
1901	José Santos Chocano, *El fin de Satán*
1902	Rubén Darío, *La caravana pasa*; Julio Herrera y Reissig, *Los maitines de la noche*; Amado Nervo, *El éxodo y las flores del camino*
1903	Enrique González Martínez, *Preludios*; José Batres Montúfar, *Las falsas apariencias [Tradiciones de Guatemala]* (narrative poetry)
1904	José Santos Chocano, *Cantos del Pacífico*; Julio Herrera y Reissig, *Los éxtasis de la montaña*
1905	Leopoldo Lugones, *Los crepúsculos del jardín*; João da Cruz e Sousa, *Últimos sonetos*; Rubén Darío, *Cantos de vida y esperanza*
1906	José Santos Chocano, *Alma América*

1907	Rubén Darío, *El canto errante*; Delmira Agustini, *El libro blanco*
1908	José Santos Chocano, *¡Fiat Lux!*
1909	Julio Herrera y Reissig, *Los peregrinos de piedra;* Leopoldo Lugones, *Lunario sentimental*
1910	Rubén Darío, *Poema del otoño;* Delmira Agustini, *Cantos de la mañana*
1911	This was the year when the Mexican poet, Enrique González Martínez, declared the imminent demise of *modernismo* with the injunction to his contemporary poets: "Wring the swan's neck"; Vicente Huidobro, *Ecos del alma*; José María Eguren, *Simbólicas*
1912	The year in which Vicente Huidobro – according to his own account – initiated the poetic movement, *Creacionismo* (Creationism); Leopoldo Lugones, *El libro fiel*; Augusto dos Anjos, *Eu*
1913	Vicente Huidobro, *Canciones en la noche*; Delmira Agustini, *Los cálices vacíos*
1914	Rubén Darío, *Canto a la Argentina*; Gabriela Mistral, *Sonetos de la muerte*
1915	Enrique González Martínez, *La muerte del cisne*; Luis Palés Matos, *Azaleas*
1916	Ramón López Velarde, *La sangre devota*
1916	Alfonsina Storni, *La inquietud del rosal*
1917	Manuel Bandeira, *A cinza das horas*; Ricardo Jaimes Freyre, *Los sueños son vida*
1918	The year in which the avant-garde movement "*Ultraísmo*" was born in Spain; César Vallejo, *Los heraldos negros*; Vicente Huidobro, *Tour Eiffel; Hallali, poème de guerre; Ecuatorial; Poemas árticos*
1919	Cecília Meireles, *Espectros*; Juana de Ibarbourou, *Las lenguas de diamante*
1920	José Juan Tablada, *Li-Po y otros poemas*; Juana de Ibarbourou, *El cántaro fresco*
1921	Vicente Huidobro, *Saisons choisies*; Carlos Pellicer, *Colores en el mar*
1922	On 13, 15, and 17 February of this year, the "Semana de Arte Moderna" (Week of Modern Art), held in the Municipal Theatre in São Paolo, had an enormous impact on literary and artistic circles in Brazil and beyond; it was also the year in which some canonic poetic works were published, including

	César Vallejo, *Trilce*; Mário de Andrade, *Paulicéa desvairada*; Gabriela Mistral, *Desolación*; and Oliverio Girondo, *Veinte poemas para ser leídos en el tranvía*
1922–30	Enriqueta Arvelo Larriva, *El cristal nervioso*
1923	Pablo Neruda, *Crepusculario*; Oswald de Andrade, *Memórias sentimentais de João Miramar*; Jorge Luis Borges, *Fervor de Buenos Aires*
1924	Pablo Neruda, *Veinte poemas de amor y una canción desesperada*; Manuel Bandeira, *O ritmo dissoluto*; Gabriela Mistral, *Ternura*
1925	Oswald de Andrade, *Pau Brasil*; Jorge Luis Borges, *Luna de enfrente*
1926	Mário de Andrade, *Losango Cáqui*; Xavier Villaurrutia, *Reflejos*
1927	Mário de Andrade, *Clã do jabuti*; Jaime Torres Bodet, *Margarita de niebla*
1928	Oswald de Andrade, *Manifesto antropófago*; Martín Adán, *La casa de cartón*
1929	Henriqueta Lisboa, *Enternecimento*; Regino E. Boti, *Kodak-Ensueño*
1930	Nicolás Guillén, *Motivos de son*; Juana de Ibarbourou, *La rosa de los vientos*
1930–39	Enriqueta Arvelo Larriva, *Voz aislada*
1931	José Lezama Lima, *Muerte de Narciso*; Nicolás Guillén, *Sóngoro Cosongo*; Vicente Huidobro, *Altazor, o el viaje en paracaídas*
1932	Ramón López Velarde, *El son del corazón*
1933	Octavio Paz, *Luna silvestre*; Pablo Neruda, *Residencia en la tierra, 1925–1931*
1934	Carlos Drummond de Andrade, *Brejo das almas*; Alfonsina Storni, *El mundo de siete pozos*
1935	Jorge de Lima, *A túnica inconsútil*; Jorge Carrera Andrade, *El tiempo manual*
1936	Outbreak of the Spanish Civil War (1936–1939) which drew an exalted response from a number of Latin American poets who were appalled by news of the savagery occurring in Spain; Henriqueta Lisboa, *Velário*; Efraín Huerta, *Línea del alba*; Pablo Neruda, *España en el corazón*
1937	In July of this year, a number of Latin American poets – including Pablo Neruda, César Vallejo, Vicente Huidobro, Octavio Paz and Nicolás Guillén – went to Spain to attend the

Second Congress of the International Association of Writers
for the Defense of Culture in order to express their solidarity
for the Republican cause; Octavio Paz, *Bajo tu clara sombra*;
Nicolás Guillén, *España; West Indies Ltd.; Cantos para sol-
dados y sones para turistas*

1938	Gabriela Mistral, *Tala*; Alfonsina Storni, *Mascarilla y trébol*
1939	José Gorostiza, *Muerte sin fin*; César Vallejo, *Poemas humanos*
1940	César Vallejo, *España, aparta de mí este cáliz*; Carlos Drummond de Andrade, *Sentimento do mundo*
1941	Octavio Paz, *Entre la piedra y la flor*; Xavier Villaurrutia, *Invitación a la muerte*
1942	João Cabral de Melo Neto, *Pedra do sono*; Octavio Paz, *A la orilla del mundo*
1943	Henriqueta Lisboa, *O menino poeta*; Nicolás Guillén, *Sóngoro Cosongo y otros poemas*
1944	César Moro, *Lettre d'amour*; Carlos Drummond de Andrade, *A rosa do povo*
1945	Gabriela Mistral wins the Nobel Prize in Literature, the first Latin American poet to do so
1945	Oswald de Andrade, *Ponta de lança*; João Cabral de Melo Neto, *O engenheiro*
1946	Mário de Andrade, *Lyra Paulistana*; Olga Orozco, *Desde lejos*
1947	Claudia Lars, *Sonetos*; Ernesto Cardenal, *Proclama del conquistador*
1948	Álvaro Mutis, *La balanza*; Rosario Castellanos, *Trayectoria del polvo*
1949	Octavio Paz, *Libertad bajo palabra*; Sebastián Salazar Bondy, *Máscara del que duerme*
1950	Pablo Neruda, *Canto general*; João Cabral de Melo Neto, *O cão sem plumas*
1951	Olga Orozco, *Las muertes*; Octavio Paz, *¿Águila o sol?*
1952	Cecília Meireles, *Doze noturnos da Holanda e o aeronauta*; Jorge de Lima, *Invenção de Orfeo*
1953	Álvaro Mutis, *Los elementos del desastre*; Pablo Neruda, *Los versos del capitán*; Augusto de Campos, *Poetamenos*
1954	Ferreira Gullar, *A luta corporal*
1954	Pablo Neruda, *Odas elementales*; Nicanor Parra, *Poemas y antipoemas*; Octavio Paz, *Semillas para un himno*
1955	Alejandra Pizarnik, *La tierra más ajena*; Claudia Lars, *Escuela de pájaros*

1955	João Cabral de Melo Neto, *Morte e vida severina: auto de Natal pernambucana*
1956	Oliverio Girondo, *En la másmedula*; Mario Benedetti, *Poemas de la oficina*
1956	The inaugural exhibition of concrete art, at the Museum of Modern Art São Paulo–*Exposição Nacional de Arte Concreta*–featured neo-avant-garde poster poems alongside artworks and marked the official launching of Brazilian concrete poetry. Notable contributors included Augusto and Haroldo de Campos, Décio Pignatari, Ronaldo Azeredo, Ferreira Gullar, and Wlademir Dias-Pino
1957	Wáshington Delgado, *Días del corazón*; Octavio Paz, *Piedra de sol*
1958	Octavio Paz, *La estación violenta*; Pablo Neruda, *Extravagario*; Roberto Juarroz, *Poesía vertical* (subsequent editions in 1963, 1965, 1969, 1974, 1976, 1982, 1984, 1988)
1959	Nicomedes Santa Cruz, *Décimas*; Eugenio Montejo, *Humano paraíso*
1960	Ernesto Cardenal, *Hora o*; Sebastián Salazar Bondy, *Confidencia en voz alta*
1961	Martín Adán, *Escrito a ciegas*; Carlos Germán Belli, *¡Oh Hada Cibernética!*
1962	Nicanor Parra, *Versos de salón*; Alejandra Pizarnik, *Árbol de Diana*; Octavio Paz, *Salamandra*
1963	Roque Dalton, *El turno del ofendido*; Enrique Lihn, *La pieza oscura*
1964	Violeta Parra, *Poesía popular y de los Andes*; Antonio Cisneros, *Comentarios reales*
1965	Alejandra Pizarnik, *Los trabajos y las noches*; Ernesto Cardenal, *Oración por Marilyn Monroe y otros poemas*
1965	Affonso Romano de Sant'Anna, *Canto e palavra*
1965	Augusto de Campos, Haroldo de Campos, and Décio Pignatari, *Teoria da poesia concreta*
1966	João Cabral de Melo Neto, *A educação pela pedra; Morte e vida Severina e outros poemas em voz alta*; Nicomedes Santa Cruz, *Canto a mi Perú*
1967	Décio Pignatari, *Poesia, pois é poesia*
1967	Jorge Luis Borges, *Obra poética 1923–1967*; Octavio Paz, *Blanco*; Gabriela Mistral, *Poema de Chile*
1968	Antonio Cisneros, *Canto ceremonia contra un oso hormiguero*; Octavio Paz, *Topoemas*

1969	Octavio Paz, *Ladera este*; Roque Dalton, *Taberna y otros lugares*
1970	Claribel Alegría, *Aprendizaje*; Mario Benedetti, *Inventario*
1971	Juan Gelman, *Cólera buey*; Alejandra Pizarnik, *La condesa sangrienta*
1971	Pablo Neruda wins the Nobel Prize in Literature
1972	Rosario Castellanos, *Poesía no eres tú (1952–1972)*; Eugenio Montejo, *Muerte y memoria*
1973	Ernesto Cardenal, *Oráculo sobre Managua*; Roque Dalton, *Poemas clandestinos*
1974	Juan Gustavo Cobo Borda, *Consejo para sobrevivir*; Olga Orozco, *Museo salvaje*
1975	Eugenio Florit, *Versos pequeños (1938–1975)*; Nicanor Parra, *Memorias de un ataúd*
1976	Ferreira Gullar, *Poema sujo*
1976	João Cabral de Melo Neto, *Museu de tudo*; José Emilio Pacheco, *Islas a la deriva*
1977	Nicanor Parra, *Sermones y prédicas del Cristo de Elqui*; Óscar Hahn, *Arte de morir*
1978	Claribel Alegría, *Sobrevivo*; Gonzalo Rojas, *Del relámpago*
1979	Enrique Lihn, *A partir de Manhattan*; Raúl Zurita, *Purgatorio*
1979	Haroldo de Campos, *Signantia: quase coelum*
1980	Néstor Perlongher, *Austria-Hungría*; Ana Cristina Cesar, *Luvas de pelica*
1981	Coral Bracho, *El ser que va a morir*; Carmen Ollé, *Noches de adrenalina*
1982	Henriqueta Lisboa, *Pousada do ser*; Eugenio Montejo, *Trópico absoluto*
1983	José Koser, *Bajo este cien*; Nicanor Parra, *Poesía política*
1984	Cecilia Vicuña, *PALABRARmás*; Haroldo de Campos, *Galáxias*
1985	Ana Cristina Cesar, *Inéditos e Dispersos*; Giannina Braschi, *La comedia profana*; María Negroni, *De tanto desolar*
1986	Armando Freitas Filho, *3x4*
1986	Raúl Zurita, *Canto a su amor desaparecido*; Blanca Varela, *Canto villano*
1987	María Mercedes Carranza, *Hola soledad*; Gloria Anzaldúa, *Borderlands/La frontera*
1988	Santiago Mutis, *Tú también eres de lluvia*; Jorge Eduardo Eielson, *Primera muerte de María*

1989	José Watanabe, *El uso de la palabra*; Armando Romero, *Las combinaciones debidas*
1990	David Huerta, *Los objetos están más cerca de lo que aparentan*; Enrique Verástegui, *Angelus Novus II*
1990	Octavio Paz wins the Nobel Prize in Literature
1991	Carlos López Degregori, *El amor rudimentario*; Paulo Leminski, *La vie en close*
1992	Homero Aridjis, *El poeta en peligro de extinción*; Óscar Hahn, *Tratado de sortilegios*
1993	Coral Bracho, *Ese espacio, ese jardín*; Raúl Zurita, *La vida nueva*
1994	Augusto de Campos, *Despoesia*
1994	Susana Thénon, *Distances*; Malú Urriola, *Dame tu sucio amor*
1995	Óscar Hahn, *Versos robados*; Juan Gustavo Cobo Borda, *El animal que duerme en cada uno y otros poemas*
1996	Omar A. García Obregón, *Pastor del tiempo*; Carlota Caulfield, *A las puertas del papel con amoroso fuego*
1997	Miguel Ángel Zapata, *Lumbre de la letra*; Marita Troiano, *Mortal in puribus*
1998	Haroldo de Campos, *Crisantempo*; Carlos López Degregori, *Aquí descansa nadie*
1999	Cecilia Vicuña, *Cloud-Net*; Blanca Varela, *Concierto animal*
2000	Jorge Eduardo Eielson, *Sin título*; Óscar de Pablo, *La otra mitad del mundo*
2001	Eduardo Chirinos, *Breve historia de la música*; Rafael Lozano-Hemmer and Guillermo Gómez-Peña, *Tech-illa Sunrise (.txt dot con Sangrita)*
2002	Ana María Uribe, *Deseo – Desejo – Desire – 3 anipoemas eróticos*; Eduardo Navas, *9_11_2001_netMemorial*
2003	Augusto de Campos, *Não: poemas*
2003	Andi Nachon, *Goa*; Wáshington Delgado, *Cuán impunemente se está uno muerto*
2004	Armando Romero, *De noche al sol*; Óscar de Pablo, *Los endemoniados*
2004	Haroldo de Campos, *Crisantempo: no espaço curvo nasce um*
2005	Miguel Ángel Zapata, *Los muslos sobre la grama*; Luz Argentina Chiriboga, *Con su misma voz*
2006	Óscar Hahn, *En un abrir y cerrar de ojos*; José Koser, *Stet*
2007	Juan Felipe Herrera, *187 Reasons Mexicanos Can't Cross the Border*; Coral Bracho, *Firefly under the Tongue*

2008	Mario Montalbetti, *El lenguaje es un revólver para dos*; Pablo Guevara, *Un iceberg llamado poesía*
2009	Armando Freitas Filho, *Lar*
2009	Armando Romero, *El árbol digital y otros poemas*; Cristina Peri Rossi, *Playstation*
2010	Ferreira Gullar, *Em alguma parte alguma*
2010	Malú Urriola, *Hija de perra y otros poemas*; Benjamín Moreno Ortiz, *Concretoons poesía digital*
2011	Ezequiel Zaidenwerg, *La lírica está muerta*; Belén Gache, *Góngora Wordtoys*
2012	José Luis Ayala, *Soñar contigo* (Aymara-Spanish edition); Carlos Germán Belli, *Los dioses domésticos y otras páginas*
2013	Mario Montalbetti, *Lejos de mí decirles*; Alejandro Crotto, *Chesterton*
2014	Enrique Verástegui, *La partitura peruana*; Blanca Varela, *Puerto supe*
2015	Augusto de Campos, *Outro*
2015	Óscar de Pablo, *De la materia en forma de sonido*; Alejandro Crotto, *Once personas*
2016	Wellington Castillo, *Huella de agonía*; Andi Nachon, *Taiga* (updated edition)

PART I

History

I

RODRIGO CACHO CASAL

Colonial Poetry

The development of colonial poetry in the territories that today belong to Spanish America and Brazil was quite different in each area. This was directly related to the policies applied by the two metropolises, Spain and Portugal, to the colonization of the New World. Since the early years of the sixteenth century Spain deployed an increasing contingent of settlers, both lay and religious, who brought with them institutions, policies, weapons, and cultural traditions. The empire was to take root in these new lands with the double intention of evangelizing its native inhabitants and exploiting its natural resources, especially precious metals. For all intents and purposes the viceroyalties of Mexico and Peru, into which the administration of the Spanish territories was divided, were part of the crown of Castile and enjoyed the same basic laws as the other Spanish kingdoms such as Leon or Navarre; in other words, America *was* Spain. Portugal, on the other hand, at first did not consider its New World enterprise as a political priority, preferring to concentrate its efforts in Africa and Asia. The American territories under Portuguese jurisdiction, as stipulated by the Treaty of Tordesillas (1494), lacked the mineral resources found in Mexico and Peru (the gold mines of Minas Gerais would not be discovered until the end of the seventeenth century), and this is why a major imperial effort akin to that of their Iberian counterpart was neither immediately sustainable nor advantageous.

The colonization of modern-day Brazil was thus slow and intermittent, and initially there were only a few isolated fortified mercantile platforms rather than fully developed cities. Olinda and Salvador were no match for impressive urban centers such as Mexico City and Lima. Major Spanish American cities soon developed a strong autonomous identity, both intellectually and economically, supported by the foundation of universities across the continent, first in Santo Domingo (1538) and a few years later in Lima and Mexico City (1551). The first printing press was established in the capital of New Spain in 1539, followed by Lima in 1584. This was not the case for

Brazil; its cities, concentrated mostly on the coast, were kept by Portugal on a tight leash, controlling and somewhat delaying their cultural growth. No printing press was allowed to operate in Brazil until the court of João VI fled Lisbon and was established in Rio de Janeiro in 1808. Students who wanted to obtain an academic degree had to travel to Portugal, since no university was founded in Brazil until 1909.

Although poetry circulated mainly via manuscript copies in Europe as well as in America, the Hispanic presses in the New World also contributed to the dissemination of local authors, fostering the rise of a new poetic identity over the turn of the sixteenth and seventeenth centuries, with seminal works such as *Arauco domado* (Arauco Tamed, 1596, published in Lima) by Pedro de Oña and *Grandeza mexicana* (Mexican Greatness, 1604, published in Mexico City) by Bernardo de Balbuena. Brazilian poets had no other choice than to print their works in Portugal, whereas the interface between Spanish America and the metropolis was more fluid. The publication of works in Spain was likely to obtain a wider readership, but, despite their technical limitations, American presses were often preferred. For instance, Eugenio de Salazar (1530–1602), born in Madrid but who resided in various American cities fulfilling administrative roles, prepared a manuscript collection of his poems before his death, *Silva de poesía*. In the opening letter addressed to his sons, he suggests Mexico City as a possible venue for its publication, "there you will be able to print it [the *Silva*], since there is a printing press, though it does not use good quality types."[1]

Mexican and Peruvian presses, however, produced only a limited number of literary texts. Most printed works were related to the administration of colonial power overseas: edicts and legal documents, university textbooks, catechisms, grammars and dictionaries of Nahuatl, Quechua, Aymara, and other indigenous languages. Spaniards imposed their language and way of life on the New World's native peoples, but they were also influenced by them. Friars and missionaries were particularly interested in native history, language and customs, firstly because this facilitated evangelization, and also because of the genuine fascination that many members of the Church felt towards pre-Columbian civilizations. Few of these groups possessed a writing system, such as Maya glyphs or Mexica pictographs, and only a handful of pre-Hispanic American codices have survived. Some were copied under Spanish supervision during the postconquest period, but the majority of the original documents were destroyed in order to eradicate indigenous religious cults, as reported by Fray Diego de Landa in sixteenth-century Yucatan

---

[1] Eugenio de Salazar, *Silva de poesía*, ed. Jaime J. Martínez Martín (Rome: Bulzoni, 2004), 25.

(c. 1566): "We found a large number of books written using their own characters, and since they were filled with diabolic superstitions and lies they were all burnt."[2]

The majority of texts that contain what we could consider to be indigenous American poetry were copied in the Latin alphabet by native scribes instructed by members of the Church. These were individuals such as the Franciscan friar Bernardino de Sahagún (1499–1590), who alongside his team of native students and collaborators educated at the Colegio de Santa Cruz de Tlatelolco collected a vast array of information regarding ancient Mesoamerican religion and culture, as well as old hymns. The sacred Maya book, *Popol Vuh* (Book of the Council), was copied and translated into Spanish by the Dominican Francisco Ximénez during the early years of the eighteenth century. Oral tradition offered the richest source of songs and hymns, and this was particularly relevant in the Inca civilization, which did not possess writing. Peruvian authors, such as the Inca Garcilaso de la Vega in his *Comentarios reales de los incas* (Royal Commentaries of the Incas, 1609), collected Quechua songs, recalling that "Inca poets were called *harauec*, which in their language means *inventor*."[3] The label is more fitting, however, to Europeans and Hispanized Indians and *mestizos* who partly erased, partly rescued, and mainly reinvented these traditional songs in the way in which they have been brought down to us.

In spite of the great racial and cultural hybridization experienced in the postconquest era, indigenous languages were seldom used by Spanish American and Brazilian poets. Traditional native songs survived in the oral tradition, but Nahuatl, Quechua, and Tupi found little space in the written text; and when they did appear these were mostly used in a religious context. For instance, Nahuatl devotional songs were performed in Mexico City during the celebrations that welcomed the arrival of relics sent by Pope Gregory XIII, as recorded by Father Pedro de Morales in his *Carta* (Letter, 1579); and Sor Juana Inés de la Cruz (1651–1695) incorporated Nahuatl in her *autos sacramentales* and *villancicos*. In Peru, Christian hymns were composed in Quechua by Fray Luis Jerónimo de Oré and included in his *Símbolo católico indiano* (Catholic Indian Symbol, 1598), followed by Juan Pérez Bocanegra's *Ritual formulario e institución de curas* (Ritual Formulary and Priestly Induction, 1631), which comprises three Quechua Marian hymns. Lastly, Father José de Anchieta (1534–1597), born in Tenerife and educated at Coimbra, was a missionary in Brazil where he learned Tupi and

[2] Diego de Landa, *Relación de las cosas de Yucatán*, ed. Miguel Rivera Dorado (Madrid: Dastin, 2002), 160.
[3] El Inca Garcilaso de la Vega, *Comentarios reales; La Florida del Inca*, ed. Mercedes López-Baralt (Madrid: Espasa Calpe, 2003), 155.

composed several religious songs in that language using Portuguese metrics, a simple style and naïve imagery, as illustrated in the following excerpt devoted to baby Jesus:

> Pitangĩ porangeté
> oroguerobiá' katú!
> Xe jarĩ, paí Jesú,
> xe moingó katú jepé:
> nde añó toroausú![4]

> (Very handsome little child,/ in him we firmly trust!/ Good Jesus, my little Lord,/ you show me the right path:/ that I shall love only you!)

Anchieta is an obvious example of the difficulties that we encounter when trying to fit early modern culture within the boundaries of a post-Romantic understanding of the history of literature, which is very dependent on concepts such as language and nationality. This Canary-born Jesuit was educated in Portugal and spent most of his adult life in Brazil. He wrote in Spanish, Portuguese, Tupi, and was also an accomplished neo-Latin poet, composing an ambitious epic poem dedicated to Mem de Sá, third governor of Brazil, *De gestis Mendi de Saa* (On the Deeds of Mem de Sá). Three countries could legitimately claim Anchieta as one of their *national* authors, though such labels would seem unfitting and limiting. He was Spanish, Portuguese, and Brazilian at the same time. Political and intellectual hybridization became even more apparent between 1580 and 1640 when Portugal was united to the crown of Castile after King Sebastian died without heirs and his uncle, Philip II of Spain, successfully imposed his dynastic claim. Then, more than ever before, the fortunes of Portugal, Spain, and America were closely interlinked; as a result, the history of colonial poetry could best be described as a constant negotiation between different languages, cultures, and traditions.

The Spanish and Portuguese conquests led to the establishment of European genres and conventions in the New World. Among these, epic and religious poetry represent the double colonial intervention of the empire and the Church in America. Inspired by Virgil and other Italian models, epic was one of the most popular poetic genres in early modern Spain, comprising a political message that usually had a propagandistic bias in favor of the Habsburg monarchy. Alonso de Ercilla, the most influential author in this mode, was also the first to publish an entire heroic poem in Spanish devoted to the New World. *La Araucana* (The Araucaniad) was issued in three parts

[4] José de Anchieta, *Obras completas, 5.1. Lírica portuguesa e tupi*, ed. Pe. Armando Cardoso, SJ (São Paulo: Loyola, 1984), 153.

(1569, 1578, 1589) and describes the Spanish campaigns against the Araucanians (Mapuche Indians) in Chile in which Ercilla took part as a soldier between 1557 and 1559. In the prologue he claims that he composed this "truthful history" while he was on the battlefield, and praises the Araucanians for their bravery regardless of their "barbaric" condition.[5]

La Araucana is a complex work and each of its parts shows variations in tone, plot, and ideological content, which granted its imitators a model that could be approached with great flexibility. The American epic became a genre in its own right, and enjoyed continuity and success between the sixteenth and the eighteenth centuries. Ercilla employed a pseudo-historical discourse, praising a variety of heroes on both sides of the conflict rather than a single leader, thus depicting the conquest as a collective enterprise coordinated by the Spanish monarchy. Yet his most significant contribution to the genre was perhaps the openness and ambiguity of its ideological message since both Spaniards and Araucanians are conceived as brave, as well as inherently vulnerable, and flawed. Galvarino's speech following his capture, when his hands are cut off by the Spaniards, is one of the most compelling examples of the atrocities of war, where the rise of violence questions the boundaries between victors and vanquished, generating only more violence like an invincible Hydra:

> diciendo así: "Segad esa garganta
> siempre sedienta de la sangre vuestra,
> que no temo la muerte ni me espanta
> vuestra amenaza y rigurosa muestra,
> y la importancia y pérdida no es tanta
> que haga falta mi cortada diestra,
> pues quedan otras muchas esforzadas
> que saben gobernar bien las espadas."[6]

> (and he said: "Cut this throat of mine/ always thirsty for your blood,/ since I do not fear death nor I am scared of/ your threats and your severe punishment,/ and my loss is not so important since/ there is no need for my severed right hand;/ there are many more brave hands left/ that know how to handle a sword with skill.")

Despite that its action is set in America, *La Araucana* was conceived in Spain within a European context. Pedro de Oña, one of its earlier imitators, adopts instead the role of the American-born poet engaging with a subject that he knows intimately well. *Arauco domado* (1596) is the first poem published by an author born in the New World (in Angol, Chile); Oña sets himself the task

---

[5] Alonso de Ercilla, *La Araucana*, ed. Isaías Lerner (Madrid: Cátedra, 2002), 69–70.
[6] Ercilla, *La Araucana*, XXII, 47.

of revising and completing Ercilla's work in order to "pay tribute to my homeland."[7] *Arauco domado* was commissioned by the outgoing viceroy of Peru, García Hurtado de Mendoza, who is praised throughout. Oña follows the pseudo-historical narrative set out by Ercilla, as did other epic authors who wrote numerous poems about Hernán Cortés. Francisco de Terrazas (died c. 1580), son of a *conquistador*, was born in Mexico and authored the epic poem *Nuevo mundo y conquista* (The New World and Conquest), only a few fragments of which are extant. What is left of his work suggests that Cortés is praised for his heroic deeds, but is also blamed for not having kept his word of rewarding his soldiers. Terrazas voices the frustration of the *conquistadors'* descendants who found that their privileges had not been granted in perpetuity. A similar message can be found in the work of another Mexican-born author who wrote an epic poem on Hernán Cortés, *El peregrino indiano* (The Indian Pilgrim, 1599) by Antonio de Saavedra Guzmán, the first American-born poet who published in Spain.

The uses of epic varied depending on the topic chosen. Certain authors focused their attention on fringe areas charting unmapped territories in the colonial imagination of the time. Juan de Castellanos wrote an ambitious poem devoted to the Caribbean, Venezuela, and New Granada, although he only managed to publish the first of four parts of his monumental *Elegías de varones ilustres de Indias* (Elegies of Illustrious Men of the Indies, 1589). The same holds true for Martín del Barco Centenera, who in *Argentina y conquista del Río de la Plata* (Argentina and the Conquest of the River Plate, 1602) describes the clashes between Spaniards and the local indigenous population of one of the largest marginal areas of Spanish America. Other authors chose to take a radically different approach, leaving aside the epic of the conquest and looking instead to medieval Spanish history and legends; for instance, we can cite Rodrigo de Carvajal y Robles's *Poema del asalto y conquista de Antequera* (Poem on the Attack and Conquest of Antequera, 1627) and Bernardo de Balbuena's *El Bernardo o victoria de Roncesvalles* (Bernardo, or the Victory of Roncesvalles, 1624). *El Bernardo* is a polemical response to the pseudo-historical epic model inspired in *La Araucana*. Balbuena holds onto Aristotelian principles and declares that "poetry ought to be an imitation of truth but not in itself truthful, describing events not as they happened but as they could have happened."[8]

A further strand of epic poetry engages with the supernatural and the divine, focusing on Jesus Christ and the lives of the saints. One early example

---

[7] Pedro de Oña, *Arauco domado*, ed. Ornella Gianesin (Como/Pavia: Ibis, 2014), 549.
[8] Bernardo de Balbuena, *El Bernardo o victoria de Roncesvalles, poema heroico* (Madrid: Diego Flamenco, 1624), ¶6.

written in Peru is Diego de Hojeda's *La Christiada* (The Chistiad, 1611), which describes Christ's passion in imitation of the neo-Latin poem by Marco Girolamo Vida, *Christias* (1535). After the arrival of the Jesuits to America and their growing importance in various aspects of the social sphere, the figure of Saint Ignatius became the subject of several religious epics. One of the earliest examples is Luis de Belmonte Bermúdez's *Vida del padre maestro Ignacio de Loyola* (Life of Father Ignacio de Loyola, 1609), followed by Pedro de Oña's *El Ignacio de Cantabria* (Ignacio of Cantabria, 1639) and Hernando Domínguez Camargo's *San Ignacio de Loyola, fundador de la Compañía de Jesús, poema heroico* (Heroic Poem on St Ignatius of Loyola, Founder of the Jesuits, 1666). Born in Bogotá in 1606, Camargo was strongly influenced by Luis de Góngora, a key figure in Spanish American and Brazilian poetry in the second half of the seventeenth century. The *Poema heroico* is one of the most complex and finest expressions of Gongorism in America, being a perfect example of what has been called the *Barroco de Indias*.

Religious poetry was present in America through a variety of genres and metrical forms. Early examples of its dissemination can be found in 1577 Mexico, when an unknown collector assembled the poetic anthology, *Flores de varia poesía* (Flowers of Various Poems). The manuscript, originally divided in five books, contains works by peninsular authors as well as others who were born or who settled in America, including Martín Cortés (son of Hernán Cortés), Fernán González de Eslava, and Francisco de Terrazas. Unfortunately, only the first book (religious poetry) and part of the second (love poetry) are extant, but this is enough to establish the literary exchange between Mexico and the metropolis. The cultural dialogue between the two continents explains also the works of the most successful early religious poet of Mexico; Eslava, who moved to the New World when he was twenty-five (1558) and there took vows, was renowned for his short plays published posthumously alongside his religious poems: *Coloquios espirituales y sacramentales y canciones divinas* (Spiritual and Sacramental Colloquia, and Divine Songs, 1610). His devotional works combine traditional Spanish motives and metrics with local themes, such as portraying Christ as a *gachopín* (i.e. a Spaniard who has just arrived from Europe):

¡Maravilla, maravilla!
Dénse a Dios gracias sin fin,
que ha venido un gachopín
de la celestial Castilla.[9]

[9] Fernán González de Eslava, *Villancicos, romances, ensaladas y otras canciones devotas*, ed. by Margit Frenk (Mexico City: El Colegio de México, 1989), 246.

(Such wonder, such wonder!/ Thanked be the Lord/ since a *gachopín* has come/ from celestial Castile.)

Eslava wrote also a number of compositions praising Mexican girls who were taking vows to become nuns, thus offering a glance into the public role of religious poetry. Devotional poetry, often accompanied by music, was very present both in the liturgy of the time and in large-scale celebrations associated with religious festivities or political events, such as the funeral of a member of the royal family. As a matter of fact, religious compositions often went hand in hand with panegyric and occasional poetry in Mexico City and Lima, as shown by various early modern accounts or *relaciones*: Cervantes de Salazar, *Túmulo imperial a las exequias de Carlos V* (Imperial Burial Mound at Charles V's Funeral, 1560); Martín de León, *Relación de las exequias en la muerte de la reina nuestra señora doña Margarita* (Account of the Funeral on the Death of Our Lady Queen Margarita, 1613); Diego Cano Gutiérrez, *Relación de las fiestas triunfales que la insigne Universidad de Lima hizo a la Inmaculada Concepción de Nuestra Señora* (Account of the Triumphal Festivities Led by the Illustrious University of Lima for the Immaculate Conception of Our Lady, 1619); Carlos de Sigüenza y Góngora, *Teatro de virtudes políticas* (Theatre of Political Virtues, 1680); and Francisco Javier Carranza, *Llanto de las piedras en la sentida muerte de la más generosa Peña* (The Weeping of the Stones at the Much Lamented Death of the Most Generous Peña, 1739).

The viceroy, the Church, the Inquisition, and the University fostered these public displays of symbolic power in which literature played a central role. Two occasional poems written in Mexico and Pernambuco, *Grandeza mexicana* and *Prosopopéia* (Prosopopoeia), are some of the best accounts of early development of Spanish American and Brazilian poetic identity. Bernardo de Balbuena was born in Spain but studied at the University of Mexico, later becoming bishop of Puerto Rico. His first published work, *Grandeza mexicana* (1604), is a collection of occasional texts: one of Spanish America's first poetic manifestos, *Compendio apologético en alabanza de la poesía* [Apologetic Compendium in Praise of Poetry]; a series of poems that earned him prizes in literary contests; a *canción* in honor of the arrival of the new Archbishop of Mexico; and, in a second issue of the book, there is also a poem for the Count of Lemos. The main piece is however an extensive poetic epistle dedicated to a lady who is about to take vows in Mexico City, and offers a sophisticated description of the beauties and riches of the city. Balbuena portrays the capital of New Spain as a space of wonder, abundance, and cultural supremacy capable of overshadowing Europe:

aquí hallará más hombres eminentes
en toda ciencia y todas facultades
que arenas lleva el Ganges en sus corrientes:
monstruos en perfección de habilidades,
y en las letras humanas y divinas
eternos rastreadores de verdades.[10]

(here you will find more eminent men/ in all subjects and disciplines/ than sands
carried in the currents of the Ganges:/ prodigies of accomplished talents,/ and
eternal pursuers of truths/ in human and sacred letters.)

Bento Teixeira's career was not as successful as Balbuena's. Son of New
Christians (i.e. descendants from converted Jews), he was born in Porto
in 1561 and moved to Brazil with his family when he was young. He
studied in the College of the Society of Jesus in Bahia, and later became
a teacher of Latin, arithmetic, and writing in Pernambuco. In 1593 he
was denounced to the Inquisition as a Judaizer, and he was later
brought to Lisbon where he was imprisoned and eventually died in
1600. In 1601 his poem *Prosopopéia* was published posthumously in
Lisbon as an appendix to *O Naufrágio que passou Jorge d'Albuquerque*
(The Shipwreck Suffered by Jorge d'Albuquerque). *Prosopopéia* is a
panegyric work in praise of Jorge de Albuquerque, captain and governor
of Pernambuco. The text is best described as an *epyllion*, or epic poem
in miniature, in which history and mythology are merged following the
example of Luís de Camões's *Os Lusíadas* (The Lusiads, 1572). The
poem takes its name from the rhetorical device known as *prosopopoeia*,
which consists in attributing human qualities and speech to inanimate
objects or imaginary characters; in this case, the sea god Proteus narrates Albuquerque's deeds. In Stanza X Teixeira directly engages with
his main source, claiming that the marine creature Triton is not wearing
a lobster shell on his head, as "described by Camões" (in *Os Lusíadas*,
VI, 17), but a rather more sophisticated sea shell, which appears in
Stanza XI:

mas ũa concha lisa e bem lavrada
de rica madrepérola trazia,
de fino coral crespo marchetada,
cujo lavor o natural vencia.
Estava nela ao vivo debuxada
a cruel e espantosa bataria

[10] Bernardo de Balbuena, *Grandeza mexicana*, ed. Luis Íñigo-Madrigal (Madrid: Biblioteca
Nueva, 2013), 84.

que deu a temerária e cega gente
aos deoses do ceo puro e reluzente.[11]

(he was wearing a smooth and well crafted/ precious nacre sea shell instead,/ carved with delicate curly coral/ whose craft exceeded nature./ There was vividly drawn/ the cruel and formidable battle/ that the reckless and blind people fought/ against the gods of the pure and bright heavens.)

Epic deeds and action are turned into speech, *prosopopéia*; art becomes an artifice that outdoes nature. Camões's almost comical lobster beret has been transformed into a complex sea shell that conjures up the Gigantomachy. Words are compared to precious material (nacre, coral), and language is twisted and enriched in this miniature heroic poem carved within a shell, which mirrors the miniature heroic style of Teixeira's work while challenging the epic tradition. *Prosopopéia* announces the artistic shift between the Renaissance and the Baroque. It also produces one of the first known poetic descriptions of the Brazilian landscape in which Stanzas XVII–XXI focus on Pernambuco's reef, frequently the victim of pirate incursions, whose etymology is said to derive from the native language *para'na* (sea) and *puca* (cave). Teixeira contributes thus to shape the Brazilian literary imagination as a hybrid space populated by Indian echoes, pirates, and mythological creatures imported from Europe.

Despite their importance and dissemination, occasional works are only one facet of colonial poetry. Other genres also circulated that had a more intimate tone, dealing particularly with love. Petrarchism was one of the most internationally successful early modern poetic trends, and its presence in America can be documented as early as 1577 in the Mexican anthology *Flores de varia poesía* mentioned above. What is left of this volume is enough to establish the predominance of love poetry above other lyric genres; the first book, devoted to religious poetry, contains sixty-one poems whereas the second, which includes the love poems, has two hundred and ninety-eight. Francisco Terrazas was one of the most talented and famous sixteenth-century Mexican poets, with sonnets that challenge the chaste love usually associated with Petrarchism:

¡Ay, basas de marfil, vivo edificio
obrado del artífice del cielo!
Colunas de alabastro que en el suelo
nos dais del bien supremo claro indicio.
Hermosos chapiteles y artificio
del arco que aun de mí me pone celo;

[11] Bento Teixeira, *Prosopopéia*, ed. Celso Cunha and Carlos Durval (São Paulo: Melhoramentos, 1977), 40.

altar donde el tirano dios mozuelo
hiciera de sí mismo sacrificio.
¡Ay, puerta de la gloria de Cupido
y guarda de la flor más estimada
de cuantas en el mundo son ni han sido!
Sepamos hasta cuándo estáis cerrada,
y el cristalino cielo es defendido
a quien jamás gustó fruta vedada.[12]

(Ah, marble pedestals, splendid edifice/ crafted by the creator of Heavens!/ Alabaster columns that on earth/ grant clear proof of the Supreme Good's existence./ Wonderful capitals and artifice/ of that arch that makes me jealous even of myself;/ altar whereupon the young tyrant god/ would go as far as sacrificing himself./ Ah, door that leads to Cupid's glory,/ fortress of the most esteemed flower/ amongst those which exist and have ever existed./ Let's see for how long can you stay closed,/ and for how long can the crystal sky be denied/ to one who has never tasted forbidden fruit.)

Terrazas's reputation soon made it to the other side of the Atlantic. Miguel de Cervantes praises him in *La Galatea* (1585) in the section of the book known as *Canto de Calíope* (The Calliope Song), which is a lengthy panegyric catalogue of contemporary Hispanic poets where there is a whole section devoted to authors from the "Antarctic region." Terrazas is the first to be mentioned in this American list because "his name is very well known both here and there [*acá y allá*]."[13] Cervantes's words speak eloquently of the cultural exchange between the metropolis and the New World, especially since Terrazas's compositions were never published during his lifetime. This also suggests that many sources and information have been lost, or are yet to be recovered, and that one should tread carefully when trying to establish the nature and the quantity of poetry produced in Spanish America and Brazil during this period.

Cervantes's *Canto de Calíope* includes another author whose work is closely related to the development of Petrarchism in America, the Portuguese-born Enrique Garcés, who emigrated to Peru where he was involved in the mining business, and politics.[14] He was also a poet and in 1591 he published in Madrid Spanish translations of Camões' *Os Lusíadas* and Petrarch's *Canzoniere* (Song Book). The final section of the latter book comprises an imitation by Garcés of Petrarch's *canzone* "Italia mia, benché

---

[12] *Flores de baria poesía. Cancionero novohispano del siglo XVI*, ed. by Margarita Peña (Mexico City: FCE, 2003), 474.
[13] Miguel de Cervantes, *La Galatea*, ed. Francisco López Estrada and María Teresa García-Berdoy (Madrid: Cátedra, 1999), 578–579.
[14] Ibid., 580–581.

'l parlar sia indarno" addressed to his fellow Peruvian readers and Philip II and turning this text into a political attack against the former viceroy of Peru, Francisco de Toledo. Petrarchism is thus employed eclectically by American poets. For instance, married love, usually alien to love poetry, is the subject of a volume published in Lima in 1602/03: *Miscelánea austral* (Austral[ian] Miscellaneous Pieces) by Diego Dávalos y Figueroa, followed by the *Defensa de damas* (Ladies' Defence), an anti-misogynistic poem in *ottava rima*. Dávalos's *Miscelánea* is composed of a series of dialogues and poems shared between his and his wife's alter egos, Delio and Celia.

All the approaches to love and Petrarchism put forward by these American authors show a clear attempt to establish themselves as an autonomous group of intellectuals who both continue and renew the Spanish literary tradition. Labels such as *austral* and *antártica* can be found in various works that appeared between the end of the sixteenth and the beginning of the seventeenth centuries in Peru, as if local authors wanted to re-appropriate the term used by Cervantes (*la región antártica*). This is the case of Dávalos's *Miscelánea austral* and Diego Mexía de Fernangil's *Parnaso antártico* (Antarctic Parnassus, 1608). The latter includes Mexía's translation of Ovid's *Heroides*, and a preliminary poetic *Discurso en loor de la poesía* (Speech in Praise of Poetry) by an unnamed "distinguished lady of this Kingdom [Peru], well versed in the Tuscan and Portuguese languages."[15] Under the auspices of the "Nymphs of the South," she praises poetry and its virtues, celebrating various authors of the "Antarctic region," where, according to her, there are countless poets based in the *Academia antártica* (Antarctic Academy) in Lima.

Little is known about this academy, which is also mentioned in other contemporary texts, but it clearly promoted the idea that Peruvian poetry was flourishing. During those same years, Mexico was also undergoing a process of literary self-affirmation, recognizable in Balbuena's *Compendio apologético en alabanza de la poesía*. Here, as in the *Discurso*, Balbuena praises the virtues of poetry and establishes a canon of Spanish poets, followed by some who are found "in our Western World."[16] *Antarctic, Austral*, the *South*, and the *Western World* are thus terms that define an autonomous literary space that acknowledges both its distance from and links to Europe, all the while proclaiming its own originality. American authors showed an incipient will to announce to Spain and the rest of the world that they no longer needed to be defined *from* Europe, such as was

---

[15] Diego Mexía de Fernangil, *Primera parte del Parnaso antártico de obras amatorias* (Seville: Alonso Rodríguez Gamarra, 1608), 9–26.

[16] Balbuena, *Grandeza mexicana*, 135r-35v.

done by Cervantes (*acá y allá*), but rather from their own geographically
marginal position with regard to the metropolis. In other words, the idea that
Mexico City and Lima are the literary periphery of Spain is questioned: *acá*
and *allá* switch referents, adopting an American perspective.

This reversal, however, should not be interpreted as a polemical or proto-
independentist response to the metropolis; Mexican and Peruvian authors
sought to join the Hispanic canon by widening its scope rather than by
denying its currency. By adopting and adapting Petrarchism, New World
authors were retracing the steps of Boscán and Garcilaso, who in the sixteenth century imported Renaissance Italianate poetry into Spain. This process of cultural transmission (*translatio studii*) took place also in America,
where love poetry exercised a very strong influence until the eighteenth
century, within both the Spanish American and the Brazilian contexts.
Manuel Botelho de Oliveira (1636–1711) and Gregório de Matos (1633–
1695) represent this trend in Brazil; both were born in Salvador and studied
in Coimbra before returning to America. Oliveira was the first Brazilian-born
author to publish a poetic book, *Música do Parnaso* (Music of Parnassus,
1705), whereas Matos's works circulated only via manuscript copies. *Música
do Parnaso* comprises a selection of texts in Portuguese, Spanish, Italian, and
Latin, and numerous love poems addressed to an idealized beloved, Anarda.
In his dedication, Oliveira applies the concept of cultural transmission to the
evolution of poetry that originated in Europe and, belatedly, was brought to
Brazil.

> Nesta América, inculta habitação antigamente de bárbaros índios, mal se podia
> esperar que as Musas se fizessem brasileiras; contudo, quiseram também pas-
> sar-se a este empório, aonde, como a doçura do açúcar é tão simpática com a
> suavidade do seu canto, acharam muitos engenhos que, imitando aos poetas da
> Itália e Espanha, se aplicassem a tão discreto entretenimento.[17]

> (In America, once the wild abode of barbaric Indians, it was hard to imagine that
> the Muses could have become Brazilian; however, they decided to move to this
> emporium too where, because the sweetness of sugar agrees with the gentleness
> of their singing, they found many authors who, imitating the Spanish and Italian
> poets, applied themselves to such a sophisticated diversion.)

At least on a rhetorical plane, Oliveira does not display the same degree of
literary confidence encountered in Spanish American authors a century earlier. The growth of Brazilian poetry is represented as an unfolding passage
from barbarism to civilization, granted by the European Muses. There are,
however, some compositions in *Música do Parnaso* in which these old

[17] Manuel Botelho de Oliveira, *Música do Parnaso* (Lisbon: Miguel Manescal, 1705), 2ᵛ.

conventions are merged with a personal perception of American identity, such as the descriptive poem *À Ilha de Maré* (The Island of Maré). A similar localism can be found in Matos despite the fact that many of his love poems are very much indebted to European authors. To a point, this is inevitable and is in line with generic conventions; Petrarchism usually portrays the inner suffering of a lover, and thus is more prone to lend itself to abstract discourse than everyday subject matter. This is not the case for descriptive poetry or another genre that Matos cultivated with passion: satire. Such texts earned him the nickname *Boca do Inferno* (The Mouth of Hell) and led to his banishment to Angola. On the occasion of his banishment he wrote a ballad where he denounced the corrupt life of Bahia and the exploitation of Brazilians by the Portuguese:

> Que os Brasileiros são bestas,
> e estarão a trabalhar
> toda a vida por manter
> maganos de Portugal.[18]

> (Since Brazilians are beasts,/ and they will work all their life/ in order to provide for/ Portuguese scoundrels.)

Social satire is the opposite of Petrarchism: it focuses on current affairs, often using a degrading language and imagery. In Spanish America this genre found one of its earliest champions in Mateo Rosas de Oquendo, who emigrated to America in the second half of the sixteenth century. His poems expose the hypocrisy of New World society, especially its vanity and its obsession with wealth, as shown in one of his most important works, the *Sátira hecha por Mateo Rosas de Oquendo a las cosas que pasan en el Pirú, año de 1598* (Satire by Mateo Rosas de Oquendo on the Things that Happen in Peru, in the Year 1598). Satire and burlesque poetry were further developed by Juan del Valle y Caviedes, who was born in Spain but spent most of his life in Lima. His most important poetic collection is *Diente del Parnaso* (The Tooth of Parnassus; also known with the longer title *Historia fatal, hazaña de la ignorancia, guerra física*; Fatal Account, Deed of Ignorance, Physical Warfare), which was compiled in 1689 but never published during his lifetime. The volume contains texts that target incompetent doctors, and shows clear indebtedness to the poetry of Francisco de Quevedo.

Quevedo's legacy can be recognized in various Brazilian and Spanish American authors, from Caviedes to Matos. The Spanish poet who left the

---

[18] Gregório de Matos, *Obra poética*, ed. by James Amado, 2 vols. (Rio de Janeiro: Record, 1990), II, 1172.

clearest mark in the second half of the seventeenth century, however, is Luis de Góngora. The complex and sophisticated *estilo culto* of his major poems stimulated the literary imagination of various generations of writers. Traces of his lavish descriptive writing can be found in Oliveira's *À Ilha de Maré*, which also seems to continue the development of baroque style following on Teixeira's "Descripção do recife de Paranambuco" (Description of the Reef of Pernambuco) included in *Prosopopéia*. Góngora's influence is most obvious in texts such as Camargo's *Poema heroico* and Sor Juana's *Primero sueño* (First Dream). Works such as these, grouped under the label of *Barroco de Indias*, often portray American nature and its artistic representation as exuberant and uncontrollable forces. This has traditionally led to regarding them as the embodiment of an incipient Creole identity willing to challenge Spain and its cultural and political hegemony.

It is frequently the case, however, that Creole discourse is better recognized a century later in the venue that fostered it: the city. In the eighteenth century poets employed the conventional mold of epic poetry to create panegyric works revolving around American urban centers and their history. Pedro Peralta y Barnuevo composed a heroic poem on *Lima fundada o conquista del Perú* (The Founding of Lima, or the Conquest of Peru, 1732), while the Brazilian Cláudio Manuel da Costa wrote the *Poema da fundação de Vila Rica* (Poem on the Founding of Vila Rica, 1773). Both authors focused their attention on the cities where they were born or spent most of their life, with a growing sense of civic and identitarian pride. A further development of this attitude is the proto-indigenism of José de Santa Rita Durão's *Camamuru. Poema épico do descubrimento da Bahia* (Camamuru. Epic Poem on the Discovery of Bahia, 1781), in which the Tupinamba play a central role. But it would indeed be anachronistic to consider these texts as the poetic equivalent of Simón Bolívar's *Carta de Jamaica* (The Jamaica Letter, 1815). Peralta, Costa, and Durão were still working within an imperialistic framework, though its process of erosion had begun. The city, which was the eradiating point of the colonial enterprise, would also be the source of its dissolution in the nineteenth century, leading poetry out of the Antarctic region and into Latin America.

2

CECILIA ENJUTO RANGEL

From Romanticism to *Modernismo*

Romanticism in Latin America has had a bad rap. Considered poor and failed as a literary movement, Octavio Paz dismissed it as "reflejo de un reflejo" (the reflection of a reflection), while Jean Franco described Romanticism as "lifeless" with rare exceptions found in the poetry of José María Heredia, José Joaquín Olmedo, and Andrés Bello, who were bridging neoclassical and Romantic aesthetics, aiming to legitimize the politics and poetics of independence movements in Latin America.[1] However, in the last few decades, critics such as Saúl Yurkievich have rescued the Romantic poets precisely because of their active engagement with politics and their poetic reconstruction of history:

> Por su anclaje vital en el presente, por su vínculo apasionado con la historia y con la problemática de actualidad, por esa manera de asumir la voz del siglo, porque escriben como hablan, los románticos inauguran el proceso de la modernidad en Hispanoamérica y, en consecuencia, forjan una prosa ... verdaderamente moderna ... La literatura romántica es literatura insurgente, literatura de ruptura, sobre todo con el anacrónico sistema político y educativo de España.[2]

> (By vital connection to the present, by its passionate link with history and with current events, by their way of assuming the voice of the century, because they write as they speak, the romantic writers inaugurate the process of the modernity in Latin America and, accordingly, forge a prose ... truly modern ... Romantic literature is insurgent literature, literature of rupture, especially in comparison to the anachronistic political and educational system of Spain.)

Yurkievich was probably referring to Argentinian Romantic poetry and the *poesía gauchesca* when he addressed how they wrote as they spoke, and

---

[1] Octavio Paz, *Los hijos del limo. Del romanticismo a la vanguardia* (Barcelona: Seix Barral, 1998), 124; Jean Franco, *An Introduction to Spanish-American literature* (Cambridge: Cambridge University Press, 1969), 45.

[2] Saúl Yurkievich, in Dario Puccini and Saúl Yurkievich, *Historia de la cultura literaria en Hispanoamérica I* (Mexico City: Fondo de Cultura Económica, 2010), 510.

although that is not a trait of all of the diverse Latin American Romantics, I concur that most of these poets fully engage with the writing of history in their poetry. In the nineteenth century, an era without Facebook or YouTube, Latin American Romantic poets such as Heredia and Antônio Gonçalves Dias, and *modernistas* such as José Martí, Rubén Darío, and Delmira Agustini, were shaping Latin American cultural politics through their poetry.

Romanticism and popular poetry formed and informed Latin American public opinion in the nineteenth century. As Gwen Kirkpatrick notes: "Still in existence today in the form of the Brazilian cordel, the Mexican corrido, the Chilean lira, and many other variations, these traditional forms took deep root in the Americas."[3] These popular traditional forms were used to signal what was the *Latin American* fabric of these poetic projects. Just as it is hard to generalize about Latin American Romantic verse, it is problematic to refer to Latin America as a "unified" space with a common history. Kirkpatrick eloquently sums up how we must begin by recognizing that Latin America in itself is a nineteenth-century cultural construction:

> In many areas indigenous groups and slave populations outnumbered criollo (European descendants born in America) elites, and centuries of colonialism had produced mestizo populations and cultures. Of course, we must draw our maps more specifically here in order not to represent Latin America as a vast, uniform, or mythic space. "Latin America" as a label had not yet been invented; instead, it was a term developed late in the nineteenth century to include areas marked by the colonial presence of Spain, Portugal, and France and their languages ... Of course, in 1800 these areas did not exist as countries but were divided into vice-royalties and other units of colonial administration. The national map of Latin America was being rearranged throughout the nineteenth century, notably in 1848 with Mexico's loss of half its territory to the United States and in 1898 with Spain's loss of its last American colonies, Cuba and Puerto Rico, which were largely administered by the United States. (Kirkpatrick, *Romantic Poetry*, 403)

In contrast to most Spanish American countries, Brazil did not become a republic until 1889, and it did not experience their tempestuous wars of independence. Decades before *modernismo* conceptualizes the need to search for a Latin American voice and aesthetics, Romantic poetry sets the stage and in many ways determines the *invention* of Latin America.

---

[3] Gwen Kirkpatrick, "Romantic Poetry in Latin America," in *Romantic Poetry*, ed. Angela Esterhammer (Philadelphia, PA: John Benjamins Publishing Company, 2002), 402.

Oscar Rivera-Rodas has examined three generations of Romantic poets in Latin America,[4] and in this brief introduction to the literary movement of Romanticism, I will only discuss José María Heredia (Cuba, 1803–1839) and Antônio Gonçalves Dias (Brazil, 1823–1864). However, as Rivera-Rodas mentioned, some poets became well known for their elegies, such as José Antonio Maitín (Venezuela, 1804–1874), and other Romantic poets saw in Heredia a precursor although their narrative work is what is more thoroughly studied, such as Esteban Echevarría (Argentina, 1805–1851), Gertrudis Gómez de Avellaneda (Cuba, 1814–1873), and José Mármol (Argentina, 1817–1871). Although it is difficult to synthesize a series of characteristics and generalizations about the literary movement, it is clear that Romanticism in Latin America privileged individual freedom, the representation of nature as a source of knowledge, the search of a "voice" of the people, and a nationalist, anti-colonialist discourse, which reacted against Spanish imperialism.

José María Heredia considered himself from Cuba, the country where he was born in 1803 but in which he lived only for six years in different time frames.[5] His father worked for the Spanish Crown in diverse judicial positions in Florida, Santo Domingo, Venezuela, and Mexico. In 1820 he briefly resided with his father in Mexico, where he wrote the first version of "En el teocalli de Cholula." But after his father's death, he returned to Cuba in 1821, where he studied law at the Universidad de la Habana, and defended abolitionist ideals and Cuba's right to independence from Spain. Lack of political freedom under the colonial rule, and an order for his imprisonment for his political activism led Heredia into exile in 1823; he lived in Boston and New York, and then in Mexico from 1825 until his death in 1839. In 1824 he wrote his ode "Niágara," inspired by the falls and the impressive, sublime landscape; and during the journey to Mexico in 1825 he wrote his famous "Himno del desterrado" (Hymn of the Exile), a "verdadero himno de combate durante muchos años de emigración cubana" (true anthem of combat during many years of Cuban emigration) (José Lezama Lima, 20).[6] Heredia has been often compared to José Martí, as they both *chose* to be Cubans, were proud of their birthplace, and were both political exiles at a very young age in the United States and Latin America. José Martí found in Heredia an example to follow: "El primer poeta de América es Heredia. Sólo él ha puesto

---

[4] See Óscar Rivera-Rodas, *La poesía hispanoamericana del siglo XIX. (Del romanticismo al modernismo)* (Madrid: Editorial Alhambra, 1988).

[5] José María Heredia, *Poesía completa*, ed. Carmen Alemany Bay (Madrid: Editorial Verbum, 2004), 12.

[6] José Lezama Lima, "José María Heredia," *Antología de la poesía cubana* (Madrid: Verbum, 2002), II, 20.

en sus versos la sublimidad, pompa y fuego de su naturaleza. Él es volcánico como sus entrañas y sereno como sus alturas" (The first poet of America is Heredia. Only he has put in his poems the sublime, pomp, and fire of its nature. He is volcanic as its entrails and serene as its heights) (Heredia, *Poesía completa*, ed. Alemany Bay, 17). Canonizing Heredia as the iconic American poet, Martí emphasized his political exile but also his Romantic sensibility. He paradoxically identified Heredia with his own verses and the sublime natural landscape they represent: fierce and serene.

Heredia's "En el teocalli de Cholula" (In the Pyramid of Cholula) reinforces the imagery of a landscape both fierce and serene like the volcano Popocatépetl, "fantasma colosal" (colossal phantom), whose eeriness inspires the poem, and decades later, Martí's vision of Heredia. The identification of the poetic self with the natural landscape is often exploited in the *topos* of ruins in Romantic poetry. Romantic poets often portray nature as the eternal, ultimate witness of history turned into ruins: "the invasion of nature is also sublime and beautiful because it destroys the emblems of tyranny and imperial power."[7] However, even if Heredia echoes the didactic lesson of the Romantic *topos* of ruins, where the remnants of the past epitomize the ephemeral nature of a great empire and its pyramids, he also subverts it by teaching us that *nothing* remains untouched by time and death, not even the "eternal" colossal volcanic mountain:

> ¡Gigante de Anáhuac! ¿Cómo el vuelo
> de las edades rápidas no imprime
> alguna huella en tu nevada frente? ...
>   Pueblos y reyes
> viste hervir a tus pies, que combatían
> cual ora combatimos, y llamaban
> eternas sus ciudades, y creían
> fatigar a la tierra con su gloria.
> Fueron: de ellos no resta ni memoria.
> ¿Y tú eterno serás? Tal vez un día
> de tus profundas bases desquiciado
> caerás; abrumará tu gran ruina
> al yermo de Anáhuac; alzáranse en ella
> nuevas generaciones, y orgullosas,
> que fuiste negarán ...
>   Todo perece
> por ley universal ... [8]

---

[7] Cecilia Enjuto Rangel, *Cities in Ruins: The Politics of Modern Poetics* (West Lafayette, IN: Purdue University Press, 2010), 11.

[8] All of the translations of Heredia's poems are the author's.

(Anahuac giant! How is it that/ the quick flight of time does not leave/a trace in your snowy forehead? ... / ... You have seen peoples and kings/ boil at your feet, fighting/ as we now fight, and they thought/ eternal their cities, and believed/ in tiring the Earth with their glory./ They were: of them nothing remains, no memories./ And will you be eternal? Perhaps one day/ from your depths, you might fall, deranged;/ overwhelmed by your great ruin/ Anahuac's wasteland;/ new generations will rise, and proud,/ will deny your existence./ All dies/ by universal law ...)

Through the apostrophe, Heredia invokes the personified volcano to signal the contrast between what seems to be a paradoxical image: the ever-present snowy volcanic mountain, which carries a fire inside, is witness to the devastation of human endeavor and reminds us that nothing remains of the glories of the past. In a surprising turn to the Romantic *topos* of ruins, Heredia questions the eternal nature of nature itself, in a visionary move that anticipates global warming and environmental disaster; the volcano itself might also be erased from its own landscape and our historical memory.

Far from idealizing the indigenous cultural legacy as a symbol of American exceptionality and the Aztec people's bond with nature, Heredia condemns the Aztec empire and its history of gratuitous violence. This critique should be analyzed as a condemnation of the Spanish empire at the end of the wars of independence. Romantic poetry, as this text shows, keeps returning to the past in order to learn from it and reinforce its political critiques in the present. There are two manuscript versions of this poem, from 1825 and 1832 in the Biblioteca Nacional de Cuba.[9] The fifty verses in which Heredia condemns the Aztec cultural practices of sacrifice and their politics of fear were introduced in the 1832 version. Manuel Pedro González, who has written extensively on Heredia, argued that both versions are quite different because these verses represent "una nota que afea la versión definitiva del poema de Heredia" (a note that disfigures the final version of Heredia's poem). He explained that "En los cincuenta versos que le añadió, impelido por su exigente religiosidad, Heredia se torna belicoso y arremete airado contra los ritos y la crueldad de los sacrificios paganos, sin acordarse de que igualmente inhumanas y fanáticas eran las sectas cristianas por aquella época, empezando por la suya propia" (In the fifty verses he added, impelled by his demanding religiosity, Heredia becomes bellicose and lashes out angrily against the rites and the cruelty of pagan sacrifices, without recalling that Christian sects at that time were just as inhuman and bigoted, starting

---

[9] Manuel Pedro González, *José María Heredia. Primongénito del Romanticismo Hispano. Ensayo de rectificación histórica* (Mexico City: Fondo de Cultura Económica, 1955), 130.

with his own (González, *Heredia*, 131).) González points out to the ethical incoherence of Heredia's critique of the racial and cultural "other" without recognizing that, as a *criollo*, a colonial subject, he is the product of the legitimized brutality of the Catholic Church and the legacy of violence of the Spanish empire. There is a correspondence between the current wars and the past, "Pueblos y reyes ... que combatían cual ora combatimos" (You have seen peoples and kings/ ... fighting/ as we now fight), but in his Romantic contemplative state, the poetic voice privileges his critique of the historical nightmare of the Aztec past. Andrew Bush argues that the two versions of "En el teocalli de Cholula" from 1820 and 1832 mark a fundamental change in Latin American poetics:

> There is a change of epoch from Neoclassicism to Romanticism between the neoclassical introduction of a timeless landscape description in that text and the insertion of an isolated poetic self, identified in history and defined by loss. When the poem is rewritten for the Toluca collection by the added recounting of a nightmare (Heredia, *Poesías completas*, includes the complete text of both versions), Heredia is already fully in the romantic world that not merely anticipated, but rather produced, Freud and our modernity.[10]

The "contemplación" (contemplation) becomes "Un largo sueño/ de glorias engolfadas y perdidas/ en la profunda noche de los tiempos" (A long dream/ of absorbed and lost glories/ in the deep night of the times). The contrast between the enslaved people and the Aztec kings and their "sacerdotes horribles salpicados/ con sangre humana rostros y vestidos" (horrific priests, their faces and dresses/ sprinkled with human blood) serves Heredia's condemnation of superstition and tyranny. With this version, "En el teocalli de Cholula" stops being just a poem about the richness of the Latin American natural landscape to become a reflection on the historical cycle of "state-sponsored" violence. Heredia stretches the use of synesthesia when "Muda y desierta, ahora te ves, pirámide" (Silent and deserted, now you are, pyramid) opposes the "grito de dolor" (cry of pain) of the past, of the victims of the heartless priests of the pyramid, which now blends with the natural landscape. The final apostrophe to the pyramid and the speaker's petition that it becomes the "ejemplo ignominioso/ de la demencia y del furor humano" (inglorious example/ of dementia and human fury) signals the need to construct a "new" Mexico, a "new" Latin America, distant from the "madness" of the past. Cholula was a great Mesoamerican sacred city,

---

[10] Andrew Bush, "Lyric poetry of the eighteenth and nineteenth centuries," in *The Cambridge History of Latin American Literature*, ed. Roberto Gonzalez Echevarría and Enrique Pupo-Walker (New York and Cambridge: Cambridge University Press, 1996), 392.

dedicated to the cult of Quetzalcóatl and his wisdom. Going to Cholula nowadays, however, it is impossible not to be appalled by the story of the famous Cholula Massacre, when Hernán Cortés led an attack against the city, following the advice of the "Tlaxcaltecas," who accused the people of Cholula of betraying the Spaniards. Jaime Montell explains how in 1519 the cholultecas were surprised, "al parecer murieron de tres a cinco mil indígenas en unas pocas horas y buena parte de la población fue incendiada burned" (apparently, from three to five thousand indigenous persons died in a few hours, and much of the population was burned).[11] Although I do not agree with González that the historical and political reflection of this text disfigures it or turns it "ugly," I am also puzzled that in a city so traumatized by the Spanish massacre of 1519, Heredia decided to recall only the Aztec cultural practices of sacrifice.

The uses of the historical past become a recurrent poetic motive throughout Romantic poetry. In reference to Heredia's "En una tempestad" (In a Storm), Raúl Coronado argues:

> Believing in his invincibility, indeed because of his proximity to God, the narrator survives in the present not by looking beyond the hurricane, past the devastation, to the rays of light piercing through the receding storm clouds but rather by remembering the present-becoming-past, mourning the devastation of what had been there before, the tearing asunder of his once far more capacious subjectivity in order to adjust to the possessive individualism of the modern world. With this spiritual awakening, of bearing witness and humbly remembering the past, the narrator is able to act in the present ... In Heredia's poem, the tempest serves as an allegory for the antinomies of modernity, the epistemic shift involved in viewing the world not as a received order but as a produced order.[12]

Just as Heredia directly addresses the volcanic mountain through the apostrophe "Gigante de Anáhuac," here he speaks to the hurricane, "Gigante de los aires, te saludo ... " (Giant of the Air, I salute you ...). Coronado suggests that the "spiritual awakening" triggered by the contemplation of the natural force of the tempest is what shapes Heredia's historical reconceptualization of modernity. This critique to the overwhelming forces of modernity is often expressed in a critique to Spanish colonialism. A recurrent Romantic *topos*, for example in Heredia and in Brazilian poet Antônio Gonçalves Dias (1823–1864), is the poetics of exile, from which diverse visions of the nation

---

[11] Jaime Montell, *La caída de México-Tenochtitlán* (Mexico City: Editorial Joaquín Mortiz, 2003), 145.
[12] Raúl Coronado, "The Poetics of Disenchantment: José María Heredia and the Tempests of Modernity," *Journal of Nineteenth Century Americanists* 1.1 (2013): 188.

or, to be more precise, the *patria* emerge. Rafael Saumel examines how Heredia becomes a symbol of Cuba when he decides to identify as Cuban: "Esa cualidad de 'iniciador' hace que Heredia esté entre los primeros cubanos en padecer varias de las enfermedades que han aquejado a la nación cubana desde el siglo XIX: exilio, tiranía, intervenciones extranjeras, fusilamientos, golpes de estado, caudillos, encarcelamiento, persecuciones, corrupción, xenofobia, separación de las familias"[13] (His role as "initiator" makes Heredia among the first Cubans to suffer from several diseases that have plagued the Cuban nation since the nineteenth century: exile, tyranny, foreign interventions, executions, coups d'état, State leaders, imprisonment, persecution, corruption, xenophobia, separation of families.)[14] Heredia's well-known "Himno del desterrado" evokes the trauma of the political exile, who has to flee his country and suffer the separation of his family. Throughout the poem the speaker uses the apostrophe to address Cuba, to make her *present* although absent, and it is towards the end of the poem that his poetics of exile and his support of Cuban independence emerge from within his critique of Spanish colonialism and its corrupt government:

> ¡Cuba! Al fin te verás libre y pura
> como el aire de luz que respiras,
> cual las ondas hirvientes que miras
> de tus playas la arena besar.
>
> Aunque viles traidores le sirvan,
> del tirano es inútil la saña,
> que no en vano entre Cuba y España
> tiende inmenso sus olas el mar.
>
> (Cuba! At the end you'll be free and pure/ as the air of light you breathe,/ as the boiling waves that you see/ kiss the sand of your beaches./ Although vile traitors serve you,/ the tyrant's malice is useless,/ not in vain between Cuba and Spain/ lies the immense sea and its waves.)

Nature once again serves as the Romantic metaphor for freedom through the imagery of the air and the waves. It is also nature, in this case the immense sea that separates the island from Spain, which legitimizes its claim for independence. Although both Heredia and Gonçalves Dias are well known for their poems on exile, Heredia's poem is more a vindication of his political critique of Spanish colonialism, the reasons why he has to flee, while Gonçalves

---

[13] This explains why someone like Leonardo Padura Fuentes would decide to write a novel based on Heredia's poetics and adventurous life, *La novela de mi vida* (2001).
[14] Rafael E. Saumell, "José María Heredia: La patria no se encuentra en ningún lugar," *Revista de Estudios Hispánicos* 43 (2009): 350.

Dias's "Canção do exílio" (Song of Exile) expresses more the *saudade* sentiment, a nationalist tone, and a *nostalgia* to return home, to a Brazil where
everything is more beautiful.

Gonçalves Dias, the son of a Portuguese shopkeeper and a mestizo woman,
wrote his famous "Canção do exílio" in 1843 while he was studying law at
the University of Coimbra in Portugal. His exile was voluntary and not
political since, as soon as he finished his studies, in 1845, he went back to
Brazil, living in Rio de Janeiro until 1856. He went to Europe several times,
but in 1864 after a short stay in France, his ship was wrecked near the shores
of Guimarães, Maranhão. There are several versions of what happened since
Gonçalves Dias was the only one who did not survive the wreckage. It seems
he fell asleep or was already sick and dying, which explains why he couldn't
move and thus drowned when the rest of the passengers abandoned the
ship.[15] "Canção do exílio," as an emblem of nationalist pride, has been
memorized by many generations of Brazilians, quoted even in the national
anthem, and has also been frequently alluded to, and parodied by, twentieth-
century poets such as Carlos Drummond de Andrade, Murilo Mendes,
Vinicius de Moraes, and Chico Buarque, among many others.

"Canção do exílio" begins with an excerpt of Goethe's ballad *Mignon* as
an epigraph, in which the speaker expresses a desire to go to an exotic land
where lemons and oranges glow and bloom. However, while in Goethe's text
the speaker seems to want to go to an ideal place, in Gonçalves Dias's poem,
the speaker wants to return home, an idealized place, tinged by *saudade* and
nostalgia.[16] As Fritz Ackermann reiterates: "Dominado pela saudade,
Gonçalves Dias dirige os seus pensamentos para a pátria distante e para
o passado. A natureza que o cerca incita-o a confrontar a realidade com
a imagem da terra natal, que traz no coração. A visão do passado suscita-lhe,
logo de início, a imagem de dois sêres da natureza brasileira, a palmeira e o
sabiá ... " (Given to nostalgia, Gonçalves Dias's thoughts turn to his distant
homeland and to the past. The nature that surrounds him leads him to

---

[15] Fritz Ackermann, *A Obra Poética de Antônio Gonçalves Dias*, trans. Egon Schaden (São
Paulo: Conselho Estadual de Cultura, Comissão de Literatura, 1964), 26.

[16] Although Gonçalves Dias is clearly in dialogue with other Romantic poets, critics such as
Sergio Alves Peixoto maintain that he is not reacting against any specific poetic movement
and stress his freedom in style to his well-known rejection of poetic conventions and
traditional norms: "Gonçalves Dias não precisa destruir mais nada. Sua poesia está
plenamente consciente de seu valor e é dela que o poeta fala, sem radicalismos e sem
agressividades. Uma poesia eminentemente romântica no que o Romantismo teria como
ponto principal: a liberdade do poeta" (Gonçalves Dias needs to destroy nothing more.
His poetry is fully conscious of its value and it is this poetry that the poet takes as his
theme, without showing himself to be radical or aggressive. An eminently romantic poetry
in which Romanticism would have as its main point the freedom of the poet.); "Gonçalves
Dias : A consciência das ilusões perdidas," *Caravelle* 68 (1997): 102.

confront reality with the image of the homeland he carries in his heart. The vision of the past brings to his mind, from the start, two emblems of Brazilian nature, the palm tree and the thrush) (Ackermann, *Gonçalves Dias*, 45). I am not convinced that an image of the past dominates the text, "Minha terra *tem* palmeiras/ Onde *canta* o sabiá" (My land has palm trees/ Where the thrush sings). The poem begins with a fixed image of an idealized space, not a past time, since it is a land symbolized by the palm trees and the song of the thrush. Evoking the birdsong as a national emblem is also a meta-literary strategy to legitimize Gonçalves Dias's own poetic song as a national anthem. Gonçalves Dias wrote the poem in Portugal, and one of the reasons why this is a nationalist text about Brazilian exceptionalism is because it is constructed through the use of contrasts between what once upon a time was the colonial land (*there*) and its imperial metropolis (*here*):

> Nosso céu tem mais estrelas,
> Nossas várzeas têm mais flores.
> Nossos bosques têm mais vida,
> Nossa vida mais amores.
>
> (Our skies have more stars,
> Our valleys have more flowers.
> Our forests have more life,
> Our lives have more love.)

The Brazilian natural landscape, through its skies, valleys, forests, and life, is simply put "more beautiful" than the European land, the "here" in Portugal. An abundance of beauty, love, and life characterizes the portrayal of the Brazilian land, to which the speaker returns through dreams that bring him a mixture of pleasure and *saudade*. The Romantic nationalist discourse is once again emphasized at the end of the poem when the speaker pleas to die in his home country, "Onde canta o sabiá" (Where the thrush sings). This contrast between the "here" and "there" evokes the traditional opposition in Brazilian *Indianist* poetry between the "us" and the "other" or "them." Wilton José Marques suggests in his essay on Gonçalves Dias's influence on Machado de Assis's Indianist poetry and his book *Americanas* (1875) that:

> Como se sabe, no desejo romântico de uma literatura nacional, o indianismo foi o mais bem sucedido passo nessa direção, pois, com sua normatização, a literatura brasileira deu vida a um símbolo que, sem colocar em perigo a realidade escravocrata, desempenhou uma missão importante ao se contrapor, no plano das representações, a imagem do colonizador luso que deveria ser desprezada, pelo menos em público, como forma de afirmação do "eu" diante do "outro." A temática do índio, visto como o "brasileiro autêntico," vem

diretamente legitimar aquilo que Antonio Candido chamou de tendência genealógica da literatura local ...[17]

(As we all know, in the Romantic desire for a national literature, Indianism was the most successful step towards that goal because, with the creation of norms, Brazilian literature gave life to a symbol, without endangering the enslaved reality which played an important role in counteracting, in terms of representations, the image of Portuguese colonizers who were to be scorned, at least in public, in order to affirm the "I" as opposed to "the other." The theme of the Indian, seen as the "Brazilian authentic self," comes directly to legitimize what Antonio Candido called the genealogical trend of local literature ...)

Although in comparison to Heredia's "Himno del desterrado," "Canção do exílio" is not as politically explicit in its critique to European colonialism, structurally and thematically it is clearly evoking Brazilian "authentic" symbols such as the palm tree and the thrush as its *indigenous* landscape, to contrast it to the "here," and distance it from the Portuguese land.

As José Luís Jobim explains in his analysis of "Canção do exílio," the use of singular and plural forms can also reveal its nationalist poetics: "The singular forms *eu* (I) and *migna* (my) highlight the subjectivity of the assertions and their relation to the individual who declares that he feels better at night in his homeland and does not want to die in Portugal. But the plural form *nossa* (our) emphasizes a national 'imagined community,'"[18] as described by Benedict Anderson. The Brazilian people become the "virtual addressee" (Jobim, "Gonçalves Dias," 107), and, as Jobim also suggests, this vision of national unity, embodied in national pride for the natural landscape, can also be found in Gonçalves Dias's poems inspired by Native Brazilians and his contributions to *Indianismo*, for example his well-known "O Canto do Piaga" (The Shaman's Song) about the Portuguese conquest or his unfinished poem "Os Timbiras" (The Timbira [Indians]). In the latter, Gonçalves Dias openly criticizes the lack of ethical and political integrity of a society that exterminates the Native Brazilians in the name of modern progress. Brazil's movement of independence from Portugal (1822) was fundamental for the reconceptualization in the mid-nineteenth century of their national identity, and poets such as Gonçalves Dias in Brazil and Heredia in Cuba were leading voices in Latin American Romantic poetry, who spoke as representatives of their "reimagined" communities.

---

[17] Wilton José Marques, "Machado de Assis & Gonçalves Dias: Encontros e diálogos," *Luso-Brazilian Review* 43.1 (2006): 53.
[18] José Luis Jobim, "Gonçalves Dias," *Portuguese Literary and Cultural Studies* 4–5 (2000): 107.

José Martí (Cuba, 1853–1895), as a poet and political writer, fought all his life in the struggle for Cuban independence from Spanish rule. Just as Heredia did, he lived most of his life in exile (in Spain, México, Guatemala, Venezuela, and New York). His famous essay "Nuestra América" (Our America) is commonly taught as a canonical text, one which defends a progressive vision of Latin American cultural identity and politics, against European and U.S. imperialist politics. Rivera-Rodas situates him as a transitional figure from Romanticism to Modernism, and this is mainly because it is difficult to categorize Martí's innovative verse, which is in dialogue with his contemporaries but not determined by their aesthetic visions. Roberto González Echevarría explains that Martí distances himself in his posthumous *Versos libres* (Free Verses) from both Romanticism and *modernismo*, to situate himself in what we might consider Latin American urban modern poetry: "Martí inaugura en *Versos libres* la poesía contemporánea de la ciudad, la poesía que ha dejado de ser simbólica (sin 'correspondencias'), en que la palabra se ha convertido en signo intercambiable y polivalente. Si el Modernismo creó una poesía urbana y cosmopolita, pero que paradójicamente pretendía manifestar la coherencia rítmica, natural del cosmos, *Versos libre* es una ruptura ... " (Martí inaugurates with *Free verses* the contemporary poetry of the city, the poetry that is no longer symbolic (not tied to "correspondences"), in that the word has become an interchangeable and versatile sign. If *modernismo* created an urban and cosmopolitan poetry, one that paradoxically sought to express the rhythmic, natural coherence of the cosmos, *Free verses* represents a breakdown.)[19] Martí opts for an aesthetics of "imperfection" rather than the *modernistas'* quest for aesthetic perfection and beauty, or the Romantic search for continuity of spirit and nature. Martí's "Amor en ciudad grande" (Love in the City), as González Echevarría thoroughly analyzes, begins by exposing the difficulties of articulating a modern poetic language. In this poem, Martí's social, political, ethical, and environmental critique of the modern city anticipates Pablo Neruda's and Federico García Lorca's urban poetry. Furthermore, Jean Franco reiterates that while "the Modernists tried to express guilt and conflict through literary symbols and images ... [Martí] by basing his imagery on everyday experiences, achieved universality" (Franco, *An Introduction*, 109). She considers that had he "not been a great political fighter, he might have been the first great twentieth-century poet, for he developed true originality" (Franco, *An Introduction*, 111).

[19] Roberto González Echevarría, "Martí y su 'Amor en ciudad grande': notas hacia la poética de *Versos libres*," in *Isla a su vuelo fugitivo: ensayos críticos sobre la literatura hispanoamericana* (Madrid: José Porrúa Turanzas, 1983), 30.

Martí's revolutionary vision of politics and poetics establishes a dialogue with his contemporaries, and although it is difficult to categorize his work, many critics consider him a *modernista*. Some critics such as Luis Monguió and Bernardo Gicovate connect Martí and Darío in their attitude to foreign cultures and cosmopolitanism, while others such as Donald Fogelquist emphasize how Martí argues in favor of knowing your own history and cultural legacy, as he does in "Nuestra América," before blindly admiring the European or the Anglo-American heritage. Aníbal González discusses Martí's work as one divided in two stages: the public, exemplified by *Ismaelillo* and *Versos sencillos* (Simple Verses), with more optimistic, *modernista* aesthetics; and the private, with *Versos libres* and *Flores del destierro* (Flowers of Exile) full of existential anguish.[20] For example, in "Amor en ciudad grande," his existential anguish is found in his criticism of a materialistic city where there is no time for love and lovemaking, where everyone treats each other as an object for pleasure or consumption: "¡O si se tiene sed, se alarga el brazo/ y a la copa que pasa se la apura!" (But if you're thirsty, reach out your arm, and drain some passing cup!).[21] Martí condemns how men treat women as mere commodities, as glasses of wine they consume and enjoy, and then discard. Martí's ethical critique reveals the dehumanizing effect of this social behavior: "¡Me espanta la ciudad! ¡Toda está llena de copas por vaciar, o huecas copas!" (The city appalls me! Full of cups to be emptied, and empty cups!). Vicente Cervera Salinas asserts: "Frente a la copa, se dibuja la estructura antitética y dual del poema, el espacio de la existencia 'natural' – como utopía del mundo hispanoamericano no 'contaminado' completamente por las fuerzas de la sociedad positivista ..."[22] (Through the cup, the antithetical structure and the duality of the poem are drawn, the space of the "natural" existence – as a utopia of the Hispanic world not completely "contaminated" by the forces of positivist society). The "natural" man is exiled from the modern city, where the social jungle of materialism and "artificiality" reigns. As most literary movements within modern poetry, we find in these *modernista* poets a conscious awareness of redefining the present through their reading of the past. As Walter Benjamin suggests with regard to Baudelaire's "Le Cygne" (The Swan), it "has the movement of a cradle

---

[20] Aníbal González, *A Companion to Spanish American Modernismo* (Suffolk: Tamesis, 2007).

[21] Martí's "Amor en ciudad grande" is translated as "Love in the City" by Esther Allen in *The Oxford Book of Latin American Poetry. A Bilingual Anthology.*

[22] Vicente Cervera Salinas, "Temor y temblor en la ciudad grande," in *La palabra en el espejo. Estudios de literatura hispanoamericana comparada* (Murcia: Universidad de Murcia, 1996), 94.

rocking back and forth between modernity and antiquity."[23] Darío, in particular, is constantly returning to symbols of antiquity, such as the swan and the Leda myth, to give them new meanings, new forms. Aníbal González suggests: "In numerous cases (Martí and Darío come immediately to mind), *modernista* poets showed from the beginning an awareness of their transitional or dual situation: they looked back nostalgically upon poetic ages that were supposedly more stable, harmonious, and coherent, while at the same time they looked ahead with foreboding to a new age in which poetry reflected change, disharmony and struggle" (González, *A Companion*, 111).

In the last two decades of the nineteenth century, *modernista* poets explored new poetic forms of expression of their experiences and aesthetic ideals. Besides Rubén Darío (Nicaragua 1867–1916), who is *modernismo*'s most influential voice; Salvador Díaz Mirón (México, 1853–1928), Manuel Gutiérrez Nájera (México, 1859–95), Julián del Casal (Cuba, 1863–93), José Asunción Silva (Colombia, 1865–96); and a younger generation of Julio Herrera y Reissig (Uruguay, 1875–1910), Leopoldo Lugones (Argentina, 1874–1938), Ricardo Jaimes Freyre (Bolivia, 1868–1933), Amado Nervo (México, 1870–1919), and Delmira Agustini (Uruguay, 1886–1914) are some of the most well-known *modernistas*, who establish an intellectual and aesthetic dialogue with Darío, although some wanted to openly distance themselves from the Nicaraguan poet, as José Asunción Silva did. In terms of *modernismo*'s key characteristics, Jean Franco sums them up as "1. The rejection of any overt message or teaching in art; 2. The stress on beauty as the highest goal; 3. The need to free verse from traditional forms" (Franco, *An Introduction*, 119). Spanish American *modernismo* in the 1880s must not be confused with Anglo-American Modernism and poets such as T.S. Eliot and Ezra Pound; or *modernismo* in Brazil, linked to the Avant Garde movements and the Week of Modern Art in 1922; or even in Spain, where *modernistas* or the Generation of 1898 were much more preoccupied with the Spanish national identity crisis and the philosophical, existential questioning it triggered. In contrast to these other historical and literary movements, Darío and the Spanish American *modernistas* found their own voice by reading and rethinking the Romantic poets, the Parnassian school of poets, and the French Symbolists, especially Baudelaire, Rimbaud, Verlaine, and Mallarmé. Although listing the characteristics of a literary movement might be a contentious enterprise, with polemic generalizations, I want to just mention some of the most traditional ways of reading Spanish

---

[23] Walter Benjamin, *The Arcades Project*, trans. Howard Eiland and Kevin McLaughlin (Cambridge, MA.: Belknap Press of Harvard UP, 1999), 356.

American *modernismo*, often associated with cosmopolitanism, a cult for the exotic, inspiration in Greek and Nordic mythology, art for art's sake, free verse, musicality, and the search for aesthetic ideals of perfection and beauty; but *modernismo* poetics has many diverse poets, and many stages with different aesthetic goals. Gerard Aching takes a stand against those who just want to consider *modernistas* as detached, politically aloof, cosmopolitan poets. As Aching persuasively argues, Darío as a journalist, writer, and diplomat, "took diplomatic appointments in Madrid, Paris, and Buenos Aires. In light of these activities, how and in what terms do critics contend that the *modernistas* evaded social issues?"[24] Darío's "Oda a Roosevelt" (Ode to Roosevelt) and "Salutación del optimista" (The Optimist's Greeting), for Pedro Salinas Darío's social poetry, show us that there are many poetic stages within *modernismo*, and that one must avoid a reading that depoliticizes his work. The fascination with French poetics and aestheticism can also be a political stand. As Aching notes:

> The politics of Spanish American *modernismo* takes place in a period in which the movement's members and readers were seeking to join and even compete with those metropolitan centers from the periphery. Cosmopolitanism was the discourse that they used to differentiate themselves from the former colonial powers only insofar as that differentiation gave them access to an equal status, to a prestige that was on par with that of former colonizers.
>
> (Aching, *The Politics*, 21)

Their cosmopolitanism or transnational preoccupations also differentiate the Spanish American *modernistas* from Spanish poets and writers, such as Miguel de Unamuno, Manuel and Antonio Machado, and Juan Ramón Jiménez, who were more concerned with their respective national, political, spiritual, intellectual crisis.

Rubén Darío was born in Nicaragua, where he exhibited enormous literary talent even as a child. When he was just fifteen he was invited to study in San Salvador, and just three years later he moved to Chile, where he published *Azul* ... (Blue ..., 1888), which was very well received by literary critics, such as the Spanish writer Juan Valera. He lived between Europe and diverse parts of Latin America as a journalist and as a diplomat; and his most influential works are *Prosas profanas* (Profane Prose Pieces, 1896) and *Cantos de vida y esperanza* (Songs of Life and Hope, 1905). His poetry is frequently "meta-poetic," reflecting on the art of writing poetry itself. As his poem "Yo persigo una forma" (I Pursue a Form) in *Prosas profanas* reveals, Darío's poetics are defined by the aesthetic quest itself, the thirst for

---

[24] Gerard Aching, *The Politics of Spanish American* modernismo. *By Exquisite Design* (Cambridge: Cambridge University Press, 1997), 4.

musicality: "Yo persigo una forma que no encuentra mi estilo ... / Y no hallo sino la palabra que huye,/ la iniciación melódica que de la flauta fluye/ y la barca del sueño que en el espacio boga ... " (I pursue a form that my style doesn't find ... / and I find but the word fleeing,/ melodic tune that flows from the flute/ and the boat of the dream that rows in space ...).[25] These images evoke his search to fix beauty and poetry through a symbolic language, where we find sculpted the Venus de Milo, "mi Bella-Durmiente" (My Sleeping Beauty), and "el cuello del gran cisne blanco que me interroga" (The Neck of the Great White Swan, Questioning Me). The swan serves as a literary sign, a question mark, or a fixed image of beauty. In "El cisne," the speaker addresses the swan through the apostrophe "¡Oh Cisne! ¡Oh sacro pájaro! ... / bajo tu blancas alas la nueva Poesía/ concibe en una gloria de luz y de armonía/ la Helena eterna y pura que encarna el ideal" (Oh Swan! Oh sacred bird! ... / under your white wings, the new Poetry/ conceives in a glory of light and harmony/ the eternal and pure Helena, who embodies the ideal). In this poem, and in a similar way in "Blasón" (Blazon), Darío exemplifies how he envisions the swan as a cultural construction, as a symbol of the new Poetry, as an emblem of beauty, and as the *modernistas*' aesthetic ideal.

Darío's swan, his eroticism, and his meta-poetic reflections are contrasted to Delmira Agustini's vision of the swan and the speaker in both "El cisne" (The Swan) and "Nocturno" (Nocturne). Aníbal González very eloquently introduces Agustini in his essay on "Modernista Poetry": "Agustini's life was tragically brief: born in 1886, she died in 1914, murdered by her abusive ex-husband, whom she had taken as a lover. The scandal of her divorce and not long after, her death, threw into sharp relief Agustini's double life: the spoiled child of a bourgeois family in a less-than-cosmopolitan Montevideo, she had always behaved correctly and had avoided the public eye (as women were expected to do in that time and place); yet, simultaneously, she wrote remarkably beautiful and profoundly erotic poems in which, like no other Spanish-language female writer before her, she openly expressed her sexuality and her desires" (González, *A Companion*, 125). It is well known that Agustini found in Darío a literary model, a "father figure," and it is very revealing how she played the role of "la Nena" (the Girl), as she was often called privately, and even publicly she was constantly underestimated as a child.[26] The mask of the woman-child is cleverly played out throughout her correspondence, and yet her poems voice a woman who conquers and

---

[25] Author's translation.
[26] For more on Agustini's "aniñamiento," see Emir Rodríguez Monegal's *Sexo y poesía en el 900 uruguayo*, Sylvia Molloy's "Dos lecturas del cisne: Rubén Darío y Delmira Agustini," and Cathy L. Jrade's *Delmira Agustini, Sexual Seduction and Vampire Conquest*.

transgresses *modernista* poetics. In her essay on Darío and Agustini, Silvia Molloy argues: "En Agustini el yo erotizado va deseando, por así decirlo, el poema: hay un erotismo de lo móvil, de lo cambiante – de lo desequilibrado si se quiere – mientras que en Darío hay el erotismo de lo fijo, o más bien de lo que se busca fijar" (In Agustini, the eroticized speaker desires, so to speak, the poem: there is an eroticism of the changeable, the transformable – of the unbalanced if you will – while in Dario, there is an eroticism of what is fixed, or rather what is sought to be fixed).[27] The mobility of this symbol in Agustini can be perceived in "El cisne" in the swan as a lover, and in "Nocturno" when the speaker identifies with a swan who flies away: "Yo soy el cisne errante de lo sangrientos rastros,/ voy manchando los lagos y remontando el vuelo" (And I am the wandering swan of the bloody trails,/ I proceed staining lakes and soaring in flight). A chromatic transgression also marks the metaphor of mobility of the swan. The swan's whiteness in Agustini is tinged by the redness of its blood, in both "Nocturno," when he flies away leaving bloody lakes, and in "El cisne," when it ends: "el cisne asusta de rojo,/ y yo de blanca doy miedo!" (the swan frightens in redness,/ and I, with my whiteness, am frightening!). The final transformation of the speaker through that erotic embrace can also be read as another metaphor of the blank page, since "El cisne" from the very beginning, just as many of Darío's texts, is both a reflection on the act of writing poetry and of constructing sexual desire.

Cathy L. Jrade identifies Agustini's swan with Darío and *modernista* poetry; she converts him into "her poetic foil and the male other of her verse. Darío becomes, in this manner, both person and poetry."[28] Agustini's "El cisne" is an act of rebelliousness against patriarchal norms and visions of female desire. From the very first stanza, she asserts her meta-poetic reflection:

> Pupila azul de mi parque
> Es el sensitivo espejo
> De un lago claro, muy claro! ...
> Tan claro que a veces creo
> Que en su cristalina página
> Se imprime mi pensamiento.[29]

> (The blue pupil of the eye of my park/ is the sensitive mirror/ of a clear, very clear lake! ... / So clear that at times I believe/ that on its crystalline page/ my thought is printed.)

---

[27] Sylvia Molloy, "Dos lecturas del cisne: Rubén Darío y Delmira Agustini," in *La sartén por el mango: encuentro de escritoras latinoamericanas*, ed. Patricia Elena González and Eliana Ortega (Río Piedras, Puerto Rico: Ediciones Huracán, 1985), 66.

[28] Cathy L. Jrade, *Delmira Agustini, Sexual Seduction, and Vampiric Conquest* (New Haven: Yale University Press, 2012), 3.

[29] The translation of Agustini's "El cisne" is found in Jrade's *Delmira Agustini*, 3.

Jrade discusses in her insightful analysis of this poem that "[e]ye and lake fuse and become the page upon which the lyric voice writes; it is the surface that reflects her literary context and upon which she projects her personal visions and sensibilities" (Jrade, *Delmira Agustini,* 154–155). I would add that besides playing with the blue reflection of the sky in the lake as a metaphor of *modernista* poetics, she is stating that the poem is a product of her "pensamiento," her thoughts, her ability to think and reflect. The speaker is embracing her authority, without an anxiety of influence, and empowers her poetics by emphasizing that they emerge from her intellect, not her soul, her body or her heart. The erotic language employed in this poem clearly transgresses *modernista* poetry and patriarchal society's limited vision of women, as it describes the sexual encounter with the personified swan: "Ningunos labios ardieron/ Como su pico en mis manos,/ Ninguna testa ha caído/ Tan lánguida en mi regazo." (No lips blazed/ as did its beak in my hands,/ no head has fallen/ as listless into my lap.) Masturbation, sexual penetration, sexual exhaustion, and even oral sex, when the speaker offers her swan "Todo el vaso de mi cuerpo" (The whole receptacle of my body), are encoded in these images. But although the speaker embraces the image of the body as receptacle, she does not lose sexual control, she does not become a submissive object of desire, but quite the contrary: these images of erotic and poetic pleasure ultimately reveal the lyric voice as an autonomous, powerful *subject* of desire, a poetic *tour de force*.

From the Romantic poetics of exile and anticolonial discourse in Heredia and Dias to *modernismo*'s meta-poetic reflections and redefinition of poetry through metaphors such as the swan, there is clearly an aesthetic and philosophical shift in Latin American nineteenth-century poetry. The process of modernization in the late nineteenth-century context challenges the oneiric images, the vision of nature, the obsession with the self, and the reconfiguration of the nation in Romantic aesthetics. While Martí's critique of the modern city is more in touch with the political and poetic questions that emerge in avant-garde art and modern urban poetry, Darío's *modernista* aesthetics show his preoccupation with a cosmopolitan, "universal" vision of poetry, highly problematic in its reification of women, but not necessarily "apolitical" or completely detached from the social struggles of its time, as his later poetic works demonstrate. Agustini's poetic drive and rhetorical risks take *modernismo* to another level. Transgressing poetic and social norms that bounded women to submissive positions, she redefines the poetics of desire in early twentieth-century Latin American poetry, setting the stage for many women poets who saw in her a model to follow.

3

ADAM JOSEPH SHELLHORSE

The Avant-Garde: From *Creacionismo* to *Ultraísmo*, Brazilian *Modernismo*, *Antropofagia*, and Surrealism

Octavio Paz understood, having experienced it himself, what constitutes the critical force of experimental writing. The writer appropriates the high modernist virtues – critique, creation, multiperspectivism, and multi-genre combination – and transforms them into ends that relate not only to the recondite world of the arts but to the fraught reality of history, thought, and politics. He makes of them a new language: "El arte de la primera mitad del siglo XX fue ante todo crítica, destrucción y recreación del lenguaje: asalto a los significados tradicionales" (The art of the first half of the twentieth century was above all critique, destruction and recreation of language: an assault on traditional meanings).[1] This language is not personal, nor is it a vehicle of expression for collective identity. For Paz, there is no other language for the writer than that of invention, transvaluation, and revelation: one that breaks with conformist representations to introduce the unsaid coming of difference. Invention, transvaluation, and revelation become the effects of a more powerful language, one more intimately entwined with the forces of life than any conventional discourse. This is what Paz never ceases to call *poesía* (poetry): a discourse no longer produced on the basis of representation, dualism, and fixity, but one which rather negates discourse to bring about new realities, new rhythms, affects, and sensations. Amplifying the purview of desire, imagination, thought, and being, experimental poetry transforms the world: it negates conventional language to introduce primordial language and experience.[2]

This chapter examines the powerful reinvention of language by Latin American poets associated with the avant-garde. It focuses on paradigmatic ideas such as *creacionismo*, *ultraísmo*, Brazilian *modernismo*, Surrealism, and the *Semana de Arte Moderna* (Week of Modern Art), through a selection of

---

[1] *Puertas al campo* (Barcelona: Seix Barral, 1989), 11.
[2] Paz, *Corriente alterna* (Mexico City: Siglo Veintiuno Editores, 1968), 54; Paz, *Pasión crítica* (Barcelona: Seix Barral, 1985), 184.

seminal writers. Comparative in scope, the chapter questions an established view about the legacy of Latin American avant-garde poetry: that it has always been dependent on European concepts.[3] Against this traditional standpoint, my investigation highlights the vanguard writers' taste for materiality, sensation, the "primitive," and will to reinvent language (including new, multidisciplinary forms of linguistic codification) as sites of critique with respect to Eurocentrism and substantialist accounts of poetry based on the metaphysics of presence. As I hope will become clear, at stake in this questioning is a new conceptualization of Latin American experimental form – one which challenges its customarily conceived cobelonging with a derived cultural aesthetics.

The Avant-Garde Age

From Europe to the Americas, it is well known that the avant-garde era articulated a sense of cultural crisis, and an openness to experimentation and change. In Latin America, it was marked by nativist utopianism, and by the building of cultural, artistic, and literary institutions, which in Europe, the vanguard movements had sought to obliterate. Moreover, arising out of the catastrophe of World War I, the Latin American avant-gardes articulate a generational coming of age, spearheaded in large part by iconoclastic poets. One can situate their zealous search for revolutionary forms, their affirmation of the originality of local cultures, and their critique of Western decadence as corresponding to the European imperial crisis, the rise of the United States as both superpower and regional hegemon (Big Brother policy), the dawning of fascism in Europe, and the Mexican and Soviet revolutions. In similar fashion, one should take into account the growth of major cities such as São Paulo, México, Santiago, Lima, and Buenos Aires, and the influx of immigrants, scientific ideas, technologies, and artistic currents. Furthermore, it is crucial to consider that many distinguished Latin American poets of the period traveled to Europe and established contacts with renowned avant-garde figures.

With respect to the rise of modernizing discourses and artistic movements in the early twentieth century, Stephen M. Hart has argued:

> The first decade of the twentieth century was characterized by a shock-cut which seemed to sweep to one side the customary ways of thinking about the

---

[3] Fernando J. Rosenberg investigates how the Latin American avant-gardes undermine the teleology of modernity as a single temporality; see "Cultural Theory and Avant-Gardes: Mariátegui, Mário de Andrade, Oswald de Andrade, Pagú, Tarsila do Amaral, César Vallejo," in *A Companion to Latin American Literature and Culture*, ed. Sara Castro-Klaren (West Sussex, UK: Wiley-Blackwell, 2008), 411; and *The Avant-Garde and Geopolitics in Latin America* (Pittsburgh, PA: University of Pittsburgh Press, 2006).

world. In 1899 Freud published his revolutionary study of dreams, *Die Traumdeutung*, in 1905 Einstein published his revolutionary theories about the energy-mass equation, and in 1909 Marinetti published his futurist manifesto which glorified the technology of the motorcar and called for the destruction of museums and libraries ... [In Brazil and in Spanish America] [t]he spell of Greco-Roman culture – and particularly its association with ruralism – had suddenly been broken.[4]

Continent-wide, classicism had died, and the narrow confines of the literary field had burst. Literature no longer seamlessly represented the elite and *la patria* as in previous *indigenismos*. And poetry itself was no longer steeped in Greco-Roman revival and mellifluous, French Parnassian symbolism, as evinced in the fin-de-siècle writings of the *modernista* generation of Darío, Bilac, and Lugones. The lyric was rather conceived as a catalyst for aesthetic and cultural thought.[5] Its task was to reinvent both world and word as part of a necessary updating of the field of cultural production. In this age of reformism, revolution, relativism, and fervor for the modern, we witness the birth, moreover, of poet seers who endeavored to attain a synthesis of the arts through typographic invention, abundance of metaphor, and collage-like open works. These luminaries linked the lyric to a new cosmopolitan "spirit" for truth, research, and invention.[6] Indeed, for the influential French poet, Guillaume Apollinaire, modern "poets [were] filling the gap," between science, cinema, technology, and the other arts (Apollinaire, "The New Spirit," 229). If the lyric had perforce become visual, multigenre, and the site of permanent revolution, this was due to the poet's desire to translate the kinetic rhythms of modernity. Many Latin American poets of the age seized this heroic, modernizing vocation for poetry as their own, and in ways that challenged a central component to Apollinaire's vision. In the widely read essay, "The New Spirit and the Poets" (1917), Apollinaire claimed that the "new spirit" and lyric would only emanate from France (Apollinaire, "The New Spirit," 236). In contradistinction, early twentieth-century Latin American subjectivities were marked by a questioning of the teleology of

[4] Stephen M. Hart, "Latin American Poetry," in *A Companion to Latin American Literature and Culture*, ed. Sara Castro-Klaren (West Sussex, UK: Wiley-Blackwell, 2008), 427–428.
[5] For superlative book-length studies on the subject, see Jorge Schwartz, *Vanguardia y cosmopolitismo en la década del veinte: Oliverio Girondo y Oswald de Andrade* (Rosario: Beatriz Viterbo Editora, 1993), and *Fervor das vanguardas: Arte e literatura na América Latina* (São Paulo: Companhia das Letras, 2013); Vicky Unruh, *Latin American Vanguards: The Art of Contentious Encounters* (Berkeley, CA: The University of California Press, 1994); and Rosenberg, *The Avant-Garde and Geopolitics in Latin America* (Pittsburgh, PA: University of Pittsburgh Press, 2006).
[6] Guillaume Apollinaire, "The New Spirit and the Poets," in *Selected Writings of Guillaume Apollinaire*, trans. and ed. Roger Shattuck (New York: New Directions Books, 1971), 228.

the modern in the first place. Never the result of blind imitation, the Latin American avant-garde's dialogue with the currents of European modernism – such as Dadaism, Surrealism, Cubism, or Futurism – was framed by dissonance, simultaneity, and the reinvention of language. Throughout this chapter, we will see how Latin American vanguard poets demonstrated a passion to attain a complex, intensive, and anti-representational medium whose purpose was to surpass the limitations of conventional poetry and lay bare a "real" commensurate with the experience of the times.

Vicente Huidobro and *Creacionismo*

In the estimation of many, the inaugural and most characteristic figure of *vanguardismo* was the visionary and polemical Chilean Vicente Huidobro (1893–1948). In conjunction with his lyrical innovations, Huidobro authored numerous statements of principle that are essential to the assessment of *vanguardismo*: "Non Serviam" (I Will Not Serve, 1914), "La creación pura" (Pure Creation, 1921), and *Manifestes* (1925). In these manifestos, poetry is assigned an epochal task: no longer will it represent reality or be bound to *modernista* rhetoric. Rather, it will create new realities adequate to the times and the inventions of technology and science: "Lo realizado en la mecánica también se ha hecho en la poesía. Os diré qué entiendo por un poema creado. Es un poema en el que cada parte constitutiva, y todo el conjunto, muestra un hecho nuevo, independiente del mundo externo, desligado de cualquier realidad que no sea la propia." (What has been achieved in mechanics has also been accomplished in poetry. I'll tell you what I mean by a created poem. It is a poem in which each constitutive part, as well as the whole ensemble, demonstrates a new thing, independent from the external world, and removed from any reality that is not its own.)[7] Having collaborated with leading figures of the avant-garde such as Apollinaire, Picasso, Tzara, Cocteau, Reverdy, Delaunay, Jacobs, Stravinsky, and translated Marinetti's futurist manifesto, Huidobro traveled to Madrid in 1918 as a proselytizer of the new, set up a literary salon in his apartment, and published four books, *Tour Eiffel, Hallali, Ecuatorial*, and *Poemas árticos* (Artic Poems). The latter two, written in Spanish, galvanized the poetry of the period and led to the birth of a new movement, *ultraísmo*, whose members included the young Argentine, Jorge Luis Borges, and a group of dissident Spaniards: Guillermo de Torre, Gerardo Diego, Juan Larrea, and Rafael Cansinos-Asséns. *Poemas árticos* is considered by René de

---

[7] Vicente Huidobro, "El creacionismo," in *Las vanguardias latinoamericanas: textos programáticos y críticos*, ed. Jorge Schwartz (Mexico City: Fondo de Cultura Económica, 2002), 116.

Costa to be the earliest avatar of avant-garde writing in Spanish, where he notes that "its poems were read and reread, studied, and imitated by a whole generation of young Spaniards ready for something new. Those who could not acquire the book itself, hand-copied its content."[8] A superlative example is the volume's second poem, "Exprés" (Express). In it, Huidobro played his hand at innovative typography, explored perspective and theme, and shunned sequential description:

Una corona yo me haría
De todas las ciudades recorridas

Londres	Madrid	Paris
Roma	Nápoles	Zurich

Silban en los llanos
        locomotoras cubiertas de algas

AQUÍ NADIE HE ENCONTRADO

De todos los ríos navegados
yo me haría un collar

El Amazonas	El Sena
El Támesis	El Rin

Cien embarcaciones sabias
Que han plegado las alas

        Y mi canción de marinero huérfano
        Diciendo adiós a las playas

Aspirar el aroma del Monte Rosa
Trenzar las canas errantes del Monte Blanco
Y sobre el cenit del Monte Cenis
Encender en el sol muriente
El último cigarro

Un silbido horada el aire

        No es un juego de agua

ADELANTE[9]

(I would make me a crown
Of all the cities I have journeyed to

---

[8] René de Costa, *Vicente Huidobro: The Careers of a Poet* (Oxford: Clarendon Press, 1984), 57.

[9] "Exprés," in *The Selected Poetry of Vicente Huidobro*, ed. David M. Guss (New York: New Directions, 1981), 46.

London   Madrid   Paris
Rome   Naples   Zurich

Locomotives seaweed-clad
                    whistle on the flatlands

I HAVE FOUND NO ONE HERE

Of all the rivers I have sailed
I would make me a necklace

        The Amazon   The Seine
        The Thames   The Rhine

A hundred wise vessels
That have folded their wings

                And my orphan sailor's song
                Bidding the shore goodbye

To take in the scent of Monte Rosa
To braid the drifting snows of Mont Blanc
And upon the Zenith of Mont Cenis
To light the last cigarette
In the dying sun

A whistle drills the air
                This is no water game

ONWARD)[10]

In his quest to renew language, the poet transforms reality. In the case of "Exprés," the motifs of modernity, travel, departure, memory, conquest, and surpassing limits configure a mental and sensory constellation full of contrasts. What counts is not the harmonic concatenation of ideas through linear, metered verse, but rather the exploration of the relationship between medium and message, and the overcoming of the limitations of traditional metered verse. The main subject of the poem is thus not travel or memory. By placing parallel themes and disparate objects in relationship such as the locomotive, boat, airplane, train timetable, and the poetic voice's *"corona"* (crown) and *"collar"* (necklace), the poem creates an ensemble of images that allegorically suggests the metamorphosis of the poetic medium and its constitutive force in modern times. As a text to be read like a painting, Huidobro's visual poem explores the idea of the radicalized medium through experimental typography and the Cubist technique of juxtaposition of the

---

[10] Vicente Huidobro, *Artic Poems*, trans. Ian Barnett, *Saltana: A Journal of Literature and Translation* (2004–2006), 7; modified.

apparently unlike. Anti-representational, freed from meter, punctuation, and utilizing displaced margins, Huidobro's "Exprés" provides the example of his ultimate aim: redoubling the expressive force of the poem in all of its constitutive parts. The poet creates not representations of objects or ideas, but renders visible their complex interplay as elements of creation. The poem thereby suggests Huidobro's oft-repeated creationist catchphrase: "arte superior al medio" (art [that is] superior to the external environment).[11] The text does not mirror a harmonious nature, but becomes a totally invented environment whose dissonant song not only celebrates its own powers of imagination and invention but parallels the creative forces of chaos and modernity.

Jorge Luis Borges and *Ultraísmo*

Another notable departure from Parnassian ornamentation is to be found in the early work of Jorge Luis Borges (1899–1986), the foremost theoretician and lyricist of Argentine *ultraísmo*. Unlike his Spanish *ultraísta* counterparts who celebrated the cultivation of all things new, and with whom he had collaborated from 1918 to 1921, this axial figure explored the problem of creating a vanguard syntax in sync with the times and adequate to Argentine experience. He will initiate this seminal project in his first book, *Fervor de Buenos Aires* (Fervor for Buenos Aires, 1923). By combining *ultraísta* tendencies such as profusion of metaphor, imagistic synthesis, and unprecedented visions, with the adoption of confessional, narrative, and philosophical threads, Borges versified not the city center but a phantasmal metropolis rooted in its margins and past. Borges's non-conformism was immediately detected by Spaniard *ultraístas* and even denounced. Even his stalwart friend and future brother-in-law, Guillermo de Torre, expressed misgivings about this new "meditative" turn in his poetics.[12] The unconventional, anti-modern dimension of this collection is felt in the initial verse: "Las calles de Buenos Aires/ ya son la entraña de mi alma./ No las calles enérgicas/ molestadas de prisas y ajetreos,/ sino la dulce calle del arrabal" (The streets of Buenos Aires/ already form the core of my soul./ Not the hurried streets/ overwhelmed with to-ing and fro-ing,/ but the sweet street of the suburb).[13] Similar to the Brazilian avant-garde, as we will soon see,

---

[11] "La creación pura (ensayo de estética)," ed. Jorge Schwartz (Mexico City: Fondo de Cultura Económica, 2002), 109.

[12] Guillermo de Torre, *Literaturas europeas de vanguardia* (Madrid: Raffael Caro Raggio, 1925), 63–64; Linda S. Maier, *Borges and the European Avant-Garde* (New York: Peter Lang Publishing, 1996), 13.

[13] Borges, *Poemas: 1922–1943* (Buenos Aires: Editorial Losada, 1943), 11.

among Borges's aims was the rediscovery of Argentine "Creole" speech, and the construction of a lyrical persona that would insert the poet into national history through the construction of exceptional perceptions and affects.[14] But perhaps the main dilemma was creating a properly Argentine poetry that was at once local and cosmopolitan, even as the volume self-reflexively explored the motifs of writing, time, modernity, and the demise of nineteenth-century Creole civilization: "La ciudad está en mí como un poema/ que no he logrado detener en palabras./ A un lado hay la excepción de algunos versos;/ al otro, arrinconándolos,/ la vida se adelanta sobre el tiempo,/ como terror/ que usurpa toda el alma" (The city resides within me like a poem/ that I have not stilled into words./ To one side there's the exception of a few verses;/ on the other, pushing them into a corner,/ life overtakes time,/ like terror/ overwhelming my soul; Borges, *Poemas: 1922–1943*, 26). The original version of "Arrabal" (Suburb), which Borges first published in Spain for *Cosmópolis* in August 1921, articulates the poet's strategy for an irreverent, regional cosmopolitanism that will have lasting repercussions for Argentine and Latin American literature:

Arrabal

A Guillermo de Torre.

El arrabal es el reflejo
    de la fatiga del viandante.
Mis pasos claudicaron
cuando iban a pisar el horizonte
y estuve entre las casas
miedosas y humilladas
juiciosas cual ovejas en manadas
encarceladas en manzanas
diferentes e iguales
como si fuesen todas ellas
recuerdos superpuestos, barajados
de una sola manzana.
El pastito precario
desesperadamente esperanzado
salpicaba las piedras de la calle
y mis miradas comprobaron
gesticulante y vano
el cartel del poniente
en su fracaso cotidiano.

---

[14] Francine Masiello, *Lenguaje e Ideología: Las escuelas argentinas de vanguardia* (Buenos Aires: Hachette, 1986), 158.

Y sentí **Buenos Aires**
y literaturicé en la hondura del alma
la viacrucis inmóvil
de la calle sufrida
y el caserío sosegado.
1921.[15]

(Suburb

For Guillermo de Torre.

The suburb is the reflection/ of the pedestrian's fatigue./ My footfalls were vanquished/ just as they were about to step on the horizon/ and I found myself between timorous,/ humiliated houses,/ as sensible as herds of sheep/ imprisoned in city blocks,/ different but equal,/ as if all of them/ were shuffled, superimposed memories/ of one city block./ The precarious, desperately/ hopeful grass/ sprinkled the stones in the street/ and my gaze verified/ gesticulating and vain/ the poster of the sunset,/ in its daily failure./ And I felt **Buenos Aires/** and I literatured in the depths of my soul/ the immobile Way of the Cross/ of the suffering street/ and the peaceful homestead./ 1921.)

"Arrabal" is exemplary of Borges's vanguard project. Dedicated to *ultraísta* paragon, de Torre, the poetic "I" takes us to the city's limits to create an exquisite vision. Yet far from the typographical experiments of the Spaniard, most notably as exhibited in *Hélices* (1918–1922), the inventive character of this poem hinges on its narrative, allegorical structure that mediates between realms of experience. Framed by the setting sun at the city's outskirts, the lyrical "I" compares the vision of stacked suburban houses and the horizon to a flock of sheep, superimposed memories, a movie poster, and the Via Crucis of Christ. In so doing, he produces a poem about the experience of witnessing and writing about the city during a specific era: the decline of the nineteenth-century city and Creole order. As a strategy for creating an Argentine literature not crippled by the pitfalls of local color, Beatriz Sarlo has argued that in early works such as these, Borges invented a mythological landscape rooted in the *orillas*, or city outskirts.[16] Never subservient to foreign or local influence, and against the grain of blindly celebrating the modern, it is also important to underscore Borges's irreverent combination of regimes of signs – the *ultraísta* and Creole narrative lyric – to produce a new poetic language. Even as he relativized the fervor for the modern, the young Borges wrote from the middle and margins of poetic tendencies to

[15] The first published version of Borges's poem, "Arrabal," is quoted from Carlos García, "La edición princeps de *Fervor de Buenos Aires,*" *Variaciones Borges,* 4 (1997): 196–97.
[16] Beatriz Sarlo, *Jorge Luis Borges: A Writer on the Edge,* ed. John King (New York: Verso, 1993), 21.

create the new. In his rediscovery of Argentine language, history, and Buenos Aires from the liminal space of the narrative *ultraísta* poem, Borges created the philosophical and sensory synthetic poem. As a reinvention of Argentine language, its task was to mediate, unvanquished, the past in the present.

Brazilian *Modernismo* and *Antropofagia*: Mário and Oswald de Andrade

Nearly a century after its irruption and outcry for liberty of expression, Brazilian *modernismo* remains the cornerstone for artistic experimentation in Brazil. It should not be confused with the Parnassian-inspired, Spanish American *modernistas*. Brazilian *modernismo* rebelled against reverence for form, and its own entrenched Parnassian tradition. As a broad-based, interdisciplinary movement that included the other arts and cultural criticism, *modernismo* was spearheaded by poetry and the desire to renovate cultural, intellectual, and artistic life. It is, in short, Brazil's symbolic, cultural, and aesthetic declaration of independence from Europe. In the words of two distinguished scholars, *modernismo*'s lasting contribution is its "poetic rediscovery of Brazil" through a "consideration of *all* (i.e., multiracial, multicultural, multiregional) aspects of Brazilian life."[17] Ushering in a cosmopolitan, creative tradition centered in the affirmation of the originality of Brazilian experience, Mário de Andrade formalized *modernismo*'s grand synthesis: (i) the permanent right to aesthetic research, (ii) updating Brazilian intelligence, and (iii) revolt against an academic, aristocratic, and Eurocentric tradition to create a new national consciousness.[18]

While multifaceted, *modernismo* is customarily divided into two phases. The first broaches the fermentation of progressive, anti-Parnassian currents in Brazil. This period commences with the uproar over the fauvist-inspired paintings of Anita Malfatti in the 1910s and spans the "constructive" vanguard phase, beginning circa 1922 and ending in 1929. The second, which we will not consider, runs roughly from 1930 to the middle of the 1940s, and is centered in the rise of the critical regionalist novel by such *modernista* scions as José Lins de Rego, Jorge Amado, and Graciliano Ramos. The point of confluence for the vanguard phase is the legendary *Semana de Arte Moderna*. A three-day festival of public performances, readings, exhibits, and lectures marking Brazil's first 100 years of independence from Portugal,

---

[17] K. David Jackson, *Haroldo de Campos: A Dialogue with the Brazilian Concrete Poet*, ed. K. David Jackson (Oxford: Centre for Brazilian Studies, 2005), 1; Charles A. Perrone, *Seven Faces: Brazilian Poetry since Modernism* (Durham, NC: Duke University Press, 1996), 2.

[18] *Aspectos da literatura brasileira* (São Paulo: Livraria Martins, 1978), 238–242.

The Week of Modern Art took place from 11 to 18 February in the Municipal Theater of São Paulo. Rejecting art for art's sake, the *Semana* sparked a dawning of critical consciousness, called for renovation and redefinition of artistic practices, and stood as a concentrated attack on cultural and literary façades. As with its European precursors, particularly international Dadaism and the Italian futurists, it descried the inseparable chasm between artists and traditional civilized existence. Constituting a yearning for contact with the people that quashed once and for all the "longing for Europe," the festival's spirit of negation was matched by a primitive constructivism.[19] Now consecrated as the symbolic watershed from which all future Brazilian thought, poetry, and art would flow, The Week of Modern Art's guiding spirit of rupture, research, synthesis, and "primitivism" led to the creation of singular works that revolutionized both the arts and the Brazilian language.

A case in point is Mário de Andrade's paean to São Paulo, *Paulicéia desvairada* (*Hallucinated City*, 1922), published in July following The Week of Modern Art.[20] The twenty-two poem volume is preceded by a statement of principles, "Extremely Interesting Preface," that launched Andrade's own lyrical "*Desvairismo*" (Hallucinism) (*Paulicéia 7*). In the "Preface," Andrade (1893–1945) reveled in his new poetic vision. Equating the lyrical impulse to the order of the unconscious, Andrade defended free verse, agrammatical syntax, "writing Brazilian," and use of exaggeration, and called for modern poetry to catch up with advances in music (*Paulicéia*, 33). Namely, it would employ non-linear polyphony to provide a total sensory and semantic effect. As poetry, "Hallucinism" might best be understood as a form of literary simultaneism where the future and the past, the Brazilian and the European, the literary and the anti-literary dissonantly merge. Turning on the concurrent arrangement of contrasting elements, linguistic heteroglossia, mixed media, and the fragmentation of the lyrical voice into elliptical sonorous chains, *Hallucinated City* is the inaugural instance of *modernista* verse. In addition to its methods of language intensification and battle cry for the new, the book was designed as a multimedial performance to disrupt the sensibilities of the middle class. As such, consider the opening stanza of the poem, "Ode ao burguês" (Ode to the Bourgeois), which Andrade recited at the central event of The Week of Modern Art: "Eu insulto o burguês ! O burguês-níquel,/ o burguês-burguês !/ A digestão bem feita de São Paulo !/ O homem-curva ! o homem-nádegas !/ O homem que sendo francês, brasileiro, italiano/ é sempre cauteloso pouco-a-pouco !"

[19] Mário de Andrade, *Entrevistas e depoimentos* (São Paulo: T.A. Queiroz, 1983), 18.
[20] *Paulicéa desvairada* (São Paulo: Casa Mayença, 1922).

(I insult the bourgeois ! The nickel-bourgeois,/ The bourgeois-bourgeois !/ The well done digestion of São Paulo/ The bent-man ! the buttocks-man !/ The man who being French, Brazilian, Italian/ is always so cautious little by little !; *Pauliceia*, 67).

If the lyrical impulse is born in the unconscious, the task of the *modernista* poet, for Andrade, was to condense this profusion into an orderly mosaic of images, references, texts, media, and sensations: "Meu querido palimpsesto sem valor !/ Crônica em mau latim/ cobrindo uma écloga que não seja de Virgilio ! . . ." (My lovely palimpsest worthless !/ Chronicle in bad Latin/ covering over an eclogue Virgil didn't write ! . . .; *Pauliceia*, 83). The hallucinated lyrical voice not only lays bare the device to shock the reader but calls attention to the fabricated character of the present: "Os jornais estampam as aparéncias/ dos grandes que fazem anos, dos criminosos que fazem/ danos . . . / Os quarenta-graus das riquezas ! O vento gela . . . / Abandonos ! Ideais palidos !/ Perdidos os poetas, os moços, os loucos !" (The newspapers stamp appearances/ of the great who make years, of the criminals who make tears . . . / The forty degrees of riches ! The wind freezes . . . / Abandoned ! Pallid ideals !/ Lost, the poets, the young, the madmen !; *Pauliceia*, 88). Such a recognition leads to the invention of a more daring syntax, capable of completely altering language and conceptions of temporality and genre. As he cannibalizes texts and media, such as the newspapers above, but also the landscape painting, the chronicle, the eclogue, the oratorio, and avant-garde polyphony in music, the poetic voice builds the poem of the city and self as a mixed media assemblage, creating an isomorphism with its linguistic Babel. Writing Brazilian to write modern, as Andrade liked to say, the achievement of *Hallucinated City* remains its powerful, primordial explorations of language as a mode of poetic polyphony and Surrealism *avant la lettre*:

> Paulicea – a grande bocca de mil dentes;
> e os jôrros dentre a lingua trissulca
> de pús e de mais pús de distinção . . .
> Giram homens fracos, baixos, magros . . .
> Serpentinas de entes frementes a se desenrolar . . .
>
> Estes homens de São Paulo,
> todos iguais e desiguais,
> quando vivem dentro dos meus olhos tão ricos,
> parecem-me uns macacos, uns macacos.
>
> (São Paulo – great mouth of a thousand teeth;/ and the gushing of its forked tongue/ of pus, and more pus of distinction . . . / Weak men whirl, short, gaunt . . . / Serpentine beings quivering, uncoiling . . . / These men of São

Paulo/ all equivalent yet different,/ when they live within my eyes so precious,/ look like monkeys to me, like monkeys; *Paulicéia*, 47–48).

Another exceptional case of Brazilian *modernista* lyric is to be found in the anti-verse of Oswald de Andrade (1890–1954). A prominent polemicist and poet-inventor, Andrade's *Pau Brasil* (1925) constitutes a turning point in Brazilian *modernismo* and a different approach to form.[21] Through emphasis on the originality of Brazil, and by means of parody, the ready-made, and cinematic montage, Andrade sought to poetically rediscover and reinvent Brazil. *Pau Brasil* is organized as a voyage of invention through history and space. While traveling, the lyrical voice provides the reader with daring, often ironic glimpses of Brazil from colonial times to the present. Never representing Brazil as a harmonious whole or unity, the poetic voice relies on perspectivism and juxtaposition, as in Cubism, to surprise and engage the reader. Across 140 poem-fragments that function as iconoclastic snapshots, and an introductory pronouncement, the lyrical voice uncovers a primitively modern and postcolonial Brazil. The poems are structured, in turn, by eleven thematic sections beginning with "History of Brazil" and culminating in "Loyde Brasileiro" (State Cruise Company). The section "Poemas de colonização" (Colonization Poems) narrates the poetic voice's musings about the colonial era in the preterit, while the segment "RP1" renders photographic flashes of modernity via immigration, technology, and emerging businesses: "Tenho uma vontade vadia/ Como um photographo ... Japonezes/ Turcos/ Migueis/ Os hoteis parecem roupas alugadas/ Negros como um compendio da historia patria" (I've got vagabond wanderlust/ Like a photographer ... Japanese/ Turks/ Michaels/ The hotels look like hired clothes/ Black like a compendium of our national history; *Pau Brasil*, 54). It is worth mentioning that *Pau Brasil* was illustrated by Andrade's lover and esteemed painter, Tarsila do Amaral. Each of the book's sections is demarcated by primitive figures signaling Brazilian particularity, such as Portuguese colonizers in caravels, palm trees, Sugarloaf Mountain, plantation houses, Afro-Brazilians at Carnival, the RP1 passenger train, São Paulo, and the ancient Araucaria trees of Minas Gerais.

Oswald's poem-inventions are founded on the technique of the ready-made. Illustrative of this point is Amaral's cover design for the book: a ready-made Brazilian flag, anticipating the style of the American painter Jasper Johns some thirty years prior. Replacing the flag's official slogan, "Order and Progress," with the words "Pau Brasil," the irreverent inscription at once recalls Brazil's first colonial product of export, the Brazilwood tree, and, through paronomasia, the phallus. Like Borges's vanguard

[21] *Pau Brasil* (Paris: Sans Pareil, 1925).

criollismo, Andrade's *Pau Brasil* project sought to disseminate a native originality with irreverence, critique, and creativity.[22] What is more, Amaral and Andrade's desacralization of official icons signals a new strategy for the Brazilian lyric: one will reinvent both poetry and Brazil only by sabotaging ready-made discourses.

Oswald's ready-made technique is nowhere more incisive than in the first thematic partition, "História do Brasil" (History of Brazil). In this section, twenty-three titled, mini-poems, such as "As meninas da gare" (Train Station Girls), "Paiz de ouro" (Gold Country), and "Sistema hydrographico" (Hydrographic System), recall modern advertising, tourism, and urban planning. They also anachronistically frame a collage of ready-made quotes, which are taken from the foundational chronicles of Brazil by European scribes, monks, missionaries, pioneers, and the Portuguese Prince Dom Pedro. The montage of poems discloses the hands of the anti-poet and cannibal of discourse. Laying bare the device by means of irony-laden titles, Andrade exposes the chronicle form and the history of Brazil proper as inventions of colonial desire. What is more, Andrade's citation collage discloses the historical mapping of Brazil as a tropical Eden, both as material outpost and as the site of future domination by the Crown in the sixteenth and seventeenth centuries.[23] Writing against this history of subjugation by means of language expropriation and Cubist perspectivism, Andrade's ready-made technique constitutes a radical metapoetics (*Pau Brasil*, 18). The "poem" devours discourse and undermines the consecrated sites of national enunciation.

Through a return to roots, Andrade's "História do Brasil" follows the volume's opening recipe in "Falação" (Speech): colonial European history, commercialism, and aristocratic erudition will be countered by a barbarian language of invention, surprise, synthesis, technology, and anti-representation. "Falação" is a shortened version of "Manifesto da Poesia Pau Brasil" (Manifesto of Pau Brasil Poetry, 1924). In this latter document, we find a more robust menu of ideas beginning with the dual emphasis on "*perceiving with liberated eyes*" and being "Brazilians only in our time" (*A utopia antropofágica*, 65, 66). Liberated vision and identity result from radical language work. Andrade's poems do not represent Brazilian reality, nor do they endeavor to speak for the nation as in nineteenth-century *indigenismo*. In effect, the manifesto never stops calling for (i) the invention of new creative processes,

[22] Against the grain of blindly following European models, it is important to note that Andrade's subversive pun, "Pau Brasil," condenses a larger *modernista* aim: to "export" Brazilian poetry for the first time (*A utopia antropofágica*, 62). See "Manifesto da Poesia Pau Brasil" (1924), in O. de Andrade, *A utopia antropofágica* (São Paulo: Globo, 2011), 59–66.

[23] On Brazil as a tropical Eden, see Darlene Sadlier, *Brazil Imagined: 1500 to the Present* (Austin, TX: University of Texas Press, 2008), 9–62.

(ii) the discovery of Brazil as an ever-changing complex of ethnicities, vegetation, and texts, and (iii) the construction of a natural and "neological" Brazilian language "without ontology."[24] The poem "Pronominais" (Pronominals) provides a parodic portrait of what this "natural" and "neological" language might look like:

Dê-me um cigarro
Diz a grammatica
Do profesor e do alumno
E do mulato sabido

Mas o bom negro e o bom branco
Da Nação Brasileira
Dizem todos os dias
Deixa disso camarada
Me dá um cigarro.

(Give me a cigarette/ Says the grammar/ Of the professor and the student/ And the smart mulatto/ But the good black and the good white/ Of the Brazilian Nation/ Every day says/ Enough with that buddy/ Gimme a smoke; *Pau Brasil*, 77–78).

The anti-poem once again sabotages official discourse. The ready-made textbook register in the first stanza sets up a subversive, anti-grammatical counterpoint: the poetization of Brazilian popular speech. Always uniting poetic frame with thematic content, the "new scale" that *Pau Brasil* seeks concerns the ways in which its poems create an isomorphic dialogue with what Andrade calls "a contemporânea expressão do mundo" (the contemporary expression of the world; *A utopia antropofágica*, 63, 65). Anti-formulaic, this latter idea refers to the twentieth-century "explosion" of new media, texts, ideas, and perspectives (*A utopia antropofágica*, 60). Devouring these techniques and ideas, the lyrical voice reinvents Brazil, the Portuguese language, and what is meant by poetry:

Longo da linha
Coqueiros
Aos dois
Aos tres
Aos grupos
Altos
Baixos.

("Longo," Coconut-trees/ In twos/ In threes/ In groups/ Tall/ Short; *Pau Brasil*, 94)

[24] *A utopia antropofágica* 61; "Manifiesto de poesía 'Palo-del-Brasil,'" in *Oswald de Andrade: obra escogida*, ed. Haroldo de Campos, trans. Héctor Olea (Caracas: Biblioteca Ayacucho, 1981), 7.

In "Longo da linha" (Along the Line,) theme, structure, and perception configure an isomorphism, or structural dialogue of mutually conditioning relationships. The poem's "line" – as geometric shape, text, idea, and chronological unfolding – articulates the perception of trees from the vantage of a moving train. Constructivist experiments such as these would greatly influence the Brazilian neo-avant-garde in the 1950s and 1960s. Above all, Andrade's constructivism would interest the Brazilian concrete poets, Augusto and Haroldo de Campos, and Décio Pignatari, who prompted Andrade's revival from obscurity.[25]

If the key to Andrade's *Pau Brasil* project resided in the reinvention of language as rediscovery of Brazil, his vision evolved with a second, more acclaimed declaration of independence in "Manifesto antropófago" (Cannibalist Manifesto, 1928). Organized as a non-linear collage of 51 aphoristic statements, "Manifesto antropófago" rewrites Brazilian history by relativizing its dependant status. It also articulates, significantly, a theory of Brazilian culture. Andrade's method is based on the indigenous Tupi rite of devouring one's adversary to acquire his powers. This antagonistic, avant-garde document brings to light and poetically performs, as in *Pau Brasil*, a rediscovery of Brazil through experimental language: "Roteiros. Roteiros. Roteiros. Roteiros. Roteiros. Roteiros. Roteiros" (Routes. Routes. Routes. Routes. Routes. Routes. Routes).[26] Just as in *Pau Brasil*, the separation between art, thought, and life is effaced. Emphasizing experimentation as the path to ever-renewed modes of thought and as a mode of cultural concretism, the manifesto vociferously proclaims European decadence (*A utopia antropofágica*, 73). It also affirms Brazil as a unique cultural, poetic, and philosophical source. Through the repeated cry of "contra" (against), fourteen times, it further proclaims war against habit, imitation,

[25] See, in particular, Décio Pignatari, "Marco Zero de Andrade," *Letras* [ALFA, FFCL de Marília] 5–6 (1964): 41–56; Haroldo de Campos, "Da razão antropofágica: diálogo e diferença na cultura brasileira," in *Metalinguagem e outras metas* (São Paulo: Editora Perspectiva 34, 1992), 231–255; Augusto de Campos, "Pós-Walds," in *Poesia antipoesia antropofagia & cia.* (São Paulo: Companhia das Letras, 2015), 258–263; and Adam Joseph Shellhorse, *Anti-Literature: The Politics and Limits of Representation in Modern Brazil and Argentina* (Pittsburgh, PA: The University of Pittsburgh Press, 2017), and "Subversions of the Sensible: The Poetics of Antropofagia in Brazilian Concrete Poetry," *Revista Hispánica Moderna* 68:2 (2015): 165–90. For theory and context of Brazilian concrete poetry in general, see Augusto de Campos, Haroldo de Campos, and Décio Pignatari, *Teoria da poesia concreta: textos críticos e manifestos (1950–1960)* (São Paulo: Ateliê, 2006); Perrone, *Seven Faces: Brazilian Poetry Since Modernism* (Durham, NC: Duke University Press, 1996); Gonzalo Aguilar, *Poesía concreta brasileña: las vanguardias en la encrucijada modernista* (Rosario: Beatriz Viterbo, 2003), and K. David Jackson, *Haroldo de Campos: A Dialogue with the Brazilian Concrete Poet* (Oxford: Centre for Brazilian Studies, 2005).
[26] "Manifesto antropófago," in O. de Andrade, *A utopia antropofágica*, 70.

calculative representational thought, and fixed ideas that have historically impeded Brazilian liberty of expression: "Somos concretistas. As idéias tomam conta, reagem, queimam gente nas praças públicas. Suprimamos as idéias e as outras paralisias. Pelos roteiros. Acreditar nos sinais, acreditar nos instrumentos e nas estrelas" (We are concretists. Ideas guard, react, end up burning people at the stake in public squares. Let us suppress ideas and other types of paralysis. For routes. Believing in signs, in instruments and in the stars; *A utopia antropofágica*, 73).

Due to its reliance on metaphor, aphorisms, heterodox sources, and a non-linear structure that emphasizes experimental process, Andrade's manifesto has long intrigued and baffled critics. What is more, few critics have explored *antropofagia* as a poetic procedure. But the fact remains *antropofagia* is a continuation and radicalization of *Pau Brasil* poetics. Cubist syntax, parody, simultaneism, and rejection of fixed ideas are all assembled to unearth a more radical experience of Brazil through language. Like "História do Brasil" in *Pau Brasil*, "Manifesto antropófago" is structured, in part, as a palimpsest, and relies on the techniques of the ready-made citation: "Tupy, or not tupy that is the question."[27] If Shakespeare is here made Brazilian through a witty ready-made pun, it is to poetically perform and announce the manifesto's decentering poetics. Synthetically assimilating Shakespeare and the Tupi with irreverence, the poetics of *antropofagia* articulates the permanent transvaluation of all that had hitherto served as model, law, grammar, and limit into a weapon or tool for Brazilian thought and art. *Antropofagia* is at once a poetics and theory of Brazil whose basis is non-unitary synthesis, critical reading, and permanent rupture. Its only law is "eating the law": "Só a antropofagia nos une. Socialmente, Economicamente. Philosophicamente ... Única lei do mundo" (Only cannibalism unites us. Socially. Economically. Philosophically. ... Sole law of the world; *Revista* 3). Even as it affirms Brazilian originality, Andrade's *antropofagia* is summarily non-identitarian. It articulates through poetic experimentation, like the *Pau Brasil* poem, a critical and creative reinvention of Brazil and its language "without ontology."[28]

In sum, as a means of quelling all "longing for Europe" and to usher in a new creative spirit for the age, Mário and Oswald de Andrade established an anti-tradition via experimental poetry (M. Andrade, *Entrevistas*, 18). Their unprecedented work and will to theory implied at once (i) rejecting the

---

[27] *Revista de Antropofagia*, facsimile ed. (São Paulo: Abril.Meta/Leve, 1975), 3.
[28] "Manifiesto de poesía 'Palo-del-Brasil,'" in *Oswald de Andrade: obra escogida*, ed. Haroldo de Campos, trans. Héctor Olea (Caracas: Biblioteca Ayacucho, 1981), 7.

diffusionist premise of modernity whereby Brazil would always be behind the times, and (ii) radically redesigning language in order to affirm Brazilian difference: a *modernista* simultaneity of creativity and critique, assimilation and invention, principle for a new poetic and political word.

César Vallejo and Lyrical Stammering

Perhaps the poet of his generation who pushed language the furthest, Peruvian César Vallejo (1892–1938) wrote his monumental *Trilce* (1922) while in jail. Long pondered as exceptional due to its polymorphous vocalizations, its methods of typographic intensification, and its obliteration of rhetoric, representation, and referents, *Trilce* articulates an incisive will to regenerate language. The collection of 77, enumerated poems without titles, is a *tour de force* of variant shades, moods, and experiments. Form and sense are smashed to pieces, so that something fresh, dreamlike, and dissonant might be created from their essential constitutive parts. If *Trilce* is an uncompromising sequence of strikes on bourgeois logic, it is also the negation of all values hitherto associated with canonical forms of poetry. Reveling in its anti-harmony through rotating modes of expression – scientific, sexual, colloquial, confessional, performative, meta-literary, and primal – *Trilce* conveys the construction and performance of a new lyrical voice. Ceaselessly interpellating speakers, voices, discourses, and the reader alike,[29] Vallejo's texts are experiments in the purest sense. They configure a stammering dialogue with language proper. Connoting the notion of three, the sweet and nonsensical, the title itself, *Trilce*, is a neologism marked by hesitation. In effect, Vallejo dramatically replaced the original designation, *Cráneos de bronce* (Bronze Skulls), while the text was being printed. To the extent that *Trilce* rewrites the world in reverse as an intensification of language and self,[30] the book does so, crucially, to translate, from language's depths, the discursive Babel, sensations, and rhythms of the modern world. The collection's stuttering speech constructs a potent, pliable language. As Vallejo's mentor Antenor Orrego wrote in the original preface: "El poeta quisiera librarse del yugo de las técnicas para expresar el crudo temblor de la Naturaleza" (The poet seeks to free himself of the yoke of techniques in order to express the raw trembling of Nature).[31] *Trilce* tends at once towards

---

[29] Michelle Clayton, *Poetry in Pieces: César Vallejo and Lyric Modernity* (Berkeley, CA: University of California Press, 2011), 78.

[30] Stephen M. Hart, "The World Upside Down in the Work of César Vallejo," in *Twentieth Century Spanish American Literature to 1960*, ed. David William Foster and Daniel Altamiranda (New York, NY: Garland Publishing, 1997), 97.

[31] *Trilce* (Lima: Talleres Tipográficos de la Penitenciaria, 1922), v.

silence and stammering, making language perform – hear, say, do – more than it says.[32]

Perceived at its inception as a failure, *Trilce* is now lauded as a breakthrough. Yet unlike his contemporaries, as Clayton reminds us, Vallejo hardly granted glimpses of the secrets of his craft, nor did he depend on intrepid metaphor and images (Clayton, *Poetry in Pieces*, 69, 74). And although he is known to have read Dadaist literature from 1919, Vallejo was certainly not affiliated with any movement.[33] In a remarkable essay, Vallejo bemoaned his contemporaries' reification of the modern.[34] By heedlessly placing gadgets in their poems to appear modern, such as airplanes and automobiles, avant-garde writers ended being conformists. Such gestures belied the lyric's requisite liberty. For Vallejo, the poet willfully invents new processes to liberate language: "El arte descubre caminos, nunca metas." (Art discovers pathways, never goals; Clayton, *Poetry in Pieces*, 134). A good example of Vallejo's vigorous idiolect is found in *Trilce*, poem "II":

II

Tiempo Tiempo.

Mediodía estancado entre relentes.
Bomba aburrida del cuartel achica
tiempo tiempo tiempo tiempo.

Era Era.

Gallos cancionan escarbando en vano.
Boca del claro día que conjuga
era era era era.

Mañana Mañana.

El reposo caliente aún de ser.
Piensa el presente guárdame para
mañana mañana mañana mañana.

Nombre Nombre.

¿Qué se llama cuánto heriza nos?
Se llama Lomismo que padece
nombre nombre nombre nombrE.

(*Trilce*, 6–7).

---

[32] Julio Ortega, *La teoría poética de César Vallejo* (Austin, TX: Del Sol Editores, 1986), 112.
[33] Stephen M. Hart, *César Vallejo: A Literary Biography* (Woodbridge: Tamesis, 2013), 96.
[34] "Estética y maquinismo," in *Las vanguardias latinoamericanas: textos programáticos y críticos*, ed. Jorge Schwartz (Mexico City: Fondo de Cultura Económica, 2002), 422.

(Time Time./ Midday doomed in nocturnal dew./ Boring lightbulb in barracks shrinks/ time time time time./ Was Was./ Roosters chant digging in vain./ Mouth of the clear day conjugates/ was was was was./ Tomorrow Tomorrow./ The warm repose still to be./ The present thinks keep me for/ tomorrow tomorrow tomorrow tomorrow./ Name Name./ What is called that which injures us?/ It's called TheSame that suffers/ name name name nameD.)[35]

As the book's second of 77 movements, "II" begins with a visual and verbal pun: it calls attention to the collection as a continuum of experiments, and to its repetition in time. Through the text's play with number, time, permutation, typography, and naming, the poem will seek to construct an untimely lyrical language capable of overcoming the redundancy of conventional language. Indeed, signaling its power of repetition as a revitalizing force, the titular "II" sets in motion the poem's principal problems: the experience of time and language as limits, and poetic renewal.

Centered in the book's project to continuously regenerate language, this poetic field is organized into four spatialized stanzas. Each begins with a two word verse, "Tiempo Tiempo" (Time Time) and is followed by a haiku-like scene suggesting one of the four seasons. Moreover, stanzas read as philosophical and oneiric riddles. The number 4 is significant because it stands for the duplication of the theme-title, and denotes, as Ortega suggests, the "experience" of the four-walled jail cell from which Vallejo wrote (Ortega, *La teoría poética*, 49). The latter reading is probable because *Trilce* is, in part, autobiographical, and includes numerous references to the poet's experience in jail. We cannot underemphasize the poem's play on the number two. What is more, each stanza ends with the stuttering repetition of theme: "time time time time." To the extent that the doubled theme-words testify to each stanza's idea, their ensuing poetic differentiation in the stanza body exemplifies their errant force: "era era era era" (was was was was). The stammering performance of theme articulates the idea of impasse – repeated throughout the text via images of stagnation, boredom, failure, entrapment, and loss of order. In *Trilce* "II," Vallejo's lyrical stammer also points to a primal force beyond and before concepts, like a drumbeat or incantation through chant.[36] Stammering repetition points to depth, movement, and an original order without concepts, to the chaotic errancy of forces that cannot be named, and to an illogical language where sounds and nouns become verbs.

---

[35] Author's translation; for an alternative translation, see *César Vallejo: The Complete Poetry: A Bilingual Edition*, ed and trans. Clayton Eshleman (Berkeley, CA: University of California Press, 2007), 169.

[36] Clayton insightfully argues that Vallejo's poetics are grounded in sound over sight, *Poetry in Pieces*, 54.

Replicating this movement of mutation, the second line of each stanza inscribes an abstract world written in reverse. For example, in stanza 1, we witness the surreal fusion of midday and night dew, and in stanza 2, rooters sing digging in vain. On the other hand, syntax is inverted in the second line of stanza 4, and in stanza 3, death is framed as a warm future to come. Anticipating the French surrealists, it is as though the poem denounced nominal designations in favor of a more penetrating, artistic reality. Or as surrealist founder André Breton might say: the poem is rather concerned with the "real functioning of thought."[37] Repetition ensures experimentation. In "II," repetition is of the order of the other, of alterity, of difference, movement, and primal force.

The movement of repetition thus flows from the affirmation of the continuing book, *Trilce*, to a particular temporal impasse – how go on? why go on writing? how avoid the language of "the Same"? From language framed by an apparent, superficial order demarcated by designation, generality, resemblance, and sameness, but also by death, memory, hope, imagination, and physical entrapment, "II" decenters language to revive it. Concerned with depth over surface limits, and the cultivation of a poetic form that thinks beyond opposition and fixed designations, Vallejo's errant text deals with orders that have no concepts: experience of perpetual difference. If conventional language is the name for symmetry and equivalence, Vallejo's poem articulates a dissymmetrical naming of thought, word, and world:

> Qué se llama cuánto heriza nos?
> Se llama Lomismo que padece
> nombre nombre nombre nombrE.

> (What is called that which injures us?/ It's called TheSame that suffers/ name name name nameD; *Trilce*, 7.)

By accentuating the poem's final letter in the sequence, "nombre nombre nombre nombrE," the poem conjoins the first-person, preterit conjugation of naming – in Spanish, *nombré* (I named) – with a babbling, primal discourse. As with Cubism, point of view, object, and theme converge. But also, as with Futurism, Vallejo renders the dynamism of his transgression typographically. Against the grain of the conventional Sameness which sticks to names and superficial designations, Vallejo gives the act of naming a constituent force. This is because the Same as nominal grammar is never sufficient. It simplifies, and does not know dynamism. Exploring its own process, even as it undoes the nominal to become force and sensation, *Trilce*'s language unfurls as a new embodiment of poetry's project to overcome habitual perception.

---

[37] André Breton, *Manifestes du surréalisme* (Paris: Gallimard, 1967), 37.

Against language's linearity and against the book as image of the world, it induces a stammering within language, a power of mutation and errancy, which multiplies its forces, and replicates, and responds to the errant forces of life.

Alejandra Pizarnik and Surrealism

We would be remiss if we were to conclude this series of portraits without accounting for surrealist poetic language and its radical reconfiguration by the legendary Argentine *poète maudit* Alejandra Pizarnik (1936–1972). For good reason, this theme has enthralled both Latin American literary scholars in general and Pizarnik readers in particular. As Nicholson's authoritative study informs, "surrealism arrived in numerous countries of [Latin America] not as the discrete movement that existed in Europe, but rather as part of a mélange of avant-garde ideas and practices ... In even broader and more diffuse ways, the exaltation of the unconscious took shape in the use of oneiric, visionary, or hallucinatory imagery, which would become hallmarks of much twentieth-century Latin American poetry."[38] Yet the question of surrealist influence in Pizarnik's poetry has only recently begun to be illuminated. In this section, we will see how Pizarnik's language is anchored in the conquests of Surrealism. For Pizarnik, Surrealism is linked to a revolutionary writing and reading method: it disorganizes the world as we customarily know it. We will also show how Pizarnik's relationship with surrealist poetics is far from derived, and that it is not simply the result of a transgressive appropriation to make artful verse. Namely, as César Aira has argued, that Pizarnik learned to make "good poetry" through the subjectivization of automatic writing and oneiric imagery.[39] For all of its mystery and darkness, Pizarnik's poetry unfolds as an endeavor to think, unveil, and prolong Surrealism at a time when it was seen as dying (Aira, *Alejandra Pizarnik*, 14). Her poetry thus points in two directions: to uncovering language and Surrealism's general essence. More precisely, as metapoetry, it signals the necessity of critically illuminating language's limits and complex constitution. By constantly laying bare the device, Pizarnik's poetry calls attention to itself not as a pure product of poetry but as a subversive and elliptical event of writing.

Pizarnik liked to speak of her "innate surrealism," of her spiritual affinities with the surrealist pantheon (Lautréamont, Rimbaud, Artaud, Bataille, and

---

[38] Melanie Nicholson, *Surrealism in Latin American Literature: Searching for Breton's Ghost* (New York, NY: Palgrave Macmillan, 2013), 8–9.

[39] César Aira, *Alejandra Pizarnik* (Rosario: Beatriz Viterbo Editora, 1998), 14, 25.

Breton), and of her natural "affective automatism."[40] From 1960 to 1964, Pizarnik lived in Paris with great joy and anguish. In the City of Light, she completely dedicated herself to poetry and supported herself as a corrections editor and translator for different literary reviews.[41] During this break-through period, she met surrealist luminaries, including Georges Bataille, Hans Arp, and Max Ernst, and befriended notable fellow travelers such as Octavio Paz, André Pieyre de Mandiargues, Julio Cortázar, and Henri Michaux. In addition, Pizarnik translated André Breton and Paul Éluard's classic of automatic writing, *L'Immaculée conception* (The Immaculate Conception), as well as works by Henri Michaux, Marguerite Duras, Antonin Artaud, Aimé Césaire, Léopold Sédar Senghor, Michel Leiris, and Yves Bonnefoy.[42] As an astute reader of the surrealist canon, Wilson under-scores how Pizarnik ultimately disagreed with Breton's all too seamless conception of freeing the unconscious, while Mackintosh has shown how Pizarnik's subversive mistranslations of *L'Immaculée conception* defy "both the male surrealists' monopoly on exploration of extreme mental states, and their delimitation of woman's role as largely passive" (Wilson, "Alejandra Pizarnik," 81; Mackintosh, "Alejandra Pizarnik," 54).

Even so, Pizarnik referred to translating, through visual imagery, the energy of the unconscious (*Diarios*, 331, 355). Like the French surrealists, she underscored the power of the imaginary and her aversion to everyday, utilitarian discourse. Yet differing from them, she eschewed automatic writ-ing's taste for the arbitrary. Breton's prolix "language without reserve" barred revision (*Manifestes*, 47). In contradistinction, Pizarnik sought a definitive style based on meticulous rewriting. As has been noted, Pizarnik corrected her miniature poems one thousand times over. One of her methods consisted in placing unfinished texts on the wall like mural-poems. In this way, she could contemplate them, word by word, from every angle (Fuentes Gómez). Another technique involved transcribing words on assorted cards. Inviting chance into the poetic process, Pizarnik would place them on her bed and arrange them like pawns on a chessboard. In effect, Pizarnik wished to

[40] Nicholson, *Surrealism*, 163; Pizarnik, *Diarios*, ed. Ana Becciu (Barcelona: Editorial Lumen, 2003), 355.

[41] Carlota Caulfield and Antonio Beneyto, "Editor's Introduction," in *From the Forbidden Garden: Letters from Alejandra Pizarnik to Antonio Beneyto* (Lewisburg, PA: Bucknell University Press, 2003), 14.

[42] Pizarnik's translation of *L'Immaculée conception* as *La inmaculada concepción* was published in 1972. For greater context, see Fiona J. Mackintosh, "Alejandra Pizarnik as Translator," *The Translator* 16.1 (2010): 43–66; Caulfield and Beneyto, *From the Forbidden Garden*; and Jason Wilson, "Alejandra Pizarnik, Surrealism and Reading," in *Árbol de Alejandra: Pizarnik Reassessed*, ed. Fiona J. Mackintosh and Karl Posso (Woodbridge: Tamesis, 2007).

establish an absolute continuity between literature and life. She saw her Paris years as an attempt to learn how to live (Caulfield and Beneyto, *From the Forbidden Garden*, 73). Steeped in the writings of Bataille, Sartre, Paz, and Heidegger, her project is marked by a search for authenticity against a backdrop of solitude, suffering, and a fully assumed death. For this reason, the specters of martyrdom and suicide haunt the pages of her *Diaries* and poems. Yet pain, isolation, and suicide are not merely personal. They are the necessary characters of a more powerful language that Pizarnik's texts summon with all their might. Poetry, in Pizarnik, becomes a suicidal conflict with discourse: by willfully suspending classical surrealist poetics, representation, and everyday usage, words do not express reality, but are able to frame, through careful arrangement, the radical alterity and limits of writing the unconscious.

Fine examples are found in arguably her masterwork, *Árbol de Diana* (1962).[43] Organized as a sequence of meditations that concern, above all, writing and the book's textual status, the volume's 38 fragments blur the boundaries between poetry and prose, and approximate drawing, painting, and philosophical reflection. Poems 24, 25, and 26 are written in explicit response to works by Wols, Goya, and Klee. In this regard, the book's visual layout is crucial. Against a backdrop of whiteness, each mini-poem takes up an entire page and appears as a constellation. The lyrical voice likens them to stars, to bones shining brilliantly in the night, and to mirrors (*Árbol de Diana*, 17, 19, 36; poems 7, 9, and 26). Furthermore, the fragments are configured as scenes in which the diminutive lyrical persona – clearly reminiscent of Pizarnik – meditates upon writing in the now, and metaphorically, on the "ferocious destiny" of her visions (*Árbol de Diana*, 16; poem 6). These illuminations envelop her in ecstasy, novelty, freedom, and overpowering sadness:

> Días en que una palabra lejana se apodera de
> mí. Voy por esos días sonámbula y transpa-
> rente. La hermosa autómata se canta, se en-
> canta, se cuenta casos y cosas: nido de hilos
> rígidos donde me danzo y me lloro en mis
> numerosos funerales. (Ella es su espejo in-
> cendiado, su espera en hogueras frías, su ele-
> mento místico, su fornicación de nombres
> creciendo solos en la noche pálida.)

> (Days in which a word from afar overpowers/ me. I journey through those days,
> somnambulant and transpa-/rent. The beautiful automaton chants to herself,

---

[43] *Árbol de Diana* (Buenos Aires: Sur, 1962).

en/chants herself, tells herself cases and things: nest of rigid/ threads where I dance myself and cry myself in my/ numerous funerals. (She is the en-/flamed mirror, her waiting in icy fires, her mystical ele-/ ment, her fornication of names/ growing alone in the pale night); *Árbol de Diana*, 27; poem 17.)

In her *Diaries*, Pizarnik likened poetry to exorcism (*Diarios*, 355). Due to its precision, poetry distills the irrational energy of the unconscious. But one is first possessed, taken hold of by "a word from afar" (*Árbol de Diana*, 27). This scene, vividly staged in the above example, is repeated throughout *Árbol de Diana*. Here, the lyrical voice – this self-described, singing and enchanted "beautiful automaton" – is compared to an "enflamed mirror" which fornicates with *names* that are born mystically of themselves. Defying Breton's dictum for automatic writing, understood as the free transcription of the unconscious, Pizarnik's poem uncovers the unconscious as a power of writing. Constantly calling attention to itself as writing, her metapoetry thinks the being of the unconscious as a writing before writing: "El poema que no digo/ el que no merezco./ Miedo de ser dos/ camino del espejo:/ alguien en mí dormido/ me come y me bebe" (The poem I do not utter/ the one I do not deserve./ Fear of being two/ the mirror's pathway:/ someone asleep in me/ eats me and drinks me; *Árbol de Diana*, 24; poem 14).

Even if the lyrical voice is staged as an "automaton," imitating Breton was never the issue. And the images attained certainly do not mean that Pizarnik has subjectivized the unconscious through brief, pure, perfect phrases (Aira, *Alejandra Pizarnik*, 25). It has been argued that the synthetic, oneiric image is the most lasting contribution of twentieth-century Surrealism (Nicholson, *Surrealism*, 233). To foreground the centrality of the image, it has likewise been claimed that the surrealists eschewed syntactic experimentation (Nicholson, *Surrealism*, 22). Pizarnik's achievement is to have turned the image reflexive and experimental:

una mirada desde la alcantarilla
puede ser una visión del mundo

la rebelión consiste en mirar una rosa
hasta pulverizarse los ojos.

(a gaze from the sewer/ can be a vision of the world/ the rebellion consists in looking at a rose/ until you pulverize the eyes; *Árbol de Diana*, 33; poem 23)

Her texts, in *Árbol de Diana*, do not imitate, aestheticize, close off, personalize, or fix the image. They rather disclose the image's provenance, that is, they reveal language's more profound structure. It is as though Breton had never thought about the nature of poetry sufficiently. Not the dictation of unconscious thought's boundlessness, Pizarnik's texts frame the unconscious as a form of self-generating, preverbal automatism – as a constituent power of language – that not only overtakes the poetic voice but produces a gallery of unforeseen images and affects that bear the signs of writing. Disclosed here as poetry's unique source, the unconscious is reproduced as a preverbal language, a regime of signs, that the poet hears, cuts up, dialogues with, meditates on, and materially distills as writing:

> un viento débil
> lleno de rostros doblados
> que recorto en forma de objetos que amar.
>
> (a frail wind/ full of folded faces/ which I cut out in form of objects to love; *Árbol de Diana*, 20; poem 10)

Text, word, image, lyrical voice, and the shadowy creatures of the unconscious are consequently designed as continuous, self-refracting mirrors. Emphasizing the now of writing, their arrangement, in *Árbol de Diana*, constitutes an infinite mirror play, in which all the component parts of the text suspend representation, fixity, and closure: "por un minuto de ver/ en el cerebro flores pequeñas/ danzando como palabras en la boca de un mudo" (for just a minute to see/ small flowers in the brain/ dancing like words in the mouth of a mute; *Árbol de Diana*, 15; poem 5). Through the critical, prose poem that negates figuration and formulae, Pizarnik renovates and prolongs surrealist poetry. Irreverently suspending the notion of a sphere of thought outside the text, and thereby anticipating the insights of philosopher Jacques Derrida, she reproduces the unconscious as always already writing: the moment of fusion in which word, perception, world, lyrical self, and inspiration become signs of writing. As Octavio Paz suggests in the book's introduction, this fusion is a "dissolution of reality" by means of a continuous "verbal crystallization," an "amalgam" of semiotic and affective forces, that "casts no shadow."[44]

Paz's luminous words eloquently condense Pizarnik's quest for independence and authenticity. They are rooted in the idea of a profound reinvention of language. The exemplary Latin American poets that we have considered are all associated with the avant-garde: from *creacionismo, ultraísmo*, Brazilian *modernismo, antropofagia*, and Surrealism. Their work testifies to the decentering of received ideas and to the radical relativization of North–South relations. On examining their poetry, there emerges a vision of experimentation that is not entirely bound to identity or nationality as customary readings would have it. Form, rather, is disclosed as a complex regime of

---

[44] Octavio Paz, "Foreword," in *Árbol de Diana*, by Alejandra Pizarnik (Buenos Aires: Sur, 1962), 7.

signs and affects. For this reason, it is by refocusing on their radicalized medium – the hybridity, collage character, stammering, and simultaneity of discourses their poems assemble – that we move beyond the classical identity paradigm and the paradigm of artistic belatedness. By reading for experimentation, we move towards Pizarnik's eloquent, silent, deathlike rebellion: the space of the critical poem that is concerned with the drama and subversion of all fixed discourses.

4

STEPHEN M. HART

Conversational Poetry

"Porque habito un susurro como un velamen,
una tierra donde el hielo es una reminiscencia,
el fuego no puede izar un pájaro
y quemarlo en una conversación de estilo calmo."

(Because I dwell in a whisper like a set of sails/ A land where ice is a reminis-
cence,/ Fire cannot hoist a bird/ And burn it in a conversation calm in style.)

José Lezama Lima, *Thoughts in Havana*[1]

The film *Paterson* (dir: Jim Jarmusch, 2016) opens with a three-minute sequence
in which we see everyday events unfolding before our eyes in an average-sized
rural American town. The viewer is at first puzzled by the self-evident care with
which apparently insignificant events such as a mass transport bus going round
a corner in a small town in New Jersey have been shot. And then the penny
drops: this is a film about the slow vision needed to be a poet, with his or her
ability to see the poetry within everyday things and everyday events. I keep this
opening sequence of *Paterson* in mind as I trace, in this chapter, the movement
plotted by the conversational mode in Latin American poetry from, roughly, the
1930s until, roughly, the 1970s. The works I refer to will – as a result of the
confines of this chapter – have to be limited, and their selection may for some
readers seem arbitrary, but an attempt has been made to plot this trajectory,
with the aim of arguing that it is a significant if under-exposed strain within the
evolution of twentieth-century Latin American verse. It was a time of the
Twilight of the Idols, a post-Vanguard when the poet turned away from rhymed
verse, metaphors, and the book, towards the rhythms of everyday speech, the
charm of common words, and the scenes of the quotidian world.[2]

[1] "Pensamientos en La Habana," trans. James Irby, in *The Oxford Book of Latin
American Poetry: A Bilingual Anthology*, ed. Cecilia Vicuña and Ernesto Livon-Grosman
(Oxford: Oxford University Press, 2009), 254, 256.
[2] For more backstory on the twilight of the idols in the poetic canon, see Stephen M. Hart,
"The Twilight of the Idols in Modernism's 1922," in *Modernisms and Modernities: Studies
in Honour of Donald L. Shaw*, ed. Susan Carvalho (Newark, DE: Juan de la Cuesta, 2006),

When thinking about the conversational mode in twentieth-century poetry, of course, *Paterson* points the way. As David Ferry points out: "Among the aspects of American poetry that are most often noticed is the freedom with which the poets use colloquial, slangy and generally non-literary language as an ordinary part of that style. As instances of this tendency one thinks at once of William Carlos Williams, E.E. Cummings, and the young T.S. Eliot."[3] True to type, the main character of Jarmusch's film, called, like the city he lives in, Paterson (Adam Driver), reads, quotes, mulls over, and, in effect, re-writes the work of William Carlos Williams, in this "prose-poem of gentle comic humility and acceptance of life."[4] Williams himself chose to write in this way, and it was a moral as well as a technical issue for him:

> For everything we do and know is tied up with words, with the phrases words make, with the grammar, which stultifies, the prose or poetic rhythms which bind us to our pet indolences and medievalisms. To Americans especially, those who no longer speak English, this is especially important. We need too often a burst of air in at the window of our prose. It is absolutely indispensable that we get this before we can even begin to think straight again. It's the words, the words we need to get back to, words washed clean. Until we get the power of thought back through a new minting of the words we are actually sunk. This is a moral question at base, but a technical one also and first.
>
> (qtd. in Ferry, 139–40).

Williams proved to be himself "a burst of air" which came in through the window of American poetry, and there is certainly evidence, which I hardly need to rehearse here, of his influence on the shape that Latin American poetry would take in the following decades. But, quite apart from Williams there was one other crucial segment of a poem written by a Latin American poet in the 1930s that would bring these ideas home. And this was the famous core verses of Pablo Neruda's "España en el corazón" (Spain in the Heart) written while the Spanish Civil War was raging:

Preguntaréis: Y dónde están las lilas?
y la metafísica cubierta de amapolas?
y la lluvia que a menudo golpeaba

175–99; and, for a thoughtful discussion of the poetry of this period described as "post-Vanguardist," see José Olivio Jiménez's introduction to his *Antología de la poesía hispanoamericana contemporánea hispanoamericana (1914–1987)*, 3rd edition (Madrid: Alianza, 1988), 7–32. See also Donald Shaw's excellent overview of this period: *Beyond the Vanguard: Spanish American Poetry After 1950* (Woodbridge: Tamesis, 2008).

[3] David Ferry, "The Diction of American Poetry," in *American Poetry*, ed. Irvin Ehrenpreis (London: Edward Arnold, 1965), 135.

[4] Peter Bradshaw, "*Paterson*: Review," *The Guardian*, May 16, 2016.

sus palabras llenándolas
de agujeros y pájaros? [5]

(You will ask: So where are the lilacs,/ where is the metaphysics blanketed in
poppies?/ and the rain that sometimes lashed/ his words, filling them/ with holes
and birds?; trans. by Adam Feinstein)

These words have been quoted in this volume by Adam Feinstein (see p. 143),
and indicate how significant they were in Neruda's trajectory.[6] Just like
Williams, Neruda saw this change in this verse-style as something technical
as well as moral. The moral issue had to do with the destruction of the
Spanish people that generals such as Francisco Franco, Emilio Mola, and
Gonzalo Queipo de Llano were conducting on the battlefields of Spain in the
name of a God, a Church, and vision of Spain that Neruda did not believe in.[7]
And it is also a technical issue because, in the poems Neruda began to write
about the war, it was clear that a new poetic idiom was emerging, one which
was simpler and easier to understand, more direct and more focused on the
everyday reality of life, rather than the extolling of absent, exotic volcanoes,
for example, or, indeed, the neo-Baroque style that José Lezama Lima uses in
the epigraph of this chapter.[8] The force of these words is extraordinary, as
anyone who has listened to a recording of them given by Neruda will
appreciate. Right at the core of Neruda's position is the idea that there is
something obscene about writing poetry when people are dying on your
doorstep. It is powerful idea, and one that even art-for-art's sakers occasionally respond to.

If the Spanish Civil War were not bad enough, World War II showed the
depths of depravity that human beings were capable of, especially in the
concentration camps of Auschwitz. And Theodor Adorno, in his famous
dictum about poetry and war, makes what I think is a similar point to
Neruda, namely, that there is something morally repulsive about writing
poetry when you turn off your human-sympathy motor in order to ramp up
your poetry-composition motor:

The more total society becomes, the greater the reification of the mind and the
more paradoxical its effort to escape reification on its own. Even the most

---

[5] "España en el corazón," *Tercera residencia* (Buenos Aires: Losada, 1976), 47.
[6] Neruda went on to explore the expressiveness of quotidian language and ordinary things in
his *Odas elementales* (1954); see D.P. Gallagher, *Modern Latin American Literature*
(Oxford: Oxford University Press, 1973), 63–66.
[7] See Paul Preston, *The Spanish Civil War* (London: Weidenfeld and Nicolson, 1986).
[8] For further discussion of the paradigm shift that occurred in poetry as a result of the
Spanish Civil War, see Stephen M. Hart, "War Within a War: Poetry and the Spanish Civil
War," in *¡No pasarán! Art, Literature and the Spanish Civil War*, ed. Stephen M. Hart
(London: Tamesis, 1988), 106–22.

extreme consciousness of doom threatens to degenerate into idle chatter. Cultural criticism finds itself faced with the final stage of the dialectic of culture and barbarism. To write poetry after Auschwitz is barbaric. And this corrodes even the knowledge of why it has become impossible to write poetry today.[9]

The main reason why I have quoted these two texts from Neruda and Adorno, respectively, is in order to make the point that when the vogue of conversational or colloquial poetry arrived in Latin America, it did so through the filter of a political sensibility that became more and more pronounced in the 1950s, 1960s, and 1970s. This was also, of course, a time of great experimentation. Poets were experimenting in lots of different ways – they were writing political poems,[10] short poems,[11] long poems,[12] exploring the connection between poetry and visual art,[13] poetry and music,[14] poetry and street art,[15] but one trait that has a connection – direct or indirect – with these many branches of poetry was the genre of "conversational poetry."

Some of the earliest explorations of poetry in the conversational mode in Latin America came out of Brazil. Carlos Drummond de Andrade (1902–1987) was perhaps the poet par excellence of this new type of poetry, one which rejected the lyricism of a previous generation.[16] For Drummond de

---

[9] Theodor Adorno, "Cultural Criticism and Society," in *Prisms*, trans. Shierry Weber Nicholsen and Samuel Weber (Cambridge, MA: MIT Press, 1983), 34.

[10] See William Rowe, "Latin American Poetry," in *The Cambridge Companion to Modern Latin American Culture*, ed. John King (Cambridge: Cambridge University Press, 2004), 136–70.

[11] See, for example, Octavio Paz's exploration of short-burst poems in the late 1950s and early 1960s; *Octavio Paz: Selected Poems*, ed. Charles Tomlinson (Harmondsworth: Penguin, 1979), 58–64, 74–76, 90–93, 112–13.

[12] For further discussion of long poems during this period, see Eduardo Chirinos, "Del poema largo y sus alrededores," in his *Abrir en prosa: nueve ensayos sobre poesía hispanoamericana* (Madrid: Visor, 2016), 151–71.

[13] In Brazil's Concrete Poetry, for example, a dialogue is established between poetry and visual art. The three most significant poets associated with this movement are Décio Pignatari (b. 1927), Augusto de Campos (b. 1931) and, arguably the key figure, Harold de Campos (1923–2003). For further discussion, see *Twentieth-Century Latin American Poetry: A Bilingual Anthology*, ed. Stephen Tapscott (Austin: TX: University of Texas Press, 1996), 375–87, and Chapter 3 in this volume.

[14] An example of this is *Nueva Canción*; for a contextual discussion, see Catherine Den Tandt and Richard A. Young, "Tradition and Transformation in Latin American Music," in *The Cambridge Companion to Modern Latin American Culture*, ed. John King (Cambridge: Cambridge University Press, 2004), 255–56.

[15] For a contextual discussion, see Vivian Schelling, "Popular Culture in Latin America," in *The Cambridge Companion to Modern Latin American Culture*, ed. John King (Cambridge: Cambridge University Press, 2004), 171–201.

[16] For further discussion of Drummond de Andrade's work, see Chapter 10.

Andrade this meant, first of all, not to dwell on one's emotions. His poem "In Search of Poetry" is set up as a dialogue in which the older poet (Andrade himself) gives some advice to a young protégé on how to write poetry. The first thing the young poet needs to remember is that he should not dwell on his feelings and emotions like the poets of yesteryear:

> Nem me reveles teus sentimentos,
> que se prevalecem do equívoco e tentam a longa viagem.
> O que pensas e sentes, isso ainda não é poesía.

> (Don't reveal your feelings to me,/ for they take advantage of misunderstandings, and take the long way round./ Whatever you may be thinking or feeling, it's still not quite poetry yet.)[17]

Just as the modern poet, Drummond de Andrade suggests, must avoid sentimentality, he must also turn from self-dramatization:

> Não dramatizes, não invoques,
> Não indagues. Não percas tempo en mentir.
> Não te aborreças.
> Teu iate de marfim, teu sapato de diamante,
> vossas mazurcas e abusões, vossos esqueletos de família
> desaparecem na curva do tempo, é algo imprestável.

> (Don't dramatize, don't invoke,/ Don't investigate. Don't waste your time lying./ Don't get exasperated./ Your ivory yacht, your diamond shoe,/ Your Polish folk dances and your superstitions, the skeletons in your family cupboard,/ Disappear over time. They're useless).[18]

Drummond de Andrade advises the young poet to steer clear of nostalgia and melancholy: "Não recomponhas/ tua sepultada e merencória infancia" (Don't reconstruct/ your gloomy, buried childhood).[19] Sentimentalism, self-dramatization, melancholy, and nostalgia were, of course, the staple diet of the Romantic poet, in Latin America as much as in Europe, from Antônio Gonçalves Dias's nostalgia for the Amerindian past as in Keats' "glutting" of "sorrow" in his "Ode on Melancholy."[20] What Drummond de

---

[17] See "Procura da poesia," in *The Penguin Book of Latin American Verse*, ed. E. Caracciolo-Trejo (Harmondsworth: Penguin, 1971), 83; editor's trans.; trans. modified.
[18] Caracciolo-Trejo, *Penguin Latin American Verse*, 83–84; editor's trans.; trans. modified.
[19] Caracciolo-Trejo, *Penguin Latin American Verse*, 84; editor's trans.; trans. modified.
[20] For discussion of Brazilian Romanticism and Arcadianism, see Stephen M. Hart, *A Companion to Latin American Literature* (Woodbridge: Tamesis, 2007), 71, and Lúcia Helena Costigan, "Court Culture, Ritual, Satire, and Music in Colonial Brazil and Spanish America," in *A Companion to Latin American Literature and Culture*, ed. Sara Castro Klaren (Oxford: Blackwell, 2008), 143–45; for Keats' "Ode on Melancholy," see

Andrade wanted was a poised exploration of the words of language itself: "Penetra surdamente no reino das palavras./ Lá estão os poemas que esperam ser escritos" (Explore quietly into the realm of words./ That's where the poems waiting to be written are).[21] Drummond de Andrade's call for a simpler and more direct form of poetry would resonate profoundly with a number of poets, and not only in Brazil. His *ars poetica* was not particularly novel. There were hints of it in the nineteenth century – in, for example, the remarkably straight-talking diction used by José Asunción Silva in "Nocturno" ("Nocturne," in Caracciolo-Trejo, *Penguin Latin American Verse*, 173–75) – as well as the early twentieth century, notably in Manuel Bandeira's "I've had enough of discreet lyricism,/ well-mannered lyricism ...," César Vallejo's "I think about your sex,"[22] as well as Neruda's lines from his Spanish Civil War verse quoted above, but, after World War II and lasting right up until the 1970s, it became more than a poetic technique, almost a way of looking at the world.[23] Indeed Drummond de Andrade's "advice" seems to be percolating just beneath the surface of João Cabral do Melo Neto's poem entitled "Uma educação pela pedra" (Education by Stone), which opens as follows:

> Uma educação pela pedra: por lições;
> para aprender da pedra, freqüentalá;
> captar su voz inenfática, impessoal
> (pela de dicção ela começa as aulas).
> A lição de moral sua resistência fria
> ao que flui e a fluir, a ser maleada;
> a de poética, sua carnadura concreta.

> (An education by stone: through lessons,/ To learn from the stone: to go to it often,/ To catch its level, impersonal voice/ (by its choice of words it begins its classes)./ The lesson in morals, the stone's cold resistance/ To flow, to flowing, to being hammered:/ The lesson in poetics, its concrete flesh.)[24]

The New Oxford Book of English Verse, ed. Helen Gardner (Oxford: Oxford University Press, 1972), 610–11.

[21] Caracciolo-Trejo, *Penguin Latin American Verse*, 84; editor's trans.; trans. modified.

[22] "Estou farto do lirismo comedido,/ do lirismo bem comportado ...," "Poética," in Caracciolo-Trejo, *Penguin Latin American Verse*, 65; "Trilce XIII," in *The Complete Poetry: A Bilingual Edition: César Vallejo*, trans. and ed. Clayton Eshleman (Berkeley, CA: California University Press, 2007), 191. The poetry of Raúl González Tuñón ought also to be mentioned as an avant-garde precedent of conversational poetry; see Rosa Sarabia, *Poetas de la poesía hispanoamericana contemporánea* (London: Tamesis, 1997), 9–49.

[23] For further discussion, see Chapter 10.

[24] *The Oxford Book of Latin American Poetry*, ed. Vicuña and Livon-Grosman, 300; editors' trans.

It is almost as if Cabral do Melo Neto's "penetration," to use the verb Drummond de Andrade uses in his "Procura da poesia," of the stone in a phenomenological sense ("catch its level") then leads to a more "impersonal," more "concrete" and "colder" poetic style which is deliberately used in order to match the "level" of the described object, namely, the stone, and its "concrete flesh." Cabral do Melo Neto's "Education by Stone" resonates with William Carlos Williams' advocacy for "words washed clean" quoted above. Indeed, the two poems by the Brazilian poets referred to above are closer in spirit to William Carlos Williams in their (at least superficially) apoliticism than to Pablo Neruda and Theodor Adorno who, as suggested above, saw a natural and causal link between politics and straight-talking.

One writer who stands with Neruda and Adorno on the issue of the link between politics and straight-talking is the Cuban poet, essayist, and intellectual Roberto Fernández Retamar (b. 1930). He is a crucial figure in this discussion not only because he wrote poems in the conversational style but because he is also the author of the first major article on the subject, published in 1975.[25] In his essay Fernández Retamar spoke – in a way that recalled the "burst of air in at the window" of the American language envisaged by William Carlos Williams – of a "new realism" in Hispano-American poetry, a new poetic manner that sought a closer, more down-to-earth relationship with the reader, moving the focal point away from the text as an art form to the world around us: in summation, reality not art. As is clear from his other works – in particular, his essay Calibán (1971) – the reality that Fernández Retamar wishes to draw the reader into is implicitly political in nature,[26] but it should be added that the poems he himself has written fit the recipe, as it were, in that they address everyday reality, do not use elaborate vocabulary or syntax, and typically have a political agenda.

When the Revolution was declared in January 1959, Fernández Retamar was among the group of Cuban left-wing intellectuals – who included Julio García Espinosa and Tomás Gutiérrez Alea – who were encouraged to design a cultural blueprint for the new political reality that was coming into being. As mentioned, Fernández Retamar wrote an important essay that invoked a new ancestral figure, Caliban, for Cuba's mulatto-mestizo future, but he also wrote poetry and, in that poetry, he combined straight-talking with political vision. "El poema de hoy" (Today's Poem), for example, uses the frame of an everyday reality to sketch out a political reality that buttresses that reality:

---

[25] Roberto Fernández Retamar, "Antipoesía y poesía conversacional en Hispanoamérica," in Para una teoría de la poesía hispanoamericana y otras aproximaciones (Havana: Casa de las Américas, 1975), 111–26.

[26] See Caliban and Other Essays, trans. Edward Baker (Minneapolis: Minnesota University Press, 1989).

El poema de hoy, cuando ya el día
quebró la frente oscura y dispersa
en múltiple caída las estrellas,
y ocupó todo el mundo el sitio
abandonado o desconocido;
el poema de hoy es el de siempre,
el de luego, el de entonces,
el solo poema que una mano
traza sin cansarse y alegre
sobre un papel que vuela vasto,
y en donde pone cielos,
astros, ígneas llamadas
que a la tarde regresarán
a conversar con nosotros.

(Today's poem – when the day had already/ Struck its dark forehead and sent/ The stars flying into various free falls,/ And the whole world was occupied/ By an abandoned or unknown place,/ Today's poem is the poem of always,/ The poem of afterwards, the poem of then,/ The only poem that a hand/ – that is happy and never grows tired –/ Draws on a piece of paper that flies into the vastness/ of space, and on which it places skies,/ Stars, burning calls,/ And, when evening falls, it/ will come back and talk with us.)[27]

"Today's Poem" turns every day, including today, into a poem, for the poem produced by today is, as the poem asserts, "el de siempre" (the poem of always). The "meaning" of today is transcendent – it flies as high as the stars in the universe – and, just as important, it returns in the evening rather like, perhaps, a boomerang paper aeroplane. The poem states that this return to the earth leads to a conversation between mankind and the day, and suggests that what occurs in the evening is a convivial conversation, that is, at the furthest remove from the lofty heights of the Old Testament or the Greek tragedies. Though not as obviously as occurs in, say, Neruda's *Canto general* (General Song, 1950), "Today's Poem" has a political message, rather like an undertow more than an explicit message. If we compare this poem to another of Fernández Retamar's poems, "Homeland" (Patria), for example, we find a similar evocation of a political reality via a synecdoche. "Homeland" is built around a number of oppositions: the mother country is associated with "certainty," "love," "promise," and "courage" – all of which is contrasted to the unnamed "enemy" (though it is obviously the United States) which is associated with "darkness" and leads to feelings of "indignation" and "anger." As

[27] "El poema de hoy," Caracciolo-Trejo, *Penguin Latin American Verse*, 218; editor's trans; trans. modified.

the poem concludes: "Eres la forma de nuestra existencia,/ Eres la piedra en que nos afirmamos,/ Eres la hermosa, eres la inmensa caja/ donde irán a romperse nuestros huesos/ para que siga haciéndose tu rostro" (You are the form of our existence,/ you are the rock on which we stand firm,/ You are the beautiful, you are the immense coffin,/ where our bones will go to be broken/ so that your countenance should continue in its making).[28] It would be difficult to see "Homeland" as anything other than a political poem – it says there is a political choice to be made, and it justifies the sacrifice of the Cuban people as a necessary hardship in order to support the objectives of the Cuban Revolution. "Today's Poem" is similar in that it also has a political agenda, although that agenda is not spelled out so clearly; the words written on the paper which is launched into space are not revealed to the reader but the context suggests that the message contained in the letter – though we never read it – is a revolutionary one. "Today's Poem," thus, is an allegory of the down-to-earth (and materialist) nature of the ideals pursued by the Revolution in Cuba; these ideals spring from everyday reality and – though touched by the vastness of the universe which they fly upwards to meet – remain rooted in the everyday, since they return in the evening, after a day's work, to mankind. The style of Fernández Retarmar's poem, indeed, echoes the semantic directness of an everyday conversation between friends.

This connection between straight-talking and politics in Latin American poetry is, as suggested, not surprising. Indeed, if we consider the list of poets that Carmen Alemany Bay deems to be authors of "poesía conversacional" (conversational poetry) – Ernesto Cardenal, Mario Benedetti, Roberto Fernández Retamar, Roque Dalton, Jaime Sabines, Sebastián Salazar Bondy, Juan Gelman, Francisco "Paco" Urondo, and Antonio Cisneros – we note that at least five of them are known as political poets.[29] The links between conversational poetry and politics, as we can see, are clear in Latin

---

[28] "Patria," Caracciolo-Trejo, *Penguin Latin American Verse*, 219; editor's trans.

[29] Carmen Alemany Bay, "Para una revisión de la poesía conversacional," *Alma mater*, 13–14 (1997): 50. Cardenal, Benedetti, Retamar, Dalton and Urondo are political poets. It is important to note that Alemany Bay does not include Nicanor Parra in this list, and this relates to the dividing line that Fernández Retamar himself draws between "poesía conversacional" and "antipoesía." This chapter, however, argues the case for the idea that Parra's work – despite its association with "antipoesía" – is a crucial voice within the conversational poetry genre, and that antipoetry is something of a misnomer as a descriptor of his poetry; it therefore includes discussion of this work. See also the Alemany Bay's book-length study, *Poética coloquial hispanoamericana* (Alicante: Universidad Publicaciones, 1997), which should be balanced by Rosa Sarabia's study on *Poetas de la poesía hispanoamericana contemporánea*, which looks at the work of Raúl González Tuñón, Nicanor Parra, Rosario Castellanos, Luisa Futoransky, and Ernesto Cardenal.

America (in the sense that at least five of the poets associated with "poesía conversacional" are also political animals), and this is diametrically opposed to the situation we find on the ground in North America.[30] But more important for the purposes of this chapter is to analyze the manner in which Latin American colloquial verse expresses its vision of the world. A writer whose work is similar in many ways to Fernández Retamar's is the Uruguayan Mario Benedetti (1920–2009), although typically his work is underwritten by a political irony that differentiates it from Fernández Retamar's work. His poem "With Your Permission" provides a flavor of his approach to the problems faced by the citizens of the Southern Cone as a result of the growth of military regimes in the 1970s and 1980s, and is a merciless attack on the notion of "authorized violence." Typical of the "bedroom politics" prevalent in Southern Cone literature of this era – one thinks especially of Luisa Valenzuela's work – the poem opens in the bedroom where a gendarme keeps watch on a woman whose lover is a dissident:

Está prohibido escribir sobre cierta violencia
así que voy a hablar de la violencia permitida
el violento autorizado asiste comprensivo y curioso
a tus cartas de amor acaricia contigo los muslos
de tu novia escucha tus murmullos tus desfallecimientos
duro e infeliz se introduce doméstico en su casa
pobre gendarme de repente promovido al horror
manoseador de secretos y mayólicas
a veces ladroncito sin vocación ni melancolía
recién llegado al crimen nuevo rico del miedo.

(It is forbidden to write about a certain class of violence/ So I will speak only of that violence which is permissible/ Authorized violence is present comprehensive and curious/ In your love letters caresses with you the thighs of your/ Sweetheart listens to your whispers your/ Expirations/ Crude and wretched he insinuates himself tamely into/ Your house/ Poor gendarme promoted suddenly to horror/ Handler of secrets and majolica/ At times a minor thief without vocation or melancholy/ A parvenu to crime and nouveau riche with fear.)[31]

[30] Of the three writers most clearly associated with conversational poetry in the United States – William Carlos Williams, E.E. Cummins, and the young T.S. Eliot – none could be seen as political, especially not T.S. Eliot for whom politics was anathema. One American poet whose work does overlap in some ways with writers such as Fernández Retamar is Allen Ginsberg; for a discussion of Ginsberg's political dissidence and the influence William Carlos Williams had on his work, see Richard Gray, *A History of American Poetry* (New York, NY: Wiley-Blackwell, 2015), 323–28. For an analysis of Williams' influence on U.S. Latino poetry, see Chapter 16 in this volume.
[31] Trans. David Arthur McMurray; *Twentieth-Century Latin American Poetry: A Bilingual Anthology*, ed. Stephen Tapscott (Austin, TX: University of Texas Press, 2006), 270.

The poem gradually builds up to a crescendo, dropping gradually more and more broad hints about how the State machinery uses violence to achieve its political ends, until we find out, midway through the poem, that "el violento autorizado tiene una descomunal tijera/ para cortar las orejas de la verdad pero después/ no sabe qué hacer con ellas" (Authorized violence owns an extraordinary pair of/ Scissors for cutting off the ears of truth but after he/ Has no idea what to do with them).[32] The finale shows that this poem is a bitter satire on the use of torture by the State as well as its use of Big-Brother technology to control the populace:

> el violento autorizado posee una formidable computadora
> electrónica capaz de informarle qué
> violencia es buena y qué violencia es mala y por
> eso prohibe nombrar la violencia execrable
> la computadora por ejemplo advirtió que este poema
> trataba de la violencia buena.

> (Authorized violence has a formidable electronic computer/ To inform him which violence is good and which/ Violence is bad so that way he can prohibit/ The mentioning of execrable violence/ The computer reported for example that this poem/ Was about good violence.)[33]

Benedetti's poem, in effect, comes full circle. It mentions the unmentionable violence committed by the State and yet, as the last stanza suggests, the State was unable to catch the nuance of its satire, and thus saw Benedetti's poem as about "good violence." The poem is, thus, not only an attack on the State's use of torture but also its fundamental political incompetence, its inability to read the symbols of life which are all around; the State, like the "parvenu to crime," "cannot understand symbols."

We find a similar type of political irony combined with an oral fluence in the work of the Mexican poet Jaime Sabines (1926–1999). In an interview he once drew attention to the difference between his work and the poets of Mount Olympus:

> Hay dos clases de poetas modernos: aquéllos, sutiles y profundos, que adivinan la esencia de las cosas y escriben: "Lucero, luz cero, luz Eros, la garganta de la luna para colores coleros," etcétera, y aquéllos que tropiezan con una piedra y dicen "pinche piedra." Los primeros son los más afortunados. Siempre encuentran un crítico inteligente que escribe un tratado "Sobre las relaciones ocultas entre el objeto y la palabra y las posibilidades existenciales de la metáfora no formulada." De ellos es el Olimpo, que en estos días se llama simplemente el Club de la Fama.

---

[32] Tapscott, *Latin American Poetry*, 271.   [33] Tapscott, *Latin American Poetry*, 271.

(There are two types of modern poet: the first, who is subtle and profound, who divines the essence of things and writes: "Heavenly body of light, zero-light, eros-light, the throat of the moon for top-hat colours," etc., and the second who bumps into a stone and says: "Crikey, a stone." The first type of poet is more fortunate. He always finds an intelligent critic to write an essay entitled "On the hidden relationships between the object and the word and the existential potential of a non-expressed metaphor." He lives on Mount Olympus, which nowadays is better known as the Club for Famous People.)[34]

Clearly, Sabines classes himself as a member of the second group, namely, not particularly famous and the type of poet who calls a spade a spade. Humor apart, Sabines' characterization suggests he is being rather harsh on himself, for his poems certainly say more than "Crikey, a stone." They have that rare gift of speaking in everyday language about everyday reality, but in such a way that there is a twist that allows the poem to mean more than it appeared to do on a first reading. "Si alguien te dice que no es cierto" (If anyone tells you it isn't true) is a good example:

Si alguien te dice que no es cierto,
dile que venga,
que ponga sus manos sobre su estómago y jure,
que atestigue la verdad de todo,
que mire la luz en el petróleo de la calle,
los automóviles inmóviles,
las gentes pasando y pasando,
las cuatro puertas que dan al este,
las bicicletas sin nadie,
los ladrillos, la cal amorosa,
las estanterías a tu espalda cayéndose,
las canas en la cabeza de tu padre,
el hijo que no tiene tu mujer,
y el dinero que entra con la boca llena de mierda,
dile que jure, en el nombre de Dios invicto
en el torneo de las democracias, haber visto y oído,
porque ha de oír también el crimen de los gatos
y un enorme reloj al que dan cuerda pegado a tu oreja;

(If anyone tells you it isn't true,/ tell them to stop by,/ and put their hands on their stomach and swear,/ bearing witness to the truth of it all./ Tell them to look at the light in the petrol in the street,/ the stationary cars,/ the passers-by who just keep going,/ the four gates that look to the east,/ the riderless bicycles,/ the bricks, the affectionate lime,/
the bookshelves falling apart behind you,/ the grey hairs on your father's head,/

[34] Qtd. in Alemany Bay, "Para una revisión," 52; author's trans.

the son your wife hasn't had/ and the money that comes in with its mouth full of shit./ Tell them to swear, in the name of God the Invincible/ and the tournament of the democracies, what they have seen and heard./ Because they must also hear the crime of the cats/ and an enormous watch which they wind up while pressed to your ear.)[35]

Although, on a superficial level, this poem may appear to be illogical since it is not clear why the speaker in the poem is demanding that someone should swear that their statement is true or, indeed, what that something is whose existence is being denied. But, as the poem develops and the images accumulate, it becomes clear that the speaker in the poem has observed that society is not functioning – in the sense that there appears to be a lack of petrol (which would explain why the cars are stationary), which is exacerbated by a failure of culture (symbolized by the broken bookshelves) and the "death" of loved ones (the father who is getting old and has grey hair and the wife who has not borne a child). A clue to the reason for the anger experienced by the speaker of the poem is found in ll. 14–16, where it appears that capitalism, Christianity, and democracy are being satirized. Yet, even while this poem may be interpreted as possessing a political edge, its power derives from its cascade of evocative images, urging us as readers to witness a tragic situation, the exact contours of which we find it difficult to work out. Perhaps most important of all, even while Sabines uses everyday words such as "light," "petrol," "cars," "bookshelves," and "money," he manages to arrange these words in such a way as to heighten their drama and allow us to conjure up a heightened perception of everyday reality without telling us explicitly what we should be seeing. In a way, we could say that, like the Russian Formalists, Sabines defamiliarizes everyday words and everyday reality, prompting us to see the stone as "more stoney."[36]

The Nicaraguan Ernesto Cardenal (b. 1925), "undoubtedly one of the most important Spanish American poets of the day,"[37] according to Fernández Retamar, is a poet whose work skillfully combines the political, the religious, and the quotidian (Cardenal was a priest as well as a revolutionary and had an urgent "desire to reconcile Christianity with communism").[38] One of his most famous poems is his "Prayer for Marilyn Monroe" which opens as follows:

[35] Caracciolo-Trejo, *Penguin Latin American Verse*, 294–95, editor's trans.; trans. modified.
[36] Victor Shklovsky, "Art as Technique," in *Literary Theory: An Anthology*, ed. Julie Rivkin and Michael Ryan (Malden, MA: Blackwell, 2004), 15–21.
[37] Fernández Retamar, "Prologue to Ernesto Cardenal," in *Caliban and Other Essays*, trans. Edward Baker (Minneapolis, MN: Minnesota University Press, 1989), 103.
[38] Gordon Brotherston, *Latin American Poetry: Origins and Presence* (Cambridge: Cambridge University Press, 1975), 173.

Stephen M. Hart

ORACIÓN POR MARILYN MONROE
Señor
recibe a esta muchacha conocida en toda la Tierra con el nombre de
    Marilyn Monroe,
aunque ése no era su verdadero nombre
(pero Tú conoces su verdadero nombre, el de la huerfanita violada a los
    9 años
y la empleadita de tienda que a los 16 se había querido matar)
y que ahora se presenta ante Ti sin ningún maquillaje
sin su Agente de Prensa
sin fotógrafos y sin firmar autógrafos
sola como un astronauta frente a la noche espacial.

(Lord accept this girl/ Called Marilyn Monroe throughout the world/
Though that was not her name/ (but you know her real name, that of the
orphan raped at nine/ the shopgirl who tried to kill herself when aged sixteen)/
who now goes into your presence without make-up/ without her Press Agent/
without her photographs or signing autographs/ lonely as an astronaut facing
the darkness of outer space.)[39]

Like the other "conversational" poets studied in this chapter, Cardenal uses
everyday words, he avoids convoluted metaphors, and he echoes the rhythms
of everyday speech. But he also expands and deepens our vision of Marilyn
Monroe. The basic idea underlying this first stanza is that Marilyn Monroe
had to appear alone before God, but Cardenal enhances the idea by drawing
attention to what she "lost" in that process (her name, her make-up, her Press
Agent, and her photographs) and ends on an image of the contrast between
the vastness of God and the smallness of a human individual (the astronaut
lost in outer space). The rest of the poem has the rhythm of a spoken prayer –
returning again and again to a plea for God's mercy – using contrasts ("she
was hungry for tranquilizers and we offered her tranquilizers"), similes ("like
a cruise on a yacht"), and metaphors ("in this world/ contaminated equally
by radioactivity and sin"; *Marilyn Monroe and Other Poems*, 76–77). Unlike
José Lezama Lima, who found it impossible to contain his poetic thoughts
within the straightjacket of everyday language, as he suggested in *Thoughts
in Havana* (see epigraph), Cardenal felt he *was* able to express his ideas
within a "conversation calm in style," and this was, indeed, where the
vigor of his poetry resides.

The Salvadorean poet, Roque Dalton (1935–1975), like Cardenal, combined politics and straight-talking in his poetry, but, unlike Cardenal, he
poured scorn on religion. "Toadstools VIII" gives a flavor of Dalton's style:

[39] Ernesto Cardenal, *Marilyn Monroe and Other Poems*, trans. Robert Pring-Mill
(London: Search Press, 1975), 75.

En mi última cárcel recé en dos ocasiones, impropio, lo sé, para el caso de un
comunista de mediana edad, pero no menos cierto. Lo que me seguirá
intrigando el resto de mi vida no es aquella concesión íntima
al miedo, sino lo que yo llamaría la concurrencia de lo
extraordinario. La primera, todo el mundo lo sabe, fue cuando el
terremoto rompió la pared de la celda. La segunda fue cuando me
dijeron que me matarían el día siguiente y que me difamarían el
fantasma rojo con toda la mierda/ de la ley

(In my last jail I prayed on two different occasions. Inconsistent, I know, in a
middle-aged Communist but true all the same. What will go on puzzling me for
the rest of my life is not that personal concession to fear but something I'd call
the chance happening of extraordinary things. The first, everybody knows, was
when the earthquake split open the wall of my cell. The second was when I was
told they'd kill me the next day and smear the red ghost with all the shit allowed
within the limits of the law.)[40]

He was given a Bible for a quarter of an hour, opened it at random and
read the verse: "Como oveja/ a la muerte fue llevado, y como cordero mudo
delante del que lo trasquila,/ así no abrió la boca. En su humillación/ su juicio
fue quitado, mas, su generación ?quién la contara?/ Porque es quitada de la
tierra su vida" (He was led like a sheep to the slaughter and, like a lamb dumb
before his shearer, so opened he not his mouth. In his humiliation his
judgement was taken way; and who shall declare his generation? For his
life is taken away from the earth). As the poem concludes: "Como milagro
que pase, padre, pero no me negará Ud. Que ello es una verdadera cabro-
nada" (As a miracle, let it pass, Father, but you can't deny that this was a
really dirty trick).[41] Many of Dalton's poems, whether written in lines like
verse or like a prose poem as here, have an oral fluidity about them which is
distinctive. The power of the Dalton poem comes from its dogged insistence
on telling life as it is – leaving no room for style or embellishment of the
facts – and in their combination of political satire and ironic self-deprecation.

Clearly, the single most important poet who can be associated with conversational poetry – even despite his more common association with the
"antipoem" – is Nicanor Parra (b.1914); born in Chillán, a small town two
hundred miles to the south of Santiago, Chile, he graduated in 1938 in
mathematics and physics at the University of Chile in Santiago and, thus,
perhaps not surprisingly, he rejected the traditional conventions of poetry,
seeing poems rather as mathematical theorems: "Maximum content, minimum of words. (...) Economy of language, no metaphors, no literary

---

[40] Trans. Hardie St. Martin; *Oxford Latin American Poetry* ed. Vicuña and Livon
Grossman, 427–28.
[41] *Oxford Latin American Poetry*, ed. Vicuña and Livon-Grosman, 427–28; trans. modified.

tropes."[42] "Like other Chileans of his generation," as Gordon Brotherston suggests, Parra "faced the problem of how to write at all and avoid the overwhelming influence of Neruda" (*Latin American Poetry*, 183); the solution he chose was a highly corrosive one. In "Roller Coaster," from *Versos del salón* (Salon Verses, 1962), for example, Parra sets out his poetic stall:

> Durante medio siglo
> la poesía fue
> el paraíso del tonto solemne.
> Hasta que vine yo
> y me instalé con mi montaña rusa.
> Suban si les parece.
> Claro que yo no respondo si bajan
> echando sangre por boca y narices.

> (For half a century/ Poetry was the paradise/ Of the solemn fool./ Until I came along/ And built my roller coaster./ Go up, if you feel like it./
> It's not my fault if you come down/Bleeding from your nose and mouth.)[43]

Whereas in the past, Parra suggests, poets ascended to Mount Olympus ("the paradise/ of the solemn fool") in order to drink in their inspiration from the spring of Castalia, nowadays they must take a ride on the modern equivalent, a roller coaster. The thrill of Parra's poetry has more in common with the modern world; it is neither gentle nor soul-uplifting. The experience of suddenly being brought down to earth is enough to give the unsuspecting reader a nose bleed. His poem "Test" is a logical extension to this idea:

> Qué es un antipoeta:
> Un comerciante en urnas y ataúdes?
> Un sacerdote que no cree en nada?
> Un general que duda de sí mismo?
> (...)
> Una advertencia a los poetas jóvenes?
> Un ataúd a fuerza centrífuga?
> Un ataúd a gas de parafina?
> Una capilla ardiendo sin difunto?
> Marque con una cruz
> La definición que considere correcta.

> (What is an antipoet:/ Someone who deals in coffins and urns?/ A general who's not sure of himself?/ A priest who believes in nothing?/ (...) A warning to

---

[42] Qtd. in Frank MacShane, "Introduction," in Nicanor Parra, *Antipoems: New and Selected*, ed. David Unger (New York: New Directions, 1985), x.

[43] Parra, *Antipoems*, 42–43.

young poets?/ A jet-propelled coffin?/ A coffin in centrifugal kerosene?/ A funeral parlour without a corpse?/ Put an X/ Next to the right answer.)[44]

Again Parra delivers a quick, sharp jab to the traditional reader of poetry, refusing to answer his own question. Parra's style is not only conversational – possessing as it does the rhythms of everyday speech – it is also self-deictically antipoetic, pouring scorn on those who attempt to beautify life in the same way they load their poems up with showy rhetorical devices. His *Letters from a Poet who Sleeps in a Chair* demonstrate that Parra's *ars poetica* encourages freedom:

> "Digo las cosas tales como son
> O lo sabemos todo de antemano
> O no sabremos nunca absolutamente nada.
> (...) Jóvenes
> Escriban los que quieran
> En el estilo que les parezca mejor
> Ha pasado demasiada sangre bajo los puentes
> Para seguir creyendo – creo yo
> que sólo se puede seguir un camino:
> En poesía se permite todo,"

> (I call a spade a spade/ We either know everything from the start/ Or we'll never know a thing./ (...)/ Young poets/ Say whatever you want/ Pick your own style/ Too much blood has gone under the bridge/ To still believe – I believe –/ That there's only one way to cross the road:/ You can do anything in poetry.)[45]

Conversational poetry has been an important strain within Latin American poetry, especially during the post-World War II period. While it often drank in the same waters that political commitment sprang from – ranging from the political undertow of Fernández Retamar's work to the satiric irony of Benedetti's verse – "poesía conversacional" always sought, in William Carlos Williams' words, to wrest the "power of thought back through a new minting of the words."

[44] Parra, *Antipoems*, 66–68.
[45] "Cartas del poeta que duerme en una silla," Parra, *Antipoems*, 90–92.

5

BEN BOLLIG

Contemporary Poetry

Any attempt to condense more than three decades of poetry from a region as vast and varied as Latin America necessarily tends to be partial, unscientific, and biased. For this and other reasons this chapter limits itself to providing a sketch of some general poetic trends during this period and more detailed – but still excessively superficial – observations about a small selection of poets who might be said to represent and at times surpass these tendencies. Despite widespread claims of poetry's irrelevance, anachronism, or willful isolation, it continues to be relevant for authors, readers, and publishers. New technologies and media have not rung the knell for writing verse, but instead provide some of the liveliest and most innovative spaces for the circulation and even composition of new poems.

As the Argentine poet Néstor Perlongher (1949–1992) stated in an essay published in 1992, although poetry does not sell a great deal, it does circulate well. Writing about Argentina, but in a phrase that could well be generalizable across the region, he observed that the end of the 1970s had witnessed a "proliferation of poets [... a] multiplication of bards."[1] This might seem surprising. As is well known, much Latin American poetry of the 1960s and 1970s combined a colloquial, communicative approach to language and structure with socio-political themes and a revolutionary intent. Roque Dalton (El Salvador, 1935–1975), Ernesto Cardenal (Nicaragua, 1925), Gonzalo Rojas (Chile, 1917–2011), Mario Benedetti (Uruguay, 1920–2009), and Juan Gelman (Argentina, 1930–2014) had all identified an almost organic connection between writing in verse and political commitment to popular mass-movements or armed revolutionary uprising. The wave of coups and military or other interventions that swept the region, and in many countries nigh on destroyed the political left in the 1970s and 1980s, violently undid this suturing of poetic creation to practical engagement. Exile, tragedy, and

---

[1] Néstor Perlongher, "Argentina's Secret Poetry Boom," *Journal of Latin American Cultural Studies* 1.2 (1992): 178.

loss would mark the later verse of many of the writers who most characterized Latin American poetry in the post-Neruda period. Dalton, Francisco "Paco" Urondo (Argentina, 1930–1976), to name but two, gave their lives to the political causes they had supported.

In the same article, Perlongher reflected that poetry in the 1980s showed "manierista" or mannerist and baroque qualities. Perhaps the most important movement or trend in Latin American poetry in the last thirty years, influential both positively and also in the (sometimes enraged) reactions it has provoked, is what Perlongher and others call the *neobarroco* or neo-Baroque. If, in overly simplistic terms, one might say that the committed or communicative poetry of the 1960s and 1970s focused on the message, be that the denunciation of social injustice, the promotion of political utopias, or the registering of the experience of revolutionary struggle, *neobarroco* poetry turned to the medium, namely the experience of language itself.

The genealogy of the *neobarroco* is complicated. Just as the poetry of Luis de Góngora (1561–1627) was overlooked and even derided for centuries in Spain, until his reappraisal by Federico García Lorca (1898–1936) and fellow members of the Generation of 1927, so too did the Latin American Colonial Baroque fail to impress strongly on later Latin American writers. But with Lorca's visits to Cuba and to Buenos Aires, one might suggest that a direct link was established between avant-garde groups in the Caribbean and the River Plate and the Spanish heirs of the Golden Age Baroque. The term *neobarroco* is widely credited to the Cuban Severo Sarduy (1937–93) and his 1974 study of the Baroque and its more recent avatars. Alejo Carpentier (1904–1980) had earlier spoken about "lo barroco" (the baroque) in relation to "lo real maravilloso" (the marvelous real) in a conference given at the Ateneo de Caracas in 1975: the *horror vacui*, and with it art that proliferates while destroying limits. Rather than a particular artistic periodization, the *barroco* was a pulse or force that returns throughout human history. As an aesthetic manifestation of a human style it was, Carpentier added, eminently suited to Latin America.

The third name in this Cuban triumvirate is, of course, José Lezama Lima (1910–1976), the later reception of whose poetry, and perhaps more importantly prose, and especially the strikingly gongorine semi-autobiographical novel, *Paradiso* (1966), is often cited by poets and theorists of the *neobarroco* as a trigger moment. Although Lezama was cosmopolitan only in his reading, and scarcely left the island, the international standing of *Paradiso* cannot be underestimated: the second edition was published in Mexico, having been edited by an Argentine, Julio Cortázar (1914–1984), resident in Paris. One might suggest that such migrations and international encounters feature prominently in the *neobarroco*'s history. In his introduction to the *neobarroco*, Perlongher traced a line from the Spanish Golden Age, through the *modernismo* of Nicaragua's Rubén Darío (1867–1916), the links between García Lorca, Surrealism, and Cuban groups (e.g. *Orígenes*) to contemporary poets.[2] The *neobarroco* was neither communicative nor translatable. Its force resides in the sensation of reading, in the physical effects of the poem on the body and mind of the reader: anti-rational, anti-colonial, and anti-*yo*. In the *neobarroco* poem, as Perlongher puts it, "todo entra en suspensión" (everything goes into suspension; Néstor Perlongher, "Prólogo," 23).

The Uruguayan writer and scholar Roberto Echavarren (b. 1944), in his study of the *neobarroco*, highlights Lezama's importance in the emergence of the new poetry, with its combination of lexical and thematic impurity and syntactical complexity.[3] For Echavarren, the *neobarroco* reacted against the shared didacticism of both the vanguards and colloquial poetry, mixing styles, registers, and references. He cites the later work of the Brazilian poet Haroldo de Campos (1929–2003), and in particular his 1984 collection *Galâxias* (Galaxies), a dense collection of prose poems – "proesia" was the term de Campos used – with its sensuous play with sounds and constantly punning syntax: "e começo aqui e meço aqui este começo e recomeço e/ arremeso e aqui me meço quando se vive sob a espécie da viagem o/ importante não é a viagem mas o começo" (I start here and I chart here with this start and a restart and/ I dart and here I chart myself when one lives under a sort of journey what's/ important isn't the journey but the start; in Echavarren, *Medusario*, 286–312).[4] De Campos was a central figure in the *concretista* or concrete poetry movement in Brazil in the 1950s and 1960s in which poets extended the scope of the calligramme into sculptural, public poetry. In his later writings he would explore the links between concrete poetry and the baroque.

It is tempting to see the *neobarroco* as a rupture with the poetry of the 1960s and 1970s, yet many of its features have their roots earlier in literary history. Likewise, in its rejection of communication, its focus on pleasure, and its seeming alienation from the political commitment of earlier poets, the *neobarroco* may seem playful, evasive, and apolitical – a postmodern diversion, one might say. Perlongher joked that such a reading mistook "ludismo" for "boludismo" (Perlongher, "Argentina's Secret," 183) – taking the

[2] Néstor Perlongher, "Prólogo," in *Medusario. Muestra de poesía latinoamericana*, (Mexico City: Fondo de Cultura Económica, 1996), 24–25.
[3] Roberto Echavarren, "Prólogo," in *Medusario. Muestra de poesía latinoamericana* (Mexico City: Fondo de Cultura Económica, 1996), 13.
[4] All translations into English are the author's unless otherwise stated in the references cited.

"ludic" for "just being a dick," one might hazard a guess in translation. But he and others argued that the *neobarroco* was a necessary response to the *de facto* closure of spaces for oppositional discourse by the coups and repression of the 1970s, an escape from the constraints of social or socialist realism, and also an outlet for the expression of (sexual, political, racial) difference, overlooked or actively repressed by class-based forms of political writing. Hippies, gay and lesbian people, *travestis*, drug users, nomads, and migrants people the poems of the *neobarroco*.

An important precursor of the *neobarroco* can thus be found, as Gustavo Guerrero notes, in the poetry of the Peruvian Rodolfo Hinostroza (1941); Hinostroza was born in Lima but moved to Cuba to study and then later to Paris. His *Contra natura* (1971) sought a synthesis of the experimentalism inherited from the avant-gardes and the use of the colloquial.[5] This involved the inclusion of drawings, doodles, mathematical equations, and non-Spanish text, in a sort of collage, shaped into drifting, sculpted lines of poetry reminiscent of the works of Stéphane Mallarmé, to name just one. Hinostroza's interests, as evidenced in his poems, included astrology, mysticism, and hallucinogens. His writing is marked by humor and eroticism, the latter often in the form of anthropomorphic metaphors, but also by a subversive, political intent: "Para arrasar el Poder/ se precisa el Poder: yo buscaré el Tao & Utopía" (To destroy Power/ one needs Power: I'll look for Tao & Utopia).[6]

If the *neobarroco* attempted to displace the traditional lyric subject or the image of the poet as "hombre nuevo," then another important innovator is the Brazilian poet Ana Cristina Cesar (1952–1983). Cesar, or "Ana C." as she is often simply known, was a precocious talent, publishing poems in her childhood, and began her adult career as one of the so-called "poetas marginais" or marginal poets in Rio de Janeiro in the 1970s. Ana C. is frequently compared to Sylvia Plath (1932–1963) and the Argentine Alejandra Pizarnik (1936–1972), in part because all three took their own lives at a young age, but more pertinently because of the provocative brilliance of their writing. She contributed to the anthology *26 poetas de hoje* (26 Poets of Today) in 1976 and then published four collections of poems and prose poems in quick succession, before her death in 1983. Posthumously her essays and translations have been published; Luciana di Leone has studied in detail what she calls the subsequent "consecration" of Ana C. as a writer.[7] Much of Cesar's work comes in the form of intimate, autobiographical writing, mixing verse

---

[5] Gustavo Guerrero, *Cuerpo plural. Antología de la poesía hispanoamericana contemporánea* (Madrid/Buenos Aires/Valencia: Pre-textos/Instituto Cervantes, 2010), 20.

[6] Rodolfo Hinostroza, *Contra natura* (Barcelona: Barral Editores, 1971), 72.

[7] Luciani di Leone, *Ana C.: As tramas da consagração* (Rio de Janeiro: 7letras, 2008).

and prose. One of her collections is, deceptively, titled *Correspondência completa* (The Complete Letters, 1979). But, as Siscar notes, what is important is less the private world of Ana C. than "a invenção que ela faz da intimidade," her inventiveness with privacy.[8] María Negroni suggests that she writes "entre el pseudo diario íntimo y la pseudo narración" (between the pseudo-private diary and pseudo-narration).[9] The poet was aware of her own myth – the precocious child writer, then the woman revealing her most intimate sexual and bodily details – and also its most strident critic. One poem, entitled "Fama e fortuna" (Fame and Fortune), begins "Assinei meu nome tantas vezes/ e agora viro manchete de jornal" (I've signed my name so many times/ and now I'm a newspaper headline).[10] Her work creates the impression of proximity, only to build distance with literary references, verbal games, and relentless, at times obscene, humor. The second-person form is strongly present, as an address to the self, the other, the reader, and even as a sort of distancing device.

Many of her poems are brief in the extreme, as short as a couplet, or even a single line. Yet their effect can be lapidary. In *Inéditos e dispersos* (Unpublished and Uncollected, 1985), we read one poem: "Aqui meus crimes não seriam de amor" (Here my crimes would not be of passion; *Inéditos e dispersos*, 127). Another, over two lines, states flatly, "a gente sempre acha que é/ Fernando Pessoa" (we always think we're/ Fernando Pessoa; *Inéditos e dispersos*, 134). Pessoa (1888–1935) was a multilingual writer both prodigious and largely unrecognized in life; more importantly, perhaps, he was one of the most brilliant practitioners of pseudonymous or so-called "heteronymic" writing, experimenting prodigiously with the link between life and fiction. *A teus pés* (At Your Feet, 1982) includes an index of names, ranging from Francisco Alvim to Walt Whitman (one of César's most admired poets, according to Siscar) by way of Billie Holiday and James Joyce. But the index comes without page numbers, and few if any of the names are directly present. One must assume, therefore, that the index provides more an indication of the palimpsestic and intertextual nature of the poems and the authorial figure they create than a useful guide to the book. As she writes in a poem entitled "Este livro" (This Book), "Meu filho. Não e automatismo. Juro. É jazz do coração. É/ prosa que dá prêmio. Un tea for two total" (My child. It's not automatic writing. I swear. It's jazz straight from the heart. It's prize-

8 Marcos Siscar, *Ana Cristina Cesar* (Rio de Janeiro: Editora da Universidade do Estado do Rio de Janeiro, 2011), 10.

9 María Negroni, *La maldad de escribir: 9 poetas latinoamericanas del siglo XX* (Montblanc, Tarragona: Igitur, 2003), 73.

10 Ana Cristina César, *Inéditos e dispersos: poesia, prosa* (São Paulo: Instituto Moreira Salles, 1998), 170.

winning prose. A total *tea for two*).[11] Just as jazz musicians can create the impression of invention on the basis of relentless preparation and studied virtuosity, so does Ana C. play with the throw-away line or the revealing slip. As Gonzalez and Treece write, her work explores "the dialectic between private and public lives, as well as reconstructing a new and original relationship with the reader."[12] Like much *neobarroco* writing, her poetry works to destabilize the lyric subject.

While the lyric subject is displaced or destabilized in *neobarroco* poetry, language itself, and in particular the pleasures of insinuation and implication, becomes the focus of many of its works. The baroque metaphor, full of high-cultural or classical references, often demanded great knowledge and erudition on the part of the reader. A writer like Góngora could "square" metaphors, combining two implicit comparisons and thus doubling the work required by the reader. Most memorably this can be found in his extended *silva*, the *Soledades* (1613, *The Solitudes*). Yet for the educated reader, the possibility of an interpretation, albeit a tortuous one, is always present. The *neobarroco* creates the sensation of difficulty, allusion, and sensuousness, but without necessarily allowing the reader to resolve the metaphor, conceit, or allusion, into a contemporary or historical referent. In short, much *neobarroco* poetry deliberately evades meaning. At the same time, signification is raised to a maximum.

Such theorizing is well illustrated by the poetry of the Mexican Coral Bracho (1951). Her writing is tactile yet, semantically, extremely slippery and evasive. Roberto Echavarren talks of a form of "poesía acuática" or aquatic poetry (Echavarren, *Medusario*, 387). As Tom Boll writes, Bracho's is "a poetic world that is sensual and exploratory, attentive to the intermittencies of the individual's experience."[13] Her long poem, "Agua de bordes lúbricos" (Slippery-edged Water) contains, in Boll's words, "a great teeming succession of liquid images" ("Introduction," 7): "Agua de medusas,/ agua láctea, sinuosa,/ agua de bordes lúbricos; espesura vidriante – Delicuescencia/ entre contornos deleitosos" (Water of jellyfish,/ milky, snaking water/ of ever-changing shapes: glossy water-flesh; melting/ into its lovely surrounding).[14] Bracho aims, in Boll's words, "to get close to the movement of water" ("Introduction," 7). Her lexis is abstract; the rhythm changeable; and the shape of the poem drifts

[11] Ana Cristina César, *A teus pés: prosa/poesia* (São Paulo: Insituto Moreira Salles, 1998), 55.

[12] Mike Gonzalez, Mike & David Treece, *The Gathering of Voices. The Twentieth-Century Poetry of Latin America* (London: Verso, 1992), 329.

[13] Tom Boll, "Introduction," in Coral Bracho & Katherine Pierpoint (translator), *Poems. Poemas* (London: Poetry Translation Centre, 2010), 6.

[14] Coral Bracho & Katherine Pierpoint (trans.), *Poems. Poemas* (London: Poetry Translation Centre, 2010), 28.

across the page, with lines short and long, left justified or tabbed. "Agua" (water) is the one constant term, but modified differently throughout the poem, showing multiple aspects of the liquid compound.

Intense, even graphic eroticism is a key characteristic of the poetry of Perlongher, Echavarren, Eduardo Espina (Uruguay, b. 1954), and others. Bracho is no different is this regard. In the poem "En la humedad cifrada" (In the ciphered humidity) she writes, "Oigo tu cuerpo con la avidez abrevada y tranquila/ de quien se impregna (de quien/ emerge,/ de quien se extiende saturado,/ recorrido/ de esperma)" (I hear your body with the short, calm keenness/ of one impregnated [one who emerges, one who stretches, saturated, overrun with sperm]; Echavarren, *Medusario*, 394). The poem is strikingly direct and sexual, yet at the same time the phrase "de quien," "of one," or perhaps "like one" sets back the speaking subject from the fleshy and liquid details. There follows a string of metaphors, "suave oráculo espeso" (smooth, thick oracle) "templo de los limos" (temple of slimes), which tempt translation as the depiction of an enthusiastic sexual scene, while at the same time creating an allusive, literary, and sensual world that for the reader may offer more pleasure than the mere depiction of sex. Language is neither communicative nor instrumental, rather a source of pleasure and provocation for the reader. Kuhnheim writes of a form of "hypersynesthesia" in Bracho's poetry.[15] This tension between what might be a transparent metaphor and a more creative, more fulfilling yet more mysterious poetic device, is a feature Bracho shares with many of her peers. Likewise the influence of recent French philosophy, Bracho begins her poem "Sobre las mesas: el destello" (On the table: the glint) with a quotation from Gilles Deleuze and Félix Guattari's *Rhizome* (in Echavarren, *Medusario*, 400). Bodies, animals, and birds populate the poem that follows, perhaps an allusion to the "becoming-animal" explored by the two Frenchmen.

A poet often associated with the *neobarroco* (and included in the important anthology *Medusario*), but whose work spans several decades and transcends any simple categorization, is the Chilean Raúl Zurita (b. 1950). A young communist detained and beaten at the time of Pinochet's *golpe de estado* (coup d'état), as an artist Zurita emerges as a member of the Colectivo de Acciones de Arte (CADA) or Art Actions Collective, along with activists and writers such as Carlos Leppe (b. 1952), Diamela Eltit (b. 1949), and Eugenio Dittborn (b. 1943), who staged performances and happenings to protest the everyday brutality of the military regime, often involving acts of violence towards themselves or large-scale interventions in public space. One

---

[15] Jill S. Kuhnheim, *Spanish American Poetry and the End of the Twentieth Century: Textual Disruptions* (Austin, TX: University of Texas Press, 2004), 119.

such action was the painting of white lines across street markings, thus turning a main road into a lengthy and very visible memorial to the murdered and disappeared of 1970s state terrorism.

The connection between poetry and art-interventions is inescapable in Zurita's works. A series of dramatic actions have accompanied his poetic output. He burnt his cheek with a hot iron and then used the image of his scar for the front cover of one collection, *Purgatorio* (Purgatory, 1979). In Rowe's words, the wound becomes a "new basis of the social" in Pinochet's Chile.[16] He attempted, thankfully without success, to blind himself with caustic liquid before a performance of sky writing, as acrobatic planes marked phrases from his *Anteparaíso* (Anteparadise, 1982) in smoke in the air over New York. And he has also created poems on the landscape of Chile, using industrial diggers to carve phrases in the Atacama Desert and on the cliffs of the Pacific coast. The latter are visible only from the sea, the former from space. As Jacobo Sefamí writes, "land art" and "body art" combine in his writing.[17]

This link between epic scale and personal risk characterizes all of Zurita's poetry. His major work, obviously inspired by Dante – a "deliberate use of Dante as a model," Rowe calls it (*Poets*, 283) – is the cycle of collections *Purgatorio, Anteparaíso,* and *La vida nueva* (The New Life, 1994). An intermediate collection, *Canto a su amor desaparecido* (1985, Song to a Disappeared Love, 1985) gives a briefer introduction of Zurita's project. It begins, in outsized type on an otherwise empty page, with a single sentence: "Ahora Zurita – me largó – ya que de puro verso y desgarro te pudiste entrar aquí, en nuestras pesadillas; ¿tú puedes decirme dónde está mi hijo?" ("Now look, Zurita," s/he snapped at me, "seeing as you've tricked and scammed your way in here, into our nightmares, are you gonna tell me where my son is?").[18] The collection records the voices of the victims of recent Chilean politics, their stories of loss, violence, and dispossession. As Gonzalez and Treece write, in Zurita's poetry "the voices of emptiness and disintegration combine with the deep and searing lament for the lost and tortured" (*Gathering of Voices*, 351). In his *Canto a su amor desaparecido*, we encounter both "a multitude of voices, a chorus of pain" and "a reconstruction of a common experience of love" (*Gathering of Voices*, 352). A lyric voice will interlude from time to time, with a song or chant. And at the center of the collection, there is a set of diagrams, showing niches in a cemetery, each

[16] William Rowe, *Poets of Contemporary Latin America. History and the Inner Life* (Oxford: Oxford University Press, 2000), 324–25.

[17] Jacobo Sefamí, "Prólogo," in Raúl Zurita, *Mi mejilla es el cielo estrellado: Antología* (Mexico City/Saltillo, Coahuila: Aldus/Instituto Coahuilense de Cultura, 2004), 19–50.

[18] Raúl Zurita, *Canto a su amor desaparecido* (Santiago de Chile: Universitaria, 1987), 7.

named after a country or region in Latin American or the post- or neo-colonial world. Short epitaphs accompany the diagrams, in the form of square, bold blocks of text.

Zurita's collections create a biblical epic of Chile, but from a secular point of view. We read shifting subject positions (in register, gender, age, and number), irruptions of violence and sex, all set against a huge, almost continental backdrop of mountains, deserts, and oceans. There are diagrams and other non-literary elements. He uses numbered points for many poems, giving a mathematical or logical feel to his work. Yet at the same time, madness – of the speaker, or of those described – is a constant threat. *Purgatorio* includes what appear to be the poet's electro-encephalograms. Zurita is a named character in many poems, often abruptly interpolated by other speaking voices. The national poetry of Gabriela Mistral (1889–1957), the formal experiments of Vicente Huidobro (1883–1948), the anti-poetry of Nicanor Parra (b. 1914), and the epic of Pablo Neruda (1904–1973) are combined and pushed to their limits in the work of Zurita. In *La vida nueva* he recorded the dreams and nightmares of poor settlers and slum-dwellers as poems. His work is at once a stunning record of the suffering Chile has undergone in recent years, and a utopian call for the possibility of a better future. Rowe points out a key difference from the poetry of the 1960s: "Zurita's concern is a refoundation of the social in ecstatic vision and not in ideology" (*Poets*, 302).

Any literary movement has its detractors and opponents, and the *neobarroco* is no exception. Even in his 1992 assessment of the contemporary poetic moment, Néstor Perlongher noted the objections to the *neobarroco* that had already emerged. Although it is risky to generalize for, as Guerrero states, the younger generation of Latin American poets demonstrates an "impresionante variedad de registros estilísticos" (an impressive array of stylistic registers),[19] one might suggest that an *objetivista or* objectivist tendency has been the most noticeable reaction to – or against – the *neobarroco* in Latin America. If *neobarroco* poetry focused on the materiality and sensuousness of language, with reference points ranging from Góngora, García Lorca, José Lezama Lima, to Brazil's *concretistas, objetivismo*, in contrast, concentrated on the creation of objects in language, and reacted to the excess and sensuality of Perlongher, Espina, Echavarren, and others with poetry that was stripped of all excess, including metaphors and even, at times, adjectives or adverbs. Poetry operates at its most indexical level, as a recording of the

[19] Gustavo Guerrero, "De un siglo a otro," in *Cuerpo plural. Antología de la poesía hispanoamericana contemporánea* (Madrid/Buenos Aires/Valencia: Pre-textos/Instituto Cervantes, 2010), 24.

observed world. Literary figures dear to *objetivista* poets are mostly Anglophone poets, including Ezra Pound, William Carlos Williams, and Louis Zukofsky. *Objetivismo* played a central role in the emergence of a new poetry scene in the 1990s, around Buenos Aires' influential literary newspaper, *Diario de poesía*, but has representatives across the continent.

Recent anthologies of Latin American poetry reflect these shifts, although it is perhaps excessive to talk of a "movement" in the literary-historical sense. Guerrero ("De un siglo," 30) sees the verse of the 1990s and 2000s as evidence of poets abandoning notions of transcendence, either of sacred transcendence as inherited from the German romantics, or of political transcendence as in social or protest poetry; in short, "la erosión y el gradual desmantelamiento del paradigma que se impone con el modernismo y las vanguardias" (the erosion and gradual dismantling of the reigning *modernista* and vanguard paradigm; "De un siglo," 30), namely that of poetry as in some way sacred. Gone too is the "compromiso político que avale un proyecto colectivo" (political commitment supporting a collective project; "De un siglo," 32). The new poetry is dominated by the image, the urban, and everyday objects, including trash. With more than fifty poets, from across the Americas, with ages ranging from thirty to fifty at the time of publication, Guerrero's anthology is with difficulty synthesized. Nevertheless, direct first-person address, the use of fragments or snippets of narrative, a contemporary, urban and everyday setting, and a certain sparseness of lexis and form can be found widely. Irony in observation marks the work of the Mexican Luis Felipe Fabre (b. 1974), or the Argentine Sergio Raimondi (b. 1968).

In the introduction to his anthology of recent poetry, Julio Ortega notes the importance of everyday speech in the work of young poets.[20] "Leemos 'poesía' en un lenguaje que ya no es 'literario' o 'poético'" (we read "poetry" in a language that is no longer "literary" or "poetic"; *El turno*, 16). For poets born after 1960, he suggests, "el acto poético es menos performativo y más dialógico" (the poetic act is less performative and more dialogic; *El turno*, 14). There is a materiality and specificity to their production; the scale is more modest; and publishing and circulation are more artisanal. Although Ortega includes a writer of sonnets, the Venezuelan Luis Gerardo Mármol Bosch (b. 1966) and a composer of what are in prosodic terms quite traditional ballads, the Argentine Paula Brudny (b. 1964), his selection is notable for its plain-speaking, first-person, direct address, often marked by metaliterary observations. Yet this is not traditional lyrical poetry; the first-person

[20] Julio Ortega, *El turno y la transición. Antología de la poesía latinoamericana del siglo XXI* (México DF: Siglo XXI, 2001), 12.

is as much a grammatical position as it is an expression of autobiography. The role of the poet seems to be to register reality, perhaps through the eyes and voice of another. In another recent anthology of young poetry, *ZurDos*, the editors write in their iconoclastic and decidedly *anti-neobarroco* introduction of the focus on the signifier rather than transcendent essences in recent poetry.[21] Similarly, Kesselman *et al.* (2012) speak of the "materialist tendency" in poetry from the 1990s and 2000s.[22]

The work of the Chilean Malú Urriola (b. 1967) both illustrates and complicates these generalizations. Her poetry conducts an at times brutal analysis of violence and sexism. Following the CADA tradition and the later novels of Diamela Eltit, her work assesses the ways in which, in a violent and sexist society, the subject incorporates such forms of discrimination into his or her psychological make-up and self-image. Much of Urriola's work is provocative and unrelenting; but her writing is not without its dark humor. Take, for example, the sequence *Los gatos de Jakobsen* (Jakobsen's Cats), in which we see Urriola play with clichés related to her own poetic voice, specifically the *poeta maldita*, the *poète maudite*, reworked as a contemporary rocker or goth: "Hay que asumir, pendeja/ que estás sola/ que te bailas un rock/ para quitarte las ganas – tú sabes de qué" (You've got to admit, bitch, that you're alone, that you dance to rock music to get rid of the urge – to you know what; Ortega, *El turno*, 101). Urriola portrays the dismissive voice of common sense, wanting rid of the annoying, unsettling "poetita de mierda" (shitty little poet; González and Araya, *ZurDos*, 316), who is constantly drunk, complaining, and refuses to comply. Urriola, however, does not give us a stable point or a fixed position from which to judge, instead obliging the reader to think through the violence of this dismissal and the internalized hatred of the poetic position. In *Dame tu sucio amor* (Give Me Your Dirty Love, 1994), Urriola takes the reader on a tour of the urban underground: "Me perdí en Buenos Aires, ebria, me hallaron en un Bunker,/ bailando en medio de travestis, un hombre pensó que yo era/ un muchacho, salimos a la calle a tomar cervezas, me/ habló de su amado por horas" (I got lost, drunk, in Buenos Aires, they found me in a dive bar,/ dancing surrounded by transvestites, a man thought I was/ a guy, we went outside to drink beers, he talked/ to me for hours about his boyfriend; González and Araya, *ZurDos*, 319). Guerrero speaks of the "atracción de la nada" (lure of the void; "De un siglo," 28) at work in her writing.

Perhaps her most ambitious project is the long poem *Hija de perra* (Daughter of a Bitch, 1996), a sequence that has been republished already

---

[21] *ZurDos. Última poesía latinoamericana: antología*, ed. Yanko González and Pedro Araya (Madrid: Bartleby, 2005), 11.

[22] *La tendencia materialista: antología crítica de la poesía de los 90*, ed. Violeta Kesselman, Ana Mazzoni and Damián Selci (Buenos Aires: Paradiso, 2012).

three times in different countries in Latin America. Here she explores the relationship between existing as a woman, existing as a writer, and the web of violence and struggle that surround these overlapping positions. The poem investigates the imbrication of hatred and self-hatred, and the fractured nature of the subject speaking in a society beset by violence. In essence, it is a long interior monologue, but in which the position of the speaker varies, and seems also to incorporate other voices, opinions, and conversations. The poem portrays a desperate fight between the urge or need to write, and the self-hatred and wider dismissal that would suppress it. It demonstrates, then, the way in which social violence is internalized by individuals. On repeated readings, the effect of these multiple voices is to show a turning in on oneself, by which hatred becomes self-hatred. Her language is direct and harsh; the setting the contemporary city, incorporating new urban tribes of goths and EMOs, and the message, a multi-layered yet acid critique of contemporary attitudes towards society's most vulnerable members.

Another writer illustrative of recent poetic trends is the Argentine Andi Nachon (b. 1970). Her *oeuvre*, to date, comprises more than half a dozen single-authored collections of poetry (many of which are represented in recent anthologies) and her own anthology of Argentine women poets. She is also a visual artist, working in film, photography and mixed media, and teaches art and design. She gives frequent readings on the Buenos Aires poetry circuit, and has also published in Chile and Brazil. Her writing occupies, in form and technique, a space between the dominant trends of the 1980s and 1990s between the *neobarroco* and *objetivismo*, while her themes take in contemporary pop culture, political memory, and resistance, and what might be termed the "psychogeography" of the city. Ambiguity – of subject or narrative position; of syntax; of geographical or physical position; and of gender – characterizes much of her work. Her poetry develops novel forms of address, in relation to comparable near-contemporary poets, not least a use of the second-person singular that is at once the poetic position and an address to the other. Explorations of space, especially that of the contemporary city, can be found in both her early collections and her volume *Taiga* (2000); later, we find subtle political engagements as in the collection *Plaza real* (2004). Some of her most recent poetry interacts with non-poetic forms, including pop and rock music, urban street culture (BMX, skating), and sci-fi and fantasy literature, including the novels of Orson Scott Card. Questions of the lyric and what a number of theorists have called "non-lyric poetry" (Baltrusch & Lourido 2012)[23] are strongly present in her work.

[23] *Non-Lyric Discourses in Contemporary Poetry*, ed. Burghard Baltrusch and Isaac Lourido (Munich: Martin Meidenbauer, 2012).

Nachon's poetry offers a sustained attempt to create a cultural space for shared experiences of the contemporary world. To do this, time and again she opens up the lyric voice to the world and the other, to the point that the control and focus implicit in the lyric are abandoned, thus creating, in her unique way, a poetic space to be shared by all.

Of the most recent poets, one must admit that it is, very likely, too early to say. But a striking tendency can be observed in some of the most notable recent poetry, namely a return to very traditional, metrically careful, poetic forms, even with additional levels of difficulty (e.g. disguising one form, such as the sonnet, within another). And within these formal constraints, the thematic ambition on display can be quite breathtaking. *El baile de las condiciones* (2011, *The Dance of Conditions*) is the fifth collection to date by the Mexican poet Óscar de Pablo (b. 1974). Beginning with three quotations from the early philosophical writings of Karl Marx, and elsewhere uniting the economist with Shakespeare and Góngora, de Pablo's collection mixes grand subjects – heresy, betrayal, gender violence, privatization, the entire culture of modern-day Mexico – with carefully worked musicality in composition, in particular the use of internal rhyme and anadiplosis. The poem "Nadie (que yo conozca) es Tolomeo III" (No One – As Far As I Know – Is Ptolomy III) shifts between ancient Egypt and today's Mexico to humorously attack contemporary political excess and corruption. In "Habla el objeto" (The Object Speaks) the electric chair speaks: "Veníd a mí vosotros que aborrecéis lo humano, yo soy la pureza, yo soy la abnegación" (Come to me all ye who abhor humanity, I am purity, I am abnegation).[24] "Canción del que te necesita" (Song of the One Who Needs You) rewrites Marx's labor theory of value as a disturbing tale of sexual exploitation or even vampirism. "Cordero con orzo el estilo de Chipre" (Cyprus-style Lamb with Orzo) threads a cookery-book recipe into the experience of political repression. And "El quijote de Tomóchic" (Don Quixote of Tomóchic) rewrites the great Spanish novel as a tale of revolutionary violence and repression in Mexico. Each poem is dense in its layering of sound, syntax, and reference, creating a collection of phenomenal poetic ambition. Despite the difficulty and complexity, these poems are by no means hermetic; and despite their clear political content, they are neither didactic nor *panfletarios* (propagandist).

Óscar de Pablo is not alone in his attempts to unite difficulty in form with thematic range and analytical acuity in contemporary Latin American poetry. Youth and ambition seem to march hand in hand. The work of the Argentine Alejandro Crotto (b. 1978) is at once entirely contemporary in

---

[24] Óscar de Pablo, *El baile de las condiciones* (México DF: Conaculta, 2011), 39.

theme and lexis, yet also marked by an overt formal and syntactical literariness that seems, today, almost deliberately anachronistic. Crotto has published two collections of poetry with the independent publisher Bajo la luna and is at once at the heart of the Buenos Aires poetry scene and something of an outsider. As well as his books, he publishes extensively online, especially in his blog, *Los porqués de la rosa*.

What is most striking about Crotto's second collection, *Chesterton* (2013), beyond the thematic, is found in its form. The second poem, "Como creciendo en el carbón la brasa" (Like the Hot Coal Growing in the Charcoal) is a sonnet in hendecasyllables, but strikingly it is constructed so that only the last syllables rhyme (as opposed to the last two, more usual in Spanish), in the form ABAB (*rima alternada*), a remarkably consistent, marked, and apparently deliberate variation on an established rhyme scheme in Spanish. There is only one concession to this pattern, the final couplet (pupila – vacila/pupil – hesitate), which in the fashion of the Shakespearean sonnet aims to summarize the argument of the piece: "Que sea nuestro cuerpo la pupila/ que se abre si hace falta y no vacila" (May our body be the pupil/ that opens if needed and does not hesitate).[25] The first twelve lines comprise one long sentence, in which a number of key terms or word roots repeat: cumplirse – cumplida (fulfill, fulfilled); pulso (pulse); sal (salt); near homophones are also used: sal – se aleja (salt – withdraws); que sea – que se abre (may it be – which opens). The poem is packed with alliteration. Subclauses, enumerations, enjambments, and marked syntax make the poem dense in signification, with meaning shifting heuristically and retroactively as one reads. As in the work of, for example, Sor Juana Inés de la Cruz (1651–1695), the poem delights in paradox, contrast, and light and shade, in particular the "brillo oscuro" (dark shine) that we see and experience. This is language charged with meaning to the maximum, Crotto using poetry to analyze the materiality of sensation. The world's mystery is a central theme for Crotto's poetry; another of his titles (again notable for its Golden Age precision) is "Si usted va y mira una gallina durante una hora o dos, va a encontrar al final que el misterio más que disminuir ha aumentado" (If You Go and Look at a Hen for an Hour or Two, You'll Find that the Mystery, rather than Diminishing, Has Grown; Crotto, *Chesterton*, 15).

"Una canción tan fría y apasionada como el alba" (A Song as Cold and Passionate as the Dawn) looks, at first glance, to be a simple piece of free verse, describing the remnants of a party, the morning after on the beach; it is reminiscent of the work of colloquial and political poets such as Ernesto Cardenal. Its content is similar to that of many contemporary objectivist

---

[25] Alejandro Crotto, *Chesterton* (Buenos Aires: Bajo la luna, 2013), 9.

poems, seeing an unidentified observer contemplating an everyday – and somewhat desolate – scene. However, with attention, one notices internal rhymes and certain rhythms, and with some rearrangement, we can set out the poem as a *lira*, heptasyllables and hendecasyllables rhyming thus: aBabB. As Quilis points out, this is a stanza form imported from Italy and perfected in Spain by Christian mystical poets such as Fray Luis de León (1527–1591) and San Juan de la Cruz (1542–1591).[26] The final couplet remains unchanged in the second arrangement, and it would also fit in a *silva* (a free combination of irregularly rhymed seven- and eleven-syllable lines). The scene on the beach will be washed away soon, by the repeated, and implacable, waves. The poem balances control and emotion; man's efforts and nature: "fría ... apasionada" (cold, passionate); "canción ... alba" (song, dawn). So form is at once polished and hidden; Crotto's poems function simultaneously in two ways. Register and prosody diverge, indeed they almost clash. This poem plays out the tension between futility and artistic work, to write so that only some will see, while describing the tide and the waves washing away man's presence on the shore or in the world.

Ezequiel Zaidenwerg (Argentina, 1981), alongside Crotto, belongs to a small group of young poets who, bucking previous trends, make traditional or even conservative poetic values central tenets of their work. Zaidenwerg published two collections of poems, *Doxa* (2007) and *La lírica está muerta* (2011, Lyric Poetry Is Dead), both with the independent publisher Vox, based in Bahía Blanca. From its title onwards, Zaidenwerg's second collection is an *ars poetica* for a new poetry: formally rigorous; steeped in literary and classical references; and with a strong first-person voice. The Song of Songs, Ovid, San Juan de la Cruz, Romantic poets writing both in Spanish and other languages, and the work of Rubén Darío, are all referenced. C.P. Kavafis and T.S. Eliot both appear. Yet at the same time, the collection deals with a series of Argentine cultural and political events and figures, including the Rosas dictatorship of the nineteenth century, the death of Che Guevara, Evita Perón's corpse, the former president Juan Domingo Perón, and corruption under President Menem in the 1990s. Zaidenwerg stages an intriguing and provocative dialogue between the formal constraints of traditional prosody and the panoply of themes available to the contemporary poet. *La lírica está muerta* takes two elements of the traditional lyric – the first-person voice and the musicality of fixed line lengths and regular rhythms – and marries them to topics more commonly associated with colloquial poetry and free verse.

[26] Antonio Quilis, *Métrica española* (Madrid: Ariel, 2009), 108.

If the work of de Pablo, Crotto, and Zaidenwerg gives an impression of ambition and skill with which young poets are addressing the page and the reader today, there are huge areas of poetic activity in new spaces and via new media, detailed comment about which space does not permit here. One must mention the online poetic network *Las afinidades electivas/ Las elecciones afectivas*, a virtual chain letter in which poets cite their influences and peers. "Cartonera" publishers, independent publishers working with street recyclers, after the model of Buenos Aires' Eloísa Cartonera, have been at the forefront of new poetry publishing in the 2000s. In Mexico City, La tortillería editorial was a prominent physical and virtual space for alternative poetry and self-publishing, years before the e-book revolution fully took hold. In Buenos Aires, Montevideo, Santiago de Chile, and other cities, performance poetry, "Slam" poetry, "sound poetry," and other forms of public engagement regularly take place. There are important examples of poetic activism, including neo-Zapatista poetry in Mexico, resistance poetry in Mapudungun in Chile, and from Patagonia, poetry in indigenous languages like Selknam and Yámana.[27] Poetry crosses languages, as in the poems in "Portunhol" of Wilson Bueno (1949–2010). In cities from Monterrey to San Miguel de Tucumán, graffiti and poetry meet in the "Acción Poética" or AP movement, marrying literary expression and political intervention.[28] These and many other adventurous projects demonstrate the continued energy and importance of poetry in Latin America.

[27] *Mamihlapinatapai. Poesía de mujeres mapuche, selknam y yámana* ed. Cristian Aliaga (Buenos Aires: Desde la gente, 2010).
[28] María Daniela Yaccar, "Mensajes plasmados en tinta negra," *Página/12* (Feb 1, 2014).

PART II

Six Key Figures

6

STEPHEN M. HART

Sor Juana Inés de la Cruz

There are, broadly speaking, four camps of opinion about the gender specificity of women's writing, which are (i) the deprecatory, (ii) the universalist
(iii) the experiential, and (iv) the epistemological. The first camp argues that
women's writing is inferior (epitomized by Nathaniel Hawthorne's 1855
reference to "a damned mob of scribbling women."[1] The second camp,
which takes the universalist stance, argues that there is no difference between
a work written by a woman and another written by a man which can be
ascribed to gender difference, a good example of which is Isabel Allende's
statement that "la literatura no tiene sexo" (literature does not have a sex).[2]
The third group, which takes the experiential approach, suggests that
women's writing is different because women's lives are different (e.g. domesticity, child-rearing, menstrual cycles).[3] The fourth camp, which is epistemological, argues that women's writing is also structurally different from men's
writing. As the French feminist theorist, Xavière Gautier, suggests: "As long
as women remain silent they will be outside the historical process. But if they
begin to speak and write as men do, they will enter history subdued and
alienated; it is a history that, logically speaking, their speech should
disrupt."[4] The work of Sor Juana Inés de la Cruz (1651–1695) is best
understood in terms of the fourth group in that it fundamentally disrupted
the society in which she lived, and it did so in different ways, as we shall see.

---

[1] Qtd. in *The New Feminist Criticism: Essays on Women, Literature, and Theory*, ed.
Elizabeth Showalter (London: Virago, 1989), 101.
[2] Lecture given at the Department of Spanish and Italian at the University of Kentucky on
October 20, 1994.
[3] A good example of this approach is the study, *Homenaje a Rosario Castellanos*, ed.
Maureen Ahern and Mary Seale Vásquez (Valencia: Albatros, 1980).
[4] "Existe-t-il une écriture de femme?" in *New French Feminisms*, ed. Elaine Marks and
Isabelle de Courtivron (New York, NY: Schoken, 1981), 162–63. For further discussion,
see Stephen M. Hart, "Is Women's Writing in Spanish America Gender-Specific?" *MLN*
110.2 (1995): 335–52.

Born into a poor family in the village of San Miguel de Nepantla near a town called Amecameca, not far from Mexico City, Juana learned to read at the age of three, and the pursuit of knowledge became her true passion. We do not know much about her early life, but we do know that when she was prohibited from attending the University in Mexico City because of her sex, she tried to attend by dressing up as a man, and even that failed. Refusing the "career" offered by marriage, in 1669 Juana took vows as a nun and entered the Convent of San Jerónimo; her cloistered life allowed her the freedom to write plays, poetry, and essays. Juana's intellectual brilliance attracted the interest of Viceroy Marquis de la Laguna, and for a time she served in his palace and, during this period (1680–1686), she became a very good friend of the Viceroy's wife, the Marquise de la Laguna and Countess of Paredes, and wrote a number of poems in their honor.[5] Her life of intellectual pleasure was ruined, however, with the publication of an essay entitled *Respuesta de la Poetisa a la muy ilustre Sor Filotea de la Cruz* (Reply to Sister Philotea), written in response to the Bishop of Puebla's recommendation that she turn her mind to spiritual rather than mundane, literary matters. The authorities silenced her; she was forced to sell her library, which she did, distributing the profits to the poor. Sor Juana died while tending the plague victims of Mexico City and, just before her death, she signed her name in blood with the words: "I, Sister Juana Inés de la Cruz, the worst in the world."

Sor Juana's disruption of the colonial and patriarchal structures of the society of New Spain, as Mexico was then known, was epitomized by her *Reply to Sister Philotea* (dated March 1, 1691, but only published posthumously in 1700), in which she alludes to her love of learning – as she says, "the desire to learn was stronger for me than the desire to eat" – and rejects the notion that women have less right to knowledge than men.[6] She attacks this gender bias ("men, who simply because they are men think themselves wise"; Sor Juana, *The Reply*, 81), and, most devastating of all, she completely turned the tables on her audience by calling the Bishop of Puebla by the feminine pseudonym he had used to admonish her originally – Sor Filotea; it was a public slap in the face. Much of Sor Juana's poetry makes more sense when read alongside her *Reply*. Her "Sátira filosófica: Poema 92" (Philosophical Satire: Poem 92), for example, opens as follows:

---

[5] See *Obras completas de Sor Juana Inés de la Cruz*, ed. Alfonso Méndez Plancarte, 3 vols. (Mexico City: Fondo de Cultura Económica, 1951), I, 40–95. Hereafter referred to as *OC*.
[6] *The Answer/La Respuesta, Including a Selection of Poems*, ed. and trans. Electa Arenal and Amanda Powell (New York, NY: University of New York, 1994), 49.

Hombres necios que acusáis
A la mujer sin razón,
Sin ver que sois la ocasión
De lo mismo que culpáis:

Si con ansia sin igual
Solicitáis su desdén,
¿por qué queréis que obren bien
si las incitáis al mal?

(You foolish and unreasoning men/ who cast all blame on women,/ not seeing
you yourselves are causes/ of the same fault you accuse:/ if, with eagerness
unequalled,/ you plead against women's disdain,/ why require them to do well/
when you inspire them to fall?; Sor Juana, *The Reply*, 156–57.)

In its direct attack on double standards, on patriarchy, and the unfair treatment of women, this poem is unique and certainly ahead of its time; as
Octavio Paz has shown, her *Reply to Sor Philotea* was shocking precisely
because its author was a woman.[7] The combination of Sor Juana's *Reply
to Sor Philotea* and poems such as her philosophical satire, "Hombres
necios ..." (Foolish Men ...) has created an image of Sor Juana as an *avant
la lettre* feminist. The enthusiasm for the image of a "modern" woman
enthralled in the past, yet rescued by modern audiences, had led to editions
of Sor Juana's work which cast her as a feminist, and a recent film goes as far
as to portray her as a lesbian.[8] We can see this process at work if we compare
the *editio princeps* of Sor Juana's work with modern, selected editions.

There were three principal tomes of her works published early on. The first
was the *Inundación castálida de la única poetisa, Musa Décima, sor Juana
Inés de la Cruz, religiosa profesa en el Monasterio de San Jerónimo en la
Imperial Ciudad de Mexico, que en varios metros, idiomas y estilos fertiliza
varios asuntos con elegantes, sutiles, claros, ingeniosos, útiles versos, para
enseñanza, recreo y admiración* (Castalian Inundation by the Unique
Poetess, Tenth Muse, Sor Juana Inés de la Cruz, a Professed Nun in the
Monastery of San Jerónimo in the Imperial City of Mexico, who in Various
Metres, Idioms and Styles Rejuvenates Various Matters with Elegant, Subtle,

[7] Octavio Paz, *Sor Juana, or the Traps of Faith*, trans. Margaret Sayers Peden (Cambridge: MA: Harvard University Press, 1988), 428.
[8] For examples of two modern editions, see *The Answer/La Respuesta, Including a Selection of Poems*, ed and trans. Electa Arenal and Amanda Powell (New York, NY: University of New York, 1994), and the Penguin edition of her work, *Poems, Protest and a Dream*, trans. Margaret Sayers Peden (Harmondsworth: Penguin, 1997). María Luisa Bemberg's film, *Yo, la peor de todas* (1990), suggests that Sor Juana had a lesbian relationship with the Vicereine; see Stephen Hart, *A Companion to Latin American Film* (Woodbridge: Tamesis, 2004), 142–43.

Clear, Ingenious and Useful Verses, for the Purposes of Learning, Recreation and Admiration), published in 1689, which contained 121 poems – including the *Primero sueño* (First Dream) – five sets of "villancicos" (Christmas carols), along with the *Neptuno alegórico* (Allegorical Neptune) and the *Explicación del arco* (Explanation of the Arch), these last two written to commemorate the arrival of the Viceroys de la Laguna in Mexico City in 1680. The second volume, entitled *Segundo tomo de las obras de soror Juana Inés de la Cruz, monja profesa en el monasterio del señor San Jerónimo de la Cuidad de México* (Second Tome of the Works of Soror (*sic*) Juana Inés de la Cruz, a Professed Nun in the Monastery of San Jerónimo in the City of Mexico), and published in 1692, contained the "autos sacramentales" (religious plays), the *Carta atenagórica* (The Athenagoric Letter), two secular plays (*Amor es más laberinto* [Love is More of a Labyrinth] and *Los empeños de una casa* [House of Desires]) and seventy more poems. The third volume, entitled *Fama y obras póstumas del fénix de México, décima musa, poetisa Americana, Sor Juana Inés de la Cruz, religiosa profesa en el convento de San Jerónimo de la Imperial Ciudad de México* (Fame and Posthumous works by the Phoenix of Mexico, the Tenth Muse, Poetess of the Americas, Sor Juana Inés de la Cruz, Professed Nun in the Convent of San Jerónimo in the Imperial City of Mexico), was published in 1700, five years after her death, and included the *Respuesta a sor Filotea*, a number of testimonies written by Sor Juana shortly before her death, along with a number of poems written by various hands celebrating Sor Juana's virtues as well as her rhetorical mastery.

All of these works, and especially the first, bear witness to the power of patronage. In the first volume, for example, alongside the "lírica personal" (Personal Lyric) as it has come to be known, are a number of poems that would normally be characterized as owing their existence to the patronage system. Thus we have poems written to celebrate the birthday of the Viceroy of Mexico, the Marquis de la Laguna,[9] a poem about the same birthday addressed to the latter's wife, the Marquise de la Laguna (OC, I, 48–50), along with four poems written to commemorate the birthday of the Vicereine herself (OC, I, 50–52, 59–60, 94, and 196–98), a poem to celebrate the baptism of their son (OC, I, 71–73), another poem written on the occasion of his first birthday (OC, I, 74–79), a poem accompanying the gift of a wooden baby-walker (OC, I, 79–81), another to celebrate their son's second birthday (OC, I, 83–84), as well as three poems wishing the Vicereine good health at Eastertide (OC, I, 81–83, 89–90, and 92–94). The eulogy of the

---

[9] There are five poems written in celebration of the Viceroy's birthday; see OC, I, 40–42, 43–45, 85–86, 95, and 193–95.

Viceroy, his wife, and their young child embodied by this set of poems was so emotive that the Vicereine took it upon herself to take the manuscript to Madrid to have it printed. And thus in 1689 – as mentioned above – *Inundación castálida* was born. But the decision to publish a wide variety of works in one volume – which was, of course, the prerogative of the dedicatee – had a sting in its tail. Nowadays it is precisely those poems which so clearly bear the hallmark of patronage which are the ones that are put to one side in favor of the more personal poems in which Sor Juana expresses her complex feelings about personal love. It is to these latter poems that we must now turn – not least because they are Sor Juana's most anthologized pieces – although we shall return later on in this chapter to the issue of how the poems written under the aegis of patronage fit together with the more personal poems.

Some of Sor Juana's most powerful poems – and these are certainly the ones that appeal to the modern reader – are her sonnets. Poem 164, "En que satisface un recelo con la retórica del llanto" (In Which She Answers a Suspicion with the Eloquence of Tears), brings us two powerful and archetypal images of love – the heart and tears – triumphally together in the last stanza to express a lover's confession:

> Esta tarde, mi bien, cuando te hablaba,
> Como en tu rostro y tus acciones veía
> Que con palabras no te persuadía,
> Que el corazón me vieses deseaba.
>
> Y amor, que mis intentos ayudaba,
> Venció lo que imposible parecía:
> Pues entre el llanto, que el dolor vertía,
> El corazón deshecho destilaba.
>
> Basta ya de rigores, mi bien, baste;
> No te atormenten más celos tiranos,
> Ni el vil recelo tu quietud contraste
>
> Con sombras necias, con indicios vanos,
> Pues ya en líquido humor viste y tocaste
> Mi corazón deshecho entre tus manos.

(This afternoon when I spake with thee beloved,/ as in thy face and thy mien I saw/ that I could not persuade thee with my words,/ the longing came for thee to see my heart,/ and love, abettor of my purposes,/ accomplished that which seemed impossible,/ for issuing with the tears that sorrow shed/ the heart dissolved in misery distilled./ Enough of cruelty, beloved, enough:/ let my harsh jealousy torment thee not/ nor vile suspicion violate thy virtue/ with foolish shadows, vain appearances,/ since now in aqueous humour thou has seen/ and held between thy hands my broken heart.)[10]

The poem is as much about persuasion and evidence as it is about the effects of love on the human frame. For the words the poetic subject used to persuade her lover of the sincerity of her love – and which, of course, are echoed by the words the poet now uses in her poem in order to persuade her readers – prove to be, initially, of little avail, and the "tyrant jealousies" appear to be prevailing. The poet's broken heart (her "corazón deshecho," translated by Samuel Beckett first as "dissolved" and then as "broken") comes to the rescue and provides, in the form of tears, the evidence that is needed to persuade her interlocutor of the authenticity of her love. As the final verse of the poem indicates, this tearful evidence falls into her lover's hands, so that he – almost literally – holds her heart in his hands. The poem uses contemporary medical knowledge about the liquid humors within the body in order to construct a witty disquisition on the struggle – a favorite trope in the Baroque tradition – between reality and appearance.

In her equally famous sonnet, "Detente, sombra de mi bien esquivo ..." (Tarry, shadow of my scornful treasure...), Sor Juana explores the tension between reality and appearance, and comes close to saying that love itself is more appearance than reality:

> Detente, sombra de mi bien esquivo,
> Imagen del hechizo que más quiero,
> Bella ilusión por quien alegro muero,
> Dulce ficción por quien penosa vivo.
>
> Si al imán de tus gracias, atractivo,
> Sirve mi pecho de obediente acero,
> ¿para qué me enamoras lisonjero
> si has de burlarme luego fugitivo?
>
> Mas blasonar no puedes, satisfecho,
> De que triunfa de mí tu tiranía:
> Que aunque dejas burlado el lazo estrecho
>
> Que tu forma fantástica ceñía,
> Poco importa burlar brazos y pecho
> Si te labra prisión mi fantasía.

[10] For original, see Sor Juana Inés de la Cruz, *Poems, Protest, and a Dream: Selected Writings*, 164; for the translation, see *Anthology of Mexican Poetry*, trans. Samuel Beckett (London: Thames and Hudson, 1958), 84.

(Tarry, shadow of my scornful treasure,/ image of my dearest sortilege,/ fair illusion for which I gladly die,/ sweet unreality for which I painfully live./ To the compelling magnet of thy grace/ since my breast as docile steel is drawn,/ why dost thou with soft ways enamour me/ if from me then in mockery thou must fly?/ And yet thou mayst nowise in triumph boast/ that over me thy tyranny has prevailed;/ for though thou breakest, mocking, the narrow coil/ that girdled the fantastic form about,/ what boots it to make mock of arms and breast/ if thou art prisoner of my fantasy?)[11]

Though the poem begins as if it were a typical poem about jilted love and the elusive lover, it enriches itself first of all with an exploration of the appearance/ reality trope, and takes that struggle to the nth power, such that it raises the possibility that appearance can be the desired term in that dialectic given its association with art, specifically with "image" (l. 2), "illusion" (l. 3), and "fiction" (l. 4). As so often in Sor Juana's verse, the poem concludes with a punchy last line; despite, or even as a result of, her lover's elusiveness, the poet can be consoled by her ability to control that image of him, by imprisoning it, i.e. the image, within her verse ("te labra prisión mi fantasía"). Although the last line suggests that this idea is a possibility rather than a fact ("si te labra prisión mi fantasía," literally, *if* my fantasy carves a prison for you; my emphasis), but it *is* actually performative since the poem *has* imprisoned her beloved by writing him into the verbal carving we are currently reading. The poet strikes back.

We find a similar exploration of the reality-appearance trope as viewed through the lens afforded by art in Poem 145, "Procura desmentir los elogios que a un retrato de la Poetisa inscribió la verdad, que llama pasión" (She endeavors to expose the praises recorded in a portrait of the Poetess by truth, which she calls passion):

> Este, que ves, engaño colorido,
> Que del arte ostentando los primores,
> Con falsos silogismos de colores
> Es cauteloso engaño del sentido:
>
> Éste, en quien la lisonja ha pretendido
> Excusar de los años los horrores,
> Y venciendo del tiempo los rigores
> Triunfar de la vejez y del olvido,
>
> Es un vano artificio del cuidado,
> Es una flor al viento delicada,
> Es un resguardo inútil para el hado:

[11] *Sor Juana's Love Poems*, trans. Joan Larkin and Jaime Manrique (Madison, WI: University of Wisconsin Press, 1997), 35; trans. Beckett, *Anthology of Mexican Poetry*, 83.

Es una necia diligencia errada,
Es un afán caduco y, bien mirado,
Es cadáver, es polvo, es sombra, es nada.

(This coloured counterfeit that thou beholdest,/ vainglorious with the excellencies of art,/ is, in fallacious syllogisms of colour,/ nought but a cunning dupery of sense;/ this in which flattery has undertaken/ to extenuate the hideousness of years,/ and, vanquishing the outrages of time,/ to triumph o'er oblivion and old age,/ is an empty artifice of care,/ is a fragile flower in the wind,/ is a paltry sanctuary from fate,/ is a foolish sorry labour lost,/ is conquest doomed to perish and, well taken,/ is corpse and dust, shadow and nothingness; Sor Juana, *The Answer*, 152–53; trans. Beckett, *Anthology of Mexican Poetry*, 85.)

Here the conclusion drawn by the poet, when reviewing a painted image of herself, seems to be opposite from that drawn when considering the way one of her poems was able to capture the image of her elusive lover. Whereas Sor Juana seems to have viewed her poem as capable, in "Detente, sombra de mi bien esquivo . . .," via her fantasy, of capturing her beloved, here the emphasis is diametrically opposed. The poet berates, in the first stanza, the "falacious syllogisms of colour" in the painting, which are "but a cunning dupery of sense," and, in the final tercets, delivers her most stinging rebuke, namely, that the copy of her body contained in the picture is nothing more than a "foolish sorry labour lost" in Beckett's wonderful Shakespearian rendering, which can be understood also – more literally – as a diligence, or missive, sent to those who will one day judge us, which has gone astray. The fact, however, that Sor Juana saw the poem as capable of capturing reality more effectively than a painting suggests that she favored writing over the visual arts, and saw the written word as offering a superior access to truth.

These three poems selected for discussion present love and/or the beloved as absent, and, as such, they speak directly and forcefully to modern audiences; other examples could have been given.[12] What is most intriguing about these love poems is their interaction with those other examples of Sor Juana's verse that are often dismissed as nothing more than patronage-poems and, therefore, are suppressed from modern selected works.[13] Some

[12] See, for example, *Sor Juana's Love Poems*, trans. Joan Larkin and Jaime Manrique.
[13] The patronage-poems do not appear, for example, in *Sor Juana's Love Poems*, trans. Joan Larkin and Jaime Manrique, nor in *The Answer/La Respuesta, Including a Selection of Poems*, ed. and trans. Electa Arenal and Amanda Powell, nor in the Penguin edition of her work, *Poems, Protest and a Dream*, already referred to, nor in *Sor Juana Inés de la Cruz: Selected Writings*, ed. and trans. Pamela Kirk Rappaport (New York, NY: Paulist Press, 2005), which emphasizes Sor Juana's devotional writings. But some of the patronage poems are included in the most recent edition available, namely, *Sor Juana Inés de la Cruz*, trans. Edith Grossman (New York, NY: W.W. Norton & Company, 2014), 14–23.

of the poems that Sor Juana addressed and dedicated to the Marquise de la Laguna, for example, appear to address her as if they were lovers. In "Solía la Señora Virreina ..." (The Vicereine Had the Custom of..), Sor Juana addresses the Vicereine as Lysi, based on the poetic name used by the Spanish poet much admired by Sor Juana, Francisco Gómez de Quevedo, in his very sensual love poems ("Si mis párpados, Lisi, labios fueran ... "),[14] and, in "Puro amor" (Pure Love), also directed at the Vicereine, Sor Juana appears to be making a confession:

> Pero ¿para qué es cansarse?
> Como a ti, Filis, te quiero;
> Que en lo que mereces, éste
> Es solo encarecimiento.
>
> Ser mujer, ni estar ausente,
> No es de amante impedimento;
> Pues sabes tú, que las almas
> Distancia ignoran y sexo.
>
> (But, why should we make ourselves weary?/ As you are, Filis, I love you;/ Which, as you deserve, is nothing/ Other than insistence;/ Since, as you know, souls ignore/ Distance and sex; OC, I, 57.)

These two stanzas have been interpreted as indicative of the existence of a sexualized lesbian love between Sor Juana and the Marquise de la Laguna.[15] But is this a misreading, or "misprision," to use Paul de Man's term?[16] If we historicize the poem and reset it within its seventeenth-century historical context, a different interpretation of these lines emerges. We should recall that Sor Juana, as a result of her social class and her illegitimacy, was dependent throughout her life on social favor, whether provided by the Church (during the period when she was a nun in the Monastery of San Jerónimo) or the Viceroys (when offered protection by the Viceroy de la Laguna and subsequently by his successor Viceroy Gaspar de la Cerda, the Eighth Count of Galve). This social favor had a different complexion in the New World to that it possessed in Europe. Though he refers to Brazil specifically, Roberto Schwarz's description of its social function has significant similarities with the role played by favor in New Spain during the seventeenth century:

[14] As Sor Juana writes: "Hete yo, divina Lysi ... " (Here I am, divine Lysi); OC, I, 52). See Quevedo's poem, "Comunicación de amor invisible por los ojos," *An Anthology of Quevedo's Poetry*, ed. R.M. Price (Manchester: Manchester University Press, 1969), 54.
[15] See http://qspirit.net/sor-juana-de-la-cruz-nun-mexico/
[16] See *Blindness and Insight: Essays in the Rhetoric of Contemporary Criticism* (New York, NY: Routledge, 1983).

Colonization, based on the monopoly of the land, produced three classes of population: the proprietor of the *latifundium*, the slave and the "free man," who was in fact dependent. (. . .) Neither proprietor, nor proletarian, the free man's access to social life and its benefits depended, in one way or another on the favor of a "big man." The caricature of this "free man" was the *agregado*. (. . .) Favor was present everywhere, combining itself with more or less ease to administration, politics, industry, commerce, the life of the city, the court, and so on. Even professions, such as medicine, or forms of skilled labor, such as the printing trade, which in Europe were on the whole free of favor, were among us governed by it. (. . .) Favor was our quasi-universal social mediation.[17]

And so it was for Sor Juana who rejected marriage as a solution, and therefore relied on favor to forge her path through life. Schwarz has also argued that this dependency-system had a direct impact on the life and work of artists in the New World. They imitated European art, he suggests, but, as far as literature was concerned, "something singular results, an emptying out of what is already hollow," leading to "ill-assortedness – unmanageable contrasts, disproportions, nonsense, anachronisms, outrageous compromises and the like," that is, the "substitution of one pastiche for another" (Schwarz, "Misplaced," 41, 44). This artistic regime of "misplaced ideas" whereby, as Schwarz suggests, "there was no proper name, since the improper use of names was part of its nature" (Schwarz, "Misplaced," 45) is, I suggest, an apt characterization of Sor Juana's verse in terms of how she worked through Quevedo and Góngora's verse.[18] It was particularly the case in those examples of her verse produced in the shadow of patronage where, as it were, the cracks in the edifice of patronage were beginning to show. Surely it is the case that Sor Juana's use of poetic names such as Filis and Lysi to address the Vicereine, derived as they clearly were from Quevedo's verse, were examples of what Schwarz calls "ill-assortedness". Even if we granted that they were similar to the *galanteos de palacio* (palace gallantries) common at the time, as Octavio Paz argues,[19] we encounter the obstacle that the *galanteos* were necessarily based on heterosexual relationships. The hypothesis that these eulogies are, in fact, misplaced in Schwarz's sense of the term is strengthened when we learn that Sor Juana used the same techniques of adulation in her poems written for and dedicated to the Vicereine who succeeded the Marquise de la Laguna, namely, the Countess of Galve, wife of Count Gaspar de la Cerda, who was New Spain's viceroy from 1688 until 1696. In one of these poems Sor Juana refers to Elvira

---

[17] Roberto Schwarz, "Misplaced Ideas: Literature and Society in Late Nineteenth-century Brazil," *Comparative Civilizations Review* 5.5 (2016): 37.
[18] For a discussion of the works Sor Juana read, see Octavio Paz, *Sor Juana, or the Traps of Faith*, 54–57.
[19] *Sor Juana, or the Traps of Faith*, 90–95.

the Countess of Galve as not only "divine," "beautiful," and "wise" but also envied by Venus and Minerva, and she refers to her own poem as a "fineza amorosa" (amorous finesse).[20] By adopting the persona Quevedo used in his love poems for Lisi in her Vicereine poems, Sor Juana was producing poems full of, to use Schwarz's words, "unmanageable contrasts" and even possibly "outrageous compromises." Likewise, when describing the love felt between the Count and Countess of Galve, Sor Juana used precisely the same images which appeared in her own love poems – such as, for example, the image of the arms as chains around the imprisoned lover, quoted above – but covered their negative associations with a positive hue:

Ofrendas – finas – a tu obsequio sean
Amantes – señas – de fino holocausto,
El pecho – rica –a mi corazón, joya,
Al cuello – dulces – cadenas mis brazos.

(Offerings – fine – may they be to your gift/ lovers – signs – of fine holocaust,/ The chest – rich – a jewel, to my heart,/ To the neck – sweet – chains are my arms; *OC*, I, 176.)

By gliding between the rhetoric of a love poem and that of a poem of obeisance, Sor Juana was in effect navigating a world of "misplaced ideas." The imagery, thus, that Sor Juana was utilizing in her poem "Puro amor" addressed to the Marquise de la Laguna – referred to above – was, rather than a coded admission of sexualized lesbian love, nothing more than an ill-assorted employment of Quevedo's rhetoric of love to describe a close Platonic friendship. Pointing in a similar direction, we should note that there were empiric obstacles that would have prevented a liaison of this kind to occur; Sor Juana was living as a cloistered nun at the time.

We might add it was not only the Vicereine who received these expressions of love from Sor Juana. Sor Juana's poem to the Marquis de la Laguna, "No habiendo logrado ver al Señor Virrey . . ." (Not Having Managed to See the Viceroy . . .), begins with a gentle chiding of his bad manners for not seeing her, then passes to a description of his many talents, and ends with the stanza:

Recibid este Romance
Que mi obligación os rinde,
Con todo lo que no digo,
Lo que digo, y lo que *dije*.

---

[20] "A la merced de alguna presea que la Excma. Señora Elvira de Toledo (Condesa de Galve), Virreina de Méjico, le presentó," *OC*, I, 117–18. The poems dedicated to the Countess of Galve are similar in tone to those written to the Vicereine de la Laguna; see *OC*, I, 117–28, as, indeed, is the poem dedicated to the Count of Galve (*OC*, I, 176–77).

(Receive this ballad/ that my obligation delivers to you,/ with everything I do
not say,/ what I say, and what I *said*; original emphasis in poem; OC, I, 47–48.)

This deliberately mysterious last stanza points to something not said or
something else which, if said, could not be reported. The tone of the poem
suggests an intimacy, or an offer of intimacy, that goes beyond the humble
expression of respect for a superior associated with verse produced within
the patronage system. Here Sor Juana is mixing poetic codes, not for the first
time, as we have seen. Quite apart from her burlesque-satirical poems (OC, I,
284–87), Sor Juana wrote to the Archbishop of Mexico, don Fray Payo
Enríquez de Ribera, asking him for a personal favor (could he confirm her,
please? OC, I, 32–38), and she also wrote a poem to a judge, "Memorial a un
juez" (Memorial to a Judge) asking him very directly not to evict a recently
widowed woman from her home; the circumstances make it very clear that
both individuals knew – despite not being named – whom Sor Juana was
referring to (OC, I, 252–53). Many of the "patronage-poems," when reread
in this light, speak to Sor Juana's desire to interrogate and test social boundaries. This suggests that those sections of her work that have normally been
undervalued or ignored as a result of being seen as patronage-poems deserve
to be seen as "symptoms" of the struggles of her inner world, and therefore
are worth revisiting.

One of Sor Juana's works whose value has never been questioned is her
Primero sueño (First Dream), a 950-line self-averred imitation of Góngora's
poetry written in honor of the Count of Galve, on whose orders French forces
attempting to invade the Spanish part of Hispaniola were defeated at the
mouth of the Guarico, on January 21, 1691, by an expeditionary force sent
from New Spain. Like Góngora's verse, the *Primero sueño* makes liberal use
of the hyperbaton, mythological culturalism, and a Latinate syntax and
vocabulary. Sor Juana's poem, however, is more philosophical than
Góngora's *Soledades* (Solitudes) in that it describes an ontological enquiry
into the nature and function of the universe; as Octavio Paz puts it, the
"language of Góngora is aesthetic; that of Sor Juana, intellectual" (*Traps
of Faith*, 358). The poem opens describing the arrival of nightfall, and how
the world, including the human body gradually falls asleep (ll. 1–265). The
second part of the poem, which is the most substantial, describes how
Fantasy begins to copy the things of the phenomenal world showing them
to the soul (ll. 290–91), and includes a section on two pyramids used as
figures of the human soul, a disquisition on the great Chain of Being followed
by an anguished awareness of the limits of human understanding as com-
pounded by the proliferation of diverse human languages and diverse species
(ll. 266–826). The final section describes the human mind waking up and

returning to the phenomenal world of everyday life (ll. 827–975). *Primero sueño* is a poetic tour de force without equal in the literary scene of the colonial period. The conclusion of the poem, in particular, is remarkable in that it suggests that, through the dream knowledge engendered by her poem, the world has become brighter and she more awake (ll. 967–975).

Sor Juana was not only the foremost poet of her day but also an outstanding verse dramatist, evident in secular plays such as *Amor es más laberinto* and *Los empeños de una casa*, as well as theological plays such as *El Divino Narciso*.[21] The latter is a Calderonian "auto sacramental" which applies a Christian dogmatic principle to a mythological story.[22] The central part of *El Divino Narciso* follows the classical story of Narcissus closely: spurning all women and even the loveliest of nymphs, Echo, Narcissus is punished by falling in love with his own image, at which point Echo becomes mute, or rather unable to do anything other than repeat what has been said to her, a technique adopted with some verve in the play.[23] Narcissus is translated into Christ and Echo into the Devil; other characters are added, such as Naturaleza Humana, Soberbia, Amor Propio, and Gracia, which broaden the perspective of the Christian allegory. Sor Juana explores the Baroque contrast between appearance and reality via the Narcissus story and re-purposes the moment when Narcissus falls in love with his own image seen in a river as the juncture when Christ falls in love with human nature:

> ¡Abre el cristalino
> de ese centro claro y frío,
> para que entre el amor mío!
> Mira que traigo escarchada
> La crencha de oro, rizada,
> Con las perlas del rocío.
> ¡Ven, esposa, a tu querido:
> rompe esa cortina clara:
> muéstrame tu hermosa cara,
> suene tu voz a mi oído!

---

[21] For an excellent translation of *Los empeños de una casa*, see *House of Desires*, trans. Catherine Boyle (London: Oberon, 2004).

[22] For further discussion of the Calderonian genealogy, see Jeremy Robbins, "Pedro Calderón de la Barca's *Eco y Narciso*: Court Drama and the Poetics of Reflection," in *Rewriting Classical Mythology in the Hispanic Baroque*, ed. Isabel Torres (Woodbridge: Tamesis, 2007), 119–27.

[23] Act IV, Scene XI; ll. 1466–1567; *El Divino Narciso*, ed. Robin Ann Rice (Navarra: Ediciones Universidad de Navarra, 2005), 255–60. For further discussion of this motif, see Stephanie Merrim, "Narciso *desdoblado*: Narcissistic Stratagems in *El Divino Narciso* and the *Respuesta a Sor Filotea de la Cruz*," *Bulletin of Hispanic Studies* 64 (1987): 111–17.

(Open the glass/ of this clear and cold centre/ and let my love in!/ Look, I bring a crest/ of curly, frost-covered gold,/ with the pearls of dew./ Come, my wife, to your lover: break open that clear curtain:/ show me your beautiful face,/ may your voice sound in my ear!, ll. 1291–1301; Sor Juana, *El Divino Narciso*, 246; the author's translation)

In a witty rewriting of theological doctrine, Sor Juana equates the point at which Narcissus thrusts his face into the surface of the stream with Christ's sacrifice on the cross – it is almost a Lacanian rewriting of the Crucifixion. Whether attacking the moral complacency of a Bishop, or the double standards of love between the sexes, or rewriting the narrative of the Crucifixion, Sor Juana fought against the subjugation and alienation of women, and placed the tension between appearance and reality – which she saw at the center of the language of art – at the heart of that battle.

Sor Juana Inés de la Cruz is a towering figure within Latin America's poetic canon. The versatility of her verse – she was an expert in a number of verse schemes, including the *lira*, the *silva*, the *redondilla*, the *décima*, the *romance*, and the sonnet – is extraordinary. Though she was clearly influenced by some of the great poets of the Spanish Golden Age, such as Quevedo and Góngora, Sor Juana took these metric forms to new heights and produced a new intervention in world literature via her intrepid mixing of codes. Perhaps most striking of all, her work emerged within the patronage system that governed the arts in the seventeenth century – whether it was the State in the form of the Viceroys or the Church – and yet she interrogated and questioned that system and, with her essay, *Reply to Sor Filotea*, made a powerful statement about the injustices suffered by women in a patriarchal society that would resonate for many years to come.

7

KAREN BENAVENTE

Gabriela Mistral

For a poet so marked by the epithets assigned to her – "Mother of America," *mater dolorosa*, "Rural Teacher," "Banished Poet," "Sterile Woman," "Powerful Consul" – there are surprisingly only two known facts that most readers associate with the figure of Gabriela Mistral: she was the first Latin American to win the Nobel Prize for Literature (1945) and she wrote maternal verses but had no natural children of her own. The apparent contradiction between her celebrated writing and her barrenness (both literal and figurative) surfaces as a recurring theme in the construction of her literary biography and the roles which ultimately defined her. Critics over the years have speculated over her "dearth" or "desolation" – that her lyrical sensibility comes from the tragedy of never bearing children – or that her lovers now dead, now fled, now married, have left her as a roaming solitary spinster who, like a female Orpheus, must compose verses while living in perpetual exile never to find a man, child or home to call her own.[1]

Gabriela Mistral is arguably one of Latin America's most daringly expressive, if not polemical, figures of the twentieth century, stirring up controversy wherever she published, spoke, or travelled.[2] We cannot read her without

[1] Alone [Hernán Diaz Arrieta], "Prólogo," in Gabriela Mistral, *Antología* (Santiago: Zig-Zag, 1940); Raul Silva Castro, *Estudios sobre Gabriela Mistral* (Santiago: Zig-Zag, 1935); Virgilio Figueroa, *La Divina Gabriela* (Santiago: Imprenta El Esfuerzo, 1933); Benjamin Carrión, *Santa Gabriela* (Quito: Editorial Casa de la Cultura Ecuatoriana, 1956). For a full bilbiography, see Patricia Rubio de Lértora, *Gabriela Mistral ante la crítica: bibliografía anotada* (Santiago: Dirección de Bibliotecas, Archivos y Museo, Centro de Investigaciones Diego Barros Arana, 1995).
[2] Many controversies arose with her sexuality and love life. See Elizabeth Horan, "Alternative destinies of Gabriela Mistral," in *Reading and Writing the Ambiente*, ed. Susana Chávez Silverman and Librada Hernández (Madison, WI: University of Wisconsin Press, 2000), 147–76; Licia Fiol Matta, *A Queer Mother for a Nation* (Minneapolis, MN: University of Minnesota Press, 2002). For Mistral's complete biographical information, see Gabriela Mistral, *Antología mayor. Vida y obra* (Santiago: Cochrane, 1992); and Jaime Concha, *Gabriela Mistral* (Santiago: Ediciones Universidad Alberto Hurtado, 2015 [1985]).

serious questions tied to her work or image. But we must remember that Gabriela Mistral carefully constructed myths of her iconic persona based on "secrets," "tragedies," or "rejections" often causing dissentions and fallings-out. Readers followed her not just because her writing seemed poignant or pertinent to themes of the day in the 1920s–1950s but also because her life could be read as a kind of a *novela*; there was always some drama that could be applied to her personal life that somehow reflected in her poetry and prose, a bit of gossip fodder (*copucha*) that made readers want to find the next poem or absorb some moral code in her prose that could be applied to them but ultimately to her.[3]

These speculations occurred from the beginning of Gabriela Mistral's career. One of Gabriela Mistral's first critics to ponder upon the mysteries of her suffering poetics to an international audience was the Chilean Arturo Torres Rioseco, who in 1920 wrote about Mistral in the Spanish magazine *Cosmópolis*.[4] He tells the anecdote that when the well-known Mexican poet Amado Nervo read her verses, he wondered what the cause was of her suffering in her first book of poems, *Desolación* (*Desolation*, 1922). Rioseco reveals to Nervo the "secret" (but not to his reader), and from then on Nervo (and the reader) is hooked and cannot stop reading or wondering. He proclaims brotherly affection and warmth for a woman who seems haunted by such tragic loss.

If we can cursorily sum up the poetry and persona of Gabriela Mistral, it may be through the contradictory wordplay and title of one of her early poems: *hallazgo* or "precious find," "discovery," "secret knowledge," or "mysterious object."[5] In almost all of her poems, readers, including the poetic subject, try to seek or find lovers, things, children, women, words, and even consolation, those hidden objects that may consume the poet's soul; and

---

[3] Palma Guillén de Nicolau, "Introducción," in Gabriela Mistral, *Desolación; Ternura; Tala; Lagar* (Mexico: Editorial Porrua, 1973), ix; and Christian Walker, "Tesoro o maletín?" *Aún no ha sido todo dicho* (Santiago: Penguin Random House Editorial Chile, 2012), Digital.

[4] Arturo Torres Rioseco, "Gabriela Mistral," *Cosmópolis* 15.3 (1920): 374. Torres Rioseco introduced Mistral's lyrics to Federico de Onís, who shortly thereafter in 1921 gave an introductory talk at the Institute of Spain in New York on Mistral's work and then published *Desolación* in 1922. It is important to note that with the exception of *Lagar* (1954) and the second edition of *Desolación* (1923), all of her poetry collections were published outside of Chile (and this also applies to poems in foreign periodicals and journals).

[5] Gabriela Mistral, *Desolación* (Santiago: Editorial Nascimiento, 1923), 267. Examples of a few poems that clearly demonstrate the poet's quest to find an object or thing include "Cosas" (*Tala*); "Niño mexicano" (*Ternura*, 1945); "¿En dónde tejemos la ronda?" (*Desolación* [1923]; *Ternura* [1924; 1945]); "País de la ausencia" (*Tala*); "La ley del tesoro" (*Tala*).

in most of the poems, the poet loses what is most dear to her. Her "búsquedas" (searches) turn into a poetic game: through "jugarretas" (playful tricks), "desvaríos" (rhapsodies), "rondas" (rounds), or "nocturnos" (nocturnes) the poetic "I" attempts to trace those mysteries through verses that connote mythic – often fantastic – possible worlds that allow her to transfigure herself or her landscape into something "other" to, offer protection from, and sometimes react violently to, people, places, and things.[6]

Mistralianist Upheavals

Traditional scholarship has built upon an archeology of knowledge based on "searching for lost facts and objects" in Mistral's life and work and has constructed original interpretations.[7] There is a library of critical reception which has extensively written on the famous case concerning Gabriela Mistral's early verses that brought her instant critical acclaim at the age of 23. In 1914 Gabriela Mistral won the highest prize for poetry for her "Sonetos de la Muerte" (Sonnets of Death) in the Floral Games among a pronounced group of (male) poets, including the popular Julio Munizaga Ossandón. A few years earlier in 1909, the same year that the "Sonetos" were dated, Gabriela Mistral was linked to the suicide of Romelio Ureta, a poor railroad worker who committed suicide with a note in his pocket signed by her (as Lucila Godoy Alcayaga, her real name). Whether Mistral had a relationship or not with the young man did not really matter. The story could be linked to her verses, particularly from *Desolación* (1922; 1923), which could allow for a richer (read: more sensationalized) reading.[8] It is important to note that this "tragic love" was never officially revoked by Mistral even though in later years she declared that she may have contrived the dramatic fiction of the suicide through the local newspaper.[9]

[6] Karen Peña, *Poetry and the Realm of the Public Intellectual* (Leeds: Legenda/ Maney 2007), 8–60.
[7] Patriarchal scholarship before 1980 (when Chilean feminists began to change the perception of Gabriela Mistral). Some typical examples include Gastón Von dem Bussche, *Visión de una poesía* (Santiago: Anales de la Universidad de Chile, 1957); Alone, *Gabriela Mistral. Premio Nobel 1945* (Santiago: Editorial Nascimiento, 1946); Norberto Pinilla, *Biografía de Gabriela Mistral* (Santiago: Editorial Tegualda, 1945); Federico de Onís, *Gabriela Mistral: Vida y Obra. Bibliografía, Antología* (New York: Instituto de las Españas, 1936); Ciro Alegría, *Gabriela Mistral íntima.* (Lima: Universo, 1968).
[8] Romelio Ureta's suicide became a source of poetic fiction for Gabriela Mistral's *Desolación*. Palma Guillén suggests that Mistral carefully organized the book so that it could be read as episodes (before, during and after) with the suicide in mind since many of the poems were written long afterwards. Guillén, "Introducción," xxi.
[9] Gabriela Mistral, *Moneda dura: Gabriela Mistral por ella misma.* Comp. Cecilia García Huidobro McA. (Santiago: Catalonia, 2005), 53.

If Mistral cannot find true love she therefore cannot have but must always pine for children or else turn to tragedy – or so the easy logic goes when analyzing Mistral's verses.[10] The poetic "I" in her poems laments or curses her barrenness to ultimately promote maternity. Her first two books, *Desolación* (1922; 1923)[11] and *Ternura* (1924; 1945),[12] appear to bemoan her fate, and in Parnassian-like sonnets and Darío-inspired alexandrine verses she rallies against God, nature, and the man who spurned her: "Pero te va a brotar víboras la tierra si vendes mi alma" (But the earth shall spew forth snakes at you if you betray my soul).[13] In other poems, she offsets this negativity by turning to the maternal song of the "lullaby" or the children's "round" in which she praises motherhood and joyous infant rhyming games. In these poems, constructed mostly in ballad (in alternating nine-syllabic) forms, mothers and children construct an idyllic sacred space of sanctity and kindred bonds.

Mistral comes to represent the perfect *modernista* poetess in the turn of the twentieth century, as one to encapsulate and symbolize ultra-feminine virtues: motherhood, patience, love of God, caring for children, promoter of education.[14] Where in "real life" she is not betrothed and bedded, in her verses or through "example," that is, through her social and educational work, she can create a hyper-real maternal persona; where she cannot find "true love," she finds solace in the Old Testament or through her conversations with God or Christ, as a Latin American Santa Teresa; where Gabriela Mistral seeks abstract "death or tragedy," she redeems herself by becoming a Whitman-like poet who converses with the soil, with American plants, with mountains and nature.[15]

Upon close scrutiny of her work and taking into consideration the patriarchal tradition in which she wrote, we find that Mistral's verses do not

[10] Alone, *Gabriela Mistral. Premio Nobel 1945*, 39–42; Federico Dussuel Díaz, "Los amores de Gabriela Mistral," in *Mensaje*, 355–60.

[11] The second edition of *Desolación* was published in Santiago in 1923 and is a more complete and accomplished collection of poems than the 1922 edition.

[12] Readers should approach *Ternura*, 1945 with care. In comparison to *Ternura*, 1924 the poems in the second edition of *Ternura*, 1945 fall rhythmically flat and have odd modifications. Jaime Quezada notices these changes and points the finger to Margaret Bates's questionable editing in *Poesías completas* (1958), but there could be other reasons for these alterations: that after Yin Yin's death in 1943 Mistral was in mourning and allowed close friends (Palma Guillén, Marta Salotti, and others) to help edit her work; Jaime Quezada, "Gabriela Mistral: Algunas referencias a *Ternura*," *Acta Literaria*, 14 (1989): 112.

[13] Gabriela Mistral, "Dios lo quiere," *Desolación*, 146.

[14] Elizabeth Horan, *Gabriela Mistral, An Artist and her people* (Washington, DC: Organization of American States, 1994).

[15] Fernando Alegría, "Gabriela Mistral," in *Walt Whitman and the World*, ed. Gay Wilson and Ed Folsom, (Iowa City, IA: Iowa City Press, 1995), 91–92.

necessarily comply with the saintly image of the maternal poet. On the surface, and according to certain themes, Mistral's life and work appear like a never-ending hall of mirrors, in which something in her verses discloses those very elements in her life, all with a certain maternal theme or pious tone. But what if the repeated tropes of motherhood and saintliness were invented constructs carefully labored over by the poet? What if the poet chose to play into the hall of smoke and mirrors – at times saintly, at times not – by donning the mask of a fictive persona to thereby disappear the "real" woman into thin air? Without revealing too much at all, Gabriela Mistral makes us forget that her poetic self is an illusory construction: Lucila Godoy Alcayaga, the humble teacher from the Valley of Elqui, is nowhere to be found. Gabriela Mistral, the lyrical speaker of "A la virgen de la colina" (To the Virgin on the Hill) and "La maestra rural" (The Rural Schoolteacher) it turns out is an achievement of craft and artifice; she is an invented poetic character who allows for her verses to construct a "virtuous" or even "violent" poetic persona that does not necessarily abide by the often contradictory authorial writer.[16]

Put another way, Gabriela Mistral may be thought of as a *dramatis persona* invented to cover Lucila Godoy Alcayaga's life.[17] Where a number of her contemporary female poets such as Alfonsina Storni, Delmira Agustini, and Juana de Ibarbourou began writing under pseudonyms such as *Tao Lao* (Storni) and *Jeannette D'Ibar* (Ibarbourou), these poets eventually returned to their original names for official recognition. Lucila Godoy Alcayaga may have begun as *Soledad* and *Alma* and later as *Gabriela Mistral*, but she never returned to her given name in her work. The very fact that Lucila Godoy Alcayaga continued to write as Gabriela Mistral (with one [famous] last name), allowed her to take poetic license with her authorial voice and play certain roles in her verses that comply with, or rebel against, conservative audiences.[18]

One such example is the very early poem "Poema del hijo" (Poem for the Child, from 1917–1918) later dedicated to Alfonsina Storni (*Desolación*, 1922).[19] The bipartite poem can be read as an epithalalium with the poet celebrating her "marriage" while at the same time longingly crying out for

[16] Elizabeth Horan, "Sor Juana and Gabriela Mistral: Locations and Locutions of the Saintly Woman," *Chasqui* 25.2 (1996): 89–103.
[17] Mistral may be likened to Fernando Pessoa's orthonym, a "man who never was." As suggested by Palma Guillén, Gabriela Mistral is not only an invention penned by Lucila Godoy Alcayaga, but also her "proud" male readers. Guillén, "Introducción," x.
[18] Gabriela Mistral appeared for the first time in print on 23 July 1908 in the periodical *El Coquimbo*.
[19] See manuscripts of "Poema del Hijo" in Archivo del Escritor. Biblioteca Nacional de Chile, AE0001464; AE0000043; AE0000065. Digital.

her dead lover and lamenting her inability to have children. But the celebratory reading can only be read in the first part of the poem. As we carefully analyze part two (and Mistral often has "respuestas" [answers] in poems to refute a one-sided poetic dialogue), we find the lyrical speaker, now older and wiser, violently blaspheming against the imaginary offspring in her womb, since those children would have betrayed her in the same treacherous way as her lover.[20]

As art imitates life, so in the recursive world of Gabriela Mistral. The "curse" of wanting and then not wanting children strangely turned into a tragic marker in Mistral's actual life, when in 1943 her adopted son Yin Yin (Juan Miguel Godoy) committed suicide at the age of 15 in Petrópolis, Brazil. The mystery surrounding his death has evolved over time in the numerous ways Mistral and others have recounted the tragedy; so too can be said of his birth, as Mistral kept secret the identity of the father as well as the circumstances of his birth.[21] In many of her lyrics in *Lagar* (1954), for instance, we can read the poet weeping for her lost son,[22] and in her posthumous "Poema de Chile" (A Poem for Chile), we find the poet exploring Chilean fantastic landscapes with her imaginary "hijo." The poem has been read as a recovery poem that seeks to rekindle those things that cannot be found: her relationship with her lost child, her motherhood and her country.[23]

The myths and legends which have perpetuated in the critical reception of her work are many and are primarily associated with the crises that constantly appear in her (pseudo)biographies. Mistral herself circulated personal stories such as being thrown out of schools, countries, and dinner parties (see "La abandonada" [The Abandoned Woman] in *Lagar*);[24] another oft-repeated Mistralianist tale was that she disliked Chile because it would not have her (see "La extranjera" [The Foreign Woman] in *Lagar*);[25] and yet another was that she had several illicit love affairs with men in power, including the poet Manuel Magallanes Moure, a close mentor and friend, and José Vasconcelos, the Minister of Education of Mexico, who invited

---

[20] Susana Münnich, *Gabriela Mistral: Soberbiamente Transgredora* (Santiago: LOM Ediciones, 2005), 35–40.

[21] Gabriela Mistral, *This America of Ours*, ed. Doris Meyer and Elizabeth Horan (Austin, TX: University of Texas Press, 2003) 4, 338.

[22] Gabriela Mistral, *Bendita mi lengua sea*, ed. Jaime Quezada (Santiago: Planeta-Ariel, 2002), 224.

[23] Soledad Falabella, *¿Qué será de Chile en el Cielo? Poema de Chile de Gabriela Mistral* (Santiago: LOM editores, 2003), 49.

[24] See quote: "Yo me sé eso de la echada," in "La palabra maldita," in Gabriela Mistral, *Selected Prose and Prose Poems*, ed. and trans. Stephen Tapscott (Austin, TX: University of Texas Press, 2002), 223.

[25] Gabriela Mistral, *Gabriela Mistral anda por el mundo*, ed. Roque Esteban Scarpa (Santiago: Editorial Andrés Bello, 1978), 9.

Mistral to Mexico in 1922 (see "Poemas del éxtasis" [Poems of Extasy] and "Himno al árbol" [Hymn to a Tree] in *Desolación*).[26]

To read Mistral's poetry in light of previous critical reception, especially before 1980, must be attempted with caution.[27] The irrevocable separation between author and lyrical subject keeps being crossed in the case of Gabriela Mistral. Whether that is because Mistral is a woman (or read: queer) or that her critics for many years have been a closed conservative group (read: Christian men) or whether because she herself promoted controversy in interviews, letters to friends, and articles (read: audacious critic) may leave more questions than answers in the close reading of her prose and poetry.

A Silent Legacy

To recontextualize Gabriela Mistral's poetic output, we must consider a singular curiosity in the whole trajectory of her work, that is, Gabriela Mistral left no obvious poetic heirs to imitate and continue her legacy.[28] Unlike other notable poets, such as Pablo Neruda, José Martí, and Rubén Darío, Gabriela Mistral did not leave a school of poets and writers to mimic and surpass her creative versification and bold prose after her death. There are several reasons for this. The first is that it was principally women poets who honored her writing, and all but for a few exceptions have been labeled "minor" poets;[29] the second is that Gabriela Mistral's work was archived and kept hidden in secret places mostly outside of Chile from 1957 to 2007 without public access; the third pertains to the Chilean dictatorship (1973–1990) which appropriated her image as a symbol of conservative values and educational didacticism; the fourth, and perhaps key to understanding the reception of Gabriela Mistral's lyrics, is that she was a poet of her time. Almost all of her poems and articles were published serially in newspapers, journals, and magazines from 1906 to 1957. There was never a week that went by during which her poems, articles, and short stories did not appear in print. Such periodicals and journals include *Revista cubana* (Cuba), *Repertorio Americano* (Costa Rica), *La Nueva Democracia*

---

[26] Gabriela Mistral, *Cartas de amor y desamor*, ed. Sergio Fernández Larraín (Barcelona: Andrés Bello, 1999); Jorge Edwards, *La otra casa: ensayos sobre escritores chilenos* (Santiago: Ediciones Universidad Diego Portales), 38.

[27] Raquel Olea, *Como traje de fiesta: loca razón en la poesía de Gabriela Mistral* (Santiago: Editorial USACH, 2009), 23–35.

[28] There is perhaps the notable exception of Pablo Neruda, who not only imitated Gabriela Mistral's style when a young poet in Temuco, Chile, but also echoes similar American themes in his later work.

[29] Some of these women poets include Rosario Castellanos, Carmen Conde, Claudia Lars and Dulce María Loynaz.

(United States), *ABC* and *La Vanguardia* (Spain), *El diario* (Bolivia), *Palabra americana* (Peru), *El Mercurio* (Chile), *La Nación* and *Sur* (Argentina), *El País* (Puerto Rico), *A Manhã* (Brazil), *Nuestro diario* (Guatemala), *El Tiempo* (Colombia), *El nuevo diario* (Venezuela), and *Excelsior* (Mexico). It is a fact now somewhat forgotten but Gabriela Mistral drew in a large following as a poet and prose writer, in print or in person, during her lifetime (to the point at times of fanaticism). It is hard for us to imagine the scale of her popularity or how widely read she was since to analyze her now requires scholars to engage in the slow process of sifting through files and archives or to access materials that are hard to obtain or no longer in print (such as old periodicals).[30] As a young woman Mistral declared her ambitions to become a famous writer; and this she did with her prolific newspaper publishing, which in times of difficulty became her only source of income.[31]

When Mistral passed away in 1957 her extraordinary output in periodicals and journals came to a sudden halt. With her materials packed away and kept under lock and key under the protection of her literary executor Doris Dana, only certain poems and prose pieces came to press (mostly from *Desolación* or *Ternura*); on occasion new material was allowed to be microfilmed in the Library of Congress in Washington DC. Generations of poets could only come across her reprints, inexpensive editions, or dog-eared books in national libraries. In the 1980s and 1990s a group of feminist poets across Latin America and rebellious writers from Santiago attempted to disseminate Mistral's poetry with their own publications and oral performances, to a limited success.[32]

It is only recently that her manuscripts papers, notes, articles, typewritten poems, and important correspondence – over 40,000 documents and artefacts – have been opened to the public. In 2007 Doris Dana's niece and heir, Doris Atkinson, donated the large collection to the Library of Chile in Santiago; and from 2008–2010 almost all of the collection was digitized. For any serious scholar wanting to study original manuscripts of Mistral's

[30] Articles, poems, and prose pieces published in the privately owned *El Mercurio* are almost impossible to recover as they are not available digitally or readily available on microfilm.

[31] On Mistral's early ambitions, see Gabriela Mistral, *Recopilación de la obra Mistraliana: 1902–1922*, Recopilación de Pedro Pablo Zegers (Santiago: RIL, 2002), 104. Palma Guillén comments how Mistral depended on income from newspapers and journals especially at moments when the Chilean government refused to support her. Guillén, "Introducción," xliv.

[32] Lila Zemborain, "La persistencia de una voz: ecos de Mistral en las poetas de hoy," in *Transatlantic Steamer: New Approaches to Hispanic and American Contemporary Poetry*, ed. by Miguel Ángel Zapata (Lima: Universidad Nacional Mayor de San Marcos, Centro de Producción Fondo Editorial; Hempstead, NY: Hofstra University, 2008), 93–103.

poems, they can be accessed easily online.[33] What is missing is the hard work: the metadata, the deciphering of difficult handwriting, the sorting through the chronology of certain poems, where they were written and when. We must also consider that there are materials that have gone missing, whether because of Mistral's extensive travels or that they may be housed elsewhere.[34]

The Authorized Book, the Deviant Poem

Gabriela Mistral wrote four books of poems during her lifetime, and they are *Desolación* (*Desolation*, 1922), *Ternura* (*Tenderness*, 1924), *Tala* (*Felling*, 1938), and *Lagar* (*Wine Press*, 1954).[35] Two additional books were published posthumously, *Lagar II* (1991) and *Poema de Chile* (*Poem of Chile*, 1968). Compared to contemporaries such as Alfonso Reyes and Jorge Luis Borges, who were actively publishing and promoting their poetry and prose collections, Mistral's book production seems but an afterthought.[36] As previously noted Gabriela Mistral wrote most of her poems for newspapers and magazines and many are yet still to be collected whether in published or manuscript form. There are dozens of Mistral's unedited notebooks with poems that have yet to be analyzed and other poems hidden away in old periodicals as the originals no longer exist.[37]

Scholars are posed with the additional aesthetic difficulty as to which version (published or not) of the poem to use. Although academic protocol decrees that the last edited book by the author is the "authorized" version, we must note that Gabriela Mistral often altered words, lines, and stanzas' meanings throughout her poetic trajectory, sometimes to deviate from

---

[33] Catálogo Bibliográfico. Archivo del Escritor. Biblioteca Nacional de Chile. www.bncatalogo.cl.

[34] It is hard to know how many private collections hold material on or by Mistral; every once in a while a document will surface and become public. Known Mistral collections include those at the Nettie Lee Benson Latin American Collection, University of Texas at Austin, the Rare Book and Manuscript Library at Barnard College and the Harvard University Houghton Library.

[35] *Desolación*'s second edtion includes more poems (published in Santiago, Chile in 1923). *Ternura* as well in its second edtion was re-edited with additional poems (some of these edits appear to have odd rhythmic choices) in 1945. *Tala* was re-edited in 1946 with poems taken out and placed in the 2nd edition of *Ternura*. *Lagar* was re-edited only a few years later in 1956, included in Margaret Bates' *Poesías completas* in 1958 and approved by Mistral.

[36] From the beginning of her career Gabriela Mistral demonstrated little interest in publishing her work in book form. As can be read in the introduction to *Desolación*, the Instituto de las Españas had to convince Mistral that it was for her own benefit.

[37] See, for instance, Gabriela Mistral. "Cuaderno [511]," Archivo del Escritor, Biblioteca Nacional de Chile, AE0015323. Digital.

common (and conservative) reading practices.[38] Three examples are the many versions of the "Sonetos de la muerte" (Sonnets of Death) which varied according to where they were published[39] and the suddenly flattened versions of "Obrerito" (Little Laborer) and "Caricia," (Caress) two beloved poems memorized by many in the 1920s only to be altered when they were republished in *Ternura*, 1945. Like Whitman, who saw publishing as an organic process, Gabriela Mistral was constantly adding to and amending her poems. Sections become longer or disappear completely. Dedications change (according to her preferences at the time of publication). Themes become more pronounced.

Out of all of her books the collection which has received the most critical acclaim (until 1980) has been *Desolación*. Not only because of the melodrama associated with it, but also, and perhaps more importantly for Mistral, it was the only book that circulated as currency for her, both in and out of the marketplace. *Desolación* was published in New York to international acclaim in 1922, and because of this she used the book as leverage for publishing bolder poems and more provocative articles, particularly outside of Chile. Numerous newspapers in the United States and Spain began to circulate her work. *Desolación* was published and reprinted without her permission (or the publishers'),[40] but it was not until much later in life (after 1945) that it mattered to Mistral. Like a coin in constant circulation, *Desolación* could be bartered and traded, copied and cut, and followers could spread the word of her tragic poetic genius.

Gender Games: Rounds, Bouts, and Pouts

On the surface there could not be two more distinct books of poetry than *Ternura* and *Tala*, published almost 20 years apart yet both among Mistral's preferred collections of poetry.[41] Published in Spain in 1924, *Ternura* has been called a "Children's Book of Verses," but Mistral later

[38] Sister Mary Charles Ann Preston, *A Study of Significant Variants in the Poetry of Gabriela Mistral* (Washington: Catholic University of America Press, 1964).

[39] Satoko Tamura, *Los sonetos de la muerte de Gabriela Mistral* (Gredos, 1998); Grinor Rojo, "'Qué no sé del amor..?' Para una nueva lectura de 'Los sonetos de la muerte' de Gabriela Mistral," *Revista ibero-americana*, LX.168–169 (1994): 673–84.

[40] See the unauthorized: Gabriela Mistral. *Nubes blancas, poesías y La oración de la maestra* (Barcelona: B. Bauzá [1925]) and the series, "Las mejores poesías de los mejores poetas" (Barcelona: Cervantes [193-]).

[41] Mauricio Ostria González, "Releyendo Ternura," in *Gabriela Mistral en verso y prosa: antología*, ed. C. Goig (Madrid: RAE-Alfaguara, 2010), 649–59; Margot Arce de Vásquez, *Gabriela Mistral: persona y poesía* (Puerto Rico: Ediciones Asomante, 1958), 70.

corrected this statement when she re-edited *Ternura* in 1945 with an addendum ("Colofón") clarifying that these poems, in particular the "lullabies" (or "canciones de cuna"), are not meant for children but mothers. They were purposely written to soothe and comfort those women, who "busc[aron] y encontr[aron], pues, una manera de hablar consigo misma[s]" (then sought and found a way to murmur to themselves).[42] Often thought of as a minor book since most of its poems appear in previous publications such as *Desolación* (1922; 1923), *Lecturas para mujeres* (*Readings for Women*, 1923; 1924), and *Tala* (1938), the poetry collection *Ternura* (1924; 1945) demonstrates a moral sensibility or tender affect in finding the "lost objects" of childhood, whether that means a "piece of straw" (La Pajita), or "[a foundling who] is-not-is of this world" ("Niño chiquito" [Small boy]) or "the child no one can see" ("La madreniña" [The girl-mother]) retaining an innocence not found anywhere else either in her other books of poetry or in her prose.

While it is true that *Ternura* has been typecast as a conservative book of verses on maternity and childhood, it could also be read as a precursor to *Tala*, the innocence before the fall from grace. To return to the "fictive" nature of her *dramatis personae*, in *Ternura* (1924) we find mothers and children engaging in monologues which involve guessing games, rounds of poetry, soothing songs, and joyous if not sentimental portraits of a time gone-by; by 1945 in the second edition Mistral purposely includes certain sections which transition into "darkness" or more sinister valleys of a desacralized space of adolescence and motherhood (read: poems from "La Desviadora [The Wandress]").

If we follow Mistral's logic on Christian symbolism and trees to denote mystic beauty and love of Christ (as found in *Desolación*), in *Tala* (1938), we find the "Felled Tree" (specifically the Araucaria).[43] There can be no redemption or resurrection, a turn back to peace before times of war. *Tala* is Mistral's responsorial gift to the "end of childhood," a symbolic offering for thousands of Spanish children who were displaced during the Spanish Civil War and could no longer return to a golden age of innocence.[44] Critics writing after 1980 have declared *Tala* an American masterpiece.[45] Mistral wrote most of the poems between 1924 and 1938 and had debated for years

[42] Gabriela Mistral, "Colofón con cara de excusa," in *Ternura* (Buenos Aires: Espasa-Calpe, 1945), 156–64.
[43] See "Cordillera" in the poem "América" of *Tala*: "Bajan de ti, bajan cantando,/ como de nupcias consumadas,/ tumbadores de las caobas y rompedor de araucarias."
[44] "Gabriela Mistral nos concede unos minutos," *El Correo de Valdívia*, May 8, 1938. Archivo del Escritor. Biblioteca Nacional AE0015668.
[45] Jaime Concha, *Gabriela Mistral* (Madrid: Júcar, 1987), p. 97.

as to where to publish the collection.[46] It would not be released until she offered her collection to Victoria Ocampo, whose publishing house, *Sur*, published the book (at its own cost) to raise funds for orphaned Basque children bombed by the Nazi Condor Legion in 1937.

Where childhood ends, so does an innocent maternity. In *Tala*, we find the calmness of motherhood and the virtuous traits of femininity – as found in *Ternura* – transition into more dangerous territory. In this poetry collection, the lyrical subject begins to refuse fixity and gender conscription and sets the stage to introduce readers to distinctive female lyricists who cannot be "found" or properly understood; they can be phantasmagoric projections of a hidden and burgeoning sexuality that will in the later collections of *Lagar* play out to become fluid, fantastic, and terrifying identities, shifting lexically through altering pronouns, neologisms and creative syntax. Although *Tala* centers its geographical space within the Americas, particularly in Chile, the women who speak hint at their deterritorialized space, without ground, home, or child. Mistral lays the groundwork for future publications, that is, *Lagar I & II* and *Poema de Chile*, where "en el secreto de la noche/ mi oración sube como las lianas,/ así cayendo y levantado,/ y tanteos como el ciego" (in the secret of the night/ [her] verse rises like the vine leaf/ falling and lifting/ tip-touching like a blind man; "La liana" [The Vine]). It is in these later collections where an ever-rising voice reimagines new poetic possibilities for transformative female *personae*: dyads and banshees, broken dolls and naked women, Greek figurines and goddesses, screaming and raging against a composed orderly world where they refuse to belong.

---

[46] Gabriela Mistral, *Carta para muchos*: España 1933–1935, ed. Karen Benavente (Santiago: Órigo-EDUFRO, 2015), 203.

8

STEPHEN M. HART

César Vallejo

"y la tórtola corta en tres su trino"
(and the turtle dove cuts her trill in three; "Telúrica y magnética," l. 57,
Poemas humanos)

"Consolado en terceras nupcias"
(Consoled by third marriages; "Un pilar soportando consuelos . . ." l. 15,
Poemas humanos)[1]

Ángel Rama once proposed that writers ought to focus on writing about the garden allotted to them in life – that is, the society in which they live rather than a remote alternative in another part of the world: "mejor cultivar el jardín que nos había tocado en suerte, con la mayor lucidez posible, y tratar de no engañarnos" (cultivate the garden which had been allotted to us, with the greatest possible lucidity, while attempting not to fool ourselves).[2] In this chapter I explore the idea that Vallejo – in a sense – took Rama's advice, but I suggest he had not one but three gardens. Vallejo brought out three collections of poetry, *Los heraldos negros* (Black Heralds), published in 1918 although it began to circulate in Lima in 1919, *Trilce*, which came out in 1922, and *Poemas humanos* (Human Poems), which was published a year after his death on April 15, 1938.[3] Vallejo also lived under the sign of three "isms," two of which were literary and the third political (*modernismo*, Dadaism and Trotskyism), and there were also three very important women in his life (Otilia Vallejo Gamboa, his niece; Otilia Villanueva Pajares, his lover in Lima; and Georgette Philippart, his wife). Vallejo's work, of course, loses its punch once you remove its autobiographical perspective, the allusions to his increasingly fragile everyday life; as Rama himself pointed out, one of the most salient characteristics of Vallejo's poetry is its

---

[1] *César Vallejo: The Complete Poetry: A Bilingual Edition*, ed. and trans. Clayton Eshleman (Berkeley, CA: California University Press), 424–25; 438–39.
[2] See Ángel Rama, *La novela en América Latina: panoramas 1920–1980* (Montevideo: Fundación Ángel Rama, 1986), 13. Rama further defined this garden as the culture which a nation constructs from contingent circumstances; see idem, 13.
[3] The first edition of the *Poemas humanos* also contained the fifteen poems of *España, aparta de mí este cáliz* (Spain, Take this Cup From Me); subsequent editions split them into separate works.

"autobiografismo" (autobiographical content).[4] It was as a result of the vogue in the early twentieth century of Freud-inspired fake biographies of writers (the artist was always "discovered" to have suffered from some type of sexual neurosis) that literary biography as a genre fell into decline.[5] The vogue nowadays is for a biographer to studiously avoid all but the most "empiric" mention of the works written by the biographee – how much the work cost to produce, what the first reviews were like – even though those works were what made the writer who he was.[6] In this chapter, though, I will explore Vallejo's literary biography and, in particular, the ways in which the intersection between time, geography, and writing can throw new light on the Peruvian poet's work. I will use the three main vectors of Vallejo's life as I see it, and map that "triple desarrollo" (triple unfolding; "Acaba de pasar el que vendrá ...," l. 2; Eshleman, *Complete Poetry*, 534–35) onto his work as follows:

> Otilia Vallejo Gamboa – *Los heraldos negros-modernismo*;
> Otilia Villanueva Pajares – *Trilce*-Dadaism; and
> Georgette Philippart – *Poemas humanos*-Trotskyism.

This analysis of the "triple unfolding" of Vallejo's life and work sees them in terms of three distinct phases, but it should be underlined that these are understood as inter-dependent worlds with strong connections between them. Otilia Vallejo Gamboa, after all, also appears in *Trilce*, and, as we shall see, there were overlaps between each of the three phases.

I

In order to excavate Vallejo's first garden, I begin with his love for his niece, Otilia Vallejo Gamboa, the eldest daughter of his brother, Víctor Clemente, and his wife, Amalia Gamboa. Otilia was approximately the same age as Vallejo – that is to say that she was more like a cousin than a niece – and she lived in the family home like the rest of the family in calle Colón no. 96 in Santiago de Chuco.[7] Otilia Vallejo Gamboa is clearly the muse of Vallejo's poem, "Ascuas" (Embers), but – for reasons of discretion – he changed her name slightly, writing Tilia rather than Otilia. As we read in the first stanza of the poem:

---

[4] In this sense Vallejo is similar to Darío whose poetry is also highly biographical; see Ángel Rama, *Rubén Darío y el modernismo* (Mexico City: Siglo XXI, 1970), 12–16.

[5] Patricia Waugh, *Literary Theory and Criticism: An Oxford Guide* (Oxford: Oxford University Press, 2006), 200–03.

[6] R.F. Foster, *W.B. Yeats: A Life, I: The Apprentice Mage 1865–1914* (Oxford: Oxford University Press, 1998).

[7] See Stephen Hart, *César Vallejo: una biografía literaria* (Lima: Cátedra Vallejo, 2014), 55.

Luciré para Tilia, en la tragedia
mis estrofas en óptimos racimos;
sangrará cada fruta melodiosa,
como un sol funeral, lúgubres vinos.
    Tilia tendrá la cruz
que en la hora final será de luz.

(In the tragedy I shall display for Tilia/ my stanzas in abundant clusters;/ each melodious fruit will bleed,/ like a funeral sun, doleful wines./ Tilia will hold the cross/ that in the final hour will be of light; Eshleman, *Complete Poetry*, 36–37.)

The poem is ambiguous, no doubt deliberately so, with regard to any suggestion of sexual contact between her and the poet. On the one hand, there is a reference to Tilia as "intacta y mártir" (virgin and martyr, l. 13), which suggests that the poet never touched her, but, on the other hand, there is a reference to her lip which was "al encresparse para el beso" (tightening for the kiss, l. 9), which appears to exceed the protocol of a Platonic relationship. The last two lines of the poem even hint at the paroxysm of sexual love: "Y en un lirio, voraz,/ mi sangre, como un virus, beberás" (And you will drink my blood/ like a virus, from a lily, voraciously!; ll. 17–18). With regard to poetic style – the theatricalization of love, the fusion between sacred and profane love, the overlapping of love, sex, and death – everything appears to point to a *modernista* self-fashioning on Vallejo's part. Indeed, we recall that Vallejo's friends "crowned" him "el primer poeta de América" (the first poet of the Americas), in a restaurant in Trujillo, Los Ñorbos, when news arrived of Rubén Darío's death; this happened in 1916, and Vallejo, at the sad news as well as the honor bestowed on him by his friends, burst into tears (Hart, *César Vallejo*, 49). In his early poems – and "Ascuas" suggests this – Vallejo was a Peruvian "Rubén Darío."[8]

This is not the only poem that appears to have been inspired by his niece. In my literary biography of Vallejo, I suggest that the opinion of Vallejo's biographer for the Trujillo period, Juan Espejo Asturrizaga – because of the close relationship he had with Vallejo over a number of years as well as the detailed information he provides about the publication of Vallejo's early poems – has been unassailable, and this has not always been positive. The testimony of other friends of Vallejo's suggests that his liaison with Otilia Vallejo Gamboa was an open secret. Espejo Asturrizaga must have known about this as much as anyone else but, in his *César Vallejo: itinerario del*

---

[8] For further discussion of Vallejo's drinking-in of *modernismo*, see Roberto Paoli, *Mapas anatómicos de César Vallejo* (Florence: D'Anna, 1981); and Jorge Cornejo Polar, "Vallejo y la vanguardia: una relación problemática," *Apuntes* 28 (1991): 73–85.

hombre, he chose not to mention the real relationship between Vallejo and Otilia Vallejo Gamboa.[9] Of course once we accept the possibility that Espejo Asturrizaga had concealed Otilia Vallejo Gamboa's trace, everything changes. There are, indeed, a number of love poems that appear to take place in a domestic setting. "El poeta a su amada" (The Poet to his Beloved), for example, discusses love in the same terms we find in "Ascuas" – sex is associated with religion (crucifixion in this case) and death, and the love is thereby "cursed" – but, most intriguingly, the poem underlines the domesticity of this "cursed" love:

> Y ya no habrán reproches en tus ojos benditos;
> ni volveré a ofenderte. Y en una sepultura
> los dos dormiremos, como dos hermanitos.

> (There will be no more reproach in your holy eyes;/ nor will I offend you ever again. In one grave/ we two will sleep, as two siblings; Eshleman, *Complete Poetry*, 58–59.)

The reference to the two lovers sleeping "as two siblings" replicates exactly what was occurring in Vallejo's life. We find the same heady mix of love, sex, and death in poem XI of *Trilce*:

> He encontrado a una niña
> en la calle, y me ha abrazado.
> Equis, disertada, quien la halló y la halle,
> no la va a recordar.

> Esta niña es mi prima. Hoy, al tocarle
> el talle, mis manos han entrado en su edad
> como en par de mal rebocados sepulcros.
> Y por la misma desolación marchóse
> > delta al sol tenebloso
> > trina entre los dos.

> > "Me he casado"
> me dice. Cuando lo que hicimos de niños
> en casa de la tía difunta.
> > Se ha casado.
> > Se ha casado.

> Tardes años latitudinales,
> que verdaderas ganas nos ha dado
> de jugar a los toros, a las yuntas,
> pero todo de engaños, de candor, como fue.

---

[9] Juan Espejo Asturrizaga, *César Vallejo: itinerario del hombre* (Lima: Mejía Baca, 1965).

(I have met a girl/ in the street, and she has embraced me./ X, expounded, whoever found her and finds her,/ will not remember her./ This girl is my cousin. Today, on touching/ her waist, my hands have entered her age/ as into a pair of badly bitewashed sepulchers./ And for that very desolation she left,/ the delta in a teneblearic sun,/ a trine between the two./ "I got married,"/ she tells me. In spite of what we did as kids/ in the house of the dead aunt./ She's married./ She's married./ Late latitudinal years, how much it made us want/ to play bulls, yoked oxen,/ but just fooling, in candor, like it was; Eshleman, *Complete Poetry*, 186–87.)

Germán Patrón Candela has argued that in this poem – because of its coded allusion to Otilia's profession ("X, expounded" alludes to the fact that Otilia was a teacher – she taught at the time in a school in Huamachuco) – Vallejo playfully combines the mathematical search for x which underlies algebra with the search for love, which a cross also stands for. The reference to her as his cousin ("This girl is my cousin") is, again, a coded reference in that it is half-true; Otilia was his niece rather than his cousin, although – given that his brother, Víctor, was many years older than him, Otilia was of a similar age to Vallejo, and therefore more like a cousin than a niece. Patrón Candela argues that – despite Espejo Asturrizaga's silence about the event – this was a poetic description of the meeting Vallejo had with Otilia Vallejo Gamboa in May 1920.[10] The poem refers to the rage of a poet who has been denied the possibility of the satisfaction of his sexual desires, which, as the poem suggests, are still raging within him. Line 17 – "how much it made us want/ to play bulls, yoked oxen" – alludes to the ambiguity of the innocence of the children's games that they played together in their aunt's house. The "dead aunt" referred to here is likely to be María de los Santos Mendoza Gurrionero, Vallejo's mother, who had died on August 8, 1918. Though she was in fact Otilia Vallejo Gamboa's grandmother, Vallejo transposes her – in the manner of an algebraic transposition – into Otilia's aunt, which she would have been had she really been Vallejo's cousin. The code used by Vallejo is, thus, revealed to be algebraic, in that it is internally consistent. The verb tense used – the present perfect ("ha dado") rather than the pluperfect – makes it clear that the desires continue into the present (of the poem). Note that the link between love, sex, and death found in "Ascuas" and "El poeta a su amada" is also present in Tr. XI. The metaphor of the "mal rebocados sepulcros" plays on the betacism of the Spanish language; by invoking the sense of "revocados" (lit. revoked) within the word "rebocados" (lit. remouthed), Vallejo is able to suggest simultaneously that the love he experienced for Otilia Vallejo Gamboa was "revocado" – that is, "revoked," or

---

[10] Germán Patrón Gambela, "El Cristo de Vallejo," *Norte* 2 (1994–1995): 10.

"outlawed" by society – and thus it was interred in the tomb of the past. The tragedy expressed by the poem – encapsulated by those "mal rebocados sepulcros" – resides in the fact that Vallejo felt that the skeleton in the cupboard could escape at any time. The portrayal in Tr. XI of love/sex as a tomb that cannot be closed has a parallel with the sense of mortality expressed in "Ascuas" and "Poeta a su amada." Vallejo's love for his niece was like an open wound that could never be healed.

II

When excavating the second garden of Vallejo's life, it is necessary to provide some details about the "elusive muse" of Vallejo's Dadaist collection of poems, *Trilce*: Otilia Villanueva Pajares. It is strange that Vallejo should have fallen in love with two young women with the same name, Otilia. The second Otilia, as we now know, lived in the Maravillas district in Lima, and Vallejo got to know her a few months after moving to Lima. On September 12, 1918, Vallejo had been promoted to the directorship of the Colegio Barrós as a result of the sudden and unexpected death of the Director. According to Espejo Asturriaga some of Vallejo's work colleagues took him out one evening after work for some socializing in the Maravillas district which was not that far away from the Colegio Barrós, and Vallejo fell in love with someone he met on that occasion: Otilia Villanueva Pajares (Hart, *César Vallejo*, 89). It is highly likely that a number of the poems in *Trilce* that focus on sex were inspired by his relationship with Otilia Villanueva Pajares and, given the at times graphic and even pornographic language used to describe these encounters, it is understandable why Vallejo's biographer decided to veil her true identity. And thus in his book, *César Vallejo: itinerario del hombre*, Espejo Asturrizaga refers to her simply as O. (Asturrizaga, *César Vallejo*, 73–74).

Sex is, of course, not the exclusive concern of *Trilce*. The collection has poems about Vallejo's mother, and about his experience of everyday life in Lima – clearly it was a shock and a paradigm shift compared to his relatively tranquil life back in Trujillo – as well as his experience of jail (Vallejo was incarcerated for 113 days as a result of the accusation that he was part of the group who burned down Carlos Santa María's business premises on August 1, 1920) – but clearly the most "dramatic" poems are those that describe his relationship with Otilia Villanueva Pajares. It was perhaps inevitable that this relationship would not last. It started in April 1919 and began to take on a dramatic twist when Otilia's family attempted to persuade Vallejo to do the decent thing and marry Otilia. But the poet refused to get married (Hart, *César Vallejo*, 95). The result was that Vallejo not only lost his lover but also his job at the Colegio Barrós, after a fisticuffs fight with Otilia's brother-in-law, Manuel Rabanal Cortegana, who was also Vallejo's work colleague. This set of events inspired poem XXXVII of *Trilce*:

He conocido a una pobre muchacha
a quien conduje hasta la escena.
La madre, sus hermanas qué amables y también
aquel su infortunado "tú no vas a volver."

Como en cierto negocio me iba admirablemente
me rodeaban de un aire de dinasta florido.
La novia se volvía agua,
y cuán bien solía llorar
su amor mal aprendido.

Me gustaba su tímida marinera
de humildes aderezos al dar las vueltas,
y como su pañuelo trazaba puntos,
tildes, a la melografía de su bailar de juncia.

Y cuando ambos burlamos al párroco,
quebróse mi negocio y el suyo
y la esfera barrida.

(I used to know a poor girl/ who I brought onto the scene./ The mother, her sisters so nice and likewise/ that unfortunate "you're not coming back" of hers./ As I was doing splendidly in a certain business,/ they surrounded me with airs of an affluent dynast./ My girlfriend turned to water,/ and how well she used to sob for me/ her half-learned love./ I enjoyed her bashful marinera/ of humble adornments circling about/ and how her kerchief would sketch dots,/ accents, to the melography of her sedgelike sawy./ And when we both sidestepped the priest,/ my business failed as did hers/and the sphere swept away; Eshleman, *Complete Poetry*, 240–41.)

The "certain business" (l. 5) referred to in the poem was Vallejo's post of director of the Colegio Barrós. This is why Otilia's mother and sisters surround Vallejo "with airs of an affluent dynast" (l. 6) – they are trying to persuade him to marry Otilia. And Otilia begins to cry and, as Vallejo says rather cynically, she sobs for his benefit "her half-learned love" (l. 9). The most poetic stanza is the third where Vallejo compares Otilia's drama to a "marinera" dance. While dancing, she appears to turn into a reed (with her "sedgelike sway," l. 13, as the poem suggests), since she was a young and slender girl – just fifteen years old – when Vallejo first met her. And the handkerchief that she holds in her hand is tracing signs in the air which form "dots,/ accents" (or, better, "tildes") spelling out the choreography of her love. The last stanza returns to the tone used at the beginning of the poem, which is anti-poetic and down-to-earth, and Vallejo notes that the two lovers "sidestepped the priest" and, as a result, Vallejo also lost his job as director of the Colegio Barrós. A few of the other poems of *Trilce*, according to Espejo Asturrizga, refer indirectly to the pressure felt by Vallejo to do the right thing. A further complication was that Otilia was pregnant, which has led to a number of poems being read as allusions to her expectant motherhood; words such as "ovario" (ovary) in Tr. IV (l. 20; Eshleman, *Complete Poetry*, 172–73), and expressions such as "Octubre habitación y encinta" (October, bedroom and pregnant) in Tr. X (l. 3, Eshleman, *Complete Poetry*, 184–85), and "los tres meses de ausencia./ Y los nueve de gestación" (The three months of absence./ And the nine of gestation) in the same poem (ll. 17–18) have been interpreted in these terms.

One intriguing feature of the love-affair Vallejo had with Otilia Villanueva Pajares in 1920–1921 is that it led to a violent paradigm shift in his poetic manner. The first stanza of Tr. IX, for example, refers directly to the lover's sex:

> Vusco volvvver de golpe el golpe.
> Sus dos hojas anchas, su válvula
> que se abre en suculenta recepción
> de multiplicando a multiplicador,
> su condición excelente para el placer,
> todo avía verdad.

> (I sdrive to ddeflect at a blow the blow./ Her two broad leaves, her valve/ opening in succulent reception/ from multiplicand to multiplier,/ her condition excellent for pleasure,/ all readies truth; Eshleman, *Complete Poetry*, 182–83.)

In 1922 such a direct reference to sex – even if couched in poetic imagery – was shocking; we need to remember that at that time *modernismo* was still in vogue – as epitomized by Rubén Darío's work – and it relied on a discreetly mythological imaginary in order to refer to sex. With this stanza Vallejo broke the molds of *modernismo*, and he did so in a violent way. Indeed, his attack on the language of *modernismo* was not restricted simply to the destruction of a metaphorical imaginary – it was an attack on language itself. Vallejo plays in this stanza on the betacism inherent in the Spanish language, writing "avía" (an archaism) instead of "había"; he also writes "vusco" rather than "busco," and adds letters to the verb "volver," turning it into "volvvver." Vallejo thereby creates new meanings as a result of playing with the phonetic fibre of language. The lines just referred to, for example, mean "todo había verdad" (all had truth) and "todavía verdad" (all had truth) simultaneously, as a result of interchanging the "b" and the "v." Vallejo's attitude towards language, as indicated by this poem, is that of a Dadaist, that is, an artist who attacks language and tears up the choir sheet of meaning.

While Vallejo wrote in positive terms about Dadaism, contacted Tristan Tzara soon after arriving in Paris, and kept up with him over the years, he did not feel the same level of sympathy for Surrealism. In fact, the first draft of "¡Oh botella sin vino! ¡oh vino que enviudó de esta botella! . . . " (Oh bottle without wine! Oh wine the widower of this bottle! . . .) deconstructs the raison d'être of the lynchpin of surrealist aesthetics, the "cadavre exquis" (exquisite cadaver). A preliminary analysis of the first autograph version of the poem shows that Vallejo wrote a number of words on the right-hand side of the paper on which he was composing the poem, and used them in order to write the poem – on the face of it this looks very much like an imitation of the arbitrariness of the surrealist formula.[11] And this raises the possibility that Vallejo was prepared to criticize Surrealism publicly, as he did in an article published in 1930, while secretly using the technique for his own poetry.[12] But, given his intimate knowledge of Paris' artistic scene, Vallejo would have known that the first poem to have been created using the surrealist method ran as follows: "Le cadavre – exquis – boira – le vin – nouveau" (The exquisite – cadaver – will drink – the – new – wine).[13] The fact that the theme of the first poem in which Vallejo "experimented" with the surrealist technique, "¡Oh botella sin vino! ¡oh vino que enviudó de esta botella! . . .," also had a very similar theme to the inaugural "exquisite cadaver" poem – Vallejo's poem is about wine and it is also about the wine bottle as a "cadaver" – means that Vallejo's poem is either an amazing coincidence or a deliberate reworking of the surrealist premise. The first stanza of Vallejo's poem is as follows:

> ¡Oh botella sin vino! ¡oh vino que enviudó de esta botella!
> Tarde cuando la aurora de la tarde
> flameó funestamente en cinco espíritus.
> Viudez sin pan ni mugre, rematando en horrendos metaloides
> y en células orales acabando.

[11] *César Vallejo: autógrafos olvidados: edición facsimilar de 52 manuscritos*, ed. Juan Fló and Stephen Hart (Woodbridge: Tamesis, 2003), 40.

[12] See Vallejo's article, "Autopsia del surrealismo," dated February 1930, in which he argued that surrealism "no representaba ningún aporte constructivo. Era una receta más de hacer poemas sobre medida, como lo son y serán las escuelas literarias de todos los tiempos" (never made any positive contribution. It's a recipe for making poems by rote, as literary schools have always done in the past and will always do in the future); see *Variedades* (March 26, 1930).

[13] See William S. Rubin, *Dada, Surrealism and Their Heritage* (New York, NY: MOMA, 1989), 83.

(Oh bottle without wine! oh wine the widower of the bottle!/ Afternoon when the aurora of the afternoon/ Flamed balefully in five spirits./ Widowhood without bread or grime, finishing in hideous metalloids/ And in oral cells ending; ll. 1–5; Eshleman, *Complete Poetry*, 448–49.)

Surely there is no coincidence here. Vallejo's poem is a self-aware and ironic dismantlement of the notion that the "cadaver" could drink "new wine," for there is no "new wine" to be had, and the wine simply ends up dead, finishing up as "hideous metalloids" (l. 4) and ending "in oral cells" (l. 5). The same idea is repeated in the second stanza which refers to how the expectation created by the wine is revealed to be nothing more than a "cruel falacia" (l. 7; cruel deceit). The poem extends the initial matrix idea – namely, that "the exquisite cadaver will drink the new wine," and turns it into an anguished exploration of the metaphor of the soul within the body expressed via the wine within the now empty bottle. Vallejo's poem, thus, not only attacks the idea expressed in the inaugural "cadavre exquis," it also attacks Surrealism's methodology, drawing the poem back to a real-life bottle which is "missing" its real-life wine, just as the body will one day "miss" its real-life soul. Vallejo's "¡Oh botella sin vino! ¡oh vino que enviudó de esta botella! ... " is, therefore, a coded attack on Surrealism that argues that their word games are trivial compared to a thoughtful enunciation of the conundrum of how the soul sits within the human body.

As we can see, Vallejo acted in the second garden of his life like a follower of Tristan Tzara – *Trilce* is an avant-garde book, but it is not *creacionista* nor *ultraísta*, nor, indeed, surrealist.[14] It's a Dadaist book. It attacks the roots of language itself, and its stance with regard to language is more radical than the attacks carried out by the other less daring squadrons of the Hispanic avant-garde.

III

César Vallejo's third garden is the one he frequented from 1927 until his death in 1938. It is the garden of politics, and also the garden in which his love for Georgette Philippart, his future wife, was born and flourished.[15] In my biography of Vallejo I have suggested that the Peruvian poet joined the Stalinist arm of Communism in 1929, but, even so, during the 1930s – and especially as a result of the arrival in Paris in 1934 of news about the destructive purges that the Soviet leader, Joseph Stalin, was carrying out in the gulags in the Soviet

[14] For discussion of these movements, see Chapter 3 in this volume.
[15] César Vallejo and Georgette Philippart were married on October 11, 1934; see Hart, *César Vallejo*, 281–82.

Union – a degree of political disillusionment grew in Vallejo's soul about the Stalinist direction that Communism was taking at that time. Only two years later the Spanish Civil War broke out and the intervention of the Soviet Union created a poisonous political atmosphere in the republican ranks, since it seemed that the Soviet Union was more interested in destroying the threat presented by the Trotskyists than shoring up the defenses of the Spanish government and the Republic. That's why a number of historians – such as Hugh Thomas – have spoken of a War within a War among the Left during the Spanish Civil War.[16] Vallejo witnessed this struggle personally when he went to Spain to participate in the Segundo Congreso de la Asociación Internacional de Escritores por la Defensa de la Cultura (Second Congress of the International Association of Writers in Defense of Culture) in the summer of 1937. Andrés Nin, a prominent Trotskyist, had mysteriously disappeared on June 20. When Vallejo arrived in Madrid on July 4, 1937, the whole city was buzzing with rumors about what had happened to him – the grim reality, though suspected at the time, only fully came out years later. Nin had been captured, tortured, and finally murdered (on June 20, 1937) by the Soviet Union's secret police, the NKVD, the People's Commissariat of Internal Affairs, which was operating in Spain at the time. According to Georgette, his wife, Vallejo returned to France and was visibly shocked by what he had seen in Spain. Whereas he had left for Spain full of enthusiasm about seeing close up the heroism of the Republican soldier, when he returned to France, he was different, nervous, sad, overwhelmed by what he had witnessed, to such an extent that he felt unable to carry on writing his poems.[17] I suggest in my biography that the main reason why he seemed so overwhelmed is that he was a closet Trotskyist at that time, and he suddenly realized the great danger he was in. As his good friend, Juan Domingo Córdoba Vargas recalls: "Trotsky era para Vallejo uno de los héroes de la revolución, el brazo derecho de Lenin, el creador, orador didáctico formidable, talento excepcional, ideólogo del partido y orientador con la revolución permanente, que lo acredita como revolucionario cien por cien, porque revolución que se estanca llega a ser superada por el normal desarrollo y desenvolvimiento posterior de los acontecimientos" (Trotsky was for Vallejo one of the heroes of the Revolution, Lenin's right-hand man, the creator, the outstanding didactic orator, an extraordinary talent, the ideologist of the Party and the leader of the permanent revolution, as a result of which he is credited with being a

[16] Hugh Thomas, *The Spanish Civil War* (Harmondsworth: Penguin, 1977).
[17] As Georgette recalls, "al regresar de España, no ha podido reanudar su labor poética" (on returning from Spain, he was unable to return to writing his poetry); see "Apuntes biográficos sobre César Vallejo," in *César Vallejo: obra poética completa* (Lima: Mosca Azul, 1970), 412.

one-hundred-percent revolutionary, because a revolution that stagnates is eventually overtaken by the normal development and subsequent course taken by events).[18] Rumors were circulating around Paris at that time that Vallejo was a Trotskyist and, as a result of his alleged allegiance to Trotskyism, Vallejo was not made editor of a Republican magazine published in Paris entitled *Nuestra España*.[19] I have also suggested elsewhere that there are two poems in which Vallejo speaks – in veiled terms – of his Trotskyism, which are "Otro poco de calma, camarada ... " (A little more calm, comrade ...) and "Al revés de las aves del monte ... " (Contrary to the mountain birds ...; Hart, *César Vallejo*, 306–27), and I would like to argue that there is another poem in which Vallejo appears to allude to Trotsky, that is, "Salutación angélica" (Angelic Salutation). Most critics see this poem as an emotional eulogy to the Bolshevik, but my interpretation differs. The poem opens as follows:

> Eslavo con respecto a la palmera,
> alemán de perfil al sol, inglés sin fin,
> francés en cita con los caracoles,
> italiano ex profeso, escandinavo de aire,
> español de pura bestia, tal el cielo
> ensartado en la tierra por los vientos,
> tal el beso del límite en los hombros.

> (Slav in regard to the palm tree,/ German with a profile to the sun, English with no limits,/ French in a rendezvous with snails,/ Italian on purpose, Scandinavian made of air,/ purely brutal Spaniard, thus the sky/ strung on the earth by the winds,/ thus the limit's kiss on the shoulders; Eshleman, *Complete Poetry*, 382–83.)

This first stanza refers to the variety of "species" of capitalist man, and here we hear of the stereotype of the Frenchman with his "snails," the Englishman with his overseas dominions (that's why he is described as "without limits"), and Vallejo then goes on to describe these different species as if they were viewed from above, that is, from the vantage-points of the heavens where the winds live ("by the winds"). The second stanza, however, suggests that the Bolshevik is someone who is able to transcend the generic character of

[18] *César Vallejo del Perú Profundo y Sacrificado*, Jaime Campodonico, ed. (Lima, 1995), 163.
[19] Hart, *César Vallejo*, 305. It was becoming more and more dangerous to express allegiance to Trotsky at that time, and this was also demonstrated when the Spanish national, Ramón Mercader, a KGB agent, executed Trotsky in Mexico City on August 21, 1940, only two years after Vallejo's death. The danger during the Spanish Civil War has been eloquently described by George Orwell in his *Homage to Catalonia*, which tells of how the KGB agents purged the Trotskyists with impunity behind republican lines during the Spanish Civil War.

nationality; his lack of "nationalism" allows him to take on a more human personality than that of the citizens of other nations:

> Mas sólo tú demuestras, descendiendo
> o subiendo del pecho, bolchevique,
> tus trazos confundibles,
> tu gesto marital,
> tu cara de padre,
> tus piernas de amado,
> tu cutis por teléfono,
> tu alma perpendicular
> a la mía,
> tus codos de justo
> y un pasaporte en blanco en tu sonrisa.

> (But you alone, Bolshevik, demonstrate,/ descending or rising from your chest,/ your confusable characteristics,/ your marital gesture,/ your paternal face,/ your lover's legs, your complexion by telephone,/ your soul perpendicular/ to mine,/ your elbows of a just man/ and a blank passport in your smile; idem.)

Because the Bolshevik is more human, he makes gestures like husbands do ("your marital gesture"), his face makes him look like a father, his legs look like lover's legs, and he is so friendly that you almost feel you can touch his skin when he talks to you on the telephone ("your complexion by telephone"). It is not surprising, given these first two stanzas, that many critics have seen this poem simply as a eulogy of the Bolshevik. This positive image seems confirmed in the third stanza when we read of the poet's desire to emulate the Bolshevik:

> Yo quisiera, por eso,
> tu calor doctrinal, frío y en barras,
> tu añadida manera de mirarnos
> y aquesos tuyos pasos metalúrgicos,
> aquesos tuyos pasos de otra vida.

> (Therefore, I would like/ your doctrinal warmth, cold and in rods,/ your added way of looking at us/ and those metallurgical steps of yours,/ your steps of another life; idem.)

The reference here to Soviet technology – the miracle of the Five-Year Plan of the Soviet Union which Vallejo saw at first hand when he visited Russia and which he described in his travelogue *Rusia en 1931* (evident here in expressions such as "in rods" and "metallurgical steps") – seems to confirm that this is a poem of praise dedicated to the Bolshevik. And thus it would be, were it not for the final stanza of the poem, which seems to go off at a tangent:

Y digo, bolchevique, tomando esta flaqueza
en su feroz linaje de exhalación terrestre:
hijo natural del bien y del mal
y viviendo talvez por vanidad, para que digan,
me dan tus simultáneas estatuas mucha pena,
puesto que tú no ignoras en quién se me hace tarde diariamente,
en quién estoy callado y medio tuerto.

(And I say, Bolshevik, taking this weakness/ in its ferocious lineage of earthly exhalation:/ the natural son of good and of evil/ and living perhaps out of vanity, to have others talk,/ your simultaneous statues make me very sad,/ because you can't but know in whom I am late daily,/ in whom I am silent and almost one-eyed; idem.)

The crucial line here is line 33 in which Vallejo addresses the Bolshevik directly and says "your simultaneous statues make me very sad." What does Vallejo mean by this? The best way to interpret these lines, I believe, is to compare them with what Vallejo said to a Soviet bureaucrat as reported in his second book on the Soviet Union, entitled *Rusia ante el segundo plan quinquenal*, which was a bit more jaundiced than the first one. As we read, for example, in the chapter "La verdad sobre la situación en Rusia" (Truth about the situation in Russia):

Semejante conducta de los burócratas llega a límites audaces, por no decir alevosos. Siguen al viajero paso a paso, ofreciéndole sus servicios de información con extrema galantería. Los he sorprendido, en ocasiones, obsta-culizando mi contacto directo con la masa, por medios astutos, candorosos y ridículos. Yo les he increpado, a veces, fraternalmente. ¿Por qué hace usted esto? Comprendo que lo que usted se propone es proporcionarme una impresión maravillosa del Soviet; pero, en verdad, lo que consigue es desfigurar la realidad objetiva de la situación.

(This type of behavior from the bureaucrats is taken to audacious if not treacherous extremes. They follow foreign visitors every step of their way, offering their services in providing information with extreme unctuousness. I have occasionally caught them obstructing my access with the people, using clever ploys which are nonetheless naive and ridiculous. I have sometimes rebuked them, in a friendly way. "Why are you doing this? I get that what you want to do is to give a marvelous impression of the Soviet Union but, to be honest, what you are in fact doing is distorting the reality of what is actually happening; author's translation.)[20]

---

[20] *Ensayos y reportajes completos*, ed. Manuel Miguel de Priego (Lima: Pontificia Universidad Católica del Perú, 2002), 323. From *Rusia ante el segundo plan quinquenal* (1965).

Indeed, in his poem, "Salutación angélica," Vallejo seems to adopt a very similar tone in addressing the Bolshevik, that is, he criticizes him "fraternally." Vallejo criticizes the "simultaneous statues" the Soviet Union is producing which are distorting reality, and these "statues" are no doubt a metaphor of the propaganda that the Soviet Union was sending simultaneously to various countries all around the world. The most intriguing lines of the poem, though, are the last two, in which Vallejo does not specify the individual who he is desperately waiting for, day in and day out. This person can be neither a capitalist – since the various incarnations of capitalism were effectively rejected by him in the first stanza of the poem – nor a Bolshevik. Since the individual concerned is someone whom the Bolshevik "can't but know," and is also someone for whom Vallejo cannot openly express his loyalty ("in whom I am silent"), and, given the date when the poem was written – sometime in the 1930s, probably in the late 1930s – it is likely that this person is none other than Leon Trotsky.

What is, finally, rather curious about Vallejo's three gardens – the first inhabited by Otilia Vallejo Gamboa, *modernismo*, and *Los heraldos negros*; the second by Otilia Villanueva Pajares, Dadaism, and *Trilce*; and the third by Georgette Philippart, Trotsky, and *Poemas humanos* – is that in all three cases, despite being "consoled by third marriages," Vallejo often felt unable to name the source of his passion.

9

ADAM FEINSTEIN

Pablo Neruda

"I have always found that the less I knew about the poet, before I began to read it, the better."[1] At the time T.S. Eliot wrote those lines, in 1929, Pablo Neruda was serving his bizarre first diplomatic mission as Chilean consul in the Far East. In Neruda's case, his remarkable life and work were so inextricably entwined that it makes little sense to untangle them.

Neruda was born Neftalí Ricardo Reyes Basoalto in Parral, central Chile, on July 12, 1904. His mother, Rosa, died two months after giving to birth to him and the family moved south to the rain-clattered, wooden-roofed town of Temuco. Neftalí's train-driver father, José del Carmen, although vehemently opposed to his son's becoming a poet, unwittingly fueled Neftalí with his lifelong passion for the natural world by driving him through the southern Chilean forests on enchanting train rides. As Neruda later recalled:

> Mi infancia son zapatos mojados, troncos rotos
> caídos en la selva, devorados por lianas
> y escarabajos, dulces días sobre la avena,
> y la barba dorada de mi padre saliendo
> hacia la majestad de los ferrocarriles.

> (My childhood was wet shoes, shattered tree trunks/ toppled in the forest, swallowed by lianas/ and beetles, days of resting gently on beds of oats,/ and the golden beard of my father, heading off/ to the majesty of the railway.)[2]

Golden-bearded or not, José del Carmen was a severe father, and in 1921, Neruda fled Temuco for the Chilean capital, Santiago, to study French pedagogy. After a sickly, solitary childhood, he quickly came to relish his new bohemian lifestyle. He chose to change his name to Pablo Neruda. The "Pablo" may have derived from one of his favorite French poets, Paul

[1] T.S. Eliot: *Selected Essays* (London: Faber and Faber, 1999).
[2] From "La frontera (1904)," *Canto General*, 2 vols (Buenos Aires: Losada, 1978), II, 183. All translations are by the author.

Verlaine, or possibly because he imagined himself as Paolo after Dante's Paolo and Francesca. Neruda himself insisted he took his surname from the Czech writer Jan Neruda. Enrique Robertson has an alternative theory: that the true origins may lie in a poster announcing a concert by the violinist, *Pablo* Sarasate, and the cellist, Wilhemina *Neruda*.[3] This is an alluring hypothesis, given the surprising instances of the violin image in Neruda's poetry.

His first collection, *Crepusculario* (Poems at Dusk) published in Santiago in 1923, is infused with melancholy. The dark shadow of tuberculosis – which killed many of Neruda's friends at the time – also hangs over many of these poems. The following year saw the publication of the book which would cement his reputation: *Veinte poemas de amor y una canción desesperada* (Twenty Love Poems and a Song of Despair). Their incoherent, postadolescent longing for fulfilling love ("I no longer love her, it's true, but perhaps I *do* love her/ Love is so short and forgetting so long") continues to exert a hold over vast numbers of readers to this day.[4] One of the leading scholars of the *Veinte poemas*, Dominic Moran, has written that, in them, "the vague sublimated longings of Neruda's literary predecessors, the *modernistas*, are replaced by urges that are unambiguously sexual, and idealized feminine figures make way for a real female body." The sense of "desperate, unassuageable but always physical yearnings is palpable even in the most intractable passages."[5] Some of the *Veinte poemas* read like delirious trances, others like dances. As Jason Wilson has pointed out, Octavio Paz's first wife, Elena Garro, linked these poems with Carlos Gardel's tangos. Wilson agrees with this assessment: "The tone of Neruda's poems fuses with tango (melancholia, the male, betrayal, revenge)."[6]

In 1926 Neruda published three books – the experimental, punctuation-free *Tentativa del hombre infinito* (Venture of the Infinite Man); the dark novella *El habitante y su esperanza* (The Inhabitant and His Hope), in some senses, a prose cousin of its predecessor – and a short collection of lyrical prose poems, *Anillos* (Rings) written with his friend Tomás Lago. But by now, Neruda was growing weary of his bohemian Santiago existence and needed a change. In 1927 he was offered that first diplomatic appointment in the Burmese capital, Rangoon. He found no point of contact with Asian culture, nor with the British colonialists. He did, however, experience what

---

[3] See Enrique Robertson Álvarez, *La pista "Sarasate": una investigación sherlokiana tras las huellas del nombre de Pablo Neruda* (Pamplona: Gobierno de Navarra/Fondo de Publicaciones, 2008.)

[4] From "Poema 20."

[5] Dominic Moran, *Pablo Neruda* (London: Reaktion Books, 2009), 32–33.

[6] Jason Wilson, *A Companion to Pablo Neruda* (Woodbridge: Tamesis, 2008), 54.

was probably his first truly satisfying love affair – with a native woman known to us only as Josie Bliss. Her jealousy eventually came to terrify him but she would inspire his magnificent poem "Tango del viudo" (Widower's Tango) which ends in heart-rending longing:

> Daría este viento del mar gigante por tu brusca respiración
> oída en largas noches sin mezcla de olvido,
> uniéndose a la atmósfera como el látigo a la piel del caballo.
> Y por oírte orinar, en la oscuridad, en el fondo de la casa,
> como vertiendo una miel delgada, trémula, argentina, obstinada ...

> (I would give up the wind over the vastness of the sea to hear your sudden breath once more on those long, unforgettable nights, mingling with the air as a whip meets the horse's pelt. And to hear you peeing in a dark corner of the house, in a trembling stream of silver, stubborn and delicate as honey ...)[7]

Neruda married for the first time in Batavia (now Jakarta) in 1930. His bride was a tall Dutch-Indonesian woman, Maria Antonia Hagenaar Vogelzang. He called her Maruca. Years later, he claimed that he had married out of loneliness: "I was a knight without a castle/ an inadmissible passenger/ a person without clothes or ... a pure wandering idiot."[8] The couple returned to Chile in April 1932.

The following year Neruda's Chilean publisher, Nascimento, brought out a luxury first edition of one of the densest and richest of all his books, *Residencia en la tierra* (Residence on Earth). "These poems indicated that I was coming to possess a territory which was indisputably mine," he told the Mexican critic Alfonso Cardona Peña. Yet he later regretted the fact that so many of the poems in this collection were "soaked in atrocious pessimism and anguish. They do not help you to live, but to die."[9] Most of the poems in the first edition of *Residencia* had, indeed, been written during those five years in the Far East which the great Neruda authority, Robert Pring-Mill, described as "a period of virtually total spiritual blackness ... His poetry turned in upon itself, recording complete disgust with existence, an increasingly morbid preoccupation with death and with the passage of time and a progressive disintegration of the world picture."[10]

---

[7] From "Tango del viudo" (Widower's Tango), *Residencia en la tierra I* (Buenos Aires: Losada, 1979), 64.
[8] From "Itinerarios" in *Estravagario* (1958).
[9] Alfredo Cardona Peña, "Pablo Neruda: Breve historia de sus libros," *Cuadernos Americanos* 9 (1950), 54–56.
[10] Robert Pring-Mill, *Pablo Neruda: A Basic Anthology* (Oxford: Oxford University Press, 1975), xxi.

It was his intense friendship with the Spanish poet Federico García Lorca, I believe, that pulled Neruda out of this "disgust with existence." Their initial encounter took place in Buenos Aires in 1933 – where Neruda was posted as consul and where Lorca was attending the Latin American première of his play, *Bodas de sangre* (Blood Wedding). They were reunited the following year in Madrid. Spain was the turning point. I do not believe, however, that Neruda was politically committed as early as 1934, as some critics have insisted. He was undoubtedly close to Communist poet friends in Madrid, especially the Spaniard Rafael Alberti and the Argentinian Raúl González Tuñón. He was unquestionably influenced by his passion for his new lover and future second wife, Delia del Carril (20 years his senior) – an Argentinian Communist aristocrat and talented painter who had studied with Fernand Léger in Paris. Yet just a year earlier, in 1933, in one of the many telling letters he wrote back from the Far East to the Argentinian critic, Héctor Eandi, Neruda had declared: " ... odio al arte proletario, proletarizante ... [y a la] invasión de odas a Moscú, trenes blindados, etc ... Yo sigo escribiendo sobre sueños" (I hate proletarian, proletarianizing arte ... [and] the invasion of odes to Moscow, tanks, etc ... I continue to write about dreams).[11] I cannot concur with Hernán Loyola's claims that several of the poems in *Residencia en la tierra* bear the hallmarks of Neruda's response to the brutally repressed miners' uprising in Asturias, northern Spain, in October 1934. They are much more about personal bitterness: in particular, his unhappy first marriage and the sickness of Neruda's only child, a daughter, Malva Marina, born with hydrocephaly in Madrid. The winter in these poems is not a political one but the winter in his heart.

What is certain is that the fascist uprising in July 1936 and Lorca's murder the following month provoked a dramatic transformation in Neruda's work, from the anguished, inward-looking verse of the *Veinte poemas* and the first *Residencia* to poems as social and political weapons. Neruda himself explicitly plays out this metamorphosis in one of his greatest poems – "Explico algunas cosas" (Let Me Explain a Few Things), from the third volume of *Residencia*, known as *España en el corazón* (Spain in My Heart):

> Preguntaréis: Y dónde están las lilas?
> Y la metafísica cubierta de amapolas?
> Y la lluvia que a menudo golpeaba
> sus palabras llenándolas
> de agujeros y pájaros?

---

[11] Letter from Pablo Neruda to Héctor Ignacio Eandi dated February 17, 1933. See *Pablo Neruda, Héctor Eandi: Correspondencia durante Residencia en la tierra*, ed. Margarita Aguirre (Buenos Aires: Editorial Sudamericana, 1980).

(You will ask: So where are the lilacs,/ where is the metaphysics blanketed in poppies?/and the rain that sometimes lashed/ his words, filling them/ with holes and birds?)[12]

Having separated from Maruca, Neruda returned to Chile with Delia in 1937. Two years later, he was back in Europe to save the lives of more than 2,000 Spanish refugees fleeing Franco's oppression by shipping them out on the *Winnipeg* from Bordeaux to Valparaíso in Chile. Some of the children stepping off the boat in Valparaíso on September 3, 1939 – the day the Second World War broke out back in Europe – would later become leading cultural, intellectual, and industrial figures in Chile. They included the painters Roser Bru and José Balmes; the historian and film director Leopoldo Castedo; the playwright José Ricardo Morales; the graphic designer Mauricio Amster; and the pianist Diana Pey Castedo and her son, Víctor Pey, the future industrialist who would return the favor by harboring Neruda during part of his remarkable year underground in Chile in the late 1940s.

At the beginning of that decade Neruda was posted as consul to Mexico City. Here, he made both friends and enemies. He drew close to the three great Mexican muralists (Diego Rivera, José Clemente Orozco, and David Alfaro Siqueiros) and fell out calamitously with Octavio Paz (while Neruda became increasingly Stalinist, Paz moved in the other direction politically). He also received the news that his daughter, Malva Marina, had died in Holland at the age of only eight. On his way back to Chile in 1943, he visited the Incan fortress of Machu Picchu in the Peruvian Andes. The long poem this experience inspired, *Alturas de Macchu Picchu* (Heights of Machu Picchu), did not merely relay his thrill at communing with his pre-Columbian forebears. He was also, in John Felstiner's view, connecting history with nature, "seeking a garden, a lost Eden like his wooded, flowery childhood."[13] Curiously, Neruda was appointed a senator for the desert region of northern Chile in 1945 a few months *before* he officially joined the Communist Party. Both were key events. The first brought him into close contact with miners and other workers. And, as he wrote in the short poem, "A mi Partido" (To My Party), the formal political allegiance was an act of brotherhood ("You've made me indestructible because I no longer end in myself") – another determined flight from the loneliness of his years in the Far East and the self-obsession of his early books.

There followed what Neruda would later call his "year of blind rats." It began in January 1948, when he was forced to flee into hiding after standing

[12] Neruda, *Tercera residencia* (Buenos Aires: Losada, 1976), 47.
[13] John Felstiner, *Can Poetry Save the Earth?* (New Haven, CT: Yale University Press, 2009), 199.

up in the Senate and condemning the treachery of Chile's President, Gabriel González Videla, for outlawing the very Communist Party which had helped him achieve power. Over the next few months, Neruda and Delia were shepherded, sometimes at the dead of night, from one safe house to another within Chile to elude the authorities. Neruda eventually escaped across the Andes on horseback into Argentina in February 1949.[14] Over the next three years, Neruda performed an intricate juggling act in Europe between Delia and his new mistress, Matilde Urrutia, a Chilean singer. In 1950, two clandestine editions came out, in Mexico and Chile, of his enormous new epic volume, *Canto General* (General Song,) much of which he had composed while living underground. Indeed, it is one of the great paradoxes in world literature that such an expansive book – in terms of geography and chronology – could be written by a poet concealed in confined spaces with little free time.

Canto general is Neruda's vast emotional response to, and celebration of, Latin America: past, present, and future. But it is also a book about treachery: both the historical betrayal of pre-Columbian cultures by the Conquistadors and his own personal betrayal at the hands of President González Videla. The epic and the personal elements of *Canto general* do not always hold together smoothly. But when they do, they offer us broad sweeps of breathtaking beauty. In sections like "El gran océano" (The Great Ocean), as Jaime Concha has put it, "the physical, the biological, the geographical and the anthropological are integrated and merge in a choral, symphonic text … There are few instances in contemporary poetry of such a close intimacy being forged between man and cosmos").[15] Two years later, Neruda published a very different collection, *Los versos del capitán* (The Captain's Verses) in Naples – anonymously, because these intimate, erotically charged poems were written to Matilde and he did not want to hurt Delia. Many, like "La noche en la isla" (Night on the Island) and "Tus manos" (Your Hands), are poignant, tender, and melodious. Yet others, such as "El desvío" (One False Step), are fueled by the ferocity of jealousy.

Neruda's next volume, *Las uvas y el viento* (The Grapes and the Wind), published in 1954, is one of the most uneven books ever written by a great poet. The book is, in essence, a chronicle of Neruda's twin passions at the time: the reconstruction of the Soviet bloc nations from the rubble of the Second World War and his love for Matilde. Much of *Las uvas y el viento* strives too hard, and too clumsily, to give voice to Neruda's political

---

[14] Pablo Larraín recently dramatized this remarkable period of the poet's life in his widely acclaimed film, *Neruda* (2016).
[15] Jaime Concha, *Cantalao*, 1.1 (2013): 47.

solidarity with his European comrades. Yet there are jewels even in this book: poems to Capri and to his great Spanish poet friend Miguel Hernández, who had died of tuberculosis in Franco's jails in 1942. And he expresses his yearning for his homeland with limpid simplicity in "Cuando de Chile":

> Oh Chile, largo pétalo
> de mar y vino y nieve,
> ay cuándo
> ay cuándo y cuándo
> ay cuándo
> me encontraré contigo . . .

> (Oh Chile, long petal/ of sea and wine and snow,/ when,/ when,/ when/ will I see you again . . .)[16]

In the mid-1950s Neruda changed tone once more and published four volumes of odes: the *Elementary Odes* (1954), *New Elementary Odes* (1956), the *Third Book of Odes* (1957), and *Voyages and Homecomings* (1959). At their best, these are exquisite gems, making the ordinary appear extraordinary. Neruda's enthusiasm is irresistibly contagious. We enjoy the world anew through his eyes: a simple artichoke is seen as a soldier, wrapped in armor and ready for battle; an onion is "more beautiful than a bird/ with blinding feathers." Just occasionally, the odes feel underworked. But mostly, they are a humanist's magical songs to friends, enemies, women, the natural world, love and poetry itself. Some are overtly political, condemning North American military aggression in Korea or U.S. appropriation of much of the Chilean copper industry. There are unexpectedly darker moments, as in the otherwise deliciously whimsical "Ode to My Suit," where he suddenly speculates that "a bullet from the enemy/ will stain you with my blood." But in general, the tone is light. Indeed, the first few lines of "Ode to Joy" – "It merely happens/ that I'm happy" – are an almost conscious rebuttal of the celebrated first line from "Walking Around" from *Residencia en la tierra* nearly two decades earlier, "It so happens I'm tired of being a man." One exhilarating ode, to the "Names of Venezuela," illustrates Neruda's love of the music of words. When the Spanish poet Gabriel Celaya approached both Neruda and Lorca in Madrid in the 1930s seeking advice on the same poem, Lorca made some general comments on word meaning, whereas Neruda scrupulously praised or criticized the sounds. It is odd, then, that Neruda's friend, Aída Figueroa, told me: "Pablo was a very charming

---

[16] From "Cuando de Chile" (When Chile?) in *Los versos del capitán* (Naples: Imprenta L'Arte Tipografica, 1952)

man ... The only thing he didn't have was an ear for music. He could hear the sounds of birds, of people's words. But not music."[17]

Interspersed in the series of books of odes is the delightful *Estravagario*, published in 1958. Much of it was written in the wake of the Khrushchev revelations at the twentieth Soviet Communist Party Congress in February 1956 and the Soviet invasion of Budapest in November the same year, both of which certainly shook Neruda. He did not say so directly, however. His doubts emerge in playful self-questioning. In "Sobre mi mala educación" (On My Bad Upbringing), he mocks his own social maladroitness (he is jealous of the natural ease of fish, guests of the sea but always immaculately dressed). Nevertheless, Robert Pring-Mill rightly pointed to *Estravagario* as marking the beginning of an autumnal period in Neruda's work. The book does lace darkness with the humor. The great poem, "El miedo" (Fear), expresses the poet's difficulty in living with himself and up to others' expectations:

> Todos pican mi poesía
> con invencibles tenedores
> buscando, sin duda, una mosca,
> Tengo miedo.
>
> Tengo miedo de todo el mundo,
> del agua fría, de la muerte ...
>
> Por eso en estos cortos días
> no voy a tomarlos en cuenta,
> voy a abrirme y voy a encerrarme
> con mi más pérfido enemigo,
> Pablo Neruda.
>
> (Everyone picks at my poetry/ with unbreakable forks,/ looking, no doubt, for a fly./ I'm afraid./ I'm afraid of everyone,/ of cold water, of death ... / That's why, on these short days,/ I'm not going to listen,/ I'm going to pen myself up/ and lock myself away/ with my most perfidious enemy,/ Pablo Neruda.)[18]

Yet despite his doubts, Neruda is fundamentally content. As he writes in "El perezoso" (Lazybones):

> Mi casa tiene mar y tierra,
> mi mujer tiene grandes ojos
> color de avellana silvestre,
> cuando viene la noche el mar

---

[17] Adam Feinstein, *Pablo Neruda: A Passion for Life* (London: Bloomsbury, 2013), 406.
[18] From "El miedo" (Fear) in *Estravagario* (Buenos Aires: Losada, 1958)

se viste de blanco y de verde
y luego la luna en la espuma
sueña como novia marina.
No quiero cambiar de planeta.

(My house has sea and land,/ my wife has big eyes/ the colour of wild hazel-
nuts./ When night falls, the sea/ dresses up in white and green/ and the moon in
the foam/ dreams like a marine bridge./ I don't want to change planets.)[19]

By now, Neruda and Delia had separated definitively and the poet was living
in quiet domesticity with Matilde. Delia had been the cultural and political
influence on Neruda. Matilde was the disciplinarian. Indeed, while Delia had
frequently teased him about his overuse of the word "raíces" (roots), he
employed it more than ever in his verse after his separation from her, as if to
reinforce his return to his origins in his new life with Matilde, the only
Chilean of his three wives. He dedicated another entire book to her in
1959: the *Cien sonetos de amor* (One Hundred Love Sonnets). Many of
these are intensely physical. In Sonnet 8, he writes: "In your embrace, I
embrace what exists." How different from the celebrated Poem 15 of the
Veinte poemas, in which, in his protracted postadolescence, he had craved
his lover's silence "because it is as if you are absent."

Not everything was running smoothly. Although Neruda supported Fidel
Castro's rebellion in Cuba and, in 1960, Havana published the first edition of
Canción de gesta (Protest Song), his collection dedicated to the Revolution,
the Cubans were outraged when he accepted an invitation to attend the PEN
Club writers' congress in New York six years later – and stopped off in Lima
on his way back home to receive an award from Peru's President Belaúnde
Terry, an opponent of the Castro regime. Most of Cuba's leading writers
signed an open letter in August 1966 condemning Neruda as a traitor to the
Left. Neruda was appalled and refused ever to return to the island. Several of
the signatories to the letter, including Roberto Fernández Retamar and
Ambrosio Fornet, have told me in Havana that they regretted the incident
and ascribed it to differences between the Cuban and Chilean Communist
Parties (one favoring the guerrilla route to revolution, the other not). Yet
Fornet said: "It was such a curious affair, because all of us who took part in
that letter were unconditional admirers of Neruda. But we thought: How
could Neruda, our great Communist hero, who had written a song to Stalin,
do such a thing?"[20] Astonishingly, *Canción de gesta* was not reprinted in
Havana until 2010.

[19] From "El perezoso" (Lazy.bones) in *Estravagario* (Buenos Aires: Losada, 1958)
[20] Ambrosio Fornet, in conversation with Adam Feinstein in Havana, Cuba, May 2011.

Pablo Neruda

The Soviet crushing of the Prague Spring in 1968 "fell on my head like a stone," Neruda wrote in a poem not long afterwards.[21] But he still felt unable to condemn Moscow publicly. Two years later, there was a new private upheaval: he fell passionately in love with his wife's niece, Alicia Urrutia. In a bid to save his marriage, Neruda asked President Salvador Allende – who in 1970 had become the world's first democratically elected Marxist head of state – to send him to Paris as Chilean Ambassador. His next book, *La espada encendida* (The Flaming Sword), which appears to be a postapocalyptic epic of spiritual and sexual renewal between Rhodo and Rosía after the expulsion of man from Paradise, is actually a retelling, in explicit terms, of his feelings for Alicia.

By now, Neruda was ill with cancer. Once in France, nevertheless, he fulfilled his ambassadorial functions – more or less. He and President Georges Pompidou spent most of a three-hour meeting discussing Baudelaire's poetry instead of renegotiating Chile's external debt.[22] In October 1971, Neruda was awarded the Nobel Prize for Literature. But the following year, illness forced him to return to Chile. He found his homeland in the grip of political and economic turmoil, with Allende's government threatened by forces both within and outside Chile, most notably the United States. The last book published in his lifetime – the largely polemic *Incitación al nixonocidio y alabanza de la revolución chilena* (Incitement to Nixonicide and Praise for the Chilean Revolution) – should be seen as part of Neruda's contribution to Unidad Popular's campaign in the March 1973 congressional elections in Chile. Within six months, Allende's government was toppled by Augusto Pinochet's brutal military coup on September 11. When soldiers raided Neruda's home at Isla Negra a few days later, he told them: "Look around you – the only thing of danger here is poetry." But poetry could not rescue Chile from fascism, just as it had not rescued Spain in 1936. Nor could it save Pablo Neruda himself. He died on September 23, 1973. His funeral in Santiago two days later turned into the first public protest against the military junta.

Eight books he had intended to leave to the world as a seventieth birthday present – seven collections of poems and his memoirs – were published posthumously in Buenos Aires in 1974. The memoirs, *Confieso que he vivido* (I Confess that I've Lived),[23] are gloriously life-affirming, if not entirely reliable. The seven collections of poems contain some of Neruda's most intensely lyrical verse. They are filled with awareness of physical

[21] "1968," in *Fin de mundo* (Buenos Aires: Losada, 1969).
[22] This was confirmed to me by the Mexican writer Carlos Fuentes.
[23] Published in English as *Memoirs* (London: Souvenir Press, 2004).

deterioration, fear of death, and a quest for peace and solitude. *Jardín de invierno* (Winter Garden) contains the hauntingly beautiful "Un perro ha muerto" (My Dog Has Died). The *Libro de las preguntas* (Book of Questions) startles with couplets spiced with childish, sometimes surreal mischief:

> Dime, la rosa está desnuda,
> o sólo tiene ese vestido?
> Que pensarán de mi sombrero
> en cien años, los polacos?

> (Tell me, is the rose naked,/ or is that its only dress?/ What will the Poles think/ of my hat, in a hundred years?)[24]

Perhaps the last poem he ever wrote was a profoundly moving love poem to Matilde, concluding:

> Fue tan bello vivir
> cuando vivías!

> El mundo es más azul y más terrestre
> de noche, cuando duermo
> enorme, adentro de tus breves manos.

> (It was so beautiful to live/ when you were alive./ The world is more blue and more earthy/ at night, when I sleep/ enormous, within your tiny hands.)[25]

In 2011 Neruda's driver, Manuel Araya, came out with claims that the poet was murdered in hospital with an injection in the stomach by Pinochet's henchmen to prevent him from leaving Chile for exile in Mexico. In other circumstances, perhaps, Neruda, who was a fanatical devotee of crime novels, might have been intrigued. His body was exhumed in April 2013 and underwent three years of forensic tests in four countries. He was reburied beside Matilde at Isla Negra in April 2016, after the scientists could find no convincing evidence of poisoning. In a dramatic new development in October 2017, however, an international team of forensic scientists meeting in Santiago unanimously rejected the official cause of Neruda's death, from cancer, and announced that they would be analyzing mysterious bacteria discovered in his remains, with the results of these new tests due within a year. Neruda's surviving family members are divided on the theory. One nephew, Rodolfo Reyes, is convinced that the

[24] From *Libro de las preguntas* (Buenos Aires: Losada, 1974)
[25] From "Final" (The End) in *El mar y las campanas* (The Sea and the Bells), 1974.

poet was poisoned, while another nephew, Bernardo Reyes, condemns the claims as sensationalist.[26]

Charles Tomlinson once wrote that Neruda "does not trust his readers."[27] I strongly disagree. Like Walt Whitman, one of his literary heroes, Neruda frequently addresses the reader as an equal, as someone who feels what Edward Hirsch has termed "the same throb of life."[28] Some of Neruda's poetry remains unrivaled in the Spanish language. Inevitably, with nearly sixty books to his name, there is unevenness. But Neruda sought to renew and enrich himself in each new collection. And, as his younger compatriot, Nicanor Parra, so memorably put it: "The Andes are also uneven."[29]

[26] See www.theguardian.com/books/2017/oct/23/pablo-neruda-experts-say-official-cause-of-death-does-not-reflect-reality (last accessed November 9, 2017)
[27] Charles Tomlinson, "Latin America Betrayed," *Times Literary Supplement*, June 28, 1991.
[28] Edward Hirsch, *How to Read a Poem* (Durham, NC: Harcourt, 1999).
[29] Nicanor Parra, *Discursos* (Santiago: Nascimiento, 1962), 9–48.

10

CHARLES A. PERRONE

Carlos Drummond de Andrade

One of the joys of reading Brazilian literature is to savor the poetry of Carlos Drummond de Andrade (1902–1987). Nearly unanimously considered Brazil's greatest poet, he left a vast poetical oeuvre of considerable thematic and stylistic variety, demonstrating longevity, versatility, and diversified aesthetic charm. He appealed to connoisseurs of *belles-lettres* and the broader reading public alike. In the pantheon of Western poetry, Drummond de Andrade merits a place alongside the greatest poets of Portugal – the giant Luis de Camões (d. 1580) and the modernist Fernando Pessoa (d. 1935) – as well as the most highly regarded Spanish American poets – Pablo Neruda, César Vallejo, Octavio Paz. Critical studies of Drummond de Andrade's life and work are plentiful; besides hundreds of articles, two or more related books have appeared *per annum* since c. 1960, mostly in Portuguese and primarily regarding his first thirty-five years of production. Quantifying his poetic output depends on the inclusion, or not, of chapbooks and lesser circumstantial or news-related items in the count. In his first collected poems (*Reunião*, 1969) ten books were credited; there were nineteen in an updated collection (1983), a second edition of which (1986) counted twenty-three.[1] It behooves anyone who desires to grasp the profile of Drummond de Andrade the poet to prefer a multilateral approach.

The opening salvo of Drummond de Andrade's modestly titled debut book, *Alguma Poesia* (Some Poetry, 1930), was "Poema de Sete Faces." This provocative "Poem of Seven Faces" fast became a signature composition. With its textual structure and historical importance, it authorizes a

---

[1] Andrade, Carlos Drummond de, *Reunião: 10 livros de poesia* (Rio de Janeiro: José Olympio, 1969); *Nova reunião: 19 livros de poesia* (Rio de Janeiro: José Olympio, 1983), 3rd expanded ed. 1986. Drummond de Andrade also published ten collections of memoirs and journalistic "chronicles" (*crônicas*), short prose pieces, anecdotal narratives, or personal commentary on current events or behavior. A complete account of editorial history is provided by Jon Tolman, "Carlos Drummond de Andrade," in *Brazilian Writers*, ed. Monica Rector (Detroit, MI: Gale, 2005), 166–83.

heptagonal organization of critical understanding of Drummond de Andrade's lyrical enterprise. On a chronological plane, his production spans seven decades: from the 1920s, when the recent college graduate agitated in upstart arts journals, to the 1980s, when the venerable dean of national poetry passed away leaving a final book to appear posthumously as *Farewell* (1996). In terms of literary history, each of the seven stanzas of the inaugural "Seven-sided poem" can be seen to reflect an aspect of the march of modern Brazilian poetry.[2] On the transnational front, a keen comparatist compared six translations of the poem into English aiming to take advantage of the best of each to distill a seventh.[3] The English-language versions of Drummond de Andrade's poetry can be grouped into seven clusters: in the 1960s John Nist issued a volume with 63 items;[4] Elizabeth Bishop's historic 1972 anthology of Brazilian poetry has a strong section on Drummond de Andrade;[5] Virgínia Araújo translated 54 poems in a theoretically framed collection done in 1980;[6] Thomas Colchie and Mark Strand edited a substantial selection (41) for a major house not long before Drummond de Andrade died;[7] and the leading translator of Portuguese-language poetry, Richard Zenith, published the most complete and best presented collection in 2015 with the felicitous title *Multitudinous Heart*.[8] The sixth and seventh groups would be translated poems appearing, respectively, in periodicals (including blogs) and other anthologies of Brazilian or Latin American poetry at both academic and trade publishers.

[2] See Charles A. Perrone, *Seven Faces: Brazilian Poetry since Modernism* (Durham, NC: Duke University Press, 1996),13–17, and notes therein for further sources in English and Portuguese.

[3] Anne Connor presented "Lost in Translation or *Poema de Sete Traduções*: A Study of 'Poema de Sete Faces' by Carlos Drummond de Andrade" at the Mid-America Conference on Hispanic Literature, University of Kansas, October 5, 2001. She has updated the study as "Poema de Sete+ Traduções: A Study of Carlos Drummond de Andrade's 'Poema de Sete Faces,'" *Delos: A Journal of Translation and World Literature* 32 (2017): 40–59.

[4] *In the Middle of the Road: Selected Poems of Carlos Drummond de Andrade*, trans. and intro John Nist (Tucson, AZ: University of Arizona Press, 1965).

[5] *An Anthology of Twentieth-Century Brazilian Poetry*, ed. Elizabeth Bishop and Emanuel Brasil (Middletown, CT: Wesleyan University Press, 1972).

[6] *The Minus Sign: Selected Poems from the* Antologia Poética, trans. and introduction Virgínia Araújo (Redding Ridge, CT: Black Swan, 1980; Manchester, UK: Carcanet, 1981).

[7] *Travelling in the Family: Selected Poems of Carlos Drummond de Andrade*, ed. Thomas Colchie and Mark Strand (New York, NY: Random House, 1986). An appendix by John Gledson comprises the most detailed and useful evaluation of these first four groups of translations; see *Influências e impasses: Drummond e alguns contemporâneos* (São Paulo: Companhia das Letras, 2003), 281–300.

[8] Carlos Drummond de Andrade, *Multitudinous Heart: Selected Poems*, trans. and intro. Richard Zenith (New York, NY: Farrar Straus Giroux, 2015).

As for poetic space, one can identify seven concentric domains of Drummond de Andrade's poetry: his family farm; the adjacent hometown; his native state of Minas Gerais; his adopted city of work and residence, Rio de Janeiro; the country of Brazil at large; the Americas; and the Western world as a whole. As far as lyric selves are concerned, one can hear seven fundamental voices (*personae*) emerge and evolve: first there was a modernist rebel; then a shy chap appeared to introspect; a third man preoccupied himself with family relations; a fourth citizen voiced profound social sympathies; number five was a metaphysician of sorts pondering words themselves; the penultimate came to sing the body, even erotically; and the seventh was an elder statesman contemplating it all. Across time, space, sense, and sentiment, then, sevens do obtain meaningfully.

As coherent or useful as such a taxonomy may be, the poet's own self-presentation somewhat confounds the heptatonic scale, the scheme of seven. Upon retirement from his public-service job (1962), Drummond de Andrade himself edited an anthology of his verse.[9] Instead of following a conventional chronological sequence of selections from each book, the author proceeded transtemporally to represent the scope of his work, choosing poems from each of his collections to distribute in nine thematic divisions. This multi-part self-characterization continues to reflect the principal lines of Drummond de Andrade's poetry even after the publication of the anthology. The poet called his operators "points of departure" or "materials." Each section had a subtitle: 1) the individual ("A Totally Twisted Self"); 2) the homeland ("A Province: This One"); 3) the family ("The Family I Gave Myself"); 4) friends ("Singing of Friends"); 5) social impact ("Better-Bitter Love"); 6) knowledge of love ("One Two Jousts"); 7) lyric itself ("Contemplated Poetry"); 8) playful exercises ("In the Square of Invitations"); and 9) a vision of, or attempt at, existence ("Efforts at Exploration and Interpretation of Being-in-the-World"). This auto-anthology opens, no surprise, with the landmark "Poem of Seven Faces." As Drummond de Andrade acknowledges, the nine departments are imprecise and overlap (which would allow collapsing a couple to have a total of seven). To be sure, any chronologically constrained classification or categorization of his poetry – as with any complex and prolific verse-maker – has hazards and traps, especially with regard to development over time, as some stylistic constants traverse the whole of his work and other aspects recur in loosely defined phases of his production.

Caveats in mind, Drummond de Andrade's poetic trajectory can be traced in broad strokes. In the 1920s, Brazilian *modernistas* sought to liberate poetry

---

[9] Andrade, Carlos Drummond de, *Antologia poética* (Rio de Janeiro: Editora do Autor, 1962).

from lingering constraints of Parnassianism and Symbolism. They combatted conservative practices by infusing verse with local awareness, including folk-life, and by revitalizing lyric through application of avant-garde techniques. Perhaps more than any other poet, Drummond de Andrade crystalized aims of *modernismo* to institute newness and to authenticate the national brand of Portuguese, while forging a personal style with universal scope. Drummond de Andrade cleared the "sacred air" of poetry by unseating the notion of "noble" thematics in favor of a more open approach. His earliest production (1930s) – often on anti-normative vanguard paths – is direct, colloquial, and experiential. Sarcastic and humorous tones abound within a somewhat individualistic focus on the quotidian. There are different perspectives in the next stage (1940s) as Drummond de Andrade explores the physical and human spheres. He ponders existential questions within the context of community, and historical events move him. His own anguish is a reflection of a generalized crisis of consciousness. In a third phase (1950s) the intimate and the social are incorporated into all-encompassing considerations of humanity and the world. Formal rigidity, rarified vocabulary, and elevated diction govern this contemplative and speculative poetry. The development of Drummond de Andrade's verse from the 1930s to the 1950s reveals a process of opening and expansion, an unfolding that can be described via a tripartite metaphor of sight and attitude. The dominant lyric self of the early poetry is ironic yet timid; he is there to observe but remains uninvolved, hardly surpassing his own limits. As the poetic "I" begins to confront his surroundings, he looks more intently at manifestations of the real. As the struggles of others are seen and internalized, existential musings lead to a project of encounter. In Drummond de Andrade's midlife stage, his textual self observes, looks at, and contemplates objects and subjects in search of essences or the roots of contradictions. Having attained such scope and level, Drummond de Andrade's speakers primarily examine anew (in books 1967 ff.) provincial origins. Later works – reflecting the predominance of paradigms over temporal progression in Drummond de Andrade's poetry – are permeated by a vigorous irony characteristic of his early verse. Naturally, with subdivisions (especially of the latter one), these "stages" or "phases," can also number seven.

Drummond de Andrade is a thoroughly modern poet capable of finding inspiration in any source or combination of elements, and of using them forcefully. He can mold everyday phenomena into poetic frames through anecdotes or articulations of utopian aspirations. Chronos (time) is his prime material passim. Critics have marveled at his ability to strike a balance between poles: from the clear, light, vulgar, straightforward to the obscure, heavy, lofty, and evocative. Comfortable with the concrete and the abstract alike, Drummond de Andrade finds linguistic structures apt for particular situations to craft poetry of discovery, be it in a rural past with mytho-mental dimensions or in the context of current relationships and modern societal values. Literary findings are not intended as truths or absolutes. Soon before his passing, Drummond de Andrade wrote: "The problem is not inventing./ It is being invented/ hour after hour and our convincing edition/ never being ready." In all his editions, a fundamental skepticism recurs. Struggles with relativism and anguish do not, however, lead to nihilism or cynicism. The multifaceted lyrical universe of Drummond de Andrade is secular at bottom; his reflections on essences and being-in-the-world do not often invoke God or notions of divinity. Over the decades, a basic dialectic between introspection and external factors remains in operation. Conveyance of disquiet may unveil emblematic poetic selves threatened by technology or by a hostile world. Drummond de Andrade seeks to apprehend a profound sense of unresolved difference and change that may affect – once again to invoke the seal of seven – the individual, the family, other affective relationships, coworkers, society at large, the nation, and mankind. When he seems to be disclosing personal positions, well-wrought devices mollify the potential for self-indulgence or confessionalism, though somewhat less so in his last two decades. Throughout, expressing feelings of oppression relates to crises in modern civilization in a view of the human condition. Great poets writing about themselves, T. S. Eliot opined, are writing about their times. In Drummond de Andrade's poetry, the intersections of private, public, and transcendent planes signal his greatness.

A feature of particular importance in assessments of Drummond de Andrade is his perspicuous attention to lexicon and expressive means. The young poet had shown his discontent by mocking exhausted values and decayed traditions, even facile commonplaces of nationalistic literature. As his *modus operandi* evolved, Drummond de Andrade expanded his pursuit of nuances, keywords, the secrets of language, and its hidden potentials. Some of his most outstanding texts invoke a metaliterary imperative to ponder words themselves and *poiesis*, the making of poetry. This urge to express may have to negotiate with the imperfections of language, with the incommunicable. In each of his several poematic approaches, there is a corresponding questioning of verbal instruments and/or the very purpose of lyric. The modernist period in Western culture has been characterized as the age of criticism. Drummond de Andrade's verse is quite self-conscious, and he is a constant critic of his own art. After the waning of *modernismo* qua movement in Brazil, its most complete poet would aver (1953): "And how boring it's become to be modern/ Now I shall be eternal."

In the interplay of sound, sense, and structuration, Drummond de Andrade's foremost interest is in meaning. Conceptual dimensions are generally more important than shape or sonority. Idea, conceit, and sometimes occurrence, overshadow pure imagery or symbolism, though words can surely be deployed and combined in unusual and provocative ways. Melopeia (melodious word formation) is not particularly robust. The notable external formal variety in Drummond de Andrade's repertory spans everything from minimalist epigrams to lengthy prose poems, from absolutely free verse to strictly metrified forms. Drummond de Andrade cultivated sonnet, ode, ballad, and elegy. If the poetry sometimes seems overly accessible, seemingly spontaneous airs may carry subtleties or surprises, i.e. simplicity may be deceptive or even duplicitous.

An imperative of challenge and provocation that characterizes Drummond de Andrade is evident in a pair of memorable selections from his first book. "In the Middle of the Road" is composed of ten simple lines. The (anti-) lyric "I" repeatedly states that "there was a stone in the middle of the road" and utters in stark, unadorned fashion that his "fatigued retinas" will never forget that. Sheer mockery? Designed to baffle? Early readers were puzzled; some staid critics laughing at the author, even suggesting that the poem might be a sign of schizophrenia or psychosis. So extended was the controversy that Drummond de Andrade, years later, was able to assemble a book consisting solely of commentaries and critiques of the neoteric set of verses. Strange as it may be, the poem can be interpreted as a sign of monotony in the human condition or as a drama of obsession (with ideas). It may be alluding to all impediments, especially those related to self-fulfillment or literary norms. "In the Middle of the Road" also qualifies as a premonition of the obtuse, hermetic mode of some of Drummond de Andrade's subsequent poetry.

The aforementioned "Poem of Seven Faces" is disjunct on the surface. The first lines relay senses of repudiation, marginality, and awkwardness that inform Drummond de Andrade's early work and never completely vanish: "When I was born, a crooked angel/ one of those who live in shadows/ said: Go on, Carlos! be *gauche* in life." Such is the initial presentation of a "twisted self" who inhabits Drummond de Andrade's poetic world. The penultimate strophe of the seven-stanza poem alludes to a well-known neoclassical Brazilian poem to promote aspects of a new poetics: "World world world so vast/ If my name were Henry the Last/ it would be a rhyme, not a solution."[10] Here Drummond de Andrade impugns rhyme and meter as technical formalities that restrict expressive plenitude. Such advocacy for artistic freedom is formulated anew via rhyme in "Consideration of the

---

[10] Translations are the author's, except here where Mike Gonzalez's and David Treece's are used. In *The Gathering of Voices: The Contemporary Poetry of Latin America* (London: Verso, 1992), 72, Gonzalez and Treece reflect the original rhyme of *mundo-Raimundo* and its effective semanteme of being king (of the world).

Poem" (1945); the poet affirms that he will not rhyme *sono* (slumber) with "the uncorresponding word" *outono* (autumn) but rather with "the word flesh/ or any other, for all are good for me." Such statements should be taken as situational, for, despite the enthusiastic prevalence of free verse in Drummond de Andrade's early years, he otherwise utilized all manners of rhyme (verse-initial, verse-final, horizontal, vertical, diagonal, internal), especially in his middle years.

As for nationalistic *modernismo*, the Drummond de Andrade of 1930 penned a numbered series of lyrical snapshots focused on his native state of Minas Gerais yet scarcely regionalist. A concluding mini-joke-poem even pokes fun at geo-ethnic fashion: "It is necessary to make a poem about Bahia ... / But I've never been there." The promotion of homegrown matter was also the object of irony in "I Have Been Brazilian Too": "I learned that nationalism is a virtue/ But there comes a time when the bars close/ and all virtues are denied." Resistance to in-vogue preferences can also be read between such lines as "A garden, hardly Brazilian ... but so lovely." An all-encompassing attitude structures "National Anthem" (in *Brejo das Almas* [Marsh of souls, 1934]); it begins in a typically promotional *modernista* gesture – "We must discover Brazil!" – only to declare, near the end of an exercise in skepticism: "We must, we must forget Brazil!" This recourse to distancing is a good measure of Drummond de Andrade's independence, of his incessant quest for revelations beyond received wisdom and set frames of reference.

The so-called "social phase" of Drummond de Andrade's poetry is defined by attitudinal and ideological shifts. The titles of his third and fourth collections clearly indicate in what directions the poet moved. While *Sentimento do mundo* (Feeling of the World; 1940) broadened horizons, *A rosa do povo* (The Rose of the People, 1945) became Drummond de Andrade's most popular book, having attracted more critical attention than any other. Therein, confidential worries and family matters are now linked to the outside world, as speakers explore such issues as mechanization, exploitation, and reification. The wry, restless personae give way to voices troubled for the Other and by farther-reaching problems of politics, society, history. Within this orientation, one of Drummond de Andrade's masterpieces is "Song for that man of the people, Charlie Chaplin," as translated by Pontiero.[11] Chaplin brilliantly portrayed the frustrations and incongruities of modern urban life. Drummond de Andrade paid homage to that cinematographic genius and his reverberations in a long (226 lines) and Whitmanesque piece

---

[11] Giovanni Pontiero, trans. and introduction, "Song for that man of the people, Charlie Chaplin," *New Directions* 39 (1979), 51 ff.

that speaks for the "abandoned, pariahs, failures, downtrodden." Drummond de Andrade's poetry of the 1940s has an existential *raison d'être* shaped by interaction and giving. The individual now operates with present imperatives: ethics, solidarity with the oppressed, and internationalism. A symptomatic poem is "Shoulders Bear the World" (1940), which establishes an urgent vantage – "Just life without mystifications" – together with "Hand in Hand," which conveys commitment: "I am shackled to life and I see my companions/ They may be taciturn but they nourish great hopes/ It is amongst them that I consider the enormity of reality." The forties were marked by the ravages of world war, and events clearly affected Drummond de Andrade's discourse in poems such as the "International Congress of Fear," "Elegy 1938," "Letter to Stalingrad," and "With the Russians in Berlin," which intone anti-fascist positions and socialist sympathies.

In the middle of the road of sociohistorical commotion, Drummond de Andrade composed two of his most powerful poems, "Residue," an enumeration of subjective and objective phenomena that illustrates the central principle of Drummond de Andrade's realm that is corrosion, and "Search for Poetry," a self-contained poetics. The latter speaks against making poetry of/from events, feelings, memories, thoughts. It proposes that those interested "penetrate quietly the kingdom of words" and contemplate the "thousands of secret faces under the neutral face" of each word. This plea might raise a question of contradiction, as so many of Drummond de Andrade's own poems derive from unrecommended sources. There is a bit of self-ironic commentary here, but occurrence, sentiment, recollection, and ideas are not really held to be, in themselves, ill-advised; what is unadvisable is direct use. Drummond de Andrade reminds us that unmediated happenings do not yield poetry; the true mission is to find linguistic tools to reformulate experience into viable art.

The next chapter in Drummond de Andrade's poetic career, beginning in the 1950s, is written with modified formal and thematic properties. The conversationally inflected and socially aware emphases of his *modernista* and *engagé* pages cede to contemporary neoclassical methods. Turning to the sonnet and other measured forms, the poet withdraws from the public square of events into an abode of philosophical tenor to reflect upon the self and the universe. This interpretative poetry is difficult to penetrate in comparison to earlier and later work. The book titles *Claro Enigma* (Clear Enigma; 1951) and *Fazendeiro do Ar* (Farmer of the Air; 1953) suggest the abstract focus of such endeavors, as do the names of poems such as "Being," "Between Being and Things," "The Contemplated Canvas," "Aspiration," "Dissolution" and "Contemplation on a Bench." This more "pure" poetry probes both carnal and psychic love, while ruminations on family and the past may prompt wonder about immortality or heredity as a cognitive category. The most critically acclaimed poem of this period (and, for some, of the Brazilian century) is "The Machine of the World," which alludes to classical content, notably Dante and Camões. Although this long lyric opens and closes on a stony road in Minas Gerais, personal accommodation and social situation are blended into a phenomenological totality with mythical and archetypical dimensions.

While poems of paradox and puzzlement are also present in *A vida passada a limpo* (A Clean Copy of Life; 1959), narrative modes and references to things at times bring to mind the more "realistic" poetry of earlier decades. Per its name, "Speculations Around the Word Man" would take verbo-ontological stances, yet the poem comprises nothing but questions, entirely lacking affirmations. This external structure is reminiscent of the much celebrated poem "José" (1942), a portrayal of setbacks, disillusionment, and potential resignation through a series of questions. For its part, the lengthy and digressive "To a Hotel under Demolition" is inspired by a real-life event and has unabashedly prosaic moments. At the end, however, the wandering poem finds unity in the metaphor of the inn; the lyric "I," he who has "lived and unlived" in the "Great Hotel of the World without management," finds himself to be "a secret guest of himself." Thus Drummond de Andrade balances narrative and lyrical imperatives, inward and outward thrusts, observation and contemplation.

The same year as his self-produced *Antologia poética*, Drummond de Andrade launched *Lição de Coisas* (Lesson of Things; 1962), which contains some material poetry. Two titles best represent the author's mixed style operating within strict binomial constraints. "The Bomb" is an extensive inquiry and counterweight to abstraction. It is composed of a series of statements about atomic explosive devices, the most intimidating invention of modern science and industry. Each line begins with "the bomb," save the last, in which "man" appears shrouded in hope that he "will destroy the bomb." This frightening lyric contrasts, but ultimately links, with the experimental "This is That," a calibrated composition made of ten numbered sets (I-X) of two-item lines. The pairs of words or neologisms result from lexical, morphological or semantic associations, e.g. "The facile the fossil/ the missle the fissil... the atom the atone... the chastity the castigate..." The concluding two lines have single items – "the bombix/ the pytx" – and connect the playful linguistic exercise to the theme of destruction. Once again philosophical, humanitarian, and creatively poetical motives blend and interpenetrate in Drummond de Andrade's poetry.

Boitempo (Oxtime) initiated a *memorialista* trilogy (1968, 1973, 1979) incorporating hundreds of items, almost all about the poet's background in

Minas Gerais. Drummond de Andrade set out to explore histories, places, and people of his childhood and adolescence. This project inherently created potential for confessionalism (self-indulgence, cathartic sentimentalism, autobiographical nostalgia), and for this reason many critics (and translators) have paid little attention to this senior verse. Yet some counter that Drummond de Andrade undertook this effort with the accrued benefits of his myriad poetic activities – modernist wrangling, committed verse, speculative divagations, metapoetics – and made poetic distance of the chronological separation from his subject matter. Detached enough to employ measures of levity and humor in his retrospection upon a parochial past, he included a few literarily self-conscious moments in the flow of recollection. There were returns to, and dramatizations of, the genesis of the brash "twisted self" of inconformity. If only about a tenth of the first set of poems of remembrance invoked Drummond de Andrade's conceptual muses, that mode did find continuation in contemporaneous volumes, e.g. *A Falta que Ama* (Loving Lack; 1968), *As impurezas do branco* (Impurities of White; 1973) and parts of *A Paixão Medida* (Measured Passion; 1980), which includes "Supposed Existence" specially translated by Gregory Rabassa (in Martins).[12] The elder bard published *Corpo* (Body; 1984), which examines multiple senses of the title word, including a side of the poet Claude Hulet saw in "Poem of Seven Faces," "a composition redolent with turgid sexuality."[13] Another of the posthumous books was the corporeally themed and explicit *O amor natural* (Natural Love, 1994), which completes one of the seven areas of operation in the poet's body of work.

The contributions of Drummond de Andrade to modern poetry can be measured in regional, national, hemispheric, and international terms. His iconoclastic role in Brazilian modernism developed into its most potent and linguistically flexible poetic arsenal. He reformulated academic verse as an idiomatic lyricism unique in its diversity of tones, depth of socio-psychological probing, and conceptual complexity. Drummond de Andrade's poetry effectively expressed multitudinous facets of the essential triad of mind-body-soul, and, following the orientational trope of this chapter, his imperatives involved seven vital topics: self-consciousness (awareness), change (metamorphosis), the mobility of feeling (sentiment), the multiplicity of being (human complexity), ethical imperatives (social concern), higher

---

[12] Wilson Martins, "Carlos Drummond de Andrade and the Heritage of *Modernismo*," *World Literature Today* 53.1 (1979), 16–19. For Rabassa translation, see 57.

[13] Claude Hulet, "Carlos Drummond de Andrade, the Romantic," in *Carlos Drummond de Andrade and His Generation*," ed. Frederick G. Williams and Sérgio Pachá (Santa Barbara, CA: Jorge de Sena Center-UCSB, 1986), 87.

inquiry (transcendence) and, most fundamentally, the instrument of attack, language itself.

Drummond de Andrade is a national institution in Brazil. Besides the enormous popularity of his prose, his poetry has been read and analyzed very widely, having profoundly influenced emerging and mature poets since the 1930s. On a related front, there are more than seventy musical settings of his poems; composers include the fellow modernist Heitor Villa Lobos and the contemporary stellar vocalist Milton Nascimento. Drummond de Andrade wrote numerous poems about his beloved Rio de Janeiro, where, among other homages, he was honored just before his death as the theme of the top samba school, Mangueira, a true sign of apotheosis. The municipality has erected a statue of him on Copacabana beach looking back at the city. As he had speculated in a postmodernist poem, Carlos Drummond de Andrade indeed ended up becoming eternal.

11

JASON WILSON

Octavio Paz

In his lifetime the Mexican poet and intellectual Octavio Paz (1914–1986) came to dominate the second half of the twentieth century. He rewrote the Mexican poetic tradition along avant-garde lines, setting up Ramón López Velarde and José Juan Tablada as founders. He became leader of a group of Mexican and Latin American poets, who shared his vision of poetry. He edited prestigious magazines that include *Plural* (1971–1976) and *Vuelta* (1976–1998). He won just about every literary prize from the Cervantes in 1981 to the Nobel Prize for Literature in 1990. To explore the reasons why he rose so high is also to ask whether, with his passing, this high reputation will survive. To appreciate his poetry is a subjective act conditioned by how well you know the work, and Octavio Paz is now saddled with his complete works in 15 volumes.[1]

---

[1] In 1949 Paz collected his work in *Libertad bajo palabra* (Mexico City: Fondo de Cultura Económica, 1949), and again in 1960 and 1968 (reprints FCE). His own selected poems appeared as *La centena (Poemas 1935–1968)* (Barcelona: Barral, 1968). In 1979 he collected his work as *Poemas (1935–1975)* (Barcelona: Seix Barral, 1979), from which, with *Árbol adentro* (Barcelona: Seix Barral, 1987), I cite. Another selected poems appeared as *Lo major de Octavio Paz: el fuego de cada día* (Barcelona: Seix Barral, 1986). He established his complete poems in two volumes, *Obra poética I (1935–1970)* (Mexico City: Fondo de Cultura Económica, 1997) and *Obra poética II (1969–1998)* (Mexico City: Fondo de Cultura Económica, 2004). Criticism is best surveyed in the wonderful annotated second edition of Hugo J. Verani, *Bibliografía crítica de Octavio Paz (1931–1998)* (Mexico City: Colegio Nacional, 1997), with a third edition promised. The best later critical studies include Tom Boll, *Octavio Paz and T. S. Eliot. Modern Poetry and the Translation of Influence* (London: Legenda, 2012;Hugo Verani,*Octavio Paz: el poema como caminata* (Mexico City: Fondo de Cultura Económica, 2013); Evodio Escalante, *Las sendas perdidas de Octavio Paz* (Mexico City: Ediciones sin nombre, 2013); Guillermo Sheridan, *Poeta con paisaje: ensayos sobre la vida de Octavio Paz* (Mexico City: Ediciones Era, 2004); Enrique Krauze, *Octavio Paz: el poeta y la Revolución* (Mexico City: Penguin Random House, Editorial México, 2014); and Jaime Perales Contreras, *Octavio Paz y su círculo intelectual* (Mexico City: Coyoacán, 2013). For a good, recent biography, see Christopher Dominguez Michael, *Octavio Paz en su siglo* (Mexico City, Aguilar, 2014). For a fine summary, see Nick Caistor, "Cien años de

Undoubtedly, Paz saw himself as a poet. If his work is a pyramid, then his poetry lies at the top. He was famously dissatisfied with his work, and often rewrote or scrapped a poem. He was also a late developer, feeling that his work began with the first edition of *Libertad bajo palabra* (Freedom on Parole) in 1949, and on through two further mutations (in 1960 and 1968), like Luis Cernuda's *La realidad y el deseo* (Reality and Desire), a poet with whom he identified. He was concerned with the fate of poetry in the critical debates of his times. Lower down the pyramid of his work came his literary and political journalism, that brought him greater fame, even notoriety, than his poetry, especially with his essays on the problems of being Mexican (*mexicanidad*) titled *El laberinto de la soledad* (The Labyrinth of Solitude, 1950), a key essay still in print. His prose output, written in the rush of life, established a power base with books, translations and essays on a myriad of subjects from Henri Michaux to Claude Lévi-Strauss, Buddhism, Sor Juana, Pessoa, and much on art and politics. His prose is polemical and bursting with energy, with its stream of semi-colons, close to his poetry, but with more emphasis on meaning. His anti-Stalinist political stance, favoring freedom, was impressive, with his critique of the *ogro filantrópico* (philanthropic ogre) carrying far beyond his poetic works. By the end of his life, you could say that Paz had become the *caudillo* he so often criticized.

However, Octavio Paz is a divided poet. His dialectical work, a continuous "vaivén" (shuttling to and fro) is based on a Paris myth, where being "afrancesado" (Frenchified) was his *destino*. Being Mexican and cosmopolitan was a constant tension. Like Julio Cortázar, he drifted toward Paris and became an outsider member of the post-War surrealist group under André Breton, before bringing this French counterculture back to Mexico as an attitude to poetry and attacking what he saw as its nationalistic distortions from his Parisian high ground, summarized in his compendium on poetry *El arco y la lira* (The Arc and the Lyre, 1957). From birth he was pulled between his Mexican roots, with his *criollo* father, a lawyer for the Zapatista revolutionary cause, and his blue-eyed mother from a Spanish family, a "niña de mil años" (a thousand-year-old little girl). He was divided between an experimentalist and a lover of traditional verse forms, between believing in the poet's intuitive wisdom and explaining in prose, often combining both. An uncertainty between prose and poetry runs through his "poetry," with two magnificent books of prose *¿Aguila o sol?* (Eagle or Sun?, 1951), and *El mono gramático* (The Grammatical Monkey, 1970), within the poetry. This constant mental movement is not necessarily

Octavio Paz" on the website *Revista de libros*, (2014), www.revistadelibros.com/articulo_imprimible.php?art=5191&t=articulos (last accessed October 1, 2016).

chronological, and can manifest itself anytime in his poems. Possibly the greatest tension is between the critical poet and the pure lyricist, seen even in individual poems. Paz was a philosopher poet, like Antonio Machado, who developed a sophisticated poetics, based on light, the other based on woman, passing time and history undermined by the "instante poético" (poetic instant) within a Platonic scheme. His best poems combined his critical view of language with rhapsodic outbursts, best exemplified in "Hacia el comienzo" (Towards the Beginning, 1964–68) where fascination with Oriental philosophies was matched by existential love poems dedicated to his new French wife.

Paz couldn't help being Mexican. He travelled abroad to civil war-torn Spain in 1937 with his first wife, Elena Garro, but it wasn't until he went to Paris as Mexican cultural attaché in 1946 that he became self-consciously Mexican. In fact, he worked in the Mexican Foreign Service until 1968 when he resigned in protest at the slaughter of students in Tlatelolco, bowing out with a poem originally titled "Limpidez" (Cleanliness).[2] From Paris he'd followed the anthropologists and archaeologists who had revived the Mexican worldview before the European Discovery and inserted himself as a spirit of that world. It may be that his analysis of the Mexican in history in *El laberinto de la soledad*, based on remaining closed up, or the role of the *fiesta* (festival), or the use of swear words partook of his own self, that these essays can be read as veiled autobiography. But with *¿Aguila o sol?* he developed a Mexican self in prose poems at odds with the politicized, folkloric view of the Mexican peasant portrayed by the Mexican muralists. For Paz being Mexican was more interior. "Mariposa de obsidian" (Obsidian Butterfly), translated into French for a surrealist magazine, was narrated by a humiliated Mexican virgin, who tells the poet "De mi cuerpo brotan imágenes: bebe en esas aguas y recuerda lo que olvidaste a nacer" (Images surge from my body; drink in these waters and remember what you forgot when you were born). It ends with a visionary request to break her in two "para leer las letras de tu destino" (in order to read the letters of your destiny; 216). The poet has been chosen to catch the spiritual energy of a forgotten Aztec fertility goddess, Itzpapálotl, as Paz points out in a note in case a reader ignores this historical association, herself the forerunner of the Virgen de Guadalupe. The same message comes in "Dama Huasteca" (Huastec Lady) where it is the poet's imagination that can awaken a stone: "Diré su secreto: de día, es una piedra al lado del camino: de noche, un río que fluye al costado del hombre" (I shall tell its secret; during the day it's a stone on the roadside: and at night it's a river that flows at the man's

---

[2] Collected as "Intermitencias del oeste (3)" (Interruptions from the West [3]) in *Ladera este* (This Side, 1968).

side; 222). At this stage Paz had too much to say to let it be said in straight lyric poetry. In "El ramo azul" (Blue Bouquet; 178–180) the poet comes into collision with the peasant's black humor and is made to kneel and offer a bouquet of blue eyes for the peasant's *novia*. He denies he has blue eyes (though Paz did) and flees the village. The peasant is given colloquial talk and the piece can be read as a short story (and has been selected as one). It's a marvelous piece about an urban poet coming into a fearful contact with real Mexico. It reads like, and was, a nightmare.

Paz accompanied his Mexican poems with prose articles, published in journals and collected in *Corriente Alterna* (Alternating Current, 1967), on the recently recovered Mexican past, and offers a double vision, one in amenable prose, that was read by many, and the other as a poem, read by few. It accounts for his popularity. From then on Mexico became part of Paz's critical vision, leading to many poems dealing with a past and fallen world, encapsulated in the city or urban scenes, similar to T.S. Eliot, to suggest "fallen" man. This "fall" is more acute in Mexico with its myth of local, revolutionary politics, most evident in the long-lined poems of *Vuelta* (Return, 1976). By the 1970s Paz had refined his satirical poems, packed with invective, to include autobiographical selves in a refined "ira" (anger) that generated a section called "Ciudad de México" (597–612). Without punctuation, the lines seem to float, and clusters of rhythmic words create the poem. The poem that gives the collection its title, "Vuelta" (Return), has the city and his memory of it enter his head as an "infestación de imágenes leprosas" (infestation of leprous images) where the act of thinking and writing seems to lead to an unknowable present. In "A la mitad de esta frase" (Midway Through This Sentence; 602–606) the poet writes from the sixth floor, as usual in Paz at night, about a Mexico City of "ladrillo y cemento" (brick and mortar) where History doesn't seem to go anywhere, matching the poet going round and round in his head. There is no "water" of salvation in this modern city. Mexico City reached one million inhabitants in 1928 and by 2015 it had mushroomed to over 23 million. No wonder that Paz continued to question it and his identity in it.

Paz is a poet of the light of the Mexican *altiplano* (high plateau), where you are closer to the sky and light inundates everything. Light is also inner light, self-knowledge and perception of it in the now, the present. It catches Paz's thinking through poetry as light also annuls the ego of the poet and his reader. As symbolic energy it is everywhere. Take the very Mexican poem "Entre la piedra y la flor" (Between the Stone and the Flower; 92–99), which he has changed considerably over time as his early neo-Marxist politics has given way to more Liberal views. It opens with "Amanecemos piedras./ Nada sino la luz. No hay nada/ sino la luz contra la luz" (We wake up to stones./ Nothing but

166

light. There is nothing/ but light against the light), as Paz attacks the way capitalism deals with sisal workers in Yucatán, where he first wrote this poem in 1937 and tidied it up in 1976. The blazing sun dominates the thinking. His later Mexican poem, *Piedra de sol* (Sunstone), which first appeared on its own in 1957 with a learned prologue that then was relegated to a note with *La estación violenta* (The Violent Season) in 1958, is held together by its monotonous verse structure of hendecasyllables. There is a Meso-American sense to the whole poem, but it expands beyond Mexico to personal and impersonal forces in Paz's life – the poem is autobiographical – and ends with dawn. It has been a nighttime exploration of woman as a symbolic force, locked up in a stone sleep (the word "piedra" [stone] is crucial in his poetics as it stands for dead matter). The sunlight wakes him up with "y el sol entraba a saco por mi frente" (and the sun entered copiously through my forehead; 277). The collection *Semillas para un himno* (Seeds for a Hymn, 1954), adds a religious tone to the coming of dawn and light. In a series of lovely, but neglected poems, Paz explores this topic of light to end, in the last poem, with "la luz se abre en las diáfanas terrazas del mediodía" (light opens in diaphanous midday terraces; 152). Midday is also a term that Paz uses to reveal a shadowless world of direct perception, where inner and outer blur as the slightly deliberate and artificial poem "Himno entre ruinas" (Hymn among the Ruins; 233–35), written in 1948, states. In alternative stanzas corresponding to day and night, it's the last and seventh stanza that solves the dialectic where the poet loses his self-consciousness to become a fruit-bearing orange tree, "atravesada por una misma y amarilla dulzura!" (shot through by the same yellow sweetness; 235). This poem exemplifies the intellect taking over and meaning becoming paramount, so that most critics have spent time analyzing it (including myself). Paz has exposed his childhood Mexican sunlight and turned it into a metaphysic.

Paz has drawn attention, as a poet, to the ways language affects the poem. He deals in the self-consciousness of thinking, so that many attitudes to words emerge, from following words on a page, to not knowing where words, as he actually writes them down, will lead. He is a language poet in its most literal sense. In one poem the word "alabastro" (alabaster; 333) appears and he can't think why. In fact, the mystery of the poet's craft is a question of words, signs, names, nouns, syllables, and images. As we shall see, puns have a role to play in this waking-up of language to a reality without language. Right at the start of his poetic career Paz wrote a poem titled "Palabra" (Word; 37); the sixteen sections of the frantic prose pieces, "Trabajos del poeta" (The Poet's Tasks; 165–177), of 1950, hunt for the "Palabra" (Word) by longing to incarnate into this word, in a way that mimics surrealist automatic writing. This experimenting with words ranges from his *Topoemas* (Topoems, 1968), with his drawings of words, in line with Brazilian Concrete poetry, to Apollinaire-type *calligrammes* shaping the poem for the eye, to poems calling up the words that you read as he writes the poem. The language theme predominates in *Salamandra* (Salamander; 1962). Paz's poetics absorbs Mallarmé's sentence, "La destruction fut ma Béatrice" (Destruction was my Beatrice) where his critical poems unpick words to leave us in a wordless experiential world. So the first step is to doubt language itself, normally the pillar of all poems. The opening poem "Entrada en materia" (Entry into Matter; 311–5), where "materia poética" (poetic matter) implies the total store of syllables and words (as in a dictionary), with the poet writing at night, freed from the day's duties, and watching the city outside and inside, converted into words and images, running in his veins. This is Paz's repeated discovery, his poetics a process of thinking-about-language. For once installed in language, sitting and writing at night, he finds that language takes over, dissolves the poem and his identity. This drive toward ignorance in the poem "El tiempo mismo" (Time Itself; 331–6) is a "no sé nada" (I know nothing; 335); Paz's contribution to the "vaivén" (shuttling to and fro) behind all his poems. The poem ends "Es la transparencia" (It's transparency; 336), where words are no longer barriers to the wordless experience (close to Buddhism and leaving him with the presence of nothing). The title poem "Salamandra" is an excursion around his associations with this word, from fireplace to the ancient Mexican Xólotl, to end with wordplay "Salamadre/ Aguamadre" (Salamother/ Watermother), a release from its fixed early meaning. In the poem "Decir: hacer" (To Speak: To Act) in *Árbol adentro* (Inner Tree, 1988), he continues to play with words that abandon him alone, when suddenly "las palabras se abren" (words open up; 13). The second section of his late "Carta de creencia" (Letter of Belief; 166–71; his last published poem), affirming his poet's lifework, Paz returns again to this radical doubt that is a poem and its link with the ego of the poet: "Las palabras son inciertas/ y dicen cosas inciertas./ Pero digan esto o aquello,/ nos dicen" (Words are uncertain/ and they say uncertain things./ But whatever they say, they speak to us). The rest of the poem plays with the word "amor" (love) as a "puente" (bridge, a slightly tired association), which ties together his two great themes, language and love.

And love leads us to Paz's greatest subject and contribution to the history of poetry. And love is allied to woman, his heterosexual other. His erotic poems establish a personal *ars combinatoria* of running water (the dream) and woman (source of all knowledge), so that through all his writing there is a dream self, with eyes closed to external reality and history, who questions the swimming woman in his mind. This continual movement allows for self-knowledge where love is no longer just a sensation, or a sexual satisfaction, but an immersion in real knowledge of the other. The literary sources of this are at the Romantic beginnings, where the dream, woman and night mix together. You could accuse Paz of putting woman on a pedestal, as did all the surrealists, and of being deeply heterosexual in terms of his continuous yin-yang of gender opposites.

Right from the start of his poetic career in the poem "Monólogo" (Monologue; 21) of 1935 the poet defines his place as lying between "la nada y el sueño" (nothingness and dream), his insomniac's hours and her red hair that "vibra con dulce violencia/ en la espalda de la noche" (vibrates with sweet violence/ on the night's back). *La nada* (Nothingness) sums up all the forces that already diverge from love. In a sonnet titled simply "II" from that same year, a "tú" (you) from his dreamscape offers her body "que en la luz abre bahías" (which opens up bays in the light; 23). One hair from this woman is enough to pull him up to salvation, as he wrote in a poem (26). Paz enriched a poetics of salvation over his lifetime. Paz as poet moves, then, between "nada" (nothing; repeated through time) and his vision of "tú" (you). The poem "La poesía" (Poetry) ends with this summary of his Romantic position: "despiértame del todo,/ hazme soñar tu sueño,/ unta mis ojos con aceite,/ para que al conocerte me conozca" (wake me up completely,/ make me dream your dream,/ smear my eyes with oil,/ so that, as it knows you, so it will know me; 106). To wake up from his alienated, lost, dead self in a poem is to make the poem's words lose their numbness. "Cuerpo a la vista" (Visible Body) closes with "Patria de sangre,/ única tierra que conozco y me conoce,/ única patria en la que creo,/ única puerta al infinito" (My blood-drenched homeland,/ the only land I know and the only one that knows me; the only land I believe in,/ the only door to infinity; 127) and clearly defines his new "patria" (repeated twice) away from his Mexican *patria* toward an infinity not yet touched. This Platonic space is made even clearer in "Más allá del amor" (Beyond Love) from 1948, which opens dramatically with "Todo nos amenaza" (everything threatens us; 131) – it's the start of the atomic age – where this "todo" (everything) is broken down in the poem to lineal time, self-consciousness and dead words. Neither love nor madness nor dreams lead to a fuller life for "una vida más vida nos reclama" (a life more full of life beckons us; 131). Here Paz recalls André Breton's plea for "la véritable vie" (real life) as a surrealist synthesis and the latter's designation of woman as source of man's change.

The poet's later poem from *Salamandra*, "Noche en claro" (Sleepless Night; 349–53), where night stands for post-Second World War darkness, is dedicated to André Breton and Benjamin Péret, two leading French surrealists, and summarizes Paz's counter views on love. His poetry is getting more realist and precise. They're in the Café de Inglaterra, in Paris, during an all-night meeting. His poetry will increase in realistic settings as his Platonism

Jason Wilson

vanishes. In an underground carriage in London he'd seen a hippy with love written on her fingers – Paz's includes his drawing of the hand and its fingers in his poem. The letters LOVE are "anillos palpitantes" (throbbing rings; an echo of Pablo Neruda's "ostras palpitantes" (throbbing oysters) from *Residencia en la tierra*); Paz has seen this "mano que das el sueño y das la resurrección" (hand that gives the dream and gives the resurrection, 351) and that leads to the ending of this poem fusing the city with the archetypal feminine "Mujer Presencia" (Woman Presence; 352; repeated on 353). He drinks sanity in her eyes; she has "todos los nombres del agua" (water's every name; 353), her "sex" reveals the other side of being. Paz is postulating an experience in a future beyond time, place and history – for Platonism still grips the poet, that promise of "something" beyond appearances.

In his long poem *Piedra de sol*, the swimming, sinuous woman inside the dreaming poet is axed on this statement: "voy por tu cuerpo como por el mundo" (I traverse your body as I do the world; 261). Only lovers, more a value than actual people, touch the root of recovery because love leads to timelessness which dissolves everything, as it does in orgasm, but here it is a metaphor not an act, to reach "oh ser total" (oh total being). Alienated twentieth-century man can only change through love. This is Paz's revolutionary, anti-political call, for then all the dividing walls fall down (alienation, abandonment, etc.) to discover "el olvidado asombro de estar vivo" (the forgotten wonder at being alive; 271). The poem "A través" (Through) from *Salamandra* brings all these elements into play again. Paz is literally writing as we read him: "escribo lo que me dicta/ el movimiento de tus pestañas" (I write dictated/ by the movement of your eyelashes; 369). The poet enters "her" as a lover, but it's more than instinctive pleasure; it's a sensation with meaning. He asks her to "reventar" (burst open) his eyes. A drop of night is on the tip of her breasts: "Al cerrar los ojos/ los abro dentro de tus ojos" (When closing my eyes/ I open them within your eyes; 369). He travels along her "white" thoughts, linking love with the blank page to reach "el reverso de la vida" (the reverse of life; 370). It's more a call to abolish consciousness than a description of the experience itself. In "Nocturno de San Ildefonso" (Nocturne in San Ildefonso) from *Vuelta* (1975), the poet surveys his life, at night. He has reincorporated punctuation but kept the irregular, floating lines. It's a critical poem about Mexican roots and student memories. It's also about poetry as a "resurrección de las presencias" (resurrection of presences; 636). The poem is being written while his wife sleeps next to him. Truth is her breathing, with her eyes closed. The poem ends "Mujer:/ fuente de la noche./ Yo me fío a su fluir sosegado" (Woman:/ source of the night./ I trust your calm flow; 639), now a set belief. Only his muse, his other, can grant him mental salvation.

A few words of conclusion on "Hacia el comienzo" (Towards the Beginning) or "Presente" (Present) as it was first titled. These Indian poems, written in the sixties, are a long love song to his second marriage to Marie José in 1966. They're fresh because they go beyond self-conscious playing with his poetics. They are contact with a real woman who liberated the poet from his Platonism. There is more realism, less speculation: "Soy real" (I am real; 459), he said in a poem and thanks to her "habito una transparencia" (I live in transparency). The poem "Maithuna" (referring to erotic couples in Indian mythology), quotes a comment from her in French about "sources," and ends "Esa noche mojé mis manos en tus pechos" (That night I soaked my hands in your breasts; 466). "Cuento de dos jardines" (The Story of Two Gardens) is a long poem that summarizes his erotic life. His first garden was from his childhood, with its magical fig tree in Mixcoac and the second a garden in Delhi, where he finds himself with his "Almendrita" (Little Almond) amongst exotic birds and a *nim* tree. From a boat near Durban (Paz associates it with Pessoa), both gardens become inner ones. The marriage of Paz and his muse is made poetically by merging his reading of Indian philosophy and poetry: "olvidé a Nagarjuna y a Dharmakirki/ en tus pechos" (I forgot Nagarjuna and Dharmakiri/ in your breasts) – the great thinkers of India are brought to life in her breasts. The poet has united Maithuna and Sunyata (emptiness as joyful release) in her "grupa" (rump; 478). It's as if the end result of philosophy is the round fruit-like *grupa*. He has been thrown into a new time where the absolute present takes over, in the sun, with bodies and mind at one. The poet has been transformed, his grey words gone: "Los signos se borran:/ yo miro la claridad (The signs fade:/ I observe clarity; 478). To help his reader Paz adds a note (there are 31 pages of notes in his *Obra poética* of 1997), but he doesn't explain "claridad" (clarity). Perhaps it's obvious that thought has been abolished, as have all words. The veil has been lifted in a direct contact between the poet and his *amada* (beloved).

Blanco, an intellectual and deliberate poem, with much work dedicated to its structure and notes on how to read it, is also a love song where the couple vanish in a scream of pleasure. The two columns are legs opening and closing, and Paz's inner eyes have been opened ("la Mirada") as her body spills into his inner world. He becomes "haz de tus imágenes/ anega-das en la música" (a sheaf of your images/ drowned in music; 496). This poem could be chanted, its structure falling away to leave a traditional love song. In "Carta de Creencia. Cantata" (Letter of Belief. Cantata) the last section has a "Coda" repeating the bliss of "nosotros" (poet, muse, and reader) that love has been a journey that ends with the lovely swaying of the bushes: "Yo hablo/ porque tú meces los follajes" (I speak/ because you make the leaves sway; 174). What lasts in Paz's poems is this exploration of love, in poetry and in prose (*La llama doble* [The Double Flame, 1993] is an essay on his history of love), that builds up a metaphysics of love based on shared experiences that transcend history by showing a more intense world, while accepting exile from the garden.

PART III

Diversity and Heterogeneity

12

SARA CASTRO-KLARÉN

Women's Poetry

"Come to see the camellia,/ born at daybreak,/ before the sun tans/its skin/ . . . The soft and white knot of friendship. The nest/ that closes upon itself – perfect."

Henriqueta Lisboa, "Camellia." 1959.[1]

"The necessity of paroxysmal dissonance at the height of the most intolerable beauty . . . The twisted thing about which I want to write."

Alejandra Pizarnik, *Journal*, August 15th, 18th, 1968.[2]

In this chapter I am going to discuss the work of two indispensable poets in the history of Latin America's poetic tradition, Henriqueta Lisboa (Brazil, 1903–1985) and Alejandra Pizarnik (Argentina, 1936–1972). Brilliant poets living in neighboring countries and a generation apart, each dedicated her life to achieving the most perfect verses by way of disciplining language to its bare minimum and living a life completely dedicated to a meditation on their gift/craft as if itself were life. Neither ever married. Probably both knew love, but it was not lasting. Pizarnik wrote at night. But for a few poems set in a secret garden, she cultivated the absence of light in nocturnal settings. Lisboa captured all the brilliance and color of the day from her beloved gardens in Minas Gerais. Although they cultivated very different aesthetics and lived in dissimilar historical circumstances, they have in common a continued and keen meditation of the question of poetics in general, and their own in particular. The work of this two epoch-making incandescent poets calls for a study in contrasts and similarities. At the core of their work there is a sustained meditation on the problem of language's capacity to communicate as well as the relationship of language to the creation of self and the emergence of the world, but the dwelling places where they rest their search register a clashing difference. Pizarnik faces a final despair, whereas Lisboa attests to an elegant and serene acceptance of the passing of death into life.

[1] See *Twentieth Century Latin American Poetry. A Bilingual Anthology*, ed. Stephen Tapscott (Austin, TX: University of Texas Press, 1996), 195. When not otherwise indicated all translations are the author's.

[2] See *Alejandra Pizarnik. A Profile*, ed. Frank Graziano, trans. Maria Rosa Fort and Frank Graziano (Durango, CO: Logbridge-Rhodes, 1987), 129.

These coincidences and divergences allow the critic to bring their work together for a discussion of two main questions: the nature of their respective inquiries, and the artistic environment in which their work appeared, and made a difference.

Each of these poets wrote and developed within a national tradition of their own in relation to the language they were born into, the artists and political generation to which they belonged by association with other writers and artists in Minas Gerais, as is the case with Henriqueta Lisboa, or Buenos Aires in the second half of the twentieth century for Pizarnik. Neither woman suffered relegation or marginalization because of their gender, although the question of gender at large is often present in their thought and aesthetic. Both received recognition from other poets and critics from the very beginnings of their careers. They were invited to join circles of artists and intellectuals that appreciated and supported their work, encouraged, and celebrated their writing and their presence as public figures in the constellations of national public intellectuals. Although the radical and brilliant poems by Alejandra Pizarnik have sometimes been compared to the far-reaching aesthetics of rupture in the poetry of César Vallejo (1892–1938), the celebration of the Argentine poet's persona and career does not in any way compare with the narrow social and artistic circles in which Vallejo moved and the relative obscurity in which he died in Paris despite the canonical importance of his trailblazing deconstruction of language, and remaking of all established poetic forms and conventions.[3]

Henriqueta Lisboa was born in Minas Gerais to a very well-established and old family. The timid, diminutive but sturdy young woman felt firmly rooted in her family, the rich artistic history of the region and the literary tradition of her country.[4] Her entire *oeuvre* seems steeped in the landscape and mythical sense of the history of Minas. Her poem to Ouro Preto (1941),[5] the birthplace of the famous colonial sculptor Aleijadinho, is but one example of the strongly held sense of place and time that animates the poetics of dwelling in her work. Ouro Preto, the hub of colonial mining and splendid Brazilian baroque, is for Henriqueta an especially good place where to live: "bõa da gente morar" (good for people to live in; *Casa de pedra* [House of Stone], 28). All good places for the poet are blessed with

<hr>

[3] See Michelle Clayton, *Poetry in Pieces. César Vallejo and Lyric Modernity* (Berkeley, CA: University of California Press, 2011), 16–19; see also Chapter Two "Invasion of the Lyric," 50–88.
[4] See Angela Vaz Leão, *Henriqueta Lisboa: O misterio da criacão poética* (Belo Horizonte: Editora PUC Minas, 2004), especially the chapter entitled "Henriqueta de Minas, Minas de Henriqueta," 85–100.
[5] Henriqueta Lisboa, *Casa de pedra. Poemas escolhidos* (São Paulo: Editora Ática, 1979), 28–31.

gardens in bloom, with things to see and touch and with birds in blissful flight. The visibility of things in all shades of the tropical palette is a prime value for her in life and art. At the end of her life, in *Pousada do ser* (Hostel of Being, 1982), she writes: "Recreio o visível/ a o meu desejo/com particular matizes/ invento o visível/ de acordo con meus própios olhos/ para que através do cotejo/ a os novos prismas/ outros ohlosos vejam" (I recreate the visible/ as I wish/ with special colors/ I invent the visible/ In accord with my eyes/ so that when compared/ under new prisms/ other eyes can see).[6] Ouro Preto's streets move along "malvas e gerânios" (mallows and geraniums). At night Ouro Preto is no less captivating to the eye for, as a camellia under the moonlight or like an old family chest, Ouro Preto invites "lembrança da familia" (family memories) left behind in the old letters and portraits of an "ingrato namorado" (ungrateful lover). Ouro Preto's romantic beauty and ties to the past lift the poet's heart. She returns to her beloved Belo Horizonte with a "coração de passarinho" (heart of a dicky bird) gladdened by the old town's beauty imbued with Brazil's historical gests. The poet's heart swells with joy with the memory of Tiradentes (1746–1792) and the rebellion of the Inconfidência Mineira (doomed movement for independence) in 1788. Like the poet, people could find a dwelling in the place where Brazil's epic heroes lived and died for the nation. Such a feeling of comfort and identity cannot only sustain a life but also death. One can, indeed, "esperar a hora da morte/ sem nenhum medo nem pena – quando nada mais espera" (wait for the hour of death/ without fear or sorrow – when nothing else is expected; *Casa de Pedra*, 28–31).

This strong sense of belonging to the historical and natural world stands in glaring contrast with Pizarnik's discomfort with the world as a geocultural tradition where she could establish a secure home. For Lisboa, before she became a poet, there existed a "casa de pedra" that was the family's home. Later, as she lived her life almost exclusively as a poet there emerged a dwelling place for her in her art. Her last collection of poems, *Pousada do ser*, stands for that sense of place crafted out of language as modulated by poetry. In a parallel and yet divergent way, Pizarnik too lived mainly as a poet in Buenos Aires and in Paris. Her favorite living spaces were the artist cafés, the brilliant parties, and her room at night. Night was the time when she wrote and tenebrous the colors of the scenes that informed the space evoked in her verses. Pizarnik's happenings occur in a landscape reminiscent of the *Wuthering Heights* film version with Laurence Olivier and Merle Oberon, were even the stones and purple ridges of the moors appear tortured and

[6] "Visibilidade," in *Presença de Henriqueta*, ed. Abigail de Oliveira Carvalho (Rio de Janeiro: Editora José Olimpo, 1992), xi.

worn out.[7] At night in her room full of dolls and cigarettes, Pizarnik inhabited her refuge, but it turned out to be a dwelling place exposed to the weathering elements. It was not a house made of stone; it turned out to be vulnerable to the wind. In "The Awakening," a poem dedicated to her first analyst Pizarnik, deploying one of her arresting surrealist images, howls: "Lord/the cage has become a bird/ and has flown away/and my heart is crazy/because it howls at death/and smiles behind the wind/at my ravings" (*The Lost Adventures*; Graziano, *Alejandra Pizarnik*, 25). Lisboa's heart, the happy little bird, flies in friendly skies knowing that flight is only an ephemeral phenomenon whereas Pizarnik's crazy heart howls behind the wind as if it were about to drop, unable to sustain its flight.

In sixty years of writing Lisboa published more than ten volumes of poetry and essays. Her critics remark on her constant exploration of new topics and creation of new forms. She does not cultivate free verse. Her poems are rather long and often rhymed. While mainly a lyrical poet, Lisboa has written some outstanding epic poems dealing with the history of Brazil. She is considered not only a force in the artistic life of Minas Gerais, but one of the outstanding poets of Brazil's star-studded twentieth century. While she lived mainly alone in a comfortable home with a beautiful library and received friends in warm but formal settings, Lisboa also taught courses at the Universidad Federal de Minas Gerais, on neo-Latin literature (French, Spanish, Italian and Portuguese). Her command of French and Latin were superb. In time, and after she came across the translation of Dante's *Divine Comedy* by the Argentine statesman and man of letters, Bartolomé Mitre (1821–1906), she translated Dante's *Purgatorio* (Purgatory), a tribute to one of the poets that she most revered. Her talent, like in the case of Pizarnik, was recognized by critics and literati barely before she turned twenty years old. She was greatly admired by many of the consecrated artists of the time. Cecília Meireles, Carlos Drumond de Andrade, and José Guimarães Rosa often wrote to her to congratulate her on her public readings of new poems and publications. They also expressed critical appreciation in public venues.[8]

---

[7] *Wuthering Heights*. 1939. Director: William Wyler. Stars: Merle Oberon, Laurence Olivier, David Niven. USA.

[8] In the second part of Lisboa's *Convívio poético* (Belo Horizonte: Imprenta Oficial, 1968), she published a series of essays written about the work of poets she most admires. Among them we find Cecília Meireles, Alfonsina Storni and Gabriela Mistral. In that volume she also includes "Lembrança de Mário." She notes the rare intelligence and generosity of the poet, trenchant prose writer and musician. For her Mário de Andrade was a hurricane strength force in Brazilian culture. Until Mário, there had not been in Brazil a creator with comparable gifts for the spontaneous expression of everything Brazilian: "o brasileiro exato quem a cultura não consiguiu domesticar o que guarda por isso toda a sua pujança primitiva. Nemhuma coacção se filtra no seu mundo poético" ("the authentic Brazilian,

Perhaps her greatest admirer was the singular and brilliant architect of the Brazilian avant-garde, Mário de Andrade (1893–1945). Along with other artists and writers, Mário gave Brazil its irreverent and radically post-colonially modern "Modernism" in his unforgettable *Macunaíma* (1925). This "mythic surrealist novel delves into Brazil's Amerindian past, recreating its horrors and grandeurs skillfully and playfully ....Though at first an incongruous mix of temporal spheres, this device allows Andrade to make some pointed references to the foibles of contemporary"[9] culture in often hilarious pages. The published correspondence between Mário and Henriqueta speaks of a deeply loving, but undefined relationship between them. Besides a shared love of letters, Henriqueta enjoyed and admired Mário as a musician. After Mário died in 1945 Henriqueta wrote the wrenching *Flor da morte* (Flower of Death, 1949).[10] In reference to the loss of Mário and also of her father, and having embraced a Christological path, Lisboa, in "Sofrimento" (Suffering) assesses her sorrow in light of our minuscule being: "O que se perdeu foi pouco/ mas era o que eu mais amava" (What was lost was not much/ but it was what I most loved; Vaz Leão, *Henriqueta Lisboa*, 111). The years after Mário's death are considered to be one of the saddest and darkest periods of her life; she managed to overcome her depression in part by engaging in profoundly spiritual meditation on the continuation of death as life. Lisboa sees her life and craft as the indefatigable pursuit of perfection in the sense of a Christlike renunciation of ego, a practice which she took as her daily bread (*Presença de Henriqueta*, 13).

Manuel Bandeira situates best the critical consensus on Lisboa's craft and poetics when he speaks of the *perfection* that she achieves: "But this perfection is not of a facile virtuosity; it is the perfection of a natural asceticism, acquired by the force of a difficult spiritual discipline, of a rigorous economic vocabulary" (Tapscott, *Latin American Poetry*, 192). Precision and clarity stand for Lisboa's style. Pizarnik's craft is also the result of precision and clarity. The Argentine poet, not unlike the girl from Minas, disputes the notion of inspiration. Neither poet believes in the power of the muses. Writing poetry is hard work and talent in and of itself is not enough. As

who has never been tamed by culture and who therefore retains his primitive force. No coercion manages to penetrate his poetic universe")(169). For the letters from Meireles to Lisboa, consult the front pages of *Presença de Henriqueta*, xii-xxv. The 42 letters that Mário de Andrade wrote to Henriqueta were published in *Querida Henriqueta: Cartas de Mário de Andrade a Henriqueta Lisboa*, ed. Padre Pauro Paulo (Rio de Janeiro: Editorial José Olimpo, 1990).
[9] For an introduction to Brazilian *modernismo* and an insightful discussion of *Macunaíma*, see Stephen M. Hart, *A Companion to Latin American Literature* (Woodbridge: Tamesis, 1999), 162–63.
[10] Vaz Leão, *Henriqueta Lisboa*, 103–16.

Pizarnik puts it: "In literature talent doesn't prove anything." (Graziano, *Alejandra Pizarnik*, 124). For her achievements in perfection Lisboa received several significant prizes in Brazil, starting in 1929 with the Olavo Bilac Prize from the Academia Mineira de Letras (Vaz Leão, *Henriqueta Lisboa*, 87). After the publication of *Pousada do ser* in 1982, she was enthroned with the Brazil Pen Club Prize and also the Machado de Assis Prize given by the Brazilian Academy of Letters.

Within the chronology of literary movements in Brazil, Lisboa is considered an heir to Brazilian and French Symbolism and to the radical subversion of form and bourgeois order of Brazilian *modernismo*. But Lisboa's meditation should not be confused with the subversion of Surrealism nor with a galloping Modernism that does dismantle the classical and Christian foundations of Western Civilization. There is no post-Nietzsche suspicion of language in Lisboa's own radical depuration of form, image, or style. When her critics speak of perfection, one of the things to notice in her verse is that the poem appears on the page after the struggle of the poet with language, diction, and rhythm; choice of figural images is over and consolidated. Lisboa, unlike Cortázar and Pizarnik, is not interested in showing or writing about the underside of the beautiful and perfected work of art. Her aesthetic calls for the serene achievement of an object at rest. She presents the sculpture in the fullness of its completion. She is interested in studying the object and its possible meaning in order to represent or rather evoke on the page the new object gained as a result of her insightful creation. What shines through is not the struggle of the artist, but rather the object in its full splendor. Lisboa thus captures the aura of the moment, the aura of the camellia in its round, private whiteness, the aura of the green parrot in its full screeching flight: "Papagaio verde/ deu un grito agudo/ Rocha numa raiva/ brusca, respondeu./ Ganhou a floresta/ un frande escaréu. Papagaios mil/ o grita gritaram/ rocha repetiu/ . . . Gritos agudíssimos!/ Mas ninguém morreu" (Green parrot/ let out a shrill scream./ Rock in sudden/ anger, replied.// A great uproar/ invaded the forest./ Thousands of parrots/ screamed together/ and rock echoed . . . ./ Very piercing screams!/ But no one died; trans. Helcio Veiga Costa, in Tapscott, *Latin American Poetry*, 193).

For the poet, the poem is, like the camellia, "O círculo/ em que se encontram os corações/ é o elo do entendimento recíproco" (the circle where hearts meet/ The bond of mutual understanding; Tapscott, *Latin American Poetry*, 195). Because meditation has borne an image, a figure that stands for thought and feeling, she is able to believe in the possibility of communication, in love, and above all in friendship. The perfectly white camellia is the symbol elaborated by Lisboa for this love that like the nun's experience is lived in a beautiful silence: "Amo em silêncio/ como as monjas/ . . . ./ Com extrema delicadeza/ como se o meu amor estivesse para morrer" (I love quietly, like the nuns/ with the utmost refinement,/ as if my beloved were about to die; Tapscott, *Latin American Poetry*, 192). The camellia, that "nest that closes upon itself" ("o ninho/ que se fecha sobre si mesmo, perfeito"; Tapscott, *Latin American Poetry*, 195), that total and perfect circularity, is the symbol for the art of the poet herself as it stands in a perfect and yet ephemeral and resplendent solitude. The camellia is one of those figures that as deployed by the poem exceeds all of its usual associations and becomes a thing in itself. It is something invented by the poet. It creates a new visibility. Camellias will never be seen again as just beautiful flowers for, from now on; they will be seen and understood as Lisboa "paints" them with an aura of total flawlessness in their untouchable whiteness. Lisboa, the paramount artist, gives the world objects that were never there before.

Lisboa's poetics is not based on reckless experimentation guided by the desire to discover something new. The new is not prized in itself. Neither is the depth of subjective of psychoanalysis, or the *fondo* so treasured by Pizarnik. Rather her poetics is oriented toward a depuration of thought, a being and living for the invisible but essential as it is given to both the senses in conjunction with intuition. Her writing stems from a serious meditation in which silence is a prized guest and facilitator. It is curious to see that at the end of her life in an essay entitled "Minha professão da fé" (My Profession of Faith), she speaks of her parents, of that "casa de pedra" (House of Stone) not in emotional or social terms but in a theological allegory. Her mother, she says, cultivated faith, hope, and charity. The father gathered in his personhood the four cardinal virtues: justice, prudence, temperance, and fortitude (*Presença de Henriqueta*, 4). Clearly in her life and in the tone, as well as in the ethical horizon of her poetry, she strove to leave a trace of the seven theological virtues. The symbol of the "casa de pedra" does not stand for any kind of oppression to be resisted, to be opposed, and to be dismantled. Quite the contrary, the image of the parents provides the poet with a substantial foundation on which she can build her art in close embrace with a life lived principally on an ethical plane of reference. In *Convívio poético* (Poetic Cohabitation, 1955) where she speaks of her preference for the French Symbolist poets, and the English Romantic poets, Gabriela Mistral, Dante, and Leopardi, Lisboa explains that for her poetry is something universally human for it speaks of the human nostalgia for the prelapsarian moment of total union (*Convívio*, 12, 44–45). She feels that it is this nostalgia that man feels for that which does not exist, or what Novalis called the "Blue flower" (*Convívio*, 12). "A flor azul que ainda não lograram ver os olhos humanos e cujo perfume enche, sem embargo, o mundo enteiro" (The blue flower that human eyes have yet to see and whose perfume fills, however, the whole world; *Convívio*, 12). Lisboa could not be further from Lacan and his psychoanalytical theory of symbolic language and the split consciousness. For Lisboa language in poetry rides on the wings of the angels: "Existe, em sentido esencial, a poesia comun ao gênero humano, aura de inspiração que o eleva acima de si próprio [. . .] Ela preside a todos os mistérios do universo e é, como a vida misma, indefinível" (There is, in the most essential sense, a poetry common to the entire human species. It is an aura of inspiration that lifts mankind above itself [. . .] Poetry presides over all the mysteries of the universe and it is, like life itself, indefinable; *Convívio*, 12). Lisboa's dwelling place in art as in life exhibited her disciplined spirit, her search for balance between silence and utterance, a discreet pursuit of classical beauty and above all prudence, restraint and serenity. This last temperamental and ethical characteristic of her person, life and art will stand in contrast with Pizarnik's journey a generation later in a different sociohistorical setting.

Alejandra Pizarnik was born Flora Pizarnik in 1939. She was lovingly known in her Russian-argentine family as Buma and Blímele. The family hispanized their last name Pozharnik ("fire" in Russian), into Pizarnik.[11] As she grew up she discovered in adolescence not only her obsessive interest in literature but her vocation as a poet. When Flora Pizarnik entered the University in Buenos Aires with an undefined interest in the humanities she began to call herself Alejandra. Alejandra was perhaps a name that she found more in tune with the Russian-Jewish origins of her family. According to her biographer Cristina Piña, at the end of her life Pizarnik, intensifying a fabled Russian ancestry that she had nurtured earlier, asked her friends to call her Sasha. This early act of renaming herself in accordance with a tradition that she chose for herself is part of the poet's endeavor to perform a life in accord with the self-given name. From the earliest adolescence Pizarnik manifested a will to fashion an identity that sprung from her deeds and self-conception as a different and rare, unique person. Staying up all night talking, laughing, and drinking in the company of artists and best friends, or writing in the solitude of her room, were the activities upon which Pizarnik grounded her performance of the artist – everything stemmed directly from her desire to plumb the unfathomable depths of subjectivity. Language was the ground that she stepped upon. Humor, sardonic remarks, sharp conceits, extravagant dress gained Flora notoriety even before she published a single verse.

When she died of an overdose of seconal sodium and other drugs (Piña, *Alejandra Pizarnik*, 18) her mother and friends found a note written with

---

[11] The information on Pizarnik's life is taken mainly from Cristina Piña's biography of Pizarnik. It is a sympathetic biography based on interviews with most of the friends and artists who knew the poet intimately and the pertinent and available documentary sources; see Cristina Piña, *Alejandra Pizarnik* (Buenos Aires: Planeta, 1991), 22.

chalk on the blackboard in her apartment. It stated her lifelong driving desire: "No quiero ir/ nada más/ que hasta el fondo" (I do not want to go/ but/ to the depths). "Fondo" can be translated as bottom, but is keeps its association with foundation and also with dregs. It is almost synonymous with "hondo" which means deep or depths. It is also refers, paradoxically, to the transparent and reflecting "substance" of a diamond. "Fondo" constitutes the principal, essential, and yet untouchable part of a person. These multiple meanings are all in play in this line. As with almost every verse she wrote Pizarnik not only exploited here the polysemic possibilities of each word, but also imbedded within them their own contradiction. The craft of intense concentration is sealed in every word in use. The reader can split the sentence and read a refusal to go someplace, any place, no place, death ("No quiero ir"/ I don't want to go), while the rest of the sentence states the contrary ("más que hasta el fondo"/ except to the bottom). The bottom is the only destination willed and acceptable in every attempt and "I don't want to go" is in fact reversed by the second part of the verse because it actually means "I (only) want to go." The "bottom" is the depth of subjectivity as both constituted and not constituted by language's failure to provide a world. In her lifelong search for answers to the mystery of life, Pizarnik explores all possible avenues, but most especially she treads the subversive and forbidden paths that may lead to that "fondo." Although she is often tormented by the suspicion or realization that such a "bottom" as a solid floor that can detain a free fall into the depths, does not exist and can neither be touched nor reached, she feels compelled to look and descend into Alice's rabbit hole. Falling ever more deeply, ever more freely, and ever more terrified seems to be the experience that encapsulates the will to touch bottom. In *Árbol de Diana* (1962) the poet's person unfolds and the speaking self invites "mi vida" (the beloved self/other) to allow herself to fall, to feel pain, to let fire embrace her in the nocturnal home: "Vida, mi vida, déjate caer, déjate doler, mi/ vida, déjate enlazar de fuego, de silencio in-/ genuo, de piedras verdes en la casa de la/ noche, déjate caer y doler, mi vida" (Life, my beloved, let yourself fall, let yourself ache, my/ life, let fire encircle you, with silence in-/ generously, with green stones in the house/ of night, let yourself fall and ache, my life).[12]

[12] Alejandra Pizarnik, *Obras Completas. Poesía y Prosa* (Buenos Aires: Corregidor, 1990), 218. These *Obras completas* do not seem to be very complete. The book *La última inocencia* (1956) for instance, is represented by only 1 page that includes two of the original sixteen poems in the original book. Cristina Piña has written an essay where she discusses the questions of the completeness of this edition. See Cristina Piña, "The "Complete" Works of Alejandra Pizarnik?" in *Árbol de Alejandra. Pizarnik Reassessed*, ed. Fiona J. Mackintosh and Karl Posso (Woodbridge: Tamesis, 2007). Since Pizarnik's

The quest to touch bottom by allowing the free fall to occur, seems to be the material question that sustains her life and art. She pursues it in her verse, prose, and theater, and even in her psychoanalytical therapy. The sessions with her analysts seemed to have been more engaged with the uncovering of layers of subjectivity than with a "therapy" (Piña, *Alejandra Pizarnik*, 54). Pizarnik started using amphetamines as an adolescent and remained addicted to amphetamines, barbiturates, alcohol and other stimulants for the rest of her life. Her house in Buenos Aires and her apartment in Paris were known as little pharmacies (Piña, *Alejandra Pizarnik*, 32, 42) among her friends.

From her debut as a literary sensation in artistic circles in Buenos Aires before she reached the age of twenty, Pizarnik's talent was recognized by almost anyone who came in contact with her. Her eccentricities in dressing and speaking with a sort of a foreign accent and strange rhythm were part of the seduction that her persona or her performance exerted on those who knew her. Her speech was arresting. She had a deep voice and a sharp tongue that could put the most unexpected and revealing spin on any trivial phrase in the give-and-take of conversation. She developed a speech style of her own. She ripped language apart. As can be seen in the verses quoted above, she introduced unexpected cuts in syntax, and even within the words themselves ("in-/genuo"). She cut up words into syllables that did not coincide with semantic units. For example she uttered "pa-raque-ve-asel-po-e-ma" (Piña, *Alejandra Pizarnik*, 55). With unanticipated and unaccustomed pauses, she redistributed the syllables – now transformed into free-floating phonemes – into new "words" in a sentence that required new assemblage and new thinking. In this way she disturbed not only the linear flow of the sentence but meaning was thrown into a sort of chaos, which in itself turned out to be revealing. Her utterances and arbitrary verse cuts presented language as a primeval cacophony of sound and letters as if belonging to an alphabetic order yet to be coded and deciphered. Multiple written examples of this creative language wrecking game can be found in her poems. Games abound and overflow meaning in the genre/gender disarticulation of the "play" *La Bucanera de Pernambuco o Hilda la Polígrafa* (1971–1972). Cultivating the taste for the absurd recommended by André Breton one of the "narrative" fragments features a pregnant male/female figure:

death a controversy and polemic has ensued as to the publication of her diaries and other texts she did not publish while alive. The diaries have been published but the editor has been faulted for acceding to Pizarnik's sister's wishes not to publish very private and scandalous entries (Piña, *Alejandra Pizarnik*, 148–49). A volume of her correspondence has also been published. It has provoked similar controversies, but the affiliation of these "letters" to the *Bucanera de Pernambuco* is nevertheless important to note. Piña has edited her own *Obras Completas*; see *Alejandra Pizarnik. Obras completas: Poesía completa y prosa selecta*, ed. Cristina Piña (Buenos Aires: Corregidor, 1993).

Desnudo como una musaraña, Flor de Edipo Chu reía de los consejos super-
fluos que nadie le daba. De repente tuvo ganas de pasear por este texto y
telefoneó a Merdon y Merdon a mí. En caso de que el lector haya olvidado el
recinto por donde Chu se pasea *encinto*, Merdon advierte que es el mismo de
antes: La boutique Coco Panel, quien, como va vestida (no va puesto que está
sentada) parece un gordo desnudo (my emphasis; Pizarnik, *Obras completas*, 191).

(Naked as a shrewmouse, Oedipus Chew Flower laughed at the superfluous
advice nobody gave him. Suddenly he felt like taking a stroll through this text
and telephoned Shithead, and Shithead called me. In case the reader's forgotten
the crash pad where pregnant Chew pads about, Shithead informs us that it is
the same as before: The boutique Coco Panel who fully clothed looks like a
naked fat man; trans. Suzanne Jill Levine, in Graziano, *Alejandra Pizarnik*, 93).

People who loved her wit, sarcasm, and inventiveness had to pay close
attention when she spoke lest they miss the pun, the witticism, the highwire
performance. Her performance of the self in language was one of a kind; it
could not be imitated nor compared. Pizarnik's astonishing talent was recognized wherever she went, be it in Buenos Aires, Paris or Mexico. She made
many loyal friends and admirers in the vibrant atmosphere of the Buenos
Aires of the late 1950s to the early 1970s and in the Paris of the early 1960s
where she went with one of the several fellowships awarded to her during her
brief life.

She was part of the café and bar scene of Buenos Aires' bohemia, an artistic
effervescence that continued in the homes of the famous and almost sacred
figures such as Oliverio Girondo, Sivina Bullrich, Victoria Ocampo, and the
magazine SUR group of artists and intellectuals. These were the circles of
brilliant artists that the Chilean novelist José Donoso, in his *Historia personal del Boom* (Personal History of the Boom Novel) called "The Argentine
Mount Olympus" or the dwelling of the Gods.[13] Pizarnik found a particular
affinity with the well-established poet Olga Orozco. Her personal and artistic
association with Orozco was strong, defining, and sustaining. Critics refer to
Orozco as Pizarnik's literary mother. Although their lives and aesthetics
remain quite apart, critics have found their parallel interest in silence and
reflection on death a thread that invites a comparative discussion of their
work. Jill S. Kuhnheim points out that Orozco embarks on a heroic quest and
"strives to overcome immoderate obstacles" such as death, physicality, and
barriers to communications.[14] Pizarnik is also interested in the possibility of

[13] *Historia personal del Boom* (Barcelona: Editorial: Anagrama Barcelona, 1972), 43–45.
[14] See Jill S. Kunheim, *Gender, Politics, and Poetry in Twentieth Century Argentina*
(Gainesville, FL: University of Florida Press, 1996), 65.

speaking through silence, but the aesthetics of each poet in dealing with the challenge of silence and death are widely different.

While Orozco writes abundant verse, graced with rich and complex visual and palpable images, Pizarnik chooses silence itself to materially state its case. She neither speaks on behalf of silence nor does silence speak in her place. For Pizarnik there is no trading of positions between utterance and silence, as we shall see below. Pizarnik writes: "Silencio/ yo me uno al silencio/ yo me he unido al silencio/ y me dejo hacer/ me dejo beber/ me dejo decir" (Silence/ I join silence/ I have joined silence/ and I abandon myself/ I let myself drink – be drunk/ I allow myself to say – be said; Pizarnik, *Obras completas*, 231). The materiality of silence is its own, it is not fused with her inability to produce verse or prose or thought. Silence is not the absence of language or lack of utterance. It registers it own, "trembling" presence, as if it were a living being of some sort, one of those silent but touchable birds she likes to evoke: "Pero el silencio es cierto/ por eso escribo/ estoy sola y escribo/ no, no estoy sola/ hay alguien aquí que tiembla" (But silence is real/ that is why I write/ I am alone and I write/ no, I am not alone/ there is someone here that trembles; Pizarnik, *Obras completas*, 278). At best silence is an unknown but certainly not a state of estrangement. Although its presence is sensed, it in no way coincides with the self: "algo cae en el silencio/ mi última palabra fue *yo*, pero me refería al alba luminosa" (Something falls in silence/ my last word was *"I"*/ but I was referring to luminous dawn; Pizarnik, *Obras completas*, 279). In contrast, Orozco struggles to make silence speak, even when she seems at peace with it.

Pizarnik's literary aesthetic resides in the tradition of French poetry of Nerval, Baudelaire, Rimbaud, Lautréamont, and Artaud. Although a great deal of Latin American poetry, from Rubén Darío's *modernismo* at the turn of the twentieth century on to the most recent work of Roberto Juarroz, a friend and contemporary of Pizarnik, exhibits a strong filiation with French intellectual and aesthetic movements, her poetry's attachment to the French tradition is defined by an affective interest in evil, in the dark bottoms of subjectivity, and in all that is subversive of the norm. An iconic image of this self is "la loba azul," the blue she-wolf prowling with unmet ripping desire (Pizarnik, *Obras completas*, 35, 67). Pizarnik's obsessive and pleasure-filled reading in the original of the work by the French *poètes maudits*, acquires its full dimensions in her encounter with the work of George Bataille on literature and evil. She delighted in the idea of catching a glimpse of Bataille in the Paris café where the *habitués* of his group gathered at the time when she was absorbed in the reading of his work on the Marquis de Sade, Baudelaire, and Jean Genet. Of the author of *Saint Genet*, Bataille wrote in *Literature and Evil*: "Genet has chosen to explore Evil as others have chosen to explore

Good. The absurdity of such an experiment is immediately obvious . . . .We explore Evil in as far as we think it Good, and inevitably, the exploration is doomed to failure or ridicule. But this does not make it any less interesting."[15] Registering affective filiations with the Marquis de Sade she delved more deeply into an exploration of the bloody and the atrocious. This affinity with Sade found full expression in her own prose narrative on the Bloody Countess, the sixteenth-century Hungarian Countess Erzébeth Bathory about whose sadistic sexual practices Valentine Penrose had in 1962 just published his sensational *La Comtesse Sanglante*. In tune with the spirit of pitiless and unrelenting rebellion of the *poètes maudits* and Sade himself Pizarnik says in *Árbol de Diana* (Diana's Tree, 1962), the book she wrote while in Paris, that for her rebellion "consiste en mirar una rosa/ hasta pulverizarse los ojos" (To stare at a rose/ until one's eyes are pulverized; Pizarnik, *Obras completas*, 212). This self-destructive act in engaging "reality" outside and yet inside the poet's quest *to see* will grow in precision and intensity with the reflection undertaken in *Extracción de la piedra de la locura* (Extraction of the Stone of Madness, 1968). The effect of the rose on the poet stands in utter contrast with the emergence of the camellia in Lisboa's poetics.

Poètes maudits, like Pizarnik and also surrealist poets like André Breton (1896–1966), live by the conviction that the poetic search is a transcendental act that can lead to an encounter with the absolute. In *Surrealism, the Road to the Absolute* (1970) Anna Balakian writes that, Mallarmé in *Igitur* explores his preoccupation with the

> Occult forces of physical life in his attempt to discover the inherent mystical qualities of material existence . . . .Instead of speculating about immortality, he seeks the absolute which denies immortality. But this absolute which is sub-servient neither to life nor to death, is not a spiritualization of reality . . . nor is it a denuding of the earthly scene [. . .] But if the absolute is not understood as the subjective perpetuation of perfected human experience after death, how will poetry convey the substance of nothingness? The existence of the absolute can be established only through the acceptance of the absurd.[16]

Automatic writing is certainly not the path. On the contrary, this search for the absolute calls for a meditation on, and disciplining of, language, and a razor-sharp choice of experiences. André Breton, in the *Second Manifesto of*

---

[15] Georges Bataille, *Literature and Evil* (New York, NY: Urizen Books, 1973), 149. The French publication date of this book is 1957 and it was the rage in the Paris of the early 1960s when Pizarnik was living there.

[16] Anna Balakian, *Surrealism, the Road to the Absolute* (New York, NY: Dutton, 1970), 42–43.

Sara Castro-Klarén

Surrealism (1930) demands an "attack of conscience . . . for everything tends
to make us believe that there exists a certain point of the mind at which life
and death, the real and the imagined . . . cease to be perceived as contradictions," and it is this point that constitutes the hope for the search of the
absolute.[17]

This attack on conscience implies an ethic of complete, fearless and limitless exploration of the relation of language to subjectivity with a special
emphasis on the examination of the dark and forbidden realms of the self.
The poet's ethical task is therefore to bond living and writing poetry in order
to create a seamless lived experience. Day pours into night like the poetic
search pours into daily living in an inseparable flow of intensity, subversion
and perhaps lucidity. The goal is to achieve one single moment of incandescence, despite the limitations and the failures of language and consciousness.
Breton longed for this moment of incandescence, for the moment when "it
will pass from absolute falseness to a new absolute that is true and poetic: the
umbrella and the sewing machine will make love . . ..the coupling of two
realities which apparently cannot be coupled on a plane which is apparently
not appropriate to them" (Breton, *Manifestoes*, 275). Octavio Paz, himself
enamored with the surrealist aesthetic of the poetic object, in his prologue to
Árbol de Diana (1962), lauds the achievement in many a poem of that
collection.[18] In this regard Piña writes that Pizarnik "attempted to make of
her life the materialization of her poetics, she tried to transform herself into
the personage of her verbal absolute" (my translation; Piña, *Alejandra
Pizarnik*, 19). This is why, in analyzing Pizarnik's poetry, the critic cannot
leave out her life. Pizarnik built in her daily life of a poet an inextricable
embrace between the act of writing poetry and the act of living the poetic
search.

Her own assessment of this embrace does not celebrate a triumph. Far
from it, it speaks of a sense of loss and maybe even regret. In her diary (April
1961) she spelled out how her life and literature had become a palimpsest of
loss: "Mi vida perdida por la literatura a causa de la literatura. Por hacer de
mi un personaje literario en la vida real, fracaso en mi interés por hacer
literatura con mi vida real, pues esta no existe; es literatura" (quoted in Piña,
Alejandra Pizarnik, 132) (Life lost for literature by fault of literature. By
making myself a literary character in real life I fail in my intent to make
literature with my real life, since the latter does not exist: it is literature;
Graziano, *Alejandra Pizarnik*, 113). In a prose poem written in 1971

[17] See André Breton, *Manifestoes of Surrealism*, trans. Richard Seaver and Helen R. Lane
(Ann Arbor, MI: University of Michigan Press, 1972), 123–24.
[18] Octavio Paz, "Árbol de Diana," in *Árbol de Diana*, by Alejandra Pizarnik (Buenos Aires:
Sur, 1962), 7.

Pizarnik, looking back on her life, seems to feel lost. She cannot find a spot where to pause and look back on the treaded path and gain perspective. "No sé dónde detenerme y morar" (I do not know where to stop and dwell; Pizarnik, *Obras completas*, 31). Moreover, language is now empty. It does not even seem to be a human thing. "El lenguaje es vacuo y ningún objeto parece haber sido tocado por manos humanas. Ellos son todos y yo soy yo" (Language is empty and no object seems to have been touched by human hands. They are everything and I, am I; Pizarnik, *Obras completas*, 31). Estranged from a past, separate from the objects, bereft of language, she asks her beloved self: "Vida, mi vida/ ¿qué has hecho de mi vida?" (Life, beloved/ what have you done with my life?; Pizarnik, *Obras completas*, 31). While theorists, and specially Lacanian readers of Pizarnik, abound on her splitting of the subject, the production of an other as mirror of a self that struggles (and fails) to be one in language, the erasure of the "I," the poet's own intimate assessment of living the ethics of the *maudit*, is that it calls for a sacrifice of a life, to be exact her life.

Pizarnik's collections of poems were published in brief books. For *Árbol de Diana* she received the prestigious Buenos Aires Municipal Prize. The first edition of the not very complete *Obras Completas* (1990) gathered in a single volume of 316 pages almost all her prose and poetry. She has been partially translated into French and into English. It is well know that she worked on a single text for many nights and that she edited by cutting down until she reached the greatest expressive value with the least number of words. Condensation and intensity are the guiding practices of her aesthetics. The poet did not only ponder the mysteries of silence as being but she also cultivated its paradoxically signifying value. Only the blank page rivals the eloquence of silence in Pizarnik's aesthetics of writing. Words are there to be sculpted to the bare minimum, for they are dangerous. "[La] lengua es el órgano del conocimiento/del fracaso de todo poema" (Language – tongue/ is the organ of knowledge/ of the failure of every poem); thus, to write requires the wielding of a knife onto language, lest the slicing knife turn on the poet: "[Escribo] como quien con un cuchillo alzado en la oscuridad" (I write as if under a knife raised in the darkness; Pizarnik, *Obras completas*, 63–64). While writing needs to be subjected to a regime of constraint and discipline, speech in dialogue, with its full orality in play, whether in conversation or in her one play, is exuberant, prodigal, extravagant and lewd.

More often than not the reader finds a single poem made up of a few verses occupying the entire page. The graphic distribution of the verses in a conical shape pointing down, underscores, aesthetically and intellectually the sense of the poem:

Sara Castro-Klarén

> "Alejandra, Alejandra
>   debajo estoy yo
>   Alejandra"

(Alejandra, Alejandra/ I'm underneath/ Alejandra"; *La última inocencia* [The Final Innocence; 1956], quoted in Piña, 93; Graziano, *Alejandra Pizarnik*, 23).

Poems sometimes appear at the bottom of a page. The blank space between the top brief poem and the bottom three of four lines occupies most of the page. Like in *Trilce* (1923) by César Vallejo, most poems do not have titles. That is the case for instance, with "En la noche del corazón./ en el centro de la idea negra./ ningún hombre es visible./ nadie está en algún jardín" (In the night of the heart/ at the center of the black idea/ no man is visible/ no one is in any garden; Pizarnik, *Obras completas*, 75), a poem that like many others simply shines in its diamantine solitude on the whiteness of the page. Under these conditions, there never was nor is there ever an Adam in the garden of Paradise.

Pizarnik could write the most arresting verses with the simplest language. She did not cultivate an ornate, glamorous or rare vocabulary nor did she craft images that referred to splendid, prestigious objects or recondite referents. The light that illuminates her canvas is night light, and briefly the light of dawn or "el alba" (the dawn). Her world is cast in shades of gray and black, with brushes of blue or lavender now and then. She speaks of blue flowers and green hearts. The atmosphere is always somberly mad. It is dictated by shades of affect rather than qualities of events outside the poetic self. The poet longs for more visibility in order to better see the objects of her imagination. Beyond the objects, like a painter, she longs to see light itself: "[Me] embriaga la luz/ no nombro más que la luz/ quería verla/ Quiero ver en vez de nombrar" (Light blinds me/ I only name the light/ I want to see it/ I want to see rather than name; Pizarnik, *Obras completas*, 31). Plain simple words are disposed on the page almost as far away from each other as possible in order to leave blank spaces through which light can pass and illuminate each word-concept. In order to extract the greatest possible meaning out of the friction of the dynamics of their separation by virtue of the verse form and their contiguity by virtue of syntactical order, the poet highlights each word in its own splendor, as if they were masterpieces in a museum. In *Figuras del presentimiento* (Figures of Premonition; 1971), one of her last texts, the poet incisively unfolds herself in a dialogue that captures a *double entendre* given in an oral exchange: "Y qué es lo que vas a decir?/ Voy a decir solamente algo/ y qué es lo que vas a hacer?/ voy a ocultarme en el lenguaje/ y por qué/ tengo miedo" (And what is it that you are going to say?/ I am only going to say something/ And what is it that you are going to do?/ I am going to hide in language/ And, that is because I am afraid; Pizarnik, *Obras completas*, 295). This minimalist aesthetic, this refusal of the splendor or the word, is the feared and longed for protection of language under which the poet seeks cover. It is fear that emits language as cover. Language is the best hiding place for the child whose memory of happy days is instantiated in the metaphor that evokes the "perfume of a bird caressed."

The minimalist pulverizing aesthetic, the will both to find a desperate moment of revelation in language and also to hide in its intricate mysteries, the nightly exercise of taming a proliferating language into the sparsest verses, may in some way be connected with the fact that Pizarnik from early on in her childhood suffered from stuttering. Surprisingly for such a brilliant conversationalist as she was, her recollections of a happy childhood are not given in the sound of language or in conversation. Childhood is rather as a world of sight, perfumes and touch: "Mi infancia y su/ perfume de pájaro acariciado" (My childhood and its/ perfume of a caressed bird; *Poemas*, 16). The perfume of a bird caressed is the kind of synesthesia with which the poet fills the otherwise blank page. In some of her prose Pizarnik deploys a much wider range of vocabulary, the kind of gross, impudent and lewd language that gave her a bad reputation in high school among the mothers of her schoolmates. This obscene vector of her dwelling in language animates the pages of *La Bucanera de Pernambuco*, a rather sadistic and lewd language-ripping text published posthumously by her friend Olga Orozco.

In *Los trabajos y las noches* (Travails and Nights, 1965) Pizarnik turns to an intense and anxious exploration of the pain and tragedy of unfound love. This period, according to her biographer, is also marked by the recurrence of bouts of depression (Piña, *Alejandra Pizarnik*, 72). Her growth as a poet, her dominion over her craft and sensibility, coincides with an increasing inability to negotiate the world of daily life. More and more she lives at night, seeking in the pained nocturnal lucidity the ever-elusive absolute of the *poètes maudits*. In 1968 she was awarded a Guggenheim Fellowship. At the time she was at work on the collection that would be published as *Extracción de la piedra de locura* (Extracting the Stone of Madness, 1968) and which announced from the first prose poem an unshakable flirtation with death. "La que murió de su vestido azul está cantando. Canta imbuída de muerte al sol de su ebriedad. Adentro de su canción hay un vestido azul, hay un caballo blanco. Hay un corazón verde tatuado con los ecos de los latidos de su corazón muerto" (The one who died because of her blue dress is singing. She sings infused with death under the sun of drunkenness. Inside her song, there is a blue dress, there is a white horse. There is a green heart tattooed with the echoes of her dead heart; Pizarnik, *Obras completas*, 263). This poem, like others in this collection, is an ode to Ophelia's death. It is painted with the absurd juxtaposition of object-images favored by surrealist aesthetics. It many ways it is reminiscent of the dreamy canvases by Henry Rousseau (1844–1910), especially "The Sleeping Gypsy."[19] The blue dress, the blue she-wolf, the blue song among the perfumed lilacs is a favorite landscape for Pizarnik's poetic self. In the following poem the lush and perfumed lilacs act out her own funerary display, shedding its petals as the vigor of life fades away. Standing for the poet, "Esta lila se deshoja/ Desde sí misma cae/ y oculta su antigua sombra/ He de morir de cosas así" (This lilac is wilting/ It falls from within me/ It hides its older vestige/ I shall die of things like this; Pizarnik, *Obras completas*, 264). This poem asks to be read in tandem with Vallejo's own prediction of death in Paris in a rainy afternoon: "Me moriré en París con aguacero,/ un día del cual tengo ya el recuerdo,/ Me moriré en París – y no me corro –/ tal vez un jueves, como es hoy, de otoño" (I will die in Paris in a downpour/ A day which I can already remember/ I will die in Paris – and I don't budge/ Maybe a Thursday, like today, in autumn).[20]

With this unmistakable romantic tone, the poet caresses her feared and yet desired death: "He de morir de cosas así." Having completed her descent to the bottom, having erased the limit between the world and language, between self and language, between life and poetry, the final scene in the story comes to pass: "Ya perdido el nombre que me llamaba/ su rostro rueda por mí" (Having lost the name that called me/ her face falls at my feet; Pizarnik, *Obras completas*, 265). Death is the loss of the mask of the poet, the loss of Alejandra as performance over the innocent Flora. This loss of language as barrier marks a coming in-distinction, in-difference between life and death. Form, syntax, convention had stood between a sort of nothingness and self. Now the poet understands that: "Murieron las formas despavoridas y no hubo más un afuera y un adentro. Nadie estaba escuchando el lugar porque el lugar no existía" (The terrified form died and there was no more outside/inside. There was nobody listening to the place because the place did not exist; Pizarnik, *Obras completas*, 265). In these poems the performance of Alejandra, the name she invented as a dwelling place in which to live, has lost its incantatory force. As a word-name-place Alejandra cannot breathe life into Flora-Alejandra any more. Even when Sasha is tried as a new power-word, the force of language in poetry to hold up a world is insufficient. The last stronghold of the imagination – artificial respiration – is overwhelmed by negative feelings and meanings. Not only was "no one listening," but if there had been someone listening, he/she would

[19] See Roger Shattuck, *Henri Rousseau* (New York: Museum of Modern Art, 1986), and Cormelia Stabenow, *Henri Rousseau 1844–1910* (Cologne: Benedikt Taschen, 1994).
[20] See César Vallejo, *Obra poética*, ed. Américo Ferrari (Paris: Colección Archivos, 1988), 339; and *The Complete Poetry of César Vallejo. A Bilingual Edition*, ed. and trans. Clayton Eshleman (Berkeley, CA: University of California Press, 2007), 380.

not have been able to perform such a task, the prospect of "listening to a place" is in itself inconceivable. Even if the cognitive order of the senses could be restored and the listener was trying to hear a word or music or even just a sound, the charge would have been futile because the place ("fondo") does not exist anyway. Thus it is not only that the absolute is not within reach, or that our imperfect senses cannot access it, but that "it" in fact does not exist. "It" may only be an effect of language, but even then, "it," the illusion of being, could have lasted longer had literature not consumed her life. This would seem to be the revelation of the *maudit* pursuit that Alejandra Pizarnik enacted in all its power in a singular and inimitable poetic flash.

As the poet reaches the inner and outer limits of the search, the place where language has collapsed as she anticipated it would in 1965 when she wrote: "Llega un día en que la poesía se hace sin lenguaje" (There comes a day when poetry is made without language; Pizarnik, *Obras completas*, 26), "Alejandra" contemplates suicide deeply immersed in melancholy. In a moment beyond death, she imagines being "Palabra o presencia seguida por animales perfumados ....Triste como si misma, hermosa como el suicidio" (Word or presence followed by perfumed animals ....Sad like only herself, beautiful like suicide; Pizarnik, *Obras completas*, 303). This melancholic vanishing of the self and the historical person into organic life as a whole is, in the end, resisted by a huge refusal to go quietly into the night. A screaming vital force arises. It is the elementary cry of the blue she-wolf and it is best captured in the poem she writes to Janis Joplin upon the day of the singer's suicide. Neither life nor death are about receiving orders ("a cantar/ dulce y a morirse luego" ([time] to sing/ sweetly and then to die; Pizarnik, *Obras completas*, 66) for poets like them. Pizarnik applauds Joplin's suicide. "Hiciste bien en morir/por eso te hablo/ por eso me confío a una niña monstruo" (You did well in dying/that is why I am taking to you/that is why I am trusting a monster little girl). Like Joplin, Pizarnik refuses to be confined to the authorship of beautiful poetry ("cantar dulce," beautiful song). With "A cantar dulce y a morirse luego/ no;/ a ladrar/" Pizarnik offers one last refusal of the things as she found them. If language has been lost and "Alejandra" can no longer perform, there is always the animal cry, the barking of a dog, the howling of a wolf, anything but surrender.

Henriqueta labored and disciplined language and living so as to build an inhabitable house of stone. There she dwelled in thought and spiritual contemplation. Alejandra, springing from her unimaginable talent with words, embarked on a search for the absolute within and beyond language. The desired object, that "fondo" of subjectivity, proved not to exist, and thus it was incapable of offering a refuge where to weather the storm of life itself.

13

STEPHEN M. HART

WITH

BRAD EPPS

LGBTQ Poetry

There is currently a split in LGBTQ studies between those who are interested in studying a set of writers in terms of their performance of LGBTQ motifs – which might, for example, take the form of mapping the coded portrayal of gay, urban cultures in Mexico, São Paolo, or Buenos Aires via the work of, say, Xavier Villarrutia (1903–1950) or Néstor Perlongher (1949–2002) – and those who prefer to produce innovative queer readings of canonized figures, by discovering, for example, homoaffectivity in the poetry of Rubén Darío or César Vallejo.[1] In this current study our aim is to bridge the gap between these two approaches.[2]

The Mexican poet, Xavier Villarrutia, is a central figure in what is broadly understood as the LGBTQ canon of Latin American poetry, and the assessment of his work has undergone a number of transitions common in this field. Similar in some ways to the poetry of the Spanish poet, Federico García Lorca (1898–1936), which was interpreted early on in terms of

---

[1] E-mail from David William Foster to Stephen Hart, August 6, 2015. Homoeroticism in Rubén Darío's work is a hotly debated topic; see Blas Matamoro, *Rubén Darío* (Madrid: Espasa, 2002); and Alberto Acereda, "'Nuestro más profundo y sublime secreto': los amores transgresores entre Rubén Darío y Amado Nervo," *Bulletin of Spanish Studies*, 89.6 (2012): 895–924. For a discussion of Vallejo's verse, see below.
For a queer reading of Gabriela Mistral, see Chapter 7 in this volume, and Licia Fiol-Matta, "The 'Schoolteacher of America': Gender, Sexuality, and Nation in Gabriela Mistral," in *¿Entiendes? Queer Readings, Hispanic Writings*, ed. Emilie L. Bergmann and Paul Julian Smith (Durham, NC: Duke University Press, 1995), 201–29. For a queer reading of Julián del Casal, see Oscar Montero, "Julián del Casal and the Queens of Havana," in *¿Entiendes?*, 92–112, and for Borges, see Daniel Balderston, "The 'Fecal Dialectic': Homosexual Panic and the Origin of Writing in Borges," in *¿Entiendes?*, 29–45.
[2] For a general introduction, see Deborah T. Meem, Michelle A. Gibson, and Jonathan Alexander, *Finding Out: An Introduction to LGBT Studies* (London: Sage, 2009). See also Judith Butler, *Gender Trouble: Feminism and the Subversion of Identity* (New York, NY: Routledge, 1990), and Alan Sinfield, *Cultural Politics: Queer Reading* (London: Routledge, 2005). For an excellent set of queer readings in Latin American and Hispanic literature, see David William Foster, *Gay and Lesbian Themes in Latin American Writing* (Austin, TX: Texas University Press, 1991), *¿Entiendes?*, and Ben Sifuentes Jáuregui, *The Avowal of Difference: Queer Latino American Narratives* (Albany, NY: SUNY Press, 2015).

Modernism and Surrealism and only elicited queer readings from the 1980s onwards,[3] Villarrutia's work was, until relatively recently, seen through the lens of his links with the significant literary group, the Contemporáneos.[4] More recent readings by critics such as Rosa García Gutiérrez point to the gay culture enunciated in Villarrutia's later poems. Of his "Nocturno de San Juan" (Nocturne in San Juan District), for example, García Gutiérrez points to sections of the poem that refer to how "the pacts of occasional sex between men are set up,"[5] which, indeed, appear hinted at in the various drawings of sailors that adorn the handwritten versions of the "Nocturne" poems included in García Gutiérrez's edition (Villarrutia, *Obra poética*, 423–26). It is now clear that Villarrutia repurposed the *modernista* Nocturne, converting it into a meditative stage for his exploration of what he calls "the secret." His poem "Nocturno de los ángeles" (Angel-Nocturne), typical of what became almost a new poetic genre in Villarrutia's hands, opens as follows:

> Se diría que las calles fluyen dulcemente en la noche.
> Las luces no son tan vivas que logren desvelar el secreto,
> El secreto que los hombres que van y vienen conocen,
> Porque todos están en el secreto
> Y nada se ganaría con partirlo en mil pedazos
> Si, por el contrario, es tan dulce guardarlo
> Y compartirlo sólo con la persona elegida.
>
> Si cada uno dijera en un momento dado,
> En sólo una palabra, lo que piensa,
> Las cinco letras del DESEO formarían una enorme cicatriz luminosa,
> Una constelación más antigua, más viva aún que las otras.
> Y esa constelación sería como un ardiente sexo
> En el profundo cuerpo de la noche,
> O, mejor, como los Gemelos que por vez primera en la vida
> se miraran de frente, a los ojos, y se abrazaran ya para siempre.

---

[3] A crucial early study was Paul Binding's *Lorca: The Gay Imagination* (London: GMP, 1985). See also Daniel Eisenberg, "Lorca and Censorship: The Gay Artist Made Heterosexual," *Angélica* [Lucena, Spain] 2 (1991): 121–45; and John K. Walsh, "A Login in Lorca's 'Ode to Walt Whitman,'" in *¿Entiendes?*, 257–78.

[4] In his introduction to Villarrutia's work, Octavio Paz focuses on the links with the Contemporáneos; see "Prólogo," in Xavier Villarrutia, *Antología*, ed. Octavio Paz (Mexico City: Fondo de Cultura Económica, 1980), 54–56. When he mentions Villarrutia's eroticism he does not allude to the fact that he was gay (56–57). Likewise Maurice Biriotti's assessment of his work, which appeared in an influential encyclopedia, does not mention his homosexuality; see "Xavier Villarrutia," in *Encyclopedia of Latin American Literature*, ed. Verity Smith (London: Fitzroy Dearborn, 1997), 843–44.

[5] Xavier Villarrutia, *Obra poética*, ed. Rosa García Gutiérrez (Madrid: Hiperión, 2005), 439.

(You would say that the streets flow sweetly in the night./ Lights are not quick enough to reveal the secret,/ The secret known to the men who come and go,/ For they are all in the street,/ And nothing were gained by dividing it into a thousand pieces/ If, on the contrary, it is so sweet to keep it/ To share along with the chosen person./ If everyone should utter, at a given moment,/ in one word only, that which he is thinking,/ the six letters of DESIRE would form a huge shining scar,/ a constellation still older, still more intense than the others./ And that constellation would be like a burning sex/ in the deep body of the night,/ or rather, like the Twins when, for the first time in their lives,/ they looked, face to face, into each other's eyes and embraced each other for ever.)[6]

Villarrutia avoids languishing in the now faded metaphors and myths of the *modernistas*; his poem has no elaborate metaphors – the most daring is the fusion between the "six letters of DESIRE" and a scar; l.10 – and he has no need of mythological stage props such as Narcissus; he simply refers to the lovers as "twins," given their gendered proximity. The poem is coded, and has – we might argue – no need to state its (in fact, open) secret. And into this dark night Villarrutia describes how the angels arrive "a poner en libertad sus lenguas de fuego,/ a decir las canciones, los juramentos, las malas palabras/ en que los hombres concentran el antiguo misterio/ de la carne, la sangre y el deseo" (to set free their tongues of fire,/ to utter the songs, oaths, and evil words/ to which men concentrate the ancient enigma/ of flesh, blood and desire; Fitts, *Anthology*, 400–01). These angels are at once celestial and malicious:

Tienen nombres supuestos, divinamente sencillos,
Se llaman Dick o John o Marvin o Louis.
En nada sino en la belleza se distinguen de los mortales.
Caminan, se detienen, prosiguen.
Cambian miradas, atreven sonrisas.
Forman imprevistas parejas.
Sonríen maliciosamente al subir en los ascensores de los hoteles
Donde aún se practica el vuelo lento y vertical.
En sus cuerpos desnudos hay huellas celestiales:
Signos, estrellas y letras azules.
Se dejan caer en las camas, se hunden en las almohadas
Que los hacen pensar todavía un momento en las nubes.
Pero cierran los ojos para entregarse mejor a los goces de su encarnación
    misteriosa,
Y cuando duermen sueñan no con los ángeles sino con los mortales.

(They bear assumed names, divinely simple./ They are called Dick or John, Marvin or Louis./ Only in their beauty are they to be distinguished from mortal men./

[6] *Anthology of Contemporary Latin-American Poetry*, ed. Dudley Fitts (Norfolk, CO: A New Directions Book, 1947), 396–99.

They walk, pause, go on again./ Exchange glances, venture smiles./ They form in casual couples./ They smile maliciously going up in hotel elevators/ where vertical slow flight is still being practiced./ On their naked bodies there are celestial marks:/ signs, stars, blue letters./ They drop into beds, sink into the pillows/ that make them think for a moment longer of the clouds./ But they close their eyes, the better to yield to the delights of their mysterious incarnation,/ and when they sleep they dream not of angels but of mortals; Fitts, *Anthology*, 400–01).

The lifts of sexual commerce are compared to the Old Testament's ladder to heaven, and their incarnation is weighted toward the world of physical mortals rather than ethereal angels, the inverse of the language of Christianity. Like the poetry of García Lorca or Luis Cernuda, Villarrutia's work, as we can see, was overwhelmed by the leitmotif of DESIRE, the only word given the prestige of capital letters in the poem.

Similar to Villarrutia's verse in terms of its emphasis on the primacy of human desire, the poetry of César Moro (1903–1956) often begins in the everyday – as in "Vienes en la noche con el humo fabuloso de tu cabellera" (You Come in the Night with the Fabulous Smoke of Your Hair), from *La tortuga ecuestre* (The Equestrian Tortoise, 1938–1939), which opens with a reference to how "you appear" and "knock at my door"; Fitts, *Anthology*, 409), and then builds the poem towards a crescendo of illumination:

> (...) quiero aprisionarte
> Y rodar por la pendiente de tu cuerpo
> Hasta tus pies centelleantes
> Hasta tus pies de constelaciones gemelas
> En la noche terrestre
> Que te sigue encadenada y muda
> Enredadera de tu sangre
> Sosteniendo la flor de tu cabeza de cristal moreno
> Acuario encerrando planetas y caudas.

> (I seek to imprison you/ and to roll down the slope of your body/ Even to the twin constellations of your feet/ in the earthly night/ that follows you enchained and dumb/ Entangled in your blood/ Supporting the dark crystal flower of your head/ Aquarium enclosing planets and pontifical trains; *Anthology*, 410–11)

which is surrealist in power and pedigree.[7] Moro, in his writings, specifically referred to surrealism as offering a defense and justification of homosexuality,

---

[7] For further discussion of the role played by surrealism in César Moro's poetry, see *César Moro y el surrealismo en América Latina*, ed. Yolanda Westphalen (Lima: Universidad Nacional Mayor de San Marcos, 2005), and, by the same author, *César Moro: la poética del ritual y la escritura mítica de la modernidad* (Lima: Universidad Nacional Mayor de San

and he chose to write in French to underline his rejection of Peru's conservative oligarchy.[8] He clearly hated Spanish as much as the Irish writer Samuel Beckett hated English. Indeed, Moro's work is as French as it is Peruvian and it embodies a violent rejection of heteronormativity in all its forms, linguistic, cultural, and religious.

One poet whose work has intriguing similarities with Moro's is the Puerto Rican Manuel Ramos Otero (1948–1990). Like Moro's poetry, Ramos Otero's is virulent and hard-hitting, but, unlike the Peruvian's, it chooses to speak to its audience directly and without metaphor. His poem, "Nobleza de sangre" (Nobility of Blood), for example, takes on some of the anger of García Lorca's poem, "Grito hacia Roma" (Shout Towards Rome) from *Poeta en Nueva York* (Poet in New York), in order to address God with an ironic tone:

> Thank you, Lord, for having sent us AIDS.
> All the junkies and faggots in New York,
> San Francisco, Puerto Rico and Haiti will be forever
> Grateful for your aplomb as Emperor of All Things and
> The Void (and, if I'm not mistaken, of Apostolic Roman Catholics).
> The heterosexuals of Central Africa are, I think,
> Ungrateful not to recognize that AIDS
> Has allowed them entrance into modernity without any prejudice,
> Though they already do know that the lack of rain and food
> Are your just stratagems as purifier and architect of souls.
> Lord, forgive bisexuals for their innate confusion,
> For believing pleasure's to be found in the variance of bodies,
> And above all forgive the irreproachable and serene moral majority
> That still knows not the sweet incision of your sword of flesh:[9]

Written at the height of the AIDS scare, the poem reads as if Manuel Ramos Otero had become the "unacknowledged legislator" speaking on behalf of all AIDS sufferers:

> Lord, I am aware that many AIDS patients who tenderly believe
> That man (and woman too, I believe) was created in your image and likeness,
> Believe that you've gone through the swarm
> Of infectious diseases that afflict us AIDS patients

Marcos, 2001). See also Jason Wilson, "The Sole Surrealist Poet: César Moro," in *Essays on Alfredo Bryce Echenique, Peruvian Literature and Culture* (London: Centre of César Vallejo Studies, 2010), 77–90.

[8] Yolanda Westphalen, *César Moro: la poética del ritual y la escritura mítica de la modernidad* (Lima: Universidad Nacional Mayor de San Marcos, 2001), 117–26. Some have argued that it was also because his partner, André Coyné, was French, but that is another story.

[9] *Puerto Rican Poetry: An Anthology from Aboriginal to Contemporary Times*, ed. and trans. Roberto Márquez (Amherst, MA: University of Massachusetts Press, 2007), 295.

(and we have certainly been patient); those sweats or nightly chills
(as if for you there's such a thing as night), Lord, that unending fatigue
that won't let me walk (much less write my poetry),
that marginalization without limits, that collective disgust of Kaposi's
    sarcoma
and the tuberculosis, of the emaciation, and the lesions on the skin.

                    (Márquez, *Puerto Rican Poetry*, 195)

In the final section of the poem, Ramos Otero questions religion, God and heteronormativity, choosing to bear AIDS as a badge of honor:

Lord, I'm going to take what little freedom I have left and, a colonial after all,
Define our identity. Let them call us the *sidious*, once and for all!
They've already committed against us those barbarities (and many more)
    they say
Were done to you (with the methods privileged by our era,
Of course). Lord, all that's left is to deal with the matter of your identity.
I'm not going to get into anything personal or invade your privacy
(which is inviolate), but what was it made you give the Americans
the franchise on the second destruction of Sodom? Freud would say:
Was it, perhaps, your total solitude, your colossal boredom, your guilt
    complex
About so many genocides, your sexual frustration with the Apostles,
Or the naïve illusion of believing that the right to love, to the secret flesh,
To life and death still belong to you by entitlement of birth?

                    (Márquez, *Puerto Rican Poetry*, 196)

"Nobility of Blood" attacks religion (God, Christ and the Apostles) as well as political structures (that is, the "Americans" who carried out the "second destruction of Sodom"), and was a rallying call for LGBTQ issues in the 1980s and 1990s throughout the Americas, written on behalf of the *sidious*, as Ramos Otero names them.[10]

The Argentine poet, Néstor Perlongher (1949–2002) was the most sophisticated and language-centric poet on LGBTQ issues of the group of writers studied in this chapter. "He co-founded the homosexual activist group Eros in Buenos Aires during the early 1970s and was a vocal member of the Frente de Liberación Homosexual de la Argentina (FLH) from 1971 until the military coup of 1976. This group attempted to draw public attention, particularly that of the left wing, to the existence and specific demands of homosexuals in Argentina. His political activity was informed by a mixture of anarchism and Trotskyism, a dynamic and

---

[10] Ramos Otero is playing poetically here with the Spanish acronym for AIDS, which is SIDA. This word-play allows Ramos Otero to suggest that the gay community – despite its detractors – is the very antonym of "insidious."

often contradictory political position."[11] We find some of this anarchism in his poem, "Tuyú," for example, which is a full frontal and angry attack on the West, on history and (the Spanish) language, on poetry, on Argentina, its conquistadors, its gauchos, on human brutality, and on supine readers:

La historia, es un lenguaje?
tiene que ver este lenguaje con el lenguaje de la historia,
o con la historia del lenguaje
en donde balbuceó
tiene que ver con este verso?
lenguas vivas lamiendo lenguas muertas
lenguas menguadas como medias
lenguas, luengas, fungosas:
este lenguaje de la historia
cuál historia?
si no se tiene por historia la larga historia de la lengua
cuentan
en un fogón
Ña Rudecinda
no roció el apero el ánima
no se hizo jabón el chajá
(gauchos fundidos, con sus lenguas de vaca, con sus trancas
con sus coyundas y sus rastras
gaucho fundido: él clava sus espuelas en el dorso – fundido-
de la lengua, como atrapado en una vizcachera)
a unos kilómetros de San Clemente, en el Tuyú
está la tumba de Santos Vega, adonde acuden las toninas
y los surfistas en sus jabas, sobre las olas de cristal
roto cristal, tercas toninas de la historia: van
donde los arponeros con sus garfios, van
donde los zafarranchos cachan: donde fundido el gaucho
saca el facón y se desgracia:
era la historia, esa desgracia!
desgracia de yacer en el Tuyú, de un yacer general
los caníbales en ese cristal las rudas olas asaetan
y tú, en esa pereza de la yertez, no jalas?
jalas de crestas cristalinas y empenachadas?

(History, is it a language?/ Does this language have to do with the language of history/ or with the history of language/ where it stuttered/ Does it have to do with this verse?/ living tongues licking dead tongues/ tongues rotting like socks/ tongues, lingering, fungous/ this language of history/ which history?/ If the long history of

[11] Ben Bollig, *Néstor Perlongher: The Poetic Search for an Argentine Marginal Voice* (Cardiff: University of Wales Press, 2008), 1.

the tongue isn't taken as a story/ they tell it/ in a gallery:/ Miz Rudecinda/ didn't the riding gear sprinkle the soul?/ didn't the screamer bird scare itself?/ [Melted gauchos, with their cow tongues, with their clubs/ with their yokes and their silver coin belts/ melted gaucho: he digs his spurs into the – melted – back/ of the tongue, as if trapped in a rabbit warren]/ a few kilometers from San Clemente, in the Tuyú/ is the tomb of Santos Vega, where the orcas come in/ and the surfers in their grass skirts, on the crystal waves/ Broken crystal, ornery orcas of history: they go/ to the harpooners with their hooks: they go/ where the deck-clearings cleave: where, melted, the gaucho/ takes out his jack-knife and disgraces himself:/ it was history, that disgrace!/ disgrace of lying in the Tuyú, of a widespread lying/ The cannibals in that crystal harassed by rude waves;/ and you, in that lethargy of rigor mortis, don't you take it lying down?/ Take crystalline, plumed crests?)[12]

Appearing to be almost a breathless, Joycean flow of language, Perlongher's poem is, in fact, highly structured. Its pivotal conceit is the similarity drawn between the affluent middle-class surfers who arrive in the modern era in Mar del Tuyú, a resort town on the Argentine Atlantic Coast, in order to enjoy its stunning scenery, beaches, and beautiful waves, and the cannibal Indians who were massacred by Spanish explorers there in the 1580s, and the two scenes are brought together through the image of the waves which bind their destinies together. Just as the Indians were (literally) speared by the waves ("Los caníbales en ese cristal las rudas olas *asaetan*," l. 30), so the modern-day tourists seem to be pulling and driving those same waves 300 years later ("Y tú, en esa pereza de la yertez, no jalas?/ Jalas de crestas cristalinas y empenachadas?"). Not only are the modern-day tourists associated with death (suggested by Perlongher's use of the verb "yacer" rather than the more normal "tenderse" or "tumbarse" for people lying on the beach), Perlongher accuses the reader of his poem ("Y tú … ") of being behind that genocide, a sardonically Argentine repurposing of Baudelaire's famous, nineteenth-century jab at his "hypocrite lecteur."[13] Perlongher clearly took no hostages when he wrote his poems.[14]

Female writers of this period attacked their subject matter in more elusive ways; as Brad Epps points out, lesbianism, "in Hispanic letters, does indeed

---

[12] Trans. Molly Weigel, *The Oxford Book of Latin American Poetry*, ed. Cecilia Vicuña and Ernesto Livon-Grosman (Oxford: Oxford University Press, 2009), 486–87.

[13] See "Préface," l. 40, *Les Fleurs du Mal* (The Flowers of Evil); Charles Baudelaire, *Selected Poems*, ed. and trans. Joanna Richardson (Harmondsworth: Penguin, 1986), 28. My interpretation of the last two lines of Perlongher's poem differs slightly from the translator's, in that I suggest the verb "jalar" to mean "to pull," and I interpret the verb in context as suggesting that the "tú" is pulling the strings of the waves, thereby continuing the decimation of the Indian subaltern in Argentina with a ruthlessness that is as harsh and unstoppable as the waves of the Atlantic Coast.

[14] For further discussion of Perlongher's poetry, see Chapter 5 in this volume.

seem all but lost: ghostwritten, as it were, in invisible ink."[15] For the writers studied here poetry was a central concern. A writer who associated poetry in a visceral sense with lesbian love – as she famously wrote to Silvina Ocampo, just eight months before her death: "I would love for you to be here, naked, by my side, reading your poems out loud" – the Argentine poet, Alejandra Pizarnik (1936–1972), is seen as a major figure within Latin American LGBTQ poetry.[16] It is clear that Pizarnik used private codes in her laconic and highly expressive poetry in order to denote private experiences, and one of these was the leitmotif of silence which, as Susana Chávez Silverman argues, she connects, via plenitude, to "the body, love and sexual pleasure."[17] In her poem "Ojos primitivos" (Primitive Eyes), Pizarnik explores this idea:

En donde el miedo no cuenta cuentos y poemas, no
forma figuras de terror y de gloria.
Vacío gris es mi nombre, mi pronombre.
Conozco la gama de los miedos y ese comenzar a cantar
despacito en el desfiladero que reconduce hacia mi desconocida que soy,
mi emigrante de sí.
Escribo contra el miedo. Contra el viento con garras que se
aloja en mi respiración.
Y cuando por la mañana temes encontrarte muerta (que no haya
más imágenes): el silencio de la comprensión, el silencio del mero
estar, en esto se van los años, en esto se fue la bella alegría
animal.

(Where fear doesn't tell tales and poems, doesn't form/ figures of terror and glory./ Gray void is my name, my pronoun./ I know the gamut of fears and that venturing to sing very/ Slowly on the narrow ledge takes me once more to my unknown/ Who I am, my own emigrant./ I write against fear. Against the wind

---

[15] "Virtual Sexuality: Lesbianismo, Loss, and Deliverance in Carme Riera's 'Te deix, amor, la mar com a penyora,'" in ¿Entiendes?, 318.

[16] Pizarnik's letter to Silvina Ocampo is dated January 31, 1972; see Susana Chávez Silverman, "Gender, Sexuality and Silence(s) in the Writing of Alejandra Pizarnik," in Árbol de Alejandra: Pizarnik Reassessed, ed. Fiona J. Mackintosh with Karl Posso (Woodbridge: Tamesis, 2007), 13–35, esp. 19. For lesbian-focused readings of Pizarnik's work see Sylvia Molloy, "From Saffo to Baffo: Diverting the Sexual in Alejandra Pizarnik," in Sex and Sexuality in Latin America, ed. Daniel Balderston and Donna J. Guy (New York, NY: New York University Press), 250–58, and Susana Chávez Silverman, "The Look that Kills: The 'Unacceptable Beauty' of Alejandra Pizarnik's in La condesa sangrienta," in ¿Entiendes? Queer Readings, Hispanic Writings, ed. Emilie L. Bergmann and Paul Julian Smith (Durham, NC: Duke University Press, 1995), 281–305.

[17] See Chávez Silverman, "Gender, Sexuality and Silence(s)," 16. The word "silence" is a multilayered term in Pizarnik's work and has a number of meanings; see Jason Wilson, "Alejandra Pizarnik, Surrealism and Reading," in Árbol de Alejandra: Pizarnik Reassessed, 88–89; and Cristina Piña, Alejandra Pizarnik: una biografía (Buenos Aires: Ediciones Corregidor, 2005), 165–66.

with claws that/ Lodges in my breath./ And when you are afraid to find yourself dead in the morning/ (and that there'll be no more images): silence of understanding,/ silence of mere being – through this the years escape, through/ this escape the beautiful animal joy.)[18]

The poem opens with a scenario of fear – which is a space occupied by the inability to write (l. 1), the loss of identity and self-knowledge (ll. 5–6), and by death (l. 9) – which is gradually converted, as a result of writing ("I write against fear," as she says, l. 7), into "beautiful animal joy" (ll. 11–12) which, juxtaposed paratactically with the "silence of mere being" mentioned in ll.10–11, suggests that this is a coded reference to "sexual pleasure" (see the quote from Chávez Silverman above). The most intriguing feature of Pizarnik's poem concerns the way in which – between the two poles of fear and sexual pleasure – the poem gravitates around a black hole of meaning, imaged as a "desfiladero que reconduce hacia mi desconocida que soy,/ Mi emigrante de sí" (literally, a ravine which takes me back to my unknown-ness of self, my emigrant from itself). The unusual playing back and forth from different pronominal expressions suggests that this emigration from the self arrives at a new reality of self-being ("emigrante de *sí*") which, as implied by the fact that the "sí" neither references "self," nor "he," nor "she," nor "it," but appears to be something altogether new, a new self-reality somewhere between "I" and "it."[19] It was in this space between the two pronouns, perhaps, that the enigma of her love which dared not speak its name truly resided, beyond fear, animal happiness and silence.[20]

The Uruguayan Cristina Peri Rossi (b. 1941) has written novels, short stories as well as poetry, and she explores, in her work, an intermediary zone between these genres.[21] Her *Indicios pánicos* (Panic Signs, 1970), which offers a devastating critique of the limitations of everyday life during a dictatorship, contains forty-six texts, some of which are free-verse poems, others bear a resemblance to Baudelaire's prose poems, and some are more like mini short stories. LGBTQ themes are present but only obliquely so, and they blend in with the political critique. Poem 2, for example, opens with a matter-of-fact description of the rigors of life, dripping with irony:

---

[18] Trans. Susan Pensak; *Woman who has Sprouted Wings: Poems by Contemporary Latin American Women Poets*, ed. Mary Crow, 2nd ed. (Pittsburgh, PA: The Latin American Literary Review Press, 1988), 47.

[19] For further discussion of the projection of subjectivity in Pizarnik's work, see Cecilia Rossi, "Alejandra Pizarnik's Poetry: Translating the Translation of Subjectivity," in *Árbol de Alejandra: Pizarnik Reassessed*, 130–47.

[20] For further discussion of Pizarnik's poetry, see Chapter 12 in this volume.

[21] Though Uruguayan Peri Rossi has lived in Spain since 1973.

> I live in a country of old people. Our birthrate is the lowest in the world and it's not reasonable to expect that it will increase in the near future, given that young couples who are still at the reproductive age emigrate to more prosperous countries. This should come as no surprise, because we don't cultivate the land, nor do we set up factories or build homes. Tourism, which was the nation's hope, has been a resounding failure; no one wants to get to know a country where the only thing you see in the streets is soldiers, a country where peace has disappeared in hotels.[22]

The description continues – elucidating how the children have disappeared from the streets, and how young people are finding it difficult to support their elderly parents – until it concludes with a jab directly not only at patriarchy but also at heteronormativity: "That's why children are no longer born nor are new cars seen. I don't know if this also accounts for the high rate of homosexuality indicated by statistics. Disillusioned with love, the young people caress one another" (Peri Rossi, *Panic Signs*, 8). The allusion to homosexuality – even if it is not alluded to directly – is integrated seamlessly into the narrative; it's a natural reaction, the poem seems to be telling us, to life in a dictatorship where everything is being taken away from you.[23] This type of casual insertion of a LGBTQ perspective into the narrative becomes almost a leitmotif technique of *Panic Signs*. In Poem 7, the statue the author caresses is "a sacrificed female astronaut" (Peri Rossi, *Panic Signs*, 13), and, in her apartment, she brushes the ceiling with her hands "as if it were a women's hips that have to be stroked with an open hand" (Peri Rossi, *Panic Signs*, 21). Poem 15, "Dialogue with the Writer," includes a question and answer that suggests how, for Peri Rossi, sexuality is intimately linked to her identity as a writer:

> "If you don't know what you're writing and you're not capable of making love to an unsatisfied woman, how can you still live?"
> "Because of a state decree: I will be preserved as a living image of a world in decline. I will be on display in the museum, preserved by refrigeration."
> (Peri Rossi, *Panic Signs*, 25).

Much of *Panic Signs* revolves around the despair of being alive, and it is a despair that brings together the political and the sexual in a disarming, fresh way. As we read in Poem 19:

---

[22] Cristina Peri Rossi, *Panic Signs*, trans. Mercedes Rowinsky-Geurts and Angelo A. Borrás (Waterloo, Ontario: Wilfrid Laurier University Press, 2002), 6.

[23] Peri Rossi's technique is not unique. As Luz María Umpierre suggests: "as a reader of Puerto Rican literature, I have yet to find a narrative text written by a woman that deals with the subject of lesbianism openly"; see "Lesbian Tantalizing in Carmen Lugo Filippi's *Milagros, Calle Mercurio*," *¿Entiendes?*, 306.

"You are very beautiful,"
   the man said to the young woman who
   had undressed for him,
but I am tired of ploughing."   (Peri Rossi, *Panic Signs*, 31).

As Poem 20 suggests, this (heterosexual) tiredness is caused by the need "to escape taxes" (Peri Rossi, *Panic Signs*, 32), and, conversely, when true love emerges, it is bathed in natural imagery: "the intimacy of your body, the rhythmical communication of your womb, your long white arms, the soft hills of your breasts nestling a lake in between them, your legs like two oars rowing gently to the sides."[24]

Fellow Uruguayan Marosa di Giorgio (1932–2004), seen by one critic as fast becoming the major twentieth-century poetic voice of the Sub-Continent,[25] draws on the language of myth, fantasy, fairy tales, and magical realism in her poetry.[26] Her poem "Bajó una mariposa a un lugar oscuro … " from *La liebre de marzo* (The March Hare, 1981) is a good example of this leitmotif in her work:

> Bajó una mariposa a un lugar oscuro; al parecer, de
> hermosos colores; no se distinguía bien. La niña más chica
> creyó que era una muñeca rarísima y la pidió; los otros
> niños dijeron: -Bajo las alas hay un hombre.
> Yo dije: -Sí, su cuerpo parece un hombrecito.
> Pero, ellos aclararon que era un hombre de tamaño natural.
> Me arrodillé y vi. Era verdad lo que decían los niños. ¿Cómo
> cabía un hombre de tamaño normal bajo las alitas?
> Llamamos a un vecino. Trajo una pinza. Sacó las alas. Y un
> hombre alto se irguió y se marchó.[27]

> (A butterfly went down to a dark place; seemingly, full of/ beautiful colors. It was difficult to make them out. The youngest girl/ thought that it was an extremely odd doll, and asked if she could have it; the other/ boys said:

---

[24] Poem 26, "The Acrobats," *Panic Signs*, 21. For further discussion of the role played by the motif of primal union with the female body, see Mary Boufis Filou, *Confronting Patriarchy: Psychoanalytic Theory in the Prose of Cristina Peri Rossi* (New York, NY: Lang, 2009), 18–46. For an excellent discussion of the role played by psychoanalysis in Peri Rossi's work in more general terms, see Geoffrey Kantaris, *The Subversive Psyche: Contemporary Women's Narrative from Argentina and Uruguay* (Oxford: Oxford University Press, 1995).

[25] Kent Johnson, "Note of Preface," in *Hotel Lautréamont: Contemporary Poetry from Uruguay*, ed. Kent Johnson and Roberto Echavarren (Bristol: Shearsman, 2011), 9.

[26] For the discussion of the role played by myth and fantasy in Marosa di Giorgio's work, see Hebert Benítez Pezzolano, *Mundo, tiempos y escritura en la poesía de Marosa di Giorgio* (Montevideo: Estuario Editora, 2012); and *Miradas oblicuas en la narrativa latinoamerica contemporánea: límites de lo real, fronteras de lo fantástico*, ed. Jesús Montoya Juárez and Angel Esteban (Madrid: Iberoamericana, 2009).

[27] *Los papeles salvajes*, ed. Daniel García Helder (Buenos Aires: Adriana Hidalgo, 2008), 33.

"There's a man under its wings."/ I said: "Yes, its body looks like a little man's."/ But, they clarified that the man was a normal size man./ I knelt down and I saw. What the boys said was true. How/ could a normal size man fit under those little wings?/ We called a neighbor. He brought some pliers. He cut off the wings. And a/ tall man stood up and walked off; author's translation)

It is, of course, possible to read this poem in gender-neutral terms as a magical event such as we might find in Gabriel García Márquez's fiction, but, given the resonance of the term "mariposa" (butterfly) in Latin American and Latino queer poetics,[28] it is difficult to see this poem as anything other than a metaphorical promotion of the larger-than-life and natural beauty of an elusive, gay man. Di Giorgio's poems are, indeed, often built around the description of the irruption of an extraordinary event within the syntax of everyday life, and the implications of this event – or even sometimes what it was – are deliberately shrouded in ambiguity. In "La naturaleza de los sueños" (The Nature of Dreams), from *Los papeles salvajes* (Savage Papers, 1991), for example, the central event of the poem is once more not clarified:

Al alba bebía la leche, minuciosamente, bajo la mirada vigilante de mi madre; pero, luego, ella apartaba un poco, volvía a hilar la miel, a bordar a bordar, y yo huía hacia la inmensa pradera, verde y gris. A lo lejos, pasaban las gacelas con sus caras de flor; parecían lirios con pies, algodoneros con alas. Pero, yo solo miraba a las piedras, a los altos ídolos, que miraban a arriba, a un destino aciago. Y, qué podía hacer; tenderme allí, que mi madre no viese, que me pasara, otra vez, aquello horrible y raro. (*Los papeles salvajes*, 45)

(At dawn I used to drink my milk, conscientiously, under the watchful eye of my mother; but, then/ she went off for a bit/ she went back to spinning honey, embroidering and embroidering, and I ran off to the immense, green and gray meadow./ In the distance the gazelles with their faces like flowers strolled by; they looked like walking lilies, winged/ cotton-pickers. But all I did was/ look/ at the stones, the lofty idols, who looked upwards, to a tragic destiny./ And, what could I do? lie there, without my mother seeing, and wait for that horrible and strange event to happen to me, again; author's translation)

The poem provides no indication as to what this event, described simply as "aquello horrible y raro" (that horrible and peculiar thing), is, which – given the references in the poems to "lirios" (lilies) and "un destino aciago" (a tragic destiny) – might indicate an experience of, or foretaste of, death. But, given the lack of details, the event described might be an experience of union with nature

[28] For a discussion of Latino poets associated with "mariposa" aesthetics, for example, see Chapter 16 in this volume.

(a rerun, as it were, of the Romantic poet's favorite experience) or even (a favorite of post-Freudian poetry) a sexual experience. Though the whole of the poem's meaning gravitates around this experience (simply called "aquello"), what happened is not made explicit. And yet, if we compare this poem with other of di Giorgio's poems, it is as likely as not to allude to some type of sexual experience, for sex is often at the center of di Giorgio's poetic world. In "Mi alma es un vampiro grueso, granate, aterciopelado ... " (My Soul is a Thick, Claret-Coloured, Velvety Vampire ...), which self-consciously draws on the symbols of Alejandra Pizarnik's poetry, the event is sexual:

> Mi alma es un vampiro grueso, granate, aterciopelado. Se
> alimenta de muchas especies y de sólo una. Las busca en la
> noche, la encuentra, y se la bebe, gota a gota, rubí por rubí.
> Mi alma tiene miedo y tiene audacia. Es una muñeca grande,
> con rizos, vestido celeste.
> Un picaflor le trabaja el sexo.
> Ella brama y llora.
> Y el pájaro no se detiene.   (*Los papeles salvajes*, 55)

(My soul is a thick, claret-coloured, velvety vampire. It/ feeds on many species and on only one. It hunts for them at/ night, and it finds it, drinks it, drop by drop, ruby by ruby./ My soul is afraid and it is courageous. It is a big doll,/ with curls and a sky-blue dress./ A hummingbird works away at her sex./ She roars and weeps./ And the bird doesn't stop; author's translation.)

The weeping, roaring sex of the poet's soul is the center of the poem. This poem is not simply a rewriting of the Romantic or, indeed, the *modernista* metaphor of the woman as flower (in this case "serviced" by a humming-bird), or even a poem about male inconstancy (given the secondary meaning of "picaflor" as a casanova). That the subject of the poem is at once a flower as well as a wild beast that roars ("brama") while it cries ("llora") clarifies that the poet's soul – again recalling Pizarnik – is mobile, labile and polymorphous.[29]

We find some of this polymorphous affectivity in a poem written by a poet who is not normally read via a LGBTQ lens. César Vallejo's poem, "Alfonso, estás mirándome, lo veo ... " (Alfonso, you are looking at me, I see ...) has, in the past, been interpreted by Vallejo scholars as a moving elegy to an individual, Alfonso de Silva, whom Vallejo met at the Legación Peruana in Paris on July 28, 1923, and with whom he subsequently developed a close

---

[29] As with Pizarnik's verse there are clear connections between Marosa di Giorgio's work and surrealism; see Natalia Font Marotte, "Visual Elective Affinities: An Elliptical Study of the Works of Angela Carter and Marosa di Giorgio," PhD Diss., University of Exeter, 2013.

friendship; Alfonso used to share the tips he received for playing his violin in various French restaurants with Vallejo, who was very much down on his luck at the time.[30] A number of these biographical details are woven – nostalgically – into the body of the poem. As a result of its statement in the opening verse that Alfonso is "looking" at Vallejo, the poem has also been interpreted in terms of a supernatural and/or uncanny experience. It is clear that the poem builds up towards a crescendo of experience of loss, especially in the fourth and fifth stanzas, and there are grounds for arguing that these two concluding stanzas of the poem express homoaffectivity in a nuanced way.[31] The fourth stanza reads as follows:

El hôtel des Ecoles funciona siempre
y todavía compran mandarinas;
pero yo sufro, como te digo,
dulcemente, recordando
lo que hubimos sufrido ambos, a la muerte de ambos,
en la apertura de la doble tumba,
de esa otra tumba con tu sér,
y de ésta de caoba con tu estar;
sufro, bebiendo un vaso de ti, Silva,
un vaso para ponerse bien, como decíamos,
y después, ya veremos lo que pasa ...

(Hôtel des Ecoles is open as always/ and they still buy tangerines;/ but I suffer, like I say, sweetly, remembering/ what we both suffered, in both our deaths,/ in the opening of the double tomb,/ of that other tomb with your being,/ and of this mahogany one of your to be;/ I suffer, drinking a glass of you, Silva,/ a glass to straighten me out, as we used to say,/ and afterward, we'll see what happens ...; Eshleman, *Complete Poetry*, 474–75)

This stanza provides details of an everyday life in the Paris of the 1920s that the two men shared (the Hôtel des Ecoles, the tangerines, the drink to set them up) and also expresses an intimacy that goes beyond the realm of the normal – some would call it paranormal – since it hints at not only a shared experience of death, but a sense in which they are joined in the "double tomb" mentioned in l.34, itself redolent of the "hermanitos" mentioned in "El poeta a su amada" (The Poet to His Love) from *Los heraldos negros* (The Black Heralds; Eshleman, *Complete Poetry*, 58,) discussed in chapter 8 of this book. The final stanza of the poem suggests a zenith of closeness between

[30] Ricardo González Vigil, *César Vallejo* (Lima: Brasa, 1985), 82–83.
[31] Here we are exploring an idea initially put to Stephen M. Hart by Georgette de Vallejo's doctor, Max Silva Tuesta, in a discussion which occurred in Lima on June 29, 2013.

the two men is achieved which is like a new hard-soft version of the consumption of the elements of Holy Communion:

> Es éste el otro brindis, entre tres,
> taciturno, diverso
> en vino, en mundo, en vidrio, al que brindábamos
> más de una vez al cuerpo
> y, menos de una vez, al pensamiento.
> Hoy es más diferente todavía;
> hoy sufro dulce, amargamente,
> bebo tu sangre en cuanto a Cristo el duro,
> como tu hueso en cuanto a Cristo el suave,
> porque te quiero, dos a dos, Alfonso,
> y casi lo podría decir, eternamente.

> (This is the other toast, among three,/ solemn, diverse,/ in wine, in world, in glass, the one that we raised/ more than once to the body/ and less than once, to the mind./ Today is even more different; today I suffer bitterly sweet,/ I drink your blood as to Christ the hard,/ I eat your bone as to Christ the soft,/ because I love you, two by two, Alfonso,/ and could almost say so, eternally; Eshleman, *Complete Poetry*, 476–77)

The reference in the poem's concluding stanza to the custom Vallejo and Alfonso had of raising a glass to "the body," Vallejo's admission that he feels an "eternal" love for Alfonso, as well as his use of the direct address "te quiero, dos a dos, Alfonso" indicate the presence of a high level of homo-affectivity in this poem.

Whether this should be seen as an indication of a "silence" in Vallejo's life and work that should be explored in greater detail is, of course, a moot point. But what is clear is that homoaffectivity, whether in the openly gay poetry of Ramos Otero, or expressed in the personally coded imagery of Pizarnik's work, or hinted at as in Vallejo's poetry, is an important current within the river of Latin American verse. Often its presence is evoked by means of what Brad Epps calls "the tension between being and coming (…), fragmentation and wholeness, recuperation and reinvention, reality and representation" ("Virtual Sexuality," 323), and it is this combination of a mysterious Otherness with its use of tantalizing encodings that subtends the best of Latin America's LGBTQ poetry.

14

ALISON KRÖGEL

Quechua/Kichwa Poetry

"Díceme que en estos tiempos se dan mucho los mestizos a componer en indio estos versos, y otros de muchas maneras, así a lo divino como a lo humano. Dios les dé su gracia para que le sirvan en todo." (I am told that at this time the mestizos are working hard at composing verses in the Indian tongue, and writing others in many ways, both in the Divine and the Human manner. May God give them grace to serve Him in everything they do);

El Inca Garcilaso de la Vega, Comentarios Reales, 1609 (Royal Commentaries of the Incas)

Writing from the Andalusian city of Córdoba in the latter half of the sixteenth century, the *mestizo* chronicler and Cusco-native Inca Garcilaso de la Vega explains in his *Comentarios Reales* (Royal Commentaries of the Incas) that even just a few decades after the arrival of Pizarro on the shores of present-day Peru, already "many mestizos" had taken to composing verses in the language of Quechua ("indio"). Interestingly, Garcilaso's brief description of the various forms and functions of poetry in the Incan empire of Tahuantinsuyu, as well as his fleeting reference to poems written "in Indian" in the years following the conquest, closes with a petition to the Divine to support these Quechua language poetic efforts. Some four centuries later, the continued composition and publication of poetry written in Quechua (as the indigenous Andean language is known in Peru and Bolivia) and Kichwa (alternately spelled as Quichua, as it is known in in Ecuador) attests to the fact that thankfully, if indeed improbably, Garcilaso's supplication has been answered.[1]

When considering the nearly five-hundred-year history of poetry written in Quechua, it is important to keep in mind that beginning in the colonial period, discursive and poetic practices in the Andean countries emerged in the midst of a space of violence, conflict, and exclusion.[2] Indeed, during the

---

[1] In this chapter I use the word "Quechua" to refer to the indigenous Andean language spoken and written by some ten million individuals principally throughout the Andean countries of Ecuador, Peru, and Bolivia. In order to respect present-day northern Andean spelling preferences, I will use the word "Kichwa" when referring specifically to the dialect of the language that is spoken and written in Ecuador.

[2] Gonzalo Espino Relucé, *Etnopoética quechua. Textos y tradición oral quechua*, PhD Diss., Universidad Nacional Mayor de San Marcos. 2007, Cyb2007, 183.

centuries following the initial conquest of Tahuantinsuyu, diverse actors and efforts have sought to silence the voices of Quechua speakers and to stamp out their artistic, cultural, and religious practices. Whether by decree of the Church, agents of the colonial government, or through a combination of ecclesiastical and political forces, on numerous occasions throughout the colonial period, the use of the Quechua language (called runasimi or "the language of the people," by its speakers) was prohibited. On repeated occasions in the colonial Andes, various archbishops, agents of the Inquisition, colonial administrators, and officials (visitadores) called for a halt in the use of "vernacular" indigenous languages and for prohibitions against indigenous instruments, clothing, and visual art, as well as Quechua-language song, dance, and theatre.[3]

Throughout the colonial period, attempts at linguistic interdictions were interspersed with attempts to "domesticate" the obstinate orality of the Quechua language in order to represent its diverse phonemes with letters of the roman alphabet and through monumental colonizing projects marked by the creation of scores of grammars, dictionaries, catechisms, and confessional manuals.[4] As a result, the efforts of a diverse cast of evangelists, agents of the Inquisition, emissaries of colonial government and Spanish, mestizo, and indigenous scribes and chroniclers has left contemporary readers with an assorted corpus of colonial-era Quechua language poetry that hints at a rich, preconquest trove of religious, epic, and amorous verses which would likely have been declaimed by either an individual or a chorus at various mourning, harvest, celebratory, or commemoratory events throughout Tahuantinsuyu.[5]

Given that Quechua verbal art is deeply oral in character and often anonymously composed, prior to the sixteenth-century arrival of Spanish aesthetic hierarchies and influences, which tended to favor individually authored poetic works, the corpus of Quechua language poetry and drama would likely have been collectively authored and performed orally in songs or recitations. Similarly, many of the "modern" poems that appear in Quechua poetry anthologies are the unattributed verses of oral song-poems or riddles which have been collected, transcribed, and edited by anthropologists, ethnomusicologists, priests, and other "Quechuists"

[3] Bruce Mannheim, *The Language of the Inka since the European Invasion* (Austin, TX: Texas University Press, 1991), 64–76; César Itier, "Literatura nisqap qichwasimipi mirayñinmanta," *Amerindia* 24 (1999): 40–41.

[4] See Noriega, *Escritura Quechua en el Perú* (Lima: Pakarina Ediciones), 1–24; and Noriega, *Poesía quechua escrita en el Perú: Antología* (Lima: CEP, 1993), 30–31.

[5] Lara, *La poesía quechua* (Mexico City: FCE, 1947); Edmondo Bendezú Aybar, *Literatura Quechua* (Caracas, Biblioteca Ayacucho, 1986).

(Quechuistas).[6] Even single-authored works of contemporary Quechua language poetry reveal in their verses the profound influence of Quechua oral culture (songs, myths, and oral histories). Yet as Jean Franco and other scholars have pointed out, the study of indigenous literatures, and indigenous language poetry in particular, is complicated by the fact that tonality and sound structures are crucial elements of both oral and written, traditional and contemporary indigenous language poetries, and these features cannot be recreated easily in translations, or even meaningfully described when using non-indigenous critical terminologies.[7] Further complicating the study of indigenous language literary histories is the fact that colonial linguistic and cultural hegemonic structures and policies, together with the intense chaos, violence, and demographic collapses that characterized the colonial period throughout the Americas, has meant that many manuscripts and voices have been lost, while work attributed to the (written) corpus of one author may in fact, have been the (oral) work of an entire community.[8]

Precolonial and Colonial Quechua Poetry

Although colonial sources of Quechua language lyrical and dramatic verse undoubtedly offer us only a very incomplete picture of preconquest poetic forms, Garcilaso's *Comentarios reales* (1609), Felipe Guaman Poma de Ayala's *Primera nueva corónica* (1615), the anonymous Quechua drama *Ollantay* (circa eighteenth century), as well the chronicles of Juan de

---

[6] See, for instance, José María Arguedas, *El canto Kechwa: con un ensayo sobre la capacidad de creación artística del pueblo indio y mestizo* (Lima: Ediciones Club del libro peruano, 1938); and his *Canciones y cuentos del pueblo quechua* (Lima: Editorial Huascarán S.A.1949); José M. B. Farfán, *Colección de textos quechuas del Perú* (Lima: Impr. del Politécnico Nacional José Pardo, 1952); Charles Kleymeyer, *Imashi! Imashi!: adivinanzas poéticas de los campesinos indígenas del mundo andino, Ecuador, Perú y Bolivia* (Quito: Ediciones Abya Yala, 1993); Lara, *La poesía quechua*; Lara, *La literatura de los Quechuas: ensayo y antología* (La Paz: Librería y editorial juventud, 1980); Juan León Mera, *Antología Ecuatoriana: cantares del pueblo ecuatoriano* (Quito: Imprenta de la Universidad Central del Ecuador, 1892); Rodrigo Montoya, Edwin Montoya and Luis Montoya, ed., *La sangre de los cerros, urqukunapa yawarnin: Antología de la poesía que se canta en el Perú* (Lima: Centro Peruano de Estudios Sociales, 1987); and Teófilo Vargas, *Aires nacionales de Bolivia* (Cochabamba: Talleres Casa Marilla, 1940), 3 vols.

[7] Jean Franco, "Some Reflections on Contemporary Writing in the Indigenous Languages of America," *Comparative American Studies* 3.4 (2005): 459; Regina Harrison, *Signs, Songs, and Memory in the Andes: Translating Quechua Language and Culture* (Austin, TX: University of Texas Press, 1989), 4–54; and Pablo Landeo Muñoz *Categorías andinas para una aproximación al willakuy* (Lima: Asamblea Nacional de Rectores, 2014).

[8] Julio E. Noriega Bernuy, *Buscando una tradición poética quechua en el Perú* (Coral Gables, FL: Centro Norte-Sur, Universidad de Miami, 1995), 149–60.

Santacruz Pachacuti Yamqui Salkamaywa (1613?), and Cristóbal de Molina (1575?) all offer fascinating glimpses of some of the forms which poetry in Tahuantinsuyu likely assumed. Two of the most well-represented of these poetic forms include the haylli (or jailli, song-poems which took the form of epic, celebratory, or agricultural songs, or sacred hymns dedicated to Andean gods such as Viracocha or Inti), and the harawi (a term frequently used to describe the passionate verses of "love poems," but which sometimes also refers to poetry, or versification in general).[9]

Like the Incan arawikus, or poet-bards before them, the composers of Quechua language verse in the postconquest Andes tended to remain anonymous within the historical record:

¿Uj kkata kusíyniy kajta	1	She who had filled the hollow, and was my only happiness
Mayqen jallppa mullppuykapun?		Which mound of bitter earth has swallowed her up?
Saqerqani qhallallajta,		I left her healthy
¿Sajra wayrachu, apakapun?		Could an evil wind have carried her away?
Purisqán pallani,	5	I follow [the hints] of her trail
Llanthunta maskkani.		I trace [the whispers] of her shadow
Kikin pay llanthuykuwanchu,		Is it she who provides me shade [as I continue on], or
Waqayníypaj ayphullanchu?		Is it only the haze left behind by my tears?[10]

One of the most well-known colonial-era Quechua poems, the powerful elegy known as "Manchay Puytu" (Ominous Storm Cloud) is anonymous, while the dozen or so late colonial poems generally attributed to the Bolivian "poet-soldier" Juan Wallparimachi Maita, are possibly not the work of a single author, but of a collective and primarily oral creative

[9] See Lara, *La poesía quechua*, 53–68; and Cáceres Romero, *Poesía Quechua del Tawantinsuyu* (Buenos Aires: Ediciones del Sol, 2009), 15–26. Although the present chapter focuses on Quechua lyrical poetry, the written Quechua literary tradition also includes a rich corpus of dramatic verse which would likely have been enjoyed in colonial times by audiences made up of illiterate, indigenous Quechua speakers, as well as bilingual Andean elites or criollos and later, during the first several decades of the twentieth century, by Andean indigenista intellectuals. Important works of written colonial Quechua drama include: *Ollantay*, *Usca Paucar*, and *Tragedia del fin de Atawallpa*. For examples of Quechua drama written during the late nineteenth and early twentieth century see works authored by Nemesio Zúñiga Cazorla, Nicanor Jara, Mariano Rodríguez, and José Salvador Cavero León studied in detail in Itier, *El teatro quechua en el cuzco* (Cusco: El Centro Bartolomé de las Casas, 2000), vol. 2.
[10] "Manchay Puitu," in Lara, *La poesía quechua*, 180. In this chapter, translations from the Spanish or the Quechua are the author's unless otherwise indicated.

Alison Krögel

process.[11] Both "Manchay Puytu" and the so-called "Wallparimachi poems" exhibit powerful imagery, elegant parallel structuring and a tone of intense lamentation, which eloquently depicts the pain and yearning associated with losing one's true love.

Republican-era Quechua Poetry

Given the forced castilianization policies, and the widespread disparagement and destruction of indigenous religions, cultural practices, and art forms during the period of Spanish colonial rule in the Andes, it is not surprising that very few examples of written Quechua poetry survive from the tumultuous years following the independence of Ecuador (1822), Peru (1824), and Bolivia (1825). Notable exceptions to this general dearth of indigenous language poetry published in the Republican-era Andes include the Kichwa language verses of the Ecuadorian poet, and former president, Luis Cordero (1833–1912) who published bilingual versions of his poems denouncing the abuses faced by indigenous Ecuadorians. Notable poems penned by Cordero in the late nineteenth century include "¡Rinimi Llacta!" (El adiós del indio), "Cushiquillca" (Coplas de contento), and "Runapag llagui" (Desventura del indio).[12] In Republican Bolivia, Quechua language promoters, educators, linguists, anthologizers, and occasional poets and dramaturges include Carlos Felipe Beltrán (1816–1898) and José David Berríos (1849–1912). Key Quechuists in Republican Peru include José Fernández Nodal (early nineteenth century–late nineteenth/early twentieth century) and José Dionisio Anchorena (1834–1906). Although much more well known for her novels (*Aves sin nido*, 1889; *Herencia, 1895*) and journalistic texts (as director of *El Perú Ilustrado*), the Cusqueñan writer and indigenista intellectual Clorinda Matto de Turner also published Quechua language poetry (see, for instance, her *Tradiciones cuzqueñas, v. 1, 1884, v.2 1886*).

Quechua Poetry in the Twentieth Century

The postindigenista corpus of twentieth-century poetry written in Quechua is often described in terms of two distinct currents inaugurated in Peru in the

[11] Noriega, "La oralización de la escritura en la poesía quechua escrita de Bolivia," *Bulletin de la Société Suisse des Américanistes* 59/60 (1996): 153. Noriega, *Poesía quechua en Bolivia* (Lima: Pakarina Ediciones, 2016), 37–39.
[12] See Cordero, "¡Rinimi Llacta!," "Cushiquillca." and "Runapag llagui" in *Poesía popular, alcances y apéndice, Indices*, ed. Isaac J. Barrera (Quito: Biblioteca ecuatoriana mínima, 1960), 60–85; and Regina Harrison, *Entre el tronar épico y el llanto elegíaco: simbología indígena en la poesía* (Quito: Abya-Yala, 1995), 111–22, 225–28.

1950s and 1960s.[13] The first of these movements is characterized by the aristocratic, Cusco-centric, "purist-Quechua" (or "modern-*misti* [mestizo]") variant that arose in 1952 with the publication of *Taki Parwa* by the Cusqueñan Kilku Warak'a (né Andrés Gutiérrez, 1909–1984), while the second is generally associated with the work of more socially engaged poet-migrants following the 1962 publication of the haylli-taki (hymn-song) "Tupac Amaru Kamaq Taytanchisman" by the renowned Peruvian writer José María Arguedas (1911–1969).[14] *Taki Parwa*, together with Warak'a's two subsequent monolingual Quechua poetry collections (*Taki ruru*, 1964 and *Yawar Para*, 1972), is generally considered to mark the inception of modern *written* Quechua poetry. Not only did Warak'a create an individually authored corpus of poetic texts, but he also managed to create verbal imagery and expressions that feel both intimate and deeply personal, while still referencing important aspects of Quechua/Andean landscapes, mythologies, and cosmovisions.[15]

Warak'a's *Taki Parwa* is written in a highbrow register of Cusqueñan Quechua and includes thirty carefully metered poems (mostly quatrains, cinquains, and sestets) composed of five, eight, or ten-syllable lines. For instance, the poem "P'uncayniykipi" (On Your Day) consists of four sestets, each integrally composed of eight-syllable lines. The gracefulness of the poem's even meter is matched by several elegantly composed (and sometimes cleverly split) semantic couplets, as evidenced in the poem's final strophe (lines 20, 22 and 21, 23). Warak'a's verses also frequently achieve a calming effect through the use of anaphoric repetition and rhythmic assonances that particularly emphasize the rounded vowel [u]. In the poem "P'uncayniykipi," examples of such [u]-centric assonances occur in the phrases "tukuy urkun," "yuraq ñukñu," and "unu rurucuncu," (lines 4, 16, and 21). These sonoral techniques are woven into "P'uncayniykipi" in order to proffer a tribute to the poem's lyrical subject, in celebration of her name day:

[13] Noriega, *Poesía quechua escrita en el Perú: Antología* (Lima: CEP, 1995), 29–30; Lienhard, *La voz y su huella* (Lima, Editorial Horizonte, 1992), 281.
[14] See Noriega's pivotal book *Buscando una tradición poética quechua en el Perú* for a study of contemporary poetry written in Quechua. For detailed readings of Arguedas' most celebrated, lengthy, and oft-cited poem, "Tupac Amaru kamaq taytanchisman" (To Our Creator Father, Tupac Amaru), see for example Antonio Cornejo Polar, "Tradición migrante e interculturalidad multicultural: El caso de Arguedas," in *Zorros al fin del milenio: Actas y ensayos del Seminario sobre la última novela de José María Arguedas*, ed. Wilfredo Kapsoli (Lima: Centro de Investigación Universidad Ricardo Palma 2004), 51; and Mazzotti, *Poéticas del flujo: migración y violencia verbales en el Perú de los 80* (Lima: Fondo Editorial del Congreso de la República, 2002), 101–04.
[15] See Odi Gonzáles, ed. and trans., "Los dos lenguajes de Kilku Warak'a," in *Taki Parwa/22 poemas: Kilku Warak'a* (Cusco: Biblioteca Municipal del Cusco, 1999), 9–10, 13–15.

Kawsay sipas t'ika mukmu	19	Vivacious lass; budding flower
amapuni ñawiykipi		may your eyes fend off any
wiqi unu rurucuncu	21	stream of tears that might blossom within you
amapuni sunquykipi		may your heart fend off any
llaki phuyu tiyacuncu	23	cloud of sorrow that might live within you
kawsay kusi wiñay wata		live happily, as each year grows older[16]

Although José María Arguedas greatly admired the work of Kilku Warak'a – calling him "the greatest Quechua poet of the twentieth century" – in Arguedas' brief prologue to "Tupac Amaru Kamaq Taytanchisman," he takes care to present his own haylli as a poem proudly written in a sociolect based largely on Cusqueñan Quechua, but which has been slightly manipulated by the poet in order for it to be linguistically comprehensible to as large a number of Quechua speakers as possible throughout the Andean countries. Given his use of some Spanish language terms which "have been adopted by both Indian and *mestizo* [Quechua speakers]," Arguedas acknowledges that his poetry will likely be met with disdain by "purist Quechuists" – intellectual elites who promoted the use of "High Quechua" or "Capac Simi," unpolluted by Spanish words.[17] Of great importance in the 1960s, 1970s, and 1980s for the dispersed communities of young Andean intellectuals studying in highland universities, or as Andean migrants (or as the children of migrants) in Lima, Arguedas closes his prologue to "Tupac Amaru Kamaq Taytanchisman" with an inspiring call to Quechua speakers and writers:

> Those of you who have a better command than I of this language, I plead to you to write. We must increase [the body] of our Quechua literature, especially in the Language that the people speak; even though the other variety, the stately and erudite, should also be cultivated with the same dedication. Let us demonstrate that contemporary Quechua is a language in which one can write poetry in a manner which is as beautiful and moving as any of the other languages perfected by centuries of literary tradition! Quechua too, is a millenary language.[18]

Arguedas famously affirmed on several occasions his belief that the semantic and sonoric richness and complexity of the Quechua language was more suited to lyrical expression than Spanish.[19] Yet in this prologue he also

[16] "P'uncayniykipi," rptd. in Odi Gonzáles, *Taki Parwa*, 26–28.
[17] Arguedas, "Taki parwa y la poesía quechua de la República," *Letras peruanas* 4.12 (1955): 73; and Arguedas, *Tupac Amaru Kamaq Taytanchisman: Haylli-Taki. A Nuestro Padre Creador Tupac Amaru: Himno-Canción* (Lima: Ediciones Salqantay, 1962), 7–8.
[18] Arguedas, *Tupac Amaru*, 9.
[19] Arguedas, *Temblar/Katatay*, ed. Sybila Arredondo (Lima I.N.C., 1972), 59; and Arguedas, *El canto Kechwa: con un ensayo sobre la capacidad de creación artística del*

directly addresses the historic problem of the Quechua writer. Namely, the fact that contemporary Quechua poetry is almost always written by bilingual intellectuals who are creators of a literature that lacks any real market or readership and whose "urban product also does not reach the monolingual Quechua population which, in practice, has still not incorporated the written form [of the Quechua language]."[20] Despite these very daunting hurdles, between 1962 and his death in 1969 Arguedas continued to write and publish poetry in Quechua, often together with his own Spanish language 'recreations' of the original poems.[21] Unfortunately, intermittent indigenous language alphabetization campaigns and "bilingual" or "intercultural" education programs and policies mounted in the Andean countries over the past 60–70 years have, as yet, failed to overcome the vast social, economic, political, and logistical challenges associated with creating a widespread community of Quechua language readers.

Nevertheless, in the years following the pivotal publications of Arguedas's and Warak'a's poetry (and since the early 1980s in particular), many innovative collections of Quechua poetry have been published in Peru, Bolivia, and Ecuador. Although generally taking the form of bilingual Quechua-Spanish poetry collections, authors such as Ariruma Kowii (1988), Carrillo Cavero (2009, 2010), and Yauri Taipe (2008) have followed Kilku Warak'a's lead in declining to provide readers with the weak and oftentimes misleading support of a translation-crutch by opting instead to publish monolingual collections of their Quechua poetry.[22] Like the first-person plural voice of Arguedas's poem "Tupac Amaru Kamaq Taytanchisman,"

pueblo indio y mestizo (Lima: Ediciones Club del libro peruano, 1938), 16; see also Mazzotti, *Poéticas del flujo: Migración y violencia verbales en el Perú de los 80* (Lima: Fondo Editorial del Congreso de la República, 2002), 100–01.

[20] Noriega, *Poesía quechua escrita en el Perú: Antología*, 40; César Itier, "Literatura nisqap qichwasimipi mirayñinmanta," *Amerindia* 24 (1999): 31–34; and Jean Franco, "Some Reflections," 464–65.

[21] Espino Relucé, *Etnopoética quechua*, 26–28; Harrison, "José María Arguedas: El substrato quechua," *Revista Iberoamericana* 49 (1983): 122. Most readers are familiar only with the six Arguedas Quechua poems compiled by Sybila Arredondo in the bilingual, posthumous collection entitled *Katatay/Temblar* (1972). According to the Peruvian literary critic Gonzalo Espino Relucé, however, a total of eighteen Quechua language poems written by Arguedas have been located to date, though not all of them were published prior to the author's death; see Espino Relucé, *Etnopoética quechua*, 27; and Mazzotti, *Poéticas del flujo*, 104.

[22] For interesting and much rarer examples of trilingual poetry collections, see Gonzáles, *Tunupa: Libro de las sirenas*, trans. Alison Krögel and José Ramón Ruisánchez (Lima: Ediciones El Santo Oficio, 2002), and Roncalla, *Escritos Mitimaes: Hacia una poética andina postmoderna* (New York, NY: Editorial Barro, 1998) for poetry in Quechua, Spanish and English; and Elvira Espejo Ayca, *Kaypijaqhaypi: Por aquí, por allá* (La Paz: Pirotecnia, 2013) who publishes trilingual Quechua-, Aymara- and Spanish-language poetry collections.

in the final decades of the twentieth century, poets writing in Quechua in the Andean countries generally lived, wrote, and worked in urban spaces, having moved away from the frigid *pampas* and distant ravines of the rural Andes: "karu qeswakunamanta, kita weraqochakuna, pampa, chiri, qoñeq allpaykuna qechuwasqankunamanta, ayqespa, mastarinakuniku lliu tawantinsuyupi... ¡Kachkaniraqkun, chaypas kachkaniraqkun, kancharisparaq!" (from the distant ravines, from the now frigid, now burning pampas that the false wiraqochas took away from us, we have fled and we have spread out across all four regions of the world... And yet we still exist, we still exist and we are shining!).[23]

While it would be impossible in these pages to explore in depth the vast corpus of twentieth- and twenty-first century Quechua poetry written and published in the Andean countries and beyond, a reading of this body of work reveals recurring examples of: lyrical poems addressed to the Beloved, Nature, Andean gods and cultural heroes, (sacred) ancestors, one's Andean community (ayllu), dramatic Andean landscapes, the memory of resplendent and sophisticated Incan forebears and their empire of Tahuantinsuyu; celebratory poems extoling the virtues of Andean (agri)culture, administration, and sociocultural and economic practices; migrants' longings for a distant Andean homeland; and denunciatory poems that call for an end to racism and oppression, and for Andean peoples to rise up against such injustices in a modern-day, turning-the-world-upside-down pachacuti. Rather more uncommon, but nevertheless present (particularly amongst women poets) are poems focused on intimate, domestic subjects – a child nursed at her mother's breast, the tattered red poncho of a beloved grandfather, or the image of a group of Quechua grandmothers happily walking into town together, arm in arm. Thematic diversity notwithstanding, some of the most striking poems of this body of work share in common their capacity to create complex and original imagery through a supple wielding of the Quechua language's adjectival richness and agglutinating plasticity in order to weave multivalenced meanings into compact (and often parallel structured) verses.

In the 1980s and 1990s, the post-Arguedian generation of bilingual Quechua poets writing primarily from Peru (Eduardo Ninamango Mallqui, Dida Aguirre, Lily Flores Palomino, Washington Córdova Huamán, Isaac Huamán Manrique, and William Hurtado de Mendoza), but also from Bolivia (Emma Paz Noya, Jaime Gutierrez Achocalla), and Ecuador (Aririuma Kowii, Auki Tituaña Males), tended to distance themselves from the creation of nostalgic, mythic imagery of heroic Andean pasts. Instead,

[23] Arguedas, *Tupac Amaru*, 16.

these poets more frequently focused on the development of poetic themes that denounced racism, poverty, (neo)colonialism, and the destruction of Andean nature and culture.[24] The literary critic José Antonio Mazzotti has characterized Peruvian poetic production in the 1980s as a "dystopic," "poetics of flow" (poéticas de flujo) that resulted from the "marked increase in internal and external migrations, a phenomenon accompanied by an unprecedented exacerbation of political violence [during the Shining Path era]."[25]

The poetry of Lily Flores Palomino is representative of this current of denunciatory, post-Arguedian Quechua poetry in that it offers up direct, vivid imagery and unadorned verses that condemn the suffering of countless indigenous Andeans. For instance, "Yuyalayay" (Hope), the penultimate poem in Flores Palomino's 1989 collection entitled *Waqalliq Takin*, begins with five lines that express with an almost oppressive force, the cruel realities faced by Andean campesinos who have been unable to free themselves from the misery meted out by hunger (1989, 100–01). The first four of these lines end with the genitive suffix /-pa/, creating a rhythmic repetition that drives the poem towards a staccato crescendo and intensifies the reader's sense of a painful and suffocating burden: "Maqakuypa/ yarqaypa/ chiripa/ nanaypa" (lines 1–4). Yet an abrupt and temporarily disorienting shift occurs in line six when a soothing assonance introduces the possibility of "hope" (yuya-layayqa). The abrupt and disconcerting ending to the poem is then presented with the rough, penetrating sounds of the occlusive postvelar /q/ in the word "wañusqata" (dead) and in the ejective occlusion of the /q'/ phoneme in the poem's final word, "marq'arikuspa" (within her arms).

[24] Mazzotti, *Poéticas del flujo*, 40; Noriega, *Escritura Quechua en el Perú* (Lima: Pakarina Ediciones), 132. Poetic precursors of this genre of dystopian Quechua verse that assertively calls for a shift in Andean power structures, denounces a host of abuses suffered by Quechua campesinos (agro-pastoralists) at the hands of exploitative wiraqocha-overlords and landowners, and laments the loss of Andean cultural forms and practices include: the poetry of the Ayacuchan poet and professor César Guardia Mayorga (Kusi Paukar), as well as the work of the Cusqueñan poet William Hurtado de Mendoza. For an analysis of Mayorga's poem, "¡Jatarichik!, see Krögel, *Food, Power, and Resistance in the Andes: Exploring Quechua Verbal and Visual Narratives* (Lanham, MD: Lexington Books, 2011), 180–84. For studies and selections of Hurtado's poetic production see Noriega, *Poesía quechua escrita en el Perú: Antología*, 305–20; Noriega, ed., *Pichka harawikuna: Five Quechua Poets, An Anthology*, trans. Maureen Ahern (New York, NY: Americas Society, Latin American Literary Review Press, 1998), 43–60; and Ángel Avedaño, *Historia de la literatura del Qosqo: Del Tiempo Mítico al Siglo XX* (Qosqo: Municipalidad de Qosqo, 1993), vol. 2, 598–601.
[25] Qtd. in *Bilingual Games: Some Literary Investigations*, ed. Doris Sommers (New York, NY: Palgrave Macmillan, 2003), 97; see also Lienhard, "Pachacuti Taki: canto y poesía quechua de la transformación del mundo," *Allpanchis* 20.32 (1998): 165–98, 190–98.

Maqakuypa	1	Behind the pummelings
yarqaypa		of the hunger
chiripa		of the cold
nanaypa		of the pain
yanqa llullaq qepanpim,	5	of the lingering deceptions
yuyalayayqa kashan		hope lies waiting
munay samita		with [optimism's] warm energy
wañusqata marq'arikuspa.		dead in her arms.[26]

With its at first disorienting and then depressing title, the poem "Yuyalayay" serves as a biting reminder of the painful and very physical privations that too many Quechua families must face on a daily basis.

Amongst students of post-Arguedian Quechua poetry, Eduardo Ninamango Mallqui stands out. His slim, impactful bilingual collection entitled *Pukutay/Tormenta* (1982) is one of the most beautifully wrought descriptions of the sorrowful, nostalgic existence of Andean migrant-exiles struggling to understand their place within highland landscapes and communities that have been violently scarred as a result of the bloody civil war waged between Shining Path insurgents and Peruvian government forces, and which claimed the lives of tens of thousands of indigenous Quechua civilians in the 1980s and 1990s. The book's title refers to an ominous "pukutay" Andean cloudscape that portends a storm of profound transformation and the upending of order within campesino communities in highland Peru during the latter half of the twentieth century. Indeed, the poems contained in this book chronicle a collection of departures, losses, and painful, cataclysmic changes.[27]

In "Poem 4" of *Pukutay*, Ninamango Mallqui subtly expresses the intense sadness that characterized this time of deep uncertainty and drastic transitions by depicting the disruption of fragile, vital connections between vegetable and human worlds. As the first-person lyrical voice of "Poem 4" nears his childhood home and interprets the signs of nature that point to the death of his grandfather, Ninamango Mallqui employs the sterile, lonesome image of a solitary cornstalk in order to express feelings of a deep and existential sadness:

[26] "Yuyalayay," in Lily Flores Flores Palomino, *Waqalliq Takin: Tañido de campanas* (Lima: Consejo Nacional de Ciencia y Tecnología, 1989), 100.
[27] Noriega, *Escritura Quechua en el Perú*, 124; Lienhard, *La voz y su huella* (Lima: Editorial Horizonte, 1992), 292–93; Mazzotti, *Poéticas del flujo*, 53.

manañan yachanichu …	9	Because I know nothing…
machu taitallaipas	11	of the grandfather
ripunña		whom they say, has already left us
sara mana poqochkaqta saqerispa	13	leaving behind the unripened cornstalks
rititas chikchipas qapinkama.		until the ice and the hail seize hold.[28]

In this strophe, the voice of the poetic-I references the Andean trope of the wakcha-orphan when describing a field of tender and still immature cornstalks that has been left unprotected now that the guiding hand of the grandfather "has departed" (ripunña, line 12). The final word of this strophe also merits particular attention, given the multivalenced meanings attached to the Quechua verb "qapiy," and given the date of the poem's initial publication at the onset of Peru's civil war. "Qapiy" means "to grab," "to seize," or "to take hold of," and is also the verb used by Quechua campesinos to refer to the way in which profound, emotional or spiritual illnesses "grab hold" of them, causing the oppressive sadness that characterizes a psychosomatic disorder known as "males de campo." Literally meaning "rural illnesses," this constellation of maladies – analogous in many ways, to post-traumatic stress disorder – includes "llakis" (painful memories), "iquyay" (weakness), and "manchay" (fear), among others.[29] Thus, although the grandfather's absence and abandonment of the family's cornstalks is not explained directly, Ninamango's use of the ominous phrase "qapinkama" in the poem's final moment alludes to the profound violence perpetrated within highland communities both during and after the civil war period in Peru.

Contemporary Quechua Poetry

With the dawn of a new century and the publication of poetry by writers such as Odi Gonzáles, Ch'aska Eugenia Anka Ninawaman, Lourdes Llasag Fernández, Mariana del Rocío Anchatuña Rojas, Lucila Lema Otavalo, Dida Aguirre, Elvira Espejo Ayca, and Godoy Félix Yauri Taipe, a new current of Quechua poetry has emerged. Written by poets who often also work as translators, educators, activists, or community organizers, this contemporary poetry often choreographs verbal gestures that flow nimbly between denunciations of a myriad of injustices and celebrations of the vitality, beauty, and

---

[28] "Poema 4," in *Pukutay/Tormenta*, ed. Eduardo Ninamango Mallqui (Lima: Tarea, Centro de Publicaciones Educativas, 1982), 20.

[29] Malvaceda E. "Ñakari: Formas culturales de sufrimiento tras la violencia política en el Perú," *Revista IIPSI* 13.2 (2010): 130; Theidon, *Intimate Enemies: Violence and Reconciliation in Peru* (Philadelphia, PA: University of Pennsylvania Press, 2013), 45.

creativity evident within urban, rural, and peri-urban Andean communities. Thus far, Quechua poetry being written and published in Andean countries (and beyond) in the twenty-first century has begun to explore new registers, rhythms, themes, and styles, while continuing to reference and engage with the rich reserves of symbols, imagery, myths, landscapes, deities, and cultural heroes of Quechua and Kichwa oral traditions, as well as with modern Quechua literary pioneers such as Arguedas.[30]

In the collection *Poesía en Quechua: Chaskaschay*, Ch'aska Eugenia Anka Ninawaman utilizes a more accessible register of Cusqueñan Quechua to celebrate and explore the symbolic and ritual diversity of the flora, fauna, and sacred spaces and beings of Peru's southern highland. Anka Ninawaman's poignant verses often celebrate (and indeed, promote) the underappreciated food resources that grow wild in the Andean countryside.[31] For instance, in her poem "Ch'awiyuyu mama" (Mother Ch'awiyuyu) the poet reveals how a Quechua women's knowledge of her community's food-landscape can guide her to nutritional treasures such as the Ch'awiyuyu plant that grows wild all year long, and can help poor women to supplement their children's nutritional needs at no cost:

Mayu patapi		Along the river's edge
q'illu sumbriru t'ikaqcha;		a yellow flower hat;
q'umir pullera ch'awicha.		a wrinkled green skirt
Inti taytaq k'anchaykusqan		under the warmth of father Sun
killa mamaq llanthuykusqan.	5	under the shadow of mother Moon
Munay munay wiñaqcha		Beautifully, beautifully you grow
phuyuq hump'inwan		covered with a dewy cloud
ch'aqchuykusqa,		gently irrigated,
hallp'aq sunqunmanta		from the heart of the land
phuturimuqcha....	10	you sprout.
hunt'aykachipuwanki.	20	You fill us completely.[32]

[30] See Juan Ulises Zevallos-Aguilar for a discussion of how, since the 1990s, Quechua poetry has moved away from lyrical representations of Andean (neoliberal) utopias in order to focus instead on themes of "ethnic recognition, identity politics, and the denunciation of problems that concern them"; see "Recent Peruvian Quechua poetry beyond Andean and neoliberal utopias," in *The Utopian Impulse in Latin America*, ed. Kim Beauchesne and Alessandra Santos (Basingstoke: Palgrave Macmillan, 2011), 275; see also Zevallos-Aguilar, *Las provincias contraatacan: regionalismo y anticentralismo en la literatura peruana del siglo XX* (Lima: UNMSM, Ediciones del Vicerrectorado Académico, 2009).

[31] Krögel, "Sara mamacha, papa mamacha: representaciones alimenticias en la poesía quechua," *Revista de crítica literaria latinoamericana* 75.1 (2012): 331–61.

[32] "Ch'awiyuyu mama," in Anka Ninawaman, Ch'aska Eugenia, *Poesía en Quechua: Chaskaschay* (Quito: Abya Yala, 2004), 96–97.

Like Anka Ninawaman, the two monolingual collections of Quechua verse published since 2009 by the Peruvian poet and musician, Ugo Facundo Carrillo Cavero also traverse a fine line between sentiments of lament and resolution. Carrillo Cavero's poems almost always allude to the possibility of finding solutions to complex social problems and a path to a brighter future. For instance, in his first collection of Quechua poetry, *Yaku-unupa yuyaynin* (Memory of the Water, 2009), Carrillo Cavero pays respectful and grateful homage to the diversity and generous productivity of Andean cultivars. One particularly striking section of this book called *"Papachanchikpa waytan uqllu waqtachanpi qillqakuna"* (Written on the Resilient Petals of Our Dear Potato's Flowers), includes thirty-eight poems, each dedicated to the beauty, resiliency, abundance, flavor, or nutritional richness of a different variety of Andean potato.[33]

Although not published in solo-authored or monolingual Quechua language volumes, since 2011 three collections of poetry published in Ecuador have focused on the work of poets writing in Kichwa and other indigenous languages. Notably, one of these anthologies, *Amanece en nuestras vidas* is dedicated exclusively to the creative work of Ecuadorian indigenous women authors. Much of this poetry is imbued with a philosophy of women-centric, community-based solidarity and problem solving that seeks, as the Aymara feminist Julieta Paredes has urged, to create and promote both the "new knowledges" of Andean women, while also celebrating the memories and achievements they have inherited from their grandmothers.[34] This recent Kichwa poetry celebrates the wisdom, resilience, and honesty of Andean women who are quite capable of overcoming obstacles in order to become the architects of their own futures.[35] The poetry of the Latacungan Kichwa poet and community

---

[33] Carrillo Cavero, *Yaku-unupa yuyaynin: La memoria del agua-Runapa Siminpi Qillqasqa* (Lima: Sol & Niebla, 2009), 57–92. For detailed studies of an exciting surge in monolingual Quechua poetry published by Carrillo Cavero since 2009, see Espino Relucé, "Ugo Carrillo: tradición y novedad en la poesía quechua contemporánea," in *El discurso de los zorros en la poética de Ugo Carrillo*, ed. Óscar Zamudio and Dante González (Lima: CEPES: Cultura y Literatura, 2013), 53–72; Krögel, "Qamllam kamallawanki: El poder transformativo de Illa y de los espacios oníricos en la poesía quechua de Ugo Facundo Carrillo Cavero," in *El discurso de los zorros en la poética de Ugo Carrillo*, ed. Óscar Zamudio and Dante González (Lima: CEPES, 2013), 19–52; Noriega, "La poética bilingüe de Hugo Carrillo Cavero," *Quehacer* 177 (2010), 94–101; and Fredy Amílcar Roncalla, "Yaku-unupa yuyaynin: Ugo Facundo Carrillo Cavero paqillqasqanmanta," in *Yaku-unupa yuyaynin: La memoria del agua-Runapa Siminpi Qillqasqa* (Lima: Sol & Niebla, 2009), 19–26; and Roncalla, *Hawansuyu Ukun Words*. Lima: Pakarina Ediciones, 2014), 95–99.

[34] Krögel, "The Dawn of our Lives," *Kilkakunawarmikuna*: The Rising Voices of Kichwa Women Poets in Ecuador," *Latin American Indian Literatures Journal* 30.1 (2016): 26–59; Juileta Paredes, *Hilando fino: desde el Feminismo Comunitario*. La Paz: Comunidad Mujeres Creando Comunidad y CEDEC, 2008), 8, 11–16.

[35] See, in particular, Llasag Fernández's poems "Allimanta purina chaki" in *Collar de historias y lunas: antología de poesía de mujeres indígenas de América Latina*, ed. Jennie

organizer, Esperanza de Lourdes Llasag Fernández merges elements of both the celebratory and denunciatory poetic currents apparent in Kichwa poetry published in Ecuador in recent years, in order to create the image of dynamic, forceful, and knowledgeable Andean women who capably organize their sisters so that their voices may be heard and their knowledge valued.[36]

Llasag Fernández's poem "Amawta" (Wise Woman) celebrates the energy, strength, unity, and confidence of both indigenous and non-indigenous Andean women.[37] The poem also cleverly deploys enjambment and the strategic use of the Kichwa first-person plural marker -chik (we) to express gratitude to both Andean "mamakunas" (female elders and community leaders or "grandmothers") and to the Pachamama/Earth mother, from whom these positive traits were originally inherited.

Urkukunamanta, sachakunamanta,		From the mountains, from the forests
panpakunamanta, llaktari allpa kawsaykunamanta		from the valleys, from the towns where they live
urpikushinalla uktalla purisha shamunkuna...	3	like winsome birds, swiftly they come walking...
Tukuykuna sinchi, kushikuylla, warmi kashkamanta	7	All strong, resilient, happy to be women
ñukanchik mamakunapak panpakana shina		like the farm plots of our venerable grandmothers
kawsayta kawsachik		full, full of our vitality
tantalla achiklla	10	so united, so radiant
Pachamama shina sumaklla		beautiful like the Pachamama,
wakinpika mana amutashka.		but at times, misunderstood.[38]

Carrasco Molina (Quito: Ministerio Coordinador de Patrimonio, 2011), 66; as well as "Mishiki Shimita kilkakuna," "Ipiku," and "mañay" in *Hatun Taki: Poemas a la Madre Tierra y a los Abuelos*, ed. Yana Lucila Lema (Quito: Ediciones Abya-Yala y Centro de Estudios sobre El Buen Vivir y Sumak Kawsay, 2013), 76, 80, 82.

[36] Krögel, "The Dawn of our Lives," Kilkakunawarmikuna: The Rising Voices of Kichwa Women Poets in Ecuador," *Latin American Indian Literatures Journal* 30.1 (2016): 26–59.

[37] Llasag Fernández, Esperanza de Lourdes, "Amawta." in *Hatun Taki*, 78.

[38] Llasag Fernández, Esperanza de Lourdes, "Amawta." in *Hatun Taki*, 78. More so than many other contemporary Kichwa poets, the work of Llasag Fernández deftly deploys several classic Quechua/Kichwa poetic elements such as semantic coupling, parallelism, internal rhyme schemes, and the repetition of particular suffixes for both semantic and sonoric effect. For instance, in line 10 of the poem "Amawta," the poet uses parallel structure to create a rhythmically balanced and semantically significant verse by adding the affective (and sometimes, augmentative) suffix "-lla" to the Kichwa words "tanta" (all) and "achik" (light). In this way, the word "tanta" takes on the meaning of "all together" (or "so united" in my translation), while "achik" comes to suggest a luminous, resplendent light ("so radiant"). Thus, the use of the suffix "-lla" not only adds a subtly positive nuance to the predeterminer "all" and to the noun "light," but adds a rhythmic parallelism to the verse.

Like the poems of Ch'aska Eugenia Anka Ninawamana and Carrillo Cavero, Llasag Fernández's work often dances on the border between the celebratory and the denunciatory, while generally leaning most of its weight towards an optimistic and celebratory space. The poem "Amawta" calls for women to realize their capacity to define themselves and their own futures and to appreciate and harness the strength and knowledge that they have inherited from their grandmothers, their kinswomen, and the Pachamama. Even if their beauty, vitality, and wisdom are not always understood or respected, the poem subtly and elegantly suggests that Andean women are more than capable of using their own agency and resilience to rectify instances of misunderstanding or ignorance.

In these few pages I have sought to offer a brief overview of some of the highlights of Quechua and Kichwa language poetry written in the Andes during the past five centuries and have suggested some ways of understanding the various movements, motivations, themes, and stylistic currents explored by the many (and at times, collective) authors of these texts. While the production, publication, dissemination, consumption, and study of poetic texts written in historically oppressed and principally oral indigenous languages has and always will be an exercise in overcoming a host of challenges, these are, nevertheless, exciting times for readers and writers of Quechua and Kichwa literature. The group of Quechua language writers, promoters, and poets involved with Pablo Landeo Muñoz in the all-Quechua language, Lima-based literary journal *Atuqpa Chupan Riwista* disseminates literary criticism written in Quechua and has done much to promote the reading of texts written in runasimi with a mind towards Quechua aesthetic preferences and categories, while *Kallpa*, a newly launched (2016) interdisciplinary *Journal of Andean Art and Culture* directed by the Quechua poet and academic Yuly Tacas, focuses on the dissemination of Quechua-language texts for a younger generation of readers and cultural activists.[39] Founded in Lima in 2011, the literary press *Pakarina Ediciones* has managed to usher towards publication an impressive number of Quechua poetry and short narrative collections and literary essays under the guidance of Dante González, a Quechua speaker, writer, academic, and editor.

Quechua literary blogs such as *Hawansuyu* (curated by the Quechua language poet, essayist, and literary critic Fredy Roncallo), *Alforja del Chuque* (maintained by the Quechua literary critic and scholar Gonzalo Espino Relucé), *Diccionario Cultural Boliviano* (edited by Elías Blanco

---

[39] Landeo, *Categorías andinas para una aproximación al willakuy* (Lima: Asamblea Nacional de Rectores, 2014); and Carolina Ortiz Fernández, *Poéticas afroindoamericanas: epísteme, cuerpo y territorio* (Lima: Parkarina Ediciones, 2014).

Mamani), as well as the all-Quechua language cultural podcast *Rimasun* (hosted and produced by New York University's Center for Latin American and Caribbean Studies), also play an important role in disseminating and promoting Quechua literature and cultural events in the Andes and beyond. The Ecuadorian government (under the auspices of its various ministries of interculturality), has, in recent years, supported the publication of bilingual poetry collections written in Kichwa and other indigenous languages, while the well-regarded and long-established press Abya-Yala continues to publish books of Kichwa poetry and Kichwa literary and cultural studies. Bolivia remains alone amongst the Andean countries in actively promoting the publication of novels written in Quechua (as well as Aymara and Guaraní) through the country's creation in 2010 of a national award honoring the year's best Bolivian novel written in an indigenous language ("El Premio Nacional de Narrativa en Idioma Originario Guamán Poma de Ayala").[40] Moreover, in recent years, Bolivian publishing houses such as Pirotecnia in La Paz have supported the publication of works of poetry written in both Aymara and Quechua by authors, such as Elvira Espejo Ayca, who are fluent in more than one indigenous Andean language and who choose to write in both of their mother tongues. Clearly then, as Fredy Roncalla asserts in his recent book *Hawansuyu: Ukun Words* "we find ourselves before the appearance of post-Arguedian Andean and trans-Andean literary spaces. In both Spanish and in Quechua, spaces and practices have begun to emerge from the thematic entrapment imposed by diglossia and [these new openings] should soon begin to bear fruit in poetry, narrative, digital technotexts, in painting, and in other areas of creation as well."[41]

---

[40] For instance, the Cochabamban Quechua writer and linguist Gladys Camacho Ríos has published the novel *Phuyup Yawar Waqaynin* (2013) that was subsequently translated into English as *The Bloody Tear of a Cloud*. In 2016 the Peruvian Quechua writer and academic Pablo Landeo published a much celebrated monolingual Quechua language novel, *Aqupampa* (Lima: Pakarina Ediciones, 2016).

[41] Fredy Amílcar Roncalla, *Hawansuyu Ukun Words* (Lima: Pakarina Ediciones, 2014), 104. While this chapter has focused on written Quechua language poetry, rich literary traditions also exist in numerous other indigenous languages throughout Latin America. See, for example, the selection of authors and poetry collections described in this volume's Guide to Further Reading.

15

MARTHA OJEDA

Afro-Hispanic Poetry

Afro-Hispanic poetry has had a long trajectory in Latin America. Literary critics continue to "unearth" long-forgotten works that date back to the nineteenth century. A brief survey of literary anthologies in the U.S., as well as monographs published in the twentieth century and the first decades of the twenty-first century, reveals that the corpus of Afro-Hispanic literature continues to gain recognition.[1] However, many of these writers have yet to be incorporated into the broader literary cannon. In other words, Afro-Hispanic literature remains at the margins of mainstream Latin American Literature, both in the U.S. and in Latin America. A thorough study of Afro-Hispanic Literatures and Cultures unveils a significant number of African-descended writers during the twentieth century, such as the following poets: Nicolás Guillén and Nancy Morejón (Cuba); Nicomedes Santa Cruz (Peru); Nelson Estupiñán Bass, Luz Argentina Chiriboga, and Adalberto Ortiz (Ecuador); Candelario Obeso (Colombia); Gerardo Maloney (Panama); Shirley Campbell and Eulalia Bernard (Costa Rica); and June Beer (Nicaragua).

The Harlem Renaissance and the Civil Rights Movement had a profound and lasting impact on the works of Black writers such as Nicolás Guillén, Manuel Zapata Olivella and Quince Duncan, among others. During the 1930s and 1940s, the *negrista* and Negritude movements were also influential among Spanish- and French-speaking Caribbean Writers. Cuban writers and artists such as Nicolás Guillén and Wilfredo Lam were discovering the multiethnic nature of their nation and promoted the study and incorporation of Afro-Cuban culture in their art. This movement reached South America in

---

[1] For publications of Afro-Hispanic writers, albeit, mostly novel writers, see Dorothy Mogsby, *Quince Duncan: Writing Afro-Costa Rican and Caribbean Identity* (Tuscaloosa, AL: The University of Alabama Press, 2014); Marvin Lewis, *Adalberto Ortiz: From Margin to Center* (Bethlehem, PA: Lehigh University Press, 2013); Antonio Tillis, *(Re)Considering Blackness in Contemporary Afro-Brazilian (Con)Texts* (New York, NY: Peter Lang, 2011) and *Critical Perspectives on Afro-Latin American Literature* (New York, NY: Routledge, 2012); Michael Handelsman, *Género, raza y nación en la literatura ecuatoriana: hacia una lectura decolonial* (Barcelona: CECAL, 2011).

the 1940s where Afro-Uruguayan poet Virginia Brindis de Salas, published *Pregón de Marimorena* (1946). Although the *indigenista* movement was predominant in Andean nations (Peru, Ecuador, Bolivia), African-descended writers participated in what Richard Jackson has called the *Afrocriollo* movement.[2] Some examples of this are Nicomedes Santa Cruz in Peru and Luz Argentina Chiriboga in Ecuador.

Richard L. Jackson, one of the pioneers in the field Afro-Hispanic literature, published two important and seminal works: *The Black Image in Latin America Literature* (1976) and *Black Writers in Latin America* (1979), which contributed to the dissemination of the works of Afro-Hispanic writers.[3] Marvin Lewis and Miriam DeCosta-Willis are also among the key Afro-American literary critics whose works have contributed to the "creation" of an Afro-Latin American literary canon within U.S. academia. Without their research, perhaps, we would not be writing about Afro-Hispanic poetry today. A common diasporic experience (slavery, oppression, emancipation, and the vindication of the African cultural heritage) leads these critics to take an interest in the literary production of Afro-Hispanic writers. This shared diasporic experience is also evident in the relationships and collaboration between Afro-American and Afro-Hispanic writers such as Nicolás Guillén and Langston Hughes.

Although Nicolás Guillén is a key figure in Afro-Hispanic poetry, this chapter will focus mainly on Nicomedes Santa Cruz, Luz Argentina Chiriboga, and Nancy Morejón, in order to highlight the works of equally accomplished poets who have not received the same generous critical attention, with the possible exception of Nancy Morejón. Slavery, emancipation, self-esteem, and national identity are predominant themes in the works of Santa Cruz, Chiriboga, and Morejón. These writers challenge official conceptions of nationhood that exclude the African cultural contributions. Morejón and Chiriboga question the dominant patriarchal systems that have marginalized women.

Nicomedes Santa Cruz

Nicomedes Santa Cruz (1925–1992), considered the most notable Afro-Peruvian poet of the twentieth century, challenged Peruvian intellectuals to question conceptions and definitions of *peruanidad* (Peruvianness) that

---

[2] *Afrocriollo* is a term used by Richard L. Jackson to refer to all the black cultural movements that emerged in Spanish-speaking Americas (*negrismo, negritud, afroantillanismo*). See *Black Writers and the Hispanic canon* (New York, NY: Twayne, 1997).

[3] Richard L. Jackson, *The Black Image in Latin America Literature* (Albuquerque, NM: University of New Mexico Press, 1976), and *Black Writers in Latin America* (Albuquerque, NM: University of New Mexico Press, 1979).

excluded the African legacy. He is also a key figure in vindicating the Afro-Peruvian heritage and its contributions to Peruvian national culture. Between the 1960s and 1970s Santa Cruz published four poetry collections, short stories and two anthologies: *Décimas* (1960), *Cumanana* (1964), *Canto a mi Perú* (I Sing to Peru, 1966), *Ritmos negros del Perú* (Black Rhythms of Peru, 1971), *Antología: décimas y poemas* (Anthology: Decimas and Poems, 1971), and *Rimactampu: rimas al Rimac* (Rimactampu: Rhymes to the Rimac River, 1972). He reached large audiences through his radio and TV programs, *Así canta mi Perú* (This is How Peru Sings), and *Danzas y canciones del Perú* (Songs and Dances of Peru), broadcast in the late 1960s and 1970s. Santa Cruz affirmed his negritude and denounced those who rejected their African heritage in poems that were widely circulated and read such as "De ser como soy me alegro" (I am Glad I Am Who I Am), "Soy un negro sabrosón" (I'm a Tasty Black), and "Cómo has cambiado, pelona" (How You've Changed, Baldy).

As a journalist, essayist, and musicologist, Nicomedes Santa Cruz published hundreds of articles to show the influence of African culture on Peruvian popular customs, history, philosophy, sports, education, language, culinary art, dance, and religion. Some of his most important newspaper articles are: "Tondero and Marinera" (1958), "La décima en el Perú" (The Decima in Peru, 1961), "El negro en el Perú" (The Negro in Peru, 1965), "Racismo en el Perú" (Racism in Peru, 1967), and "De Senegal a Malambo" (From Senegal to Malambo, 1973). These articles were a vehicle for raising awareness of the social conditions of blacks in Peru and the Americas, and were published in major newspapers and magazines such as *Caretas, El Comercio*, and *Expreso* – the latter being the most widely read magazine among the popular classes. "El negro en Iberoamérica" (The Black in Ibero-America, 1988) is one of his most important essays, and it was here that he unveiled the unrecorded and forgotten history of blacks and their contributions to the Hispanic world. Nicomedes and his sister Victoria Santa Cruz also contributed to the reconstruction of Afro-Peruvian music and dance. They both collected, performed, and recorded forgotten Afro-Peruvian rhythms such as *festejo, zaña, landó, samba-malato, panalivio*, and *socabón*. Nicomedes compiled and released a total of sixteen records between 1957 and 1980.[4]

---

[4] The first album was titled *Gente Morena* (Colored People) and the last was *Décimas y poemas* (Decimas and Poems). These included mostly poems recited with musical accompaniment known as *cumananas* and *socabón*. The other two albums that stand out are *Cumanana* (1964) and *Socabón* (1975) because they underscored the contributions of the African-descended population to Peruvian traditional musical folklore and dance. Each album contained two long-plays and a 67-page booklet explaining the origins of the songs

Although Santa Cruz's poetic output in the 1960s and 1970s had a high social profile in Peru, his poetry had little impact in academic circles. Richard L. Jackson's pioneering research in the 1980s, however, bucked the trend and galvanized interest in Santa Cruz's work; articles on his work began appearing in various publications ranging from scholarly journals to literary magazines in the U.S. A number of books on the poetry of Nicomedes Santa Cruz came out, and these helped to expand his Afro-Peruvian's readership in a global sense, thereby introducing him to new international literary circles.[5] In Peru, Estuardo Núñez, one of the leading Peruvian literary critics of his time, published his article: "La literatura peruana de la negritud" where he declared that "[d]entro de las letras peruanas, Santa Cruz ha afirmado la nueva conciencia de la negritud" (Santa Cruz has given rise to a new consciousness of negritude in Peruvian literature).[6]

Furthermore, in the late 1980s, Peruvian literary critics began to reevaluate the distinctiveness of the national literary canon. In *La formación de la tradición literaria en el Perú (The Formation of Peruvian Literary Tradition,* 1989), for example, Antonio Cornejo Polar and Fernando Carrillo highlighted the so-called "marginal traditions" (tradiciones marginales) referring to indigenous and popular literatures. In an interview with Arroyo, Cornejo Polar acknowledged that his limited knowledge of the subject did not allow him to study these literary traditions thoroughly; however, he did underline the importance of recognizing the multilingual and multicultural nature of Peruvian Literature.[7] Pointing in a similar direction, Francisco Carrillo, another important literary critic, called for "a reordering of the literary starting with a frank and open vindication of all that vast literature that is just now being studied and compiled and it ranges from Quechua, Aymara, and Amazonian literatures to the novels of the Peruvian black world and to what has been called popular or oral literature."[8] It is crucial to emphasize

included in the album; see Martha Ojeda, "Nicomedes Santa Cruz and Black Cultural Traditions in Peru: Renovating and Decolonizing the National Imaginary," in *Critical Perspectives on Afro-Latin American Literature,* ed. Antonio Tillis (New York, NY: Routledge, 2012), 214.

[5] For example, Teresa Salas and Henry Richards edited *Asedios a la poesía de Nicomedes Santa Cruz* (Quito: Editora Andina, 1982) and, the following year, Marvin Lewis published *Afro-Hispanic Poetry 1940–1980: From Slavery to Negritud in South American Verse* (Columbia, MO: University of Missouri Press, 1983). Lewis is one of the first literary critics to study the work of Santa Cruz within an Afro-Peruvian sociohistorical context.

[6] Estuardo Núñez, "La literatura peruana de la negritud," *Hispanoamérica,* 10.28 (1981): 27.

[7] Carlos Arroyo, *Hombres de letras: historia y crítica Literaria en el Perú* (Lima: Ediciones Memoria Angosta, 1992), 61.

[8] "un reordenamiento de lo literario a partir de una reivindicación, franca y abierta, de toda esa vastísima literatura que recién se encuentra en proceso de estudio y de recopilación y

these critical efforts to incorporate the so-called "marginal literatures" into the national literary corpus. According to Carrillo, a key obstacle to incorporating these literatures into the main literary corpus, is "the lack of sufficient text compilation" as well as "the lack of a suitable theoretical-epistemological apparatus that would not seek to exclude the contribution of anthropology and other social sciences and that uses clearly different categories to those that are used for the study of erudite (canonical) literature."[9] This fact underscores the need to establish a non-Eurocentric theoretical apparatus and critical methods, since the existent ones have had a tendency to exclude the diverse expressions and non-Western literary traditions. For example, Santa Cruz's work has been catalogued as popular and underestimated even by those (Antonio Cornejo Polar and Carrillo) who are questioning the basic premises and the validity of these literary classifications.

Santa Cruz's poetic and ideological evolution, from *Décimas* to the *Black Rhythms of Peru*, is marked by three specific periods: Negritude (the early poetry collections), socio-political commitment (from the 1960s to the mid-1970s), and hemispheric and international vision (last poetry collections). Indeed, Richard Jackson had underscored the evolution of Santa Cruz' poetic vision towards a pluricultural, and hemispheric ideology in his seminal study, *Black Literature and Humanism Latin America.*[10] *Décimas* (1960), Cruz's first published poetry collection, is representative of the process of cultural and ethnic vindication, and is characterized by the exclusive use of the *décima* as a poetic form.[11] In this collection Santa Cruz rescues Afro-Peruvian folklore and affirms his ethnic identity and cultural heritage in poems such as "Ritmos negros del Perú" (Black rhythms of Peru), "Soy un negro sabrosón" (I Am a Tasty Black), and "De ser como soy me alegro" (I Am glad I Am who I Am; *Décimas*, 29). Salas, Kattar-Goudiard and Núñez[12] consider Santa Cruz the

que va desde las literaturas quechua, aymara, y amazónicas hasta la novelística del mundo negro peruano y lo que se ha dado en llamar la literatura popular u oral"; qtd. in Arroyo, *Hombres*, 39.

[9] "la falta de recopilación suficiente de textos, sino también por la carencia de un aparato teórico-epistemológico idóneo que no excluya el aporte de la antropología y de otras ciencias sociales y que maneje categorías evidentemente distintas a las que se utilizan para el estudio de la literatura erudita" (qtd. in Arroyo, *Hombres*, 40).

[10] *Black Literature and Humanism in Latin America* (Athens, GA: University of Georgia Press, 1988).

[11] Santa Cruz, *Décimas*, 2nd edition (Lima: Libreria Studium, 1966). A *décima* is a poetic form of ten-verse stanzas with (abbaaccddc) rhyme scheme. The *decimista* is the person who uses this poetic form. Santa Cruz is mainly known as a *decimista* but he also used other poetic forms.

[12] See Teresa Caijao and Henry J. Richards, "Nicomedes Santa Cruz y la poesía de su conciencia de negritud," *Cuadernos Americanos*, 202 (1975): 182–99; Jeannette Kattar-Goudiard and René L. F. Durand, *Nicomedes Santa Cruz, poeta negro del Perú:*

Peruvian poet of negritude because the above-mentioned poems transmit a pronounced feeling of pride and appreciation for this ethnic heritage:

> De ser como soy me alegro
> ignorante es quien critica.
> Que mi color sea negro
> eso a nadie perjudica.

> (I am glad I am who I am/ He who criticizes [me] is ignorant./ The fact that I am black/ does not harm anyone.)   (*Décimas*, 59)[13]

Cumanana (1964) marks a decisive moment in the explorations of Santa Cruz's artistic and sociopolitical commitment. In this collection, the poet finds his own voice: he uses a variety of poetic forms, his poetry has a militant tone, and his aim is to denounce a clearly unjust society. Santa Cruz chooses to use a politically charged language and questions the very nature of "art for art's sake," which is symptomatic of the period and the political turmoil sweeping throughout Latin America. In "Talara, no digas 'yes'" (Talara, Don't Say Yes), Santa Cruz supported the campaign for the nationalization of oil and condemned the American appropriation of oil wells in northern Peru.

A close reading of his poetry reveals that, despite his preferential use of the *décima*, Nicomedes employs a variety of strophes, and his poetic language is essentially contestatory. His poems express the non-conformism that emanates from the prevalent oppression and injustice. One of the predominant metaphors in his poetry is the "rhyme-spear" (rima-lanza). In "Johannesburg," the poet fences with his rhyme:

> Quiero aguda mi rima
> como punta de lanza.
> Que otra mano la esgrima
> si alcanza.

> (I want my rhyme sharp/ as a spearhead./ May another hand brandish it/ if he can.)[14]

Canto a mi Perú (1966) includes poems that are more nationalistic in nature and ideologically aligned to the tenets of the Peruvian Revolution. It also continues to focus on the themes predominant in the two preceding poetry collections. In poems like "Cantares" (Songs), "Pasaje Obrero" (The Worker's Bus Fare), and "Piedra, piedra" (Stone, Stone) Santa Cruz vindicates the

presentación y selección de poemas (Dakar: Centre de Hautes Études Afro-Ibéro-Amériques, Université de Dakar, 1970); and Núñez, "La literatura," 27.

[13] Unless otherwise noted, all translations are the author's.

[14] *Cumanana: Décimas de pie forzado y poemas* (Lima: Librería Editorial Juan Mejía Baca, 1964), 85.

worker, supports agrarian reform and denounces social injustice. "Patria o muerte!" (Motherland or Death) contains the most explicit revolutionary language that reflects the sentiment of a disenfranchised sector of Peruvian society in the 1960s:

> Yo grito revolución
> Y ataco todo gobierno
> Que en olvido sempiterno
> Sotierra la Educación.
>
> . . . .
>
> Mi alma es revolucionaria
> Porque a como dé lugar
> Estoy dispuesto a luchar
> Por Nuestra Reforma Agraria.

> (I shout revolution/ and I attack any government/ that in everlasting negligence/ buries Education./ (. . .)/ My soul is revolutionary/ because however I can/ I am ready to fight/ for Our Agrarian Reform.)[15]

Ritmos Negros del Perú (1971) has a profoundly internationalist dimension. These poems contain a universal message of cultural solidarity between Latin America and the rest of the world. Santa Cruz's wish for a multicultural and inclusive society stands out in the poem "América Latina." The poems "Johanesburgo" and "Congo Libre" (Free Congo) stress the poet's support for the oppressed, and the African peoples' struggle for liberation. In the last stanza of "Congo Libre," the poetic voice emphatically declares his desire for Congo to achieve true freedom:[16]

> Africa, tierra sin frío,
> Madre de mi obscuridad,
> Cada amanecer ansío
> Cada amanecer ansío
> Cada amanecer ansío
> Tu completa libertad.

> (Africa, land without coldness,/ Mother of my darkness,/ every dawn I long/ every dawn I long/ every dawn I long/ your complete freedom.)[17]

The poem shifts from a focus on the purely personal level to a concern for more universal human values, and shows a deep commitment to

---

[15] *Canto a mi Perú* (Lima: Librería Studium, 1966), 109–10.
[16] This poem was composed following the Congo's independence in June 30, 1960; see *Obras Completas: Poesía (1949–1989)*, compiled by Pedro Santa Cruz (Lima: Libros en Red, 2004), vol. 1, 287.
[17] *Ritmos negros del Perú* (Buenos Aires: Editorial Losada, 1971), 80.

building a new brotherhood that is simultaneously multiethnic and multicultural.

During the last fifteen years of his life, Nicomedes Santa Cruz devoted himself to writing essays and although his poetical compositions were almost nonexistent, it is precisely during this time that he reflected upon his poetic creation. In 1991, in his essay "The Black and his Song: The Adventure of Oral and Written Poetry in America," Nicomedes provided a penetrating analysis of his creative process, in particular where he underlines the oral and collective nature of his poetical production:

> we, the singers that have begun from the most orthodox *troubadouresque* tradition, we have our voice as a principal tool and the *repentista* improvisation as vital creative mechanism. Then, the daily exercise of addressing the public present (live), allows us to exercise a sort of energetic tuning with the auditorium, whose flow and ebb perfect our singing to the just measure and to the exact demand of our audience, not matter how numerous and heterogeneous they may be.[18]

It is evident that Santa Cruz privileges orality and performance, he writes for the people and about the people; as he himself suggests, "my song comes from the people/ and my song goes to the people."[19] Through performance, orality, and the marriage of poetry, music, and song, Santa Cruz endows poetry with its original qualities. It is critical to emphasize this artistic gift possessed by Nicomedes who had the ability to recite continuously up to twenty poems in addition to improvising new *décimas* on the spot. With this technique he was following the popular tradition of the *countrapunteo* (poetic duel) and his admirable memory allowed him to preserve a vast repertoire.[20] Santa Cruz was the poet-chronicler of his people and of his epoch. His main goal was to safeguard the collective memory of his ethnic group, to put his poetry at the service of the people and to use it as an instrument of liberation.

---

[18] "los cantores que hemos empezado a partir de la más ortodoxa tradición trovadoresca, tenemos como principal herramienta la voz y como vital mecanismo creativo la improvisación repentista. Luego, el ejercicio cotidiano de dirigirnos a un público presente (en vivo), nos permite ejercitar una suerte de sintonía energética con el auditorio, cuyo flujo y reflujo nos va afinando el canto a la justa medida y a la exacta exigencia de nuestra audiencia, por muy numerosa y heterogénea que ésta sea"; see "El Negro y su canto: aventura de la poesía oral y escrita en América," in *Afroamericanos y V Centenario: ponencias V encuentro de antropología y misión* (Madrid: Editorial Mundo Negro, 1992), 168.

[19] "mi canto del pueblo viene/ y mi canto al pueblo va." See "Canto lo que el pueblo siente," of 1974.

[20] *Socabón* and *cumananas* are two types of poetry performed by Santa Cruz. The *socabón* (sung *décimas* with musical accompaniment) and the *cumananas*, (the tradition of singing improvised popular folk songs in *desafío*) will be a part of his unmistakable style.

Santa Cruz's mastery of language, his diversity of topics, his skillful handling of varied poetic forms, his use of rhyme and rhythm, and rhetorical skills such as humor and satire place him among the most original and representative Latin American poets of his time. Moreover, because Santa Cruz incorporates Inca and African myths, and Spanish folklore, his *décimas* represent the coexistence of three literary traditions; that is to say, the syncretism of the Spanish, African, and indigenous cultures. As recognition for his cultural contributions, in 2002, Peru's National Cultural Institute paid an official tribute to Nicomedes Santa Cruz, recognizing him as an "Honorable representative of the cultural heritage of the nation ... granting him the highest posthumous recognition for his invaluable contribution to Peruvian culture."[21] In 2004 the Universidad Nacional Mayor de San Marcos hosted the First International Conference dedicated to Nicomedes Santa Cruz's artistic production. Finally, Santa Cruz's work has paved the way for many contemporary Afro-Peruvian writers such as Lucía Charún-Illescas, Delia Zamudio, Gregorio Martínez, Antonio Galves Ronceros, José Campos Dávila, Maritza Joya, Máximo Justo Torres (Majustomo), and Mónica Carillo (Oru).

Luz Argentina Chiriboga

Luz Argentina Chiriboga (b. 1940) was born in Esmeraldas, Ecuador. She earned a degree in biology from the Universidad Central of Quito, Ecuador. Chiriboga is a prolific author who has authored six novels, essays, children's books, and seven poetry collections, among them are: *La contraportada del deseo* (The Underbelly of Desire, 1992), *Manual de Ecología para niños* (Ecology Manual for Children, 1992), *Palenque* (1999), *Capitanas de la historia* (The Female Captains of History, 2003), *Con su misma voz* (In Her Own Voice, 2005). In 1991 she published *Tambores bajo mi piel* (Drums Under My Skin), which is considered the first novel published by an Afro-Latina writer. Her other novels are: *Jonatás y Manuela* (1994) and *En la noche del viernes* (On Friday Night, 1997), *Cuéntanos abuela* (Tell Us, Granny, 2002), *Desde la sombra del silencio* (From the Shadow of Silence, 2004), and *Este mundo no es de las feas: Crónica de sueños* (This World is not for Ugly Women: A Chronicle of Dreams, 2006). Chiriboga's works have been translated to English, Italian, and French and, according to DeCosta-Willis, her poetry and fiction is shaped by the "prevailing ideology of international feminism" ("Afra-Hispanic," 250). On the one hand, her works

---

[21] See www.librosenred.com/autores/nicomedessantacruz.html (last accessed October 26, 2017).

reflect Chiriboga's aim to vindicate women's contribution to nation building; on the other, her writings undermine established societal norms that oppress women.

In *La contraportada del deseo* (1992), Chiriboga uses erotic imagery and figurative language to vindicate a woman's rights to her body, sexuality, and desire, thereby challenging prevailing codes of what is acceptable in "proper señoritas:"

> Cuando la luna
> rasga el amanecer
> crepitantes fuegos
> exploran mi subsuelo.
> Sonámbulos deseos
> gimen en mis ansias,
> los siento retorcerse
> abriendo surcos en todas mis parcelas.

> (When the moon/ rips the early morning/ burning fires/ explore my subsoil./ Somnambulistic desires/ moan in my excitement/ I feel them contorting/ opening furrows/ in all my parts.)[22]

The words "rips, burning fires, desires, moan, excitement" evoke the sensuality and eroticism in her treatment of female sexuality and desire in this poem. The collection's title itself, *Contraportada del deseo* (the Underbelly of Desire) underscores the main theme of the poem. The "underbelly," in this context, refers to the forbidden/hidden aspect of female desire, which has been tamed and censored in most Latin American societies. I concur with DeCosta-Willis's assertion that such a representation of female desire is "a form of social and aesthetic resistance" to dominant ideologies.[23]

Palenque (1999) is divided in three parts and contains 30 *décimas*.[24] Poems such as "La trata" (Slave Trade), "Travesía" (The Crossing), "Plantación" (Plantation), and "Palenque" explore the themes of the middle passage and slavery. The second part of the collection focuses on themes of rebellion and liberty exemplified in the poems "Jonatás" and "Manuela." Part three highlights a sense of pride in one's heritage and place of origin as

---

[22] *La Contraportada del deseo* (Quito: Talleres Gricos ABYA-YALA, 1992), 91–92; trans. Clementina Adams; see *Common Threads: Themes in Afro-Hispanic Women's Literature* (Miami, FL: Ediciones Universal, 1998), 203–04.

[23] Miriam DeCosta-Willis, "Afra-Hispanic Writers and Feminist Discourse," in *Women in Africa and the African Diaspora: A Reader*, eds. Rosalyn Terborg-Penn and Andrea Benton Rushing (Washington, DC: Howard University Press, 1996), 253.

[24] *Palenque* (Quito: Editorial Instituto Andino de Artes Populares, 1999). It is noteworthy that this poetic form is predominant among the Afro-Hispanic poets throughout Latin America. See footnote 11 in this chapter for a description of the *décima*.

well as self-esteem. In Chiriboga's case this means a sense of pride for the Esmeraldas region of Ecuador, which represents the space of the Afro-Ecuadorean community. In "La trata," the poetic voice condemns the unjust and abusive nature of the slave trade:

Los millones de africanos
llegados cual mercancía
trabajaron noche y día
para sus amos tiranos.
Aquellos falsos cristianos,
mercaderes del dolor,
amasaron el terror.
En esa cruel desventura
esa fue la coyuntura
que tuvo el conquistador.

(Millions of Africans/ brought in like merchandise/ worked night and day/ for their tyrant masters./ Those false Christians,/ merchants of pain,/ they amassed terror./ In that cruel misfortune/ that was the situation/ that the conquistador had; *Palenque*, 22–24)

The last stanza of the poem, quoted above, criticizes the hypocrisy of those *conquistadores* who claimed to be Christians yet inflicted pain and suffering on the slaves. It is significant that "El Palenque" closes the first part of this collection, because it symbolizes the resistance and the refusal to be enslaved:

Símbolo de resistencia
del negro en la esclavitud
luchando en su plenitud
por su justa independencia.

(Symbol of resistance/ of Blacks in slavery/ fighting in full force/ for their righteous independence.)

(...)

Fue el mágico territorio
donde vio la libertad,
en él la fraternidad
Tuvo glorioso santuario.
Abandonó el Rosario
rezado por exigencia
para ganar indulgencia
y el amo no fuera cruel.
Negro, tenías tu cuartel,
símbolo de Resistencia.

(It was the magic territory/ where he saw freedom/ in there, fraternity/ had a glorious sanctuary./ He abandoned the Rosary/ prayed to by obligation/ in order to gain indulgence/ and to avoid the master's cruelty./ Negro, you had your barracks,/ symbol of resistance.)

(. . .)

Fue su mayor convicción
guerrear con tenacidad,
en pro de su identidad
y de la unificación.
Hay que aprender la lección
y renovar su presencia,
pues el PALENQUE es la esencia
de toda la africanía
que luchó con valentía
por su justa independencia.

(It was his greatest conviction/ To fight with tenacity/ For this identity/ And unification./ We must learn the lesson/ And renew its presence,/ for the PALENQUE is the essence/ Of all the Africanness/ Who fought with courage/ For their righteous independence; *Palenque*, 46–48)

Furthermore, in the second stanza, "El Palenque" underscores the importance of learning and remembering that this space was a site of resistance for those who fought for freedom ("independencia"). In other poems, Chiriboga often equates the slaves' struggle for freedom with Ecuador's struggle for independence from colonial rule.

Capitanas de la historia (2003), as the title suggests, is an homage to women leaders who have shaped the history of Latin America and have contributed to key historical moments such the Wars of Independence. However, most of these women leaders have been excluded from the official history books; therefore, Chiriboga brings them back to center stage. In poems such as "Manuela Sáenz," she writes these important women back into history. Manuela Sáenz is not depicted only as Bolivar's assistant and lover, but as an essential contributor to the Wars of Independence in Latin America:

A Manuela Revolución
Yo la contemplo radiante
Con Jonatás adelante
Fraguando la subversión.

(Manuela Revolution/ I contemplate her, joyful/ with Jonatás in front/ forging rebellion.)[25]

---

[25] *Capitanas de la Historia: Poesía* (Quito: L. Argentina, 2002), 55.

(...)

Fue rebelde e inteligente,
Caminó hacia el confín
Por dar al cepo su fin
Y a América un nuevo frente.
Introdujo diligente
Una estrategia brillante.
Porque fue beligerante
Y ayudó a romper la aldaba
Que el continente aplastaba
Yo la contemplo radiante.

(She was rebellious and intelligent/ She walked towards the edge/ To end oppression/ And to give America, a new front/ She diligently introduced/ A brilliant strategy/ Because she was a militant/ And she helped to break the lock/ That was crushing the continent/ I gaze at her, joyful; *Capitanas*, 56)

Manuela Saénz becomes the epitome of Revolution. The poet cleverly changes her last name to "Revolución." In doing so, Manuela is transformed to represent the heart of the revolution that leads to independence from the Spanish colonial powers. In an effort to shine the spotlight on the marginalized and forgotten voices, Chiriboga also dedicates a poem to Jonatás. She was one of Manuela Sáenz's slaves who played an important role advancing the revolutionary cause. One must note that, in *Capitanas de la historia*, the poem "Jonatás" precedes "Manuela Sáenz," which thereby symbolically highlights her essential role in raising awareness of the inhumane nature of slavery. Jonatás, then, becomes the single most influential person in encouraging Manuela, her mistress, to fight for freedom, independence, and the end of slavery.

Simón Saénz la compró
para esclava de Manuela,
ella no iría a la escuela,
fue lo que él imaginó.
Ella al rato ideó
que su gran Manuela entienda
que el negro esclavo con rienda
tenía un trato humillante,
brutal delito flagrante
por el dueño de hacienda.

(Simon Saenz bought her/ As a slave for Manuela/ She wouldn't go to school/ It's what Simon imagined/ Jonatás soon had an idea/ To make Manuela understand/ That the controlled black slave/ Had humiliating treatment/ It was a flagrant brutal crime/ By the plantation owner; *Capitanas*, 51–52)

Jonatás pronto la tornó
Mujer de inmensa valía
Que demostró gran valentía
Y hasta carcel soportó.
Esta esclava le quitó
A Manuelita la venda
Para entrar en la contienda
Llamada Liberación.
Ella fue revelación
Y se volvió una leyenda.

(Jonatás soon changed her/ Into an immensily valuable woman/ Who showed
great courage/ Who even endured jail/ This slave removed/ Manuelita's blind-
fold/ so she entered the fight/ called Liberation/ Jonatás was the revelation/ And
she became a legend; *Capitanas*, 51–52).

With "Jonatás," the poet delves into the historical past in order to identify
key moments where women and slaves have been agents in the process of
liberation. By composing these two poems, Chiriboga participates in a
process of historical revisionism to include the voices of those who have
been omitted from it. The fact that these poems were published in *Palenque*
and that Chiriboga also published a novel titled *Jonatás y Manuela*, highlight
her commitment to ensuring their rightful place in history. It is evident that
Chiriboga's work, both in prose and poetry, seeks to explore themes of
slavery, nationhood, and identity from the black female perspective while
vindicating women's rights.

Nancy Morejón

Nancy Morejón (b. 1944) is without a doubt one of the best known and most
anthologized Afro-Latina poets in the U.S. She has published more than ten
poetry collections, numerous essays, and literary criticism. Her poetry has
been translated into several languages, including French, Italian, and
Russian. She has also won many literary awards, among them, Cuba's
National Prize for Literature in 2001. Her poetry collections include:
Mutismos (Silences, 1962), *Amor, ciudad atribuida* (Love, an Attributed
City, 1964), *Richard trajo su flauta y otros argumentos* (Richard Brought
Along his Flute and Other Arguments, 1967), *Parajes de una época* (The
Places of an Epoch, 1979), *Octubre imprescindible* (Indispensable October,
1983), *Cuaderno de Granada* (Granada Notebook, 1984), *Piedra pulida*
(Polished Stone, 1986), and *Paisaje célebre* (Famous Landscape, 1993).
Salient themes in her poetry are *mestizaje*, slavery, the revolution, and
feminism. Much like Nicolás Guillén, who was her mentor, Morejón calls

attention to the *mestizo* nature of Cuban culture. In poems like "Amo a mi amo" (I love my Master), she examines issues of slavery, oppression, and the sexualization of the female body while subverting *negrista* representations of the black woman's body. Her poetic output saw a couple of hiatuses from 1968 to 1979 and 1988 after the publication of *Piedra Pulida* (1986). Some critics have pointed out that the hiatus in her publishing poetry during the 1970s might have been caused by Morejón's participation in cultural and artistic groups that vindicated the situation of blacks in Cuba at a time when this act could have been interpreted as undermining the revolutionary ideology. William Luis states that "Morejón was probably silenced because of her alleged affiliation with individuals and organizations that had a racial agenda" but, according to DeCosta-Willis, Morejón denied any association with these groups.[26] It is worth noting that Morejón's poetry seems to reflect the shifts, and perhaps the contradictions in the revolutionary discourse of the 1960s and 1970s, a point that has been further explored by William Luis.[27]

"Mujer Negra" (Black Woman) from *Parajes de una época* (1979), the most anthologized of her poems, is a powerful piece that, in essence, narrates the history of slavery in Cuba from the vantage point of a black woman who has been uprooted from her homeland, subjugated, and violated. In forty-nine verses and six stanzas, the poet sums up the uprising process undertaken by the black slave woman, which seems to parallel the liberation process brought about by the Cuban revolution:

> Me fui al monte.
> Mi real independencia fue el palenque
> y cabalgué entre las tropas de Maceo.
>
> (I left for the hills./ My real independence was the free slave fort./ I rode with the troops of Maceo.)[28]

The final stanza alludes to the triumph of the Cuban Revolution of 1959, creating a parallelism between the slave's emancipation and the freedom sought by the Revolution:

> bajé de la Sierra
> para acabar con capitales y usureros,

[26] Qtd. in *Singular like a Bird: The Art of Nancy Morejón*, ed. Miriam DeCosta-Willis (Washington, DC: Howard University Press, 1999), 7.
[27] See William Luis, "Race, Poetry and Revolution in the Work of Nancy Morejón," in *Singular like a Bird*, ed. DeCosta-Willis, 45–67.
[28] Nancy Morejón, Juanamaría Cordones-Cook, and Gabriel Abudu, *Looking Within: Selected Poems, 1954–2000. Mirar Adentro: Poemas Escogidos, 1954–2000* (Detroit, MI: Wayne State University Press, 2003), 202.

con generales y burgueses.
Ahora soy: sólo hoy tenemos y creamos.

(I came down from the Sierra/ to put an end to capitals and usurer,/ to generals
and to bourgeois./ Now I exist: only today do we own, do we create; *Looking
Within*, 203)

The poem concludes with an optimistic tone of solidarity and camaraderie:
"Iguales míos, aquí los veo bailar/ alrededor del árbol que plantamos para el
comunismo./ Su pródiga madera ya resuena" (My equals here I see you
dance/ around the tree we are planting for communism./ Its prodigal wood
resounds; *Looking Within*, 203). According to C. RoseGreen-Williams, this
poem can be inscribed in the process of revisionism of Cuban history, which
was common in the 1960s and 1970s; it is also a counterdiscourse of the
narratives of Africa as a "heartland," highlighted by Caribbean poets such as
Edward Brathwaite and other French *négritude* poets.[29]

In "Mujer Negra," the poetic voice affirms her "Cubanness" while
acknowledging her African ancestry. As RoseGreen-Williams points out
the poem shows a sense of agency rather than victimhood; in this poem,
the black slave woman takes her future and life in her own hands and carves
out an identity for herself (RoseGreen-Williams, *Singular Like a Bird*, 192).
To borrow from Carlos Aguirre, she becomes an "agent of her own freedom"
(agente de su propia libertad). This agency is highlighted by the declaratives:
"Me rebelé. Anduve/ Me sublevé" (I rebelled. I walked/ I rose up). These
verses help advance the poem and act as pillars of the creation or foundation
of her future and identity. Finally, the stanza that reads: "Trabajé mucho
más./ Fundé mi mejor canto milenario y mi esperanza./ Aquí construí mi
mundo" (I worked much more./ I created my best millennial song as well as
my hope./ I built my world here) underscores the notion of agency, while
establishing a sense of homeland and belonging ("Aquí construí mi mundo";
Looking Within, 203). In other words, the poetic voice forges a new identity
rooted in Cubanness.

While "Mujer Negra" focuses on the history of slavery and the revolutionary process, drawing parallelisms between the situation of black slaves
and all Cubans under the oppressive rule of the Batista regime, "Amo a mi
Amo" highlights the physical and psychological domination of women.
Typical of Morejón's poetry, the poem concludes with the vindication of
the subjugated self; there is a refusal to be enslaved, and a sense of liberation,
both literally and metaphorically. On the other hand, the political undertones of the poem are noticeable: the oppressed who gain consciousness of

---

[29] C. RoseGreen-Williams, "Re-writing the History of Afro-Cuban Woman: Nancy
Morejón's 'Mujer Negra,'" in *Singular like a Bird*, 192.

their condition, and later craft ways to rebel either passively or actively: "Oyendo hablar a los viejos guardieros, supe. Que mi amor/ da latigazos en las calderas del ingenio" (Hearing the old field guards talking, I learned/ that my love/ gives lashings in the cauldrons of the sugar mill). The awareness of injustice and oppression compels the slave woman to rebel:

¿Por qué le sirvo?
¿A dónde va en su espléndido coche
Tirado por caballos más felices que yo?
(...)
Maldigo
(...)
Amo a mi amo, pero todas las noches
Cuando atravieso la vereda florida hacia el
     Cañaveral donde a hurtadillas hemos hecho el
     Amor,
Me veo cuchillo en mano, desollándolo como una res sin
     Culpa.
Ensordecedores toques de tambor ya no me dejan
Oír ni sus quebrantos, ni sus quejas.

(Why must I serve him?/ Where could he go in his splendid carriage,/ drawn by horses happier than me?/ (...)/ I curse/(...)/ I love my master, but every night/ when I cross the flowery pathway to the cane fields/ where we have surreptitiously made love,/I can see myself with knife in hand, butchering him like/ some innocent animal./ Deafening drumbeats no longer let me/ hear his sorrows, or his complaints./ The tolling bells call me./

Morejón's poetic craft is evinced by her mastery of poetic language, use of metaphors, rhythm, and the ambiguities in the poem. At first glance, the slave woman can be seen as oppressed and objectified, but a careful reading shows that the "master" is not in a position of control and power. The verses in the first stanza: "abanico todo su cuerpo cundido de llagas y balazos" (I fan his whole body, full of sores and bullet wounds) and the penultimate stanza: "I can see myself with knife in hand, butchering him like/ some innocent animal" create an image of a helpless and injured man. It is an image that subverts representations of powerful *conquistadores*. Although in the first part of the poem, the master-slave interactions seem to portray what Gutiérrez has called "another deeper variant of the master-slave syndrome" in "Amo a mi amo" (215),[30] the poem concludes with the mental/psychological liberation

---

[30] Maricela A. Gutiérrez, "Nancy Morejón's Avenging Resistance in 'Black Woman' and "I love My Master': Examples of a Black Slave Woman's Path to Freedom," in *Singular like a Bird*, ed. DeCosta-Willis, 215.

from bondage. This subversion and liberating process starts, symbolically, with the objectification of the master. The poetic voice focuses on the master's "hands, feet, eyes, and lips," which is an interesting reversal of the female's objectified body. In sum, in "Amo a mi amo," the slave woman participates in the process of othering the master; thus, transforming herself from object to subject.

In conclusion, it is evident that Afro-Hispanic poets share similar concerns about exploring the historical past in order to inscribe the Black Latino experience into the national imaginary of their respective countries. The struggle for freedom from slavery in Santa Cruz, Chiriboga, and Morejón is equated with the corresponding struggle of each nation for freedom from colonial bondage and imperial domination. These poets, each in his or her own way, ask the reader to question conventional definitions of identity and nationhood.

16

MICHAEL DOWDY

U.S. Latino/a Poetry

In 2012 Juan Felipe Herrera (b. 1948) was appointed Poet Laureate of California. In 2015 he was appointed Poet Laureate of the United States. Herrera was the first Latino to be appointed to each position. Most reports emphasized variations on this theme, noting that he is the son of Mexican migrant workers. Equally notable, though overlooked in responses to his 2015 appointment, is the incongruence between Herrera's surreal, propulsive critiques of U.S. imperialism in Latin America and the official nature of the position. Although Herrera's arrival at the pinnacle for civic-minded poets culminates two centuries of poetry by writers of Latin American descent in the U.S., his appointment obscures his repudiations of state-sponsored violence and capitalist exploitation, from Mexico to Chile. For example, his antic list poem "187 Reasons Mexicanos Can't Cross the Border" taunts anti-immigrant nativists with the survival of Latinos, even as it catalogues the forces that dehumanize them. With "reasons" like "Because the CIA trains better with brown targets," "Because our accent is unable to hide U.S. colonialism," and "Because the North is really South," Herrera disorients the ideologies and geographies that relegate Latin America to the "backyard" of its civilized, beneficent "Good Neighbor."[1] Herrera may be poet laureate of "America," in the narrow national register, but he is equally a poet of América, the continent, in the dissident tradition of Pan-American hemispherism.

Herrera exemplifies this chapter's premise: understanding U.S. Latino/a poetry requires knowledge of the traditions and contexts of Latin American poetry. Cataloguing the range of forms and practices in Latino poetry calls for a hemispheric lens that foregrounds historical relations and migratory routes between north and south. The uneven, unpredictable history of Latino poetry underscores the role of north-south relations in

[1] Juan Felipe Herrera, *187 Reasons Mexicanos Can't Cross the Border: Undocuments 1971–2007* (San Francisco: City Lights, 2007), 29–30.

developing its aesthetic tools and sensibilities. The major national groups of Latinos, moreover, from Mexico, Puerto Rico, and Cuba, have unique relationships to U.S. empire with different historical flashpoints: 1848, when the Treaty of Guadalupe Hidalgo ceded California and much of the Southwest to the U.S.; 1898, when the U.S. colonized Cuba and Puerto Rico; and 1959, when Fidel Castro's revolution sent scores of Cubans into exile in Florida. Chicano (Mexican-American), Nuyorican (New York Puerto Rican), and Cuban-American poetries comprise key parts of Latino poetry, which is itself a fundamental part of U.S. American poetry. If each archive requires a customized critical approach attuned to an unfolding historical relation to the U.S., the pluralistic field of Latino poetry generates a complementary demand to be conceptualized as a poetics of relation – to Latin America and the U.S., and their points of friction, contact, and exchange.

This chapter maps a literary history of U.S. Latino poetry, from its diffuse origins in the nineteenth century to the heterogeneous contemporary scene. This approach highlights the contributions of influential figures such as Alurista (b. 1947), Pedro Pietri (1944–2004), Lorna Dee Cervantes (b. 1954), and Gloria Anzaldúa (1942–2004), but emphasizes how Latino poets have encountered and appropriated Latin American symbols, histories, and traditions. Latino poets' engagements with the region vary in thickness. Some were born, or have lived and worked, in Latin American countries. Some have searched there for antecedents and inspiration. Some have styled themselves as part of Latin American traditions. Many have translated Latin American poets into English.

Part I considers questions about Latino poetry's origins, genealogies, and definitions. When does Latino poetry begin? Who counts as a Latino poet? Part II describes the development of Chicano and Nuyorican poetries in the "movement era," from the mid-1960s to the mid-1970s. Part III discusses key figures from the "post-movement" era, during the 1980s and 1990s, exploring how Latino poetry expanded, often via feminist and queer paradigms, to reflect on conflicts in Central America and on the U.S-Mexico borderlands. At the same time, the Nuyorican Poets' Cafe in New York City solidified the role of performance in Latino poetics. Part IV surveys the dizzying aesthetic range of Latino poetry in the new millennium, as it simultaneously enters the mainstream and comprises a vanguard of North American letters. The chapter concludes with microsketches of contemporary Latino poets whose hemispheric literary practices include poetry, translation, criticism, teaching, and editing.

I

Defining the parameters of Latino poetry is difficult in part because "Latino" is not a racial, ethnic, linguistic, or national category but an imaginary construct encompassing persons of Latin American descent in the U.S. Whereas "Hispanic" is a U.S. Census term from the 1970s with assimilationist connotations, "Latino" enfolds productive contradictions and ambiguities that militate against essentializing cultural nationalisms and racisms alike. Raúl Coronado uses the term "proleptically" to refer to early nineteenth-century Spanish speakers in the U.S., largely in what is now Texas. His historicization is useful for periodizing Latino poetry:

> I use "Latino" as a way to conceptualize the experiences of these communities as they sedimented over time, a sedimentation that may also have had its detours and reverse-formations, but that nonetheless contributed to the formation of Latino literary and intellectual culture. "Latino," in this sense, refers less to a subject-position than it does to a literary and intellectual culture that emerges in the interstices between the United States and Spanish America. Because it emerged in that space it does not have clear temporal and spatial boundaries. [...] [I]t is precisely the non-national specificity of "Latino" that makes the term particularly useful, given the intractability of the nation as an overpowering concept in organizing fields of knowledge.[2]

Coronado's methodology facilitates an expansive canon of Latino poetry. José Martí, who spent fifteen years in New York, where he wrote most of his poems and essays, many for Latin American periodicals, might be read as a Latino poet rather than a Cuban exile. "Nuestra América" would be a founding document of Latino poetics "in the interstices between" north and south. Similarly, Puerto Rican poets such as Clemente Soto Vélez and Julia de Burgos would be read as foundational Latino poets. William Carlos Williams, whose mother was Puerto Rican, has already been reclaimed as Latino, beginning with a study by the New York Puerto Rican poet Julio Marzán (b. 1946).[3] Williams has influenced Latino poets as different as the Nuyorican Victor Hernández Cruz (b. 1949) and Rosa Alcalá (b. 1969), child of immigrants from Franco's Spain and, like Williams, a native of Paterson, New Jersey. Ernest Fenollosa, another influential poet of Spanish descent who traced his heritage to indigenous Mexico, would be read as Latino.[4]

---

[2] Raúl Coronado, *A World Not to Come: A History of Latino Writing and Print Culture* (Boston, MA: Harvard University Press, 2013), 29–30.
[3] Julio Marzán, *The Spanish American Roots of William Carlos Williams* (Austin, TX: University of Texas Press, 1994).
[4] David Colón, "The Hispanic Fenollosa," *Jacket 2* (2015). Available at: <http://jacket2.org/commentary/hispanic-fenollosa>.

Michael Dowdy

Rather than consider these poets "proto-Latino," to adapt "proto-Chicano" from Américo Paredes (1915–1999), they would be incorporated into the longue *durée* of Latino poetry, with its attendant ambiguities. After all, when does a Mexican poet in the U.S. become a Latino poet? Is this shift a function of time, self-identification, publication and marketing, racialized interpellation into the state, the acquisition of citizenship or residency papers, or some combination thereof? While this question is significant, it remains secondary to the movement of bodies, ideas, and cultures across the hemisphere. Critics such as Kirsten Silva Gruesz explore how writers have shuttled between south and north in the Americas since the late eighteen hundreds. This movement intensified in the twentieth century – in the aftermath of the Mexican Revolution of 1910; in the 1930s with mass deportations of Mexicans (many of them U.S. citizens) during the Great Depression; during the Bracero guest worker program (1942–1964) that brought five million Mexican men to the U.S.; in the 1980s, with the debt crisis and wars in Central America; and in the 1990s with NAFTA and neoliberal entrenchment.

Cruz has suggested that Latino poetry is defined by a "tremendous coming and going" and "Spanish and English constantly breaking into each other like ocean waves."[5] This description fits a range, from Martí, who traveled to promote Cuban independence, to the Mexican "migrant imaginary," in Alicia Schmidt Camacho's terms.[6] Poetry played a significant part in the nineteenth-century development of Latino culture, forming an elliptical throughline to the late 1960s, when poets and poetry played central roles in the Chicano (Mexican-American) and Puerto Rican civil rights movements. "Because of its brevity, mobility, association with the voice, and status as a prestige genre," Gruesz writes, lyric poetry was the most common genre in Spanish-language periodicals in this early era. Poetry was also the most translated, circulating north and south in broadsides, pamphlets, and newspapers.[7]

Such uncertain, mobile ontologies and canons underlie Latino poetry. Whereas the languages of Latin American poetry include Spanish, Portuguese, Quechua, and Nahuatl, among others, Latino poetry's primary language has shifted from Spanish, in the nineteenth century, to English, beginning with Paredes's iconic poem "The Mexico-Texan" (1934). But this

[5] *Panoramas* (Minneapolis, MN: Coffee House, 1997), 122; *Red Beans* (Coffee House, 1991), 89–90.
[6] *Migrant Imaginaries: Latino Cultural Politics in the U.S.-Mexico Borderlands* (New York, NY: New York University Press, 2008).
[7] Kirsten Silva Gruesz, *Ambassadors of Culture: The Transamerican Origins of Latino Writing* (Princeton, NJ: Princeton University Press, 2002), xii–xiii.

248

evolution oversimplifies. In rejecting monolingualism, Latino poetry moves within and outside of English- and Spanish-language traditions. Anzaldúa's linguistic taxonomy, in her seminal book *Borderlands/La Frontera: The New Mestiza* (1987), lists the languages she speaks:

1. Standard English
2. Working class and slang English
3. Standard Spanish
4. Standard Mexican Spanish
5. North Mexican Spanish dialect
6. Chicano Spanish (Texas, New Mexico, Arizona, and California have regional variations)
7. Tex-Mex
8. *Pachuco* (called *Caló*)[8]

This list exemplifies the polyvocality of the field. For other Latino poets, especially those in the Nuyorican tradition, such a list might include African-American vernacular English (AAVE). Broadly understood, "[t]he unstable relation" between the "popular oral" and "literary written" dimensions of Mexican migrant poetry (Schmidt Camacho, *Migrant Imaginaries*, 45) applies to much Latino poetry, from the 1960s to the present. The corrido tradition, detailed by José E. Limón, the bracero ballads from the 1940s and 1950s, and today's *narcocorridos* offer a similar lineage in which popular forms and lyric subjectivities converge.[9] These multilingual and multiregister qualities intensified in the movement era, when Chicano and Nuyorican poets invented new languages of collective identity.

II

Although periodization questions follow this prehistory into the present, critics agree that the bedrock of Latino poetry was produced in the movement era, beginning in the mid-1960s. In California and the Southwest, *movimiento* poetry propelled Chicano activism. In New York, Nuyorican poetry developed alongside the Puerto Rican Movement and the radical activist group the Young Lords. These poetries share many qualities and contexts. First and foremost, they emphasized and often complicated the relationship between artistic production and political activity, agitation, and resistance. Poetry was an important mode of collective subject formation,

[8] *Borderlands/La Frontera: The New Mestiza* (San Francisco, CA: Aunt Lute, 1987), 55.
[9] *Mexican Ballads, Chicano Poems: History and Influence in Mexican-American Social Poetry* (Berkeley, CA: University of California Press, 1992).

political protest, and the galvanization of community spirit. Chicano Movement poetry and Nuyorican poetry helped to develop forms of cultural nationalism, in which a documentary impulse guided poets' attempts to make visible the lives of communities that had been rendered invisible through conquest and colonization. But poets did not merely record the lives of the oppressed; they performed new identities that aimed to decolonize their communities, arts, languages, and lands. It is possible to discern in Latino poetry a throughline from the precursor era to the present, in which movement-era poetry serves as the knotty connective tissue. Since the beginning, Latino poets have lived and worked in multiple standard and non-standard languages (including forms of Spanglish), switching between registers and codes, both oral and written, exposing the limits and imperial undertones of monolingualism (Spanish *or* English), and demonstrating myriad forms of social and political engagement.

The poetry of *el movimiento* reinscribes indigenous Mexico into Chicano identity. The archive is replete with Aztec symbols, a codex of images that collectively created the ideal image of the warrior-poet who fights to reclaim the homeland of Chicanos: Aztlán, the place of the Aztecs. This myth-making is rooted in appropriations, none more prominent than the neologism "Floricanto," the *movimiento* term for poetry derived from the Nahuatl words for "flower" and "song." Chicanos became members of "La Raza," the race of descendants of the Aztecs who would gain control of their ancestral lands. The epic poem "Yo Soy Joaquín" (1967), by Rodolfo "Corky" Gonzales (1928–2005), shows the historical scope of this imaginary. Gonzales, like many other poets, was a prominent activist. This passage in the declaratory, triumphant poem imagines Chicano identity emerging from the colonial encounter, producing a *mestizaje* of conqueror and conquered, indigenous and Spanish. The prosaic verse also indicates why the poem endures largely as a document of cultural pride rather than aesthetic excellence:

> I am Cuauhtémoc, proud and noble,
> leader of men, king of an empire civilized
> beyond the dreams of the gachupín Cortés,
> who also is the blood, the image of myself.
> I am the Maya prince.
> I am Nezahualcóyotl, great leader of the Chichimecas.
>
> I am the sword and flame of Cortes the despot
> And I am the eagle and serpent of the Aztec civilization.
> I owned the land as far as the eye
> could see under the Crown of Spain,

and I toiled on my Earth and gave my Indian sweat and blood
for the Spanish master who ruled with tyranny over man and
beast and all that he could trample
But ... THE GROUND WAS MINE.[10]

Although Ricardo Sánchez (1941–1995) and José Montoya (1932–2013) were significant figures, no poet exerted more influence on *movimiento* aesthetics than Alurista (b. 1947). Born in Mexico City, Alurista immigrated to the U.S. as a teenager. He is best known for his preamble to "El Plan Espiritual de Aztlán." This manifesto for social action, liberation, and autonomy was adopted in 1969 at the National Chicano Youth Liberation Conference in Denver, where Gonzales's organization Crusade for Justice was based. Beginning with "In the spirit of a new people," the preamble offers a masculinist, programmatic vision of a Chicano nation rooted in "forefathers" and secured via "brotherhood," simultaneously emergent and ancient.[11]

While the direct influence of Latin American poetry on Chicano Movement poetry is minimal, parallel events in Mexico retain a symbolic resonance in the cultural production of Chicano poets. 1968 may not resonate in the U.S. as it does in Mexico, but the Mexican Student Movement and the Tlatelolco massacre seeped into the poetic consciousness, flashing up in Herrera, Margarita Cota-Cárdenas (b. 1941), and others. Similarly, resistance to the war in Vietnam influenced the sensibilities of Chicano poetry, culminating in the Chicano Moratorium protest march in East Los Angeles on August 29, 1970.

Nuyorican poetry has a more oblique and less prescriptive relationship to social movements, as well as a more diffuse and less obvious debt to Latin American cultures. The Nuyorican tradition, Urayoán Noel argues, developed in relation to "the new American poetries" of the 1950s and 1960s, the voice- and breath-driven aesthetics of Beat, Objectivist, Black Mountain, New York School, and Black Arts Movement poets.[12] But Dadaism and Surrealism, especially as filtered through Latin American poetries, also shaped Nuyorican aesthetics. Noel identifies *Inventory* (1964), by Frank Lima (1939–2013), as the first book of Nuyorican poetry. Yet Cruz, whose *Snaps* was published in 1968, and Pietri, who first read his epic "Puerto Rican Obituary" in 1969, were the seminal figures. Their divergent poetics evolved dramatically over the decades, exemplifying Nuyorican poetry's

---

[10] "Yo Soy Joaquín" is available at: <www.latinamericanstudies.org/latinos/joaquin.htm>.
[11] "El Plan Espiritual de Aztlán" is available at: <www.umich.edu/~mechaum/Aztlan.html>.
[12] *In Visible Movement: Nuyorican Poetry from the Sixties to Slam* (Iowa City, IA: University of Iowa Press, 2014).

restless innovation, frenetic mobility, and fraught relationship to politics. As Raphael Dalleo and Elena Machado Sáez argue, Pietri epitomizes the difficulty of periodizing an archive that bridges the eras with aesthetic and thematic continuities while relating differently to movement-era and "post-Sixties" political-economic formations.[13]

Cruz's work shows the influence of Pan-Latin American and Caribbean musical traditions. His polylinguistic play, cacophonous sound effects, and score-like typographies enact a rhythmic movement on the page. These movements juxtapose the dissonant geographies of the island and New York, transforming Manhattan's ice, concrete, and skyscrapers with humidity, mangoes, and palm trees. His poem "An Essay on William Carlos Williams" distills the transgression of generic categories central to Latino poetics. Declaring "[t]he tongue itself carries/ the mind" (*Red Beans*, 52), Cruz locates in Williams the unfinished spontaneity of Nuyorican poetry. For this reason, Noel identifies Williams as one of its two literary-historical cornerstones.

Like Cruz, Pietri was born in Puerto Rico and moved to New York as a child. A veteran of the war in Vietnam, Pietri unflinchingly renders the lived experience of imperialism with an anarchist glee. Just as Cruz uses Williams to create his *ars poetica*, Pietri pays homage to Jorge Brandon, an island *declamador* and *trovador* whom Noel sees as the second cornerstone for Nuyorican poetry, to imagine his own. "Traffic Misdirector" illustrates the importance of the oral tradition, improvisation, mobility, and absurdity to Nuyorican poetry:

> the greatest living poet
> in new york city
> was born in Puerto Rico
> his name is Jorge Brandon
> he is over 70 years old
> he carries his metaphor
> in brown shopping bags
> inside steel shopping cart
> he travels around with
> on the streets of manhattan
> he recites his poetry
> to whoever listens
> & when nobody is around
> he recites to himself[14]

[13] *The Latino/a Canon and the Emergence of Post-Sixties Literature* (New York, NY: Palgrave, 2008).
[14] *Selected Poetry* (San Francisco, CA: City Lights, 2015), 71.

Pietri's skinny lines and phonetic spellings recall Soto Vélez but without his elevated *vanguardia* rhetoric that places poetry and revolution on a pedestal. As the above poem's alternative genealogy and antic revaluation of "high" and "low" cultures indicates, Pietri bears more the influence of Nicanor Parra's irreverent anti-poetry: "Don't expect me to explain anything/ All I can truly say about myself/ Is that after monday comes tuesday" (58).

Like *movimiento* poetry, Pietri's most influential poem, "Puerto Rican Obituary," focuses on the decolonization of the minds and bodies of his community. First performed at a Young Lords rally in 1969, it nonetheless displays the ways in which Nuyorican poetry was less programmatic and more ungovernable in its relationship to political activism. Unlike much Chicano Movement poetry, Nuyorican poetry tends to states of abjection rather than cultural pride, and problems rather than solutions:

> All died yesterday today
> and will die again tomorrow
> passing their bill collectors
> on to the next of kin
> All died
> waiting for the garden of eden
> to open up again
> under a new management (3–4)

This is a different sort of epic than "Yo Soy Joaquín." Juan, Miguel, Milagros, Olga, and Manuel, the poem's five archetypal Nuyoricans, displaced from their cultural origins, die repeatedly. The latter "died hating all of them," "because they all spoke broken English/ more fluently than he did" (10).

Ultimately, Puerto Rico's colonial status as a U.S. "Commonwealth" created a darker, more anxious aesthetic than *el movimiento*. Though Chicano Movement poetry engaged with deprivations of poverty and oppression, and though the poetries share many characteristics, including their multiple "broken" languages, the equally abundant political energies of Nuyorican poetry were more diffuse. The forms of belonging nurtured by cultural nationalism are tested by the very mobilities afforded by Puerto Ricans' second-class citizenship, and by the tensions between "here" and "there" (New York and the island) identified by the groundbreaking scholar Juan Flores.[15] Whereas Nuyorican poetry is diasporic, Chicano nationalism mostly disavowed transnational imaginaries, as Schmidt Camacho argues. Finally, New York's hyperurban spatiotemporality, claustrophobia, and hustle, evident in the "barrio"

---

[15] *From Bomba to Hip-Hop: Puerto Rican Culture and Latino Identity* (New York, NY: Columbia University Press, 2000).

or "street" poetry of Pietri and Jesús "Papoleto" Meléndez (b. 1950) foreclose utopian impulses. For Nuyoricans, Aztlán is the paradoxically unreachable and omnipresent island of Puerto Rico.

III

Critical periodizations such as "post-Sixties" and "post-movement" suggest departures from the movement era, but the later poetry often maintains continuities. The feminist, queer, border, performance, and hemispheric poetries of the 1980s and after scrutinize, even reject, the masculinist hierarchies of the earlier era, but from within Chicano, Nuyorican, and Latino traditions. In the 1980s, Chicano poetry takes aesthetic turns toward (i) experimental forms apart from narrow conceptions of identity politics and political protest (Alurista's *Spik in Glyph?* [1981] and Herrera's *Exiles of Desire* [1983]); (ii) lyric forms, in the North American tradition (Cervantes's *Emplumada* [1981]); and (iii) border poetics (Anzaldúa's *Borderlands*). In the U.S. Puerto Rican context, the Nuyorican Poets Cafe, which originally opened in 1974 in the apartment of Miguel Algarín (b. 1941), became the epicenter of Slam poetry. At the same time, the New York Puerto Rican poet Martín Espada (b. 1957) disavowed Nuyorican aesthetics but affirmed its oppositional political identity. His first book, *The Immigrant Iceboy's Bolero* (1982), staked his claim as a poet of the Americas.

In these decades, Latino poetry's consciousness of north-south relations matured. This awareness mapped two geographies, one centered in Mexico, the other with an expansive hemispherism. Often, as Herrera's writing tacitly admits, Mexico serves as a synecdoche for Latin America. Comparing *Emplumada* and *Borderlands* is instructive of the divergent uses of Mexico in Chicano poetics. Cervantes's "Oaxaca, 1974" begins: "México,/ I look for you all day in the streets of Oaxaca."[16] Surrounded by children she cannot understand, essences escape her. Her alienation is rooted in language, her necessary if fruitless search rejecting the presence of Mexico in Chicano identity assumed in "Yo Soy Joaquín." "My name," she laments, "hangs about me like a loose tooth" (44). Likewise, "Visions of Mexico while at a Writing Symposium in Port Townsend, Washington" begins: "When I'm that far south, the old words/ molt off my skin, the feathers/ of all my nervousness" (45). This anxiety leads Schmidt Camacho to conclude that *Emplumada* departs from Chicano nationalism, while Raúl H. Villa sees

[16] *Emplumada* (Pittsburgh, PA: University of Pittsburgh Press, 1981), 44.

Emplumada revising it through feminist lenses.[17] (Cervantes, who came of age during the movement, tends to Villa's view.) Whether the U.S.-Mexico border is a barrier or a bridge, as Schmidt Camacho writes (162), it becomes a fault line in Latino poetics. Cervantes sees a barrier, Anzaldúa a bridge.

Borderlands invents a genre – the border text – by obliterating generic categories and questioning the binary logic of Western philosophy. Anzaldúa's multilingual (Spanish, English, Nahuatl, and Caló) text combines historiography, ethnography, mythology, poetry, lyric essay, folklore, and *testimonio* to create a "new *mestiza* consciousness" that rejects such divisions. Rafael Pérez-Torres maps in Chicano poetry a broad shift from collective to individual subjectivities between the eras.[18] In Anzaldúa, however, a collective *indigenismo* remains, but it is queered, rooted in Indian women's historical resistance, and centered in ambiguities more common to Nuyorican than *movimiento* poetics. She defines Chicano identity capaciously:

> *Nosotros los Chicanos* straddle the borderlands. On one side of us, we are constantly exposed to the Spanish of the Mexicans, on the other side we hear the Anglos' incessant clamoring so that we forget our language. Among ourselves we don't say *nosotros los americanos, o nosotros los españoles, o nosotros los hispanos*. We say *nosotros los mexicanos* (by *mexicanos* we do not mean citizens of Mexico; we do not mean a national identity, but a racial one). We distinguish between *mexicanos del otro lado* and *mexicanos de este lado*. Deep in our hearts we believe that being Mexican has nothing to do with which country one lives in. Being Mexican is a state of soul – not one of mind, not one of citizenship. Neither eagle nor serpent, but both. And like the ocean, neither animal respects borders. (62)

It is difficult to overstate Anzaldúa's influence on Latino poetics, despite her adaptation of José Vasconcelos's racial essentialisms. Her thick description and theorization of the border, along with her cognitive mapping of a new identity, extended Latino poetry's concerns with naming, identity, language, and belonging.

The Nuyorican Poets Cafe dramatized these concerns, evolving from its counterinstitutional roots to MTV performances. Three generations of Nuyorican poets, led by Edwin Torres (b. 1958), Willie Perdomo (b. 1967), and Mayda del Valle (b. 1978, in Chicago), emerged alongside Slam poets of many ethnic-racial backgrounds. Consequently, the term "Nuyorican" became "a metonymy of the physical space of the Cafe, decontextualized

---

[17] Raúl H. Villa, *Barrio-Logos: Space and Place in Urban Chicano Literature and Culture* (Austin, TX: University of Texas Press, 2000).

[18] *Movements in Chicano Poetry: Against Myths, Against Margins* (New York, NY: Cambridge University Press, 1995).

from community histories and cultural identifications" (Noel, *In Visible Movement*, 124). Pietri and other artists simultaneously developed absurdist-anarchist spaces such as the New Rican Village and the El Puerto Rican Embassy website (1994) that combined numerous impulses – utopian vanguard, satirical, anti-realist, and anti-documentary – to critique the continued colonization of Puerto Rico and, implicitly, the movement era's representational forms.

Like these artists, Espada's poetry is grounded in *independentista* politics. Yet when he describes discovering a tradition, "an artistry of dissent," in the poetry of Neruda and Ernesto Cardenal, he implies that Nuyorican poetry lacks artistry.[19] Rather than *exteriorismo*, Cardenal's poetics of quotation and fragmentation exemplified in "Zero Hour," Espada's highly crafted figurative language, which rejects Nuyorican poetry's unfinished improvisations, resembles Cervantes's and honors Neruda's. Espada has been called "the Pablo Neruda of North American authors" by the Chicana poet Sandra Cisneros (b. 1954), an attribution trumpeted from book jackets and marketing materials. His writing locates in the figure of Neruda poetry's power to give voice to the voiceless of the Americas, in the mode of "The Heights of Machu Picchu": "I come to speak for your dead mouths." Teresa Longo's anthology of essays examines the ways Neruda is appropriated in North America, including by Latino poets such as Tino Villanueva (b. 1941) and Marcos McPeek Villatoro (b. 1962).[20] No poet has translated Neruda, in the broadest sense of the term, more frequently and deftly than Espada, whose *Republic of Poetry* depicts his trip to Chile for the 2004 Neruda centennial.[21]

Espada's hemispheric poetry touches down in more places in Latin America and pays homage to more writers – beyond Neruda and Cardenal, Roque Dalton, Rubén Darío, Eduardo Galeano, Subcomandante Marcos, Soto Vélez, and Raúl Zurita feature prominently – than any other North American poet. His travels provide a lens for (i) assessing the Latin American canon from a Latino perspective and (ii) reading "Latino by Latin American," as I argue elsewhere.[22] The latter approach emphasizes divergent modes for poeticizing north-south relations. Herrera's hemispheric poetics, for instance, is distilled in a sign he recorded from the May 1, 2006, "Day Without an Immigrant" march in Los Angeles for the rights for the

---

[19] Martín Espada, *Poetry Like Bread: Poets of the Political Imagination from Curbstone Press* (Willimantic, CT: Curbstone, 2000), 17.

[20] *Pablo Neruda and the U.S. Culture Industry* (New York, NY: Routledge, 2002).

[21] *The Republic of Poetry* (New York, NY: Norton, 2006).

[22] Michael Dowdy, *Broken Souths: Latina/o Poetic Responses to Neoliberalism and Globalization* (Tucson, AZ: University of Arizona Press, 2013).

undocumented: "Yo nací en América soy Americano ok" (*187 Reasons*, 62). This "line" exemplifies Herrera's hemispherism: "found," fragmentary, estranged, unstable, and colloquial, winking at Bolívar and Martí. In contrast, Espada strives for lucidity, originality, narrative heft, and lyric concision.

Their poems about El Salvador illuminate these differences. Both employ "datelines." Herrera's "Nightpainters" has "THE DUSK OF LA GUARDIA NACIONAL OF EL SALVADOR." Espada's widely anthologized "The Skull Beneath the Skin of the Mango" has "El Salvador, 1992." Herrera begins: "They observe the wounds. Only observance is possible here in the daylight. At night, they will refigure with the palette of moonlight, with the turpentine of fever." Espada begins: "The woman spoke/ with the tranquility of shock:/ the Army massacre was here."[23] They share a commitment to document the horrors of U.S.-backed death squads in El Salvador, including the massacre at El Mozote (1981), Espada's subject. Although each insists that Latino poets can write the hemisphere and that a sense of belonging can be nurtured transnationally, Herrera distorts and haunts while Espada illuminates, reveals.

IV

Poets working on the margins or outside of Chicano and Nuyorican traditions during these decades highlight the challenge of surveying Latino poetry's formal, experimental, and performance practices. These traditions are internally diverse, and the field of Latino poetry into which they are incorporated magnifies this pluralism. Seminal texts such as Gary Soto's *Elements of San Joaquin* (1977), Jimmy Santiago Baca's *Martín and Meditations on the South Valley* (1987), and Sandra Cisneros's *My Wicked Wicked Ways* (1994) disrupt narrow mappings of Chicano poetry in ways too numerous and complex to delineate here. Rafael Campo's AIDS poems and gay sonnets in *What the Body Told* (1996) likewise bend the trajectories of Cuban-American poetry and lead a turn to formalism in Latino poetry.[24] The twenty-first century has seen a proliferation of (i) poets descending from nations apart from the main national groups; (ii) poets developing innovative

---

[23] Martín Espada, *Alabanza: New and Selected Poems 1982–2002* (New York, NY: Norton, 2002), 109; Juan Felipe Herrera, *Half of the World in Light: New and Selected Poems* (Tucson, AZ: University of Arizona Press, 2008), 37.
[24] On formalism, see Frederick Luis Aldama, *Formal Matters in Contemporary Latino Poetry* (New York, NY: Palgrave, 2013). On Baca and Cisneros, see John Alba Cutler, *Ends of Assimilation: The Formation of Chicano Literature* (New York, NY: Oxford University Press, 2015).

forms of literary practice and activism; and (iii) poets transforming the intersections between North and Latin American poetries. There is considerable overlap across these dimensions.

Of numerous poets in the first category, Carmen Giménez Smith (b. 1971), of Peruvian, and Mauricio Kilwein Guevara (b. 1961), of Colombian descent, deserve particular notice. Giménez Smith's "So You Know Who We Are" underscores the class and gender dimensions of Latino poetry's nomadism, turning it to mock-confession:

> The wisteria and bill collectors colluded
> to swallow our household whole, so we dismantled
> it, rivet and splinter, made two piles on the lawn:
>
> 1. belongings the quality of lead,
> 2. belongings the quality of dandruff.
>
> (...)
>
> My father insisted that staying
> was akin to calcifying. He hated geologic
> permanence buried in heaps under us.
> He buried his employ instead.
> My mother sewed nickels into her hem.[25]

While traces of Latin America dot Giménez Smith's poems, Kilwein Guevara's idiosyncratic genealogies proliferate. His surreal prose poems, hallucinatory lists, and lyric meditations address the Costa Rican poet Eunice Odio, record "found" poems in Oaxaca, narrate Colombian history from the conquest to Plan Colombia crop dusters, and grapple with Borges's legacy.

New literary formations range among individual inventions, loose affiliations, and organized groups. "Antropoesía," poetry with an ethnographic sensibility, theorized by Renato Rosaldo (b. 1941), underlines the documentary underpinnings of Latino poetry. The "performance autology" of the Dominican Josefina Baez (b. 1960) highlights Latino poetry's performativity. "Mariposa" poetics, created by Rigoberto González (b. 1970), enacts a queer Latino aesthetic. CantoMundo nurtures Latino poets through workshops and readings. The Undocupoets have successfully agitated for the rights of undocumented poets. Finally, Rodrigo Toscano (b. 1964) inverts "Latin American poetry" with "American Latin Poetry" (A.L.P.) to parody all such formations, especially vanguard ones, and to critique capitalism's commodification of literature.

---

[25] *Odalisque in Pieces* (Tucson, AZ: University of Arizona Press, 2009), 2.

Latino poets' engagements with Latin American cultures, histories, and poetries have also widened. Anthologies by Mónica de la Torre (b. 1968) and Marjorie Agosín (b. 1955) translate contemporary Mexican and Latin American women's poetry, respectively.[26] The poet-critic-curator Roberto Tejada (b. 1964) edited Octavio Paz's *Vuelta* while living in Mexico City, where he founded *Mandorla: New Writing from the Americas*. Alcalá translates Cecilia Vicuña (b. 1949), who like Agosín is read as Chilean and Latina. Alcalá teaches in the hemisphere's only bilingual MFA program, at the University of Texas-El Paso, shaping future generations of Latin American poets. These examples suggest some of the ways in which literary influence now moves from Latino to Latin American, reversing the general historical direction of influence.

In addition to his seminal study of Nuyorican poetry cited above, the Puerto Rican poet Noel (b. 1976) has developed a vanguard hemispheric poetics incorporating traditional *décimas* and digital forms, from smart phones to search engines. His poetry draws from poets across Latin America, from Pablo de Rokha to Haroldo de Campos. "Trill Set" (mis) translates César Vallejo's "Trilce" by reading it in Spanish through speech recognition software. A performance piece "scored for two voices," Noel instructs us to read "his" perverted version with the original or Clayton Eschelman's translation. The last stanza of section seven is:

> Ahora hormigas minuteras
> se adentran dulzoradas, dormitadas, apenas
> dispuestas, y se baldan,
> quemadas pólvoras, altos de a 1921.

Noel's rendering is:

> I'll without a miasma of fairness
> sentiment was allowed less of me got us up in us
> these boisterous East divided them
> in my less blue for us I did close the Amiga was he imposed think you will know[27]

Whereas Espada's poems are reverential, if often ironic, Noel's absurdist virtuosity mines the randomness and contingency of commodity circulation, poetry included. He thus offers an alternative angle on the Latin American canon, dramatizing the mistranslations defining north-south relations, not to mention the difficulty of translating Vallejo.

[26] De la Torre and Michael Wiegers, *Reversible Monuments: Contemporary Mexican Poetry* (Port Townsend, WA: Copper Canyon, 2002); Agosín, *These Are Not Sweet Girls: Poetry by Latin American Women* (Fredonia, NY: White Pine Press, 1994).
[27] *Hi-Density Politics* (Buffalo, NY: BlazeVox, 2010), 75.

In calling himself a "falso-Chileno," Daniel Borzutzky (b. 1974) critiques the modes of authenticity circumscribing Latino writing. Like Zurita, whose poetry he translates, his poetry is haunted by state violence, though Borzutzky's is more narrative, obsessive, grotesque. And like Espada, he finds uncanny convergences in the Pinochet coup of September 11, 1973, and the terrorist attacks of September 11, 2001. Here's part of "The Immigrant, Vanishing Sun":

> I do not know how to talk about myself without talking about my country. I do not know how to talk about my country without talking about all the bodies it has destroyed. I do not know how to talk about my city without talking about all the bodies it keeps underground. I do not know how to talk about ghosts without talking about myself. [...] I am an immigrant standing on a mountain in a city of glass and there are bodies trying to climb buildings that decompose on one side of a line. It is like this everywhere: the city is decomposing and its decomposition provides the only means by which we can understand ourselves. We sing a song called "Thank you to Life" and we mean it even though we hate every second of being alive. It is forgetting that enables us to see that there might be breath in the mud pits of the sinking valley.[28]

These negations ("I do not") merge Chile and the U.S. into "my country." "[M]y city" alludes to Chicago, where Borzutzky lives, and Santiago. The "city of glass" refers to Neruda's home in Isla Negra; Espada's "City of Glass," which is dedicated to Neruda (*Republic of Poetry*, 22–23); the World Trade Center Towers; and the gilded neoliberal metropolis. Finally, the figurative "mountain" immigrants climb echoes the "flipped over mountains flashing in the night" in Borzutzky's translation of Zurita.[29] In short, Borzutzky writes the north-south circuits of violence Latinos have traveled for centuries.

In conclusion, U.S. Latino/a poetry occupies a unique position. At the vanguard of North American letters, it is also entering the U.S. canon, to which Herrera's appointments attest. Due in part to the forms and locations of their political engagement, Longo argues for reading Latino poets within the Latin American canon.[30] Yet this approach minimizes the unique perspectives afforded to poets in the north and reinforces the historical hierarchy of prestige between Latin American and Latino writers. Instead, Latino poetry disrupts U.S. and Latin American canons equally, pushes beyond them, and forms a mobile archive in the interstices of north and south.

---

[28] *In the Murmurs of the Rotten Carcass Economy* (New York, NY: Nightboat Books, 2015), 35–36.
[29] *The Country of Planks* (South Bend, IN: Action Books, 2015), 68.
[30] Teresa Longo, "A Poet's Place, 2004," *Crítica Hispánica* 28.1 (2006): 181–96.

17

THEA PITMAN

(New) Media Poetry

"In a world in which we are constantly bombarded by the detritus of information technology, from irritating e-mail spamming to ravishing computer viruses, some may argue that the place of poetry should be a removed and quieter realm that provides a respite from the twirling chaos of the technology-inflected contemporary life," writes protean Brazilian artist and poet Eduardo Kac.[1] However, Kac (b. 1962) has no intention of offering us poetry as "a substitute for a walk in the park, sunbathing or meditation"; for him poetry should engage fully in the way that "language is malleably and constantly expanded and transformed" through the media that surround us, both old and new, and the resultant works should seek to "reshape [...] the media and transform [...] technology into an instrument of the imagination" (Kac, *Media Poetry*, 10).

Kac's enthusiastic embrace of the potential for technological inventions of all sorts to be used for poetic purposes is by now long-standing. He created poems with ASCII computer code and with holographic technologies in the early 1980s, and he exhibited networked "minitel" poems at a group exhibition in São Paulo entitled "Arte On-Line" in 1985. In 1996 he edited the first anthology dedicated to "new media poetry" where an international group of writers including Giselle Beiguelman (Brazil, b. 1962) and André Vallias (Brazil, b. 1963), as well as Ladislao Pablo Györi (Argentina, b. 1963), offered commentary and reflection on their "new media" poetic experiments thus far.

Kac's fascination with interrogating and exploiting the newest technologies of the day in his poetic works clearly emerged in an environment in the big urban centres of Brazil where he found like-minded artists and poets, as well as institutions that could just about be persuaded to support and provide exhibition space for his work (because this kind of poetry needs more than just the pages of a book to exist, and before the advent of the internet,

[1] Eduardo Kac, ed., *Media Poetry: An International Anthology* (Bristol: Intellect, 2007), 9.

installations in exhibitions or other public spaces, e.g. electronic billboards, were the preeminent form of distribution). That fascination with the conjunction of poetry and (new) media has since spread across the region with particular "nodes" of activity around the River Plate, and in Chile and Mexico, and it continues to grow with international acknowledgement of its vibrancy coming in the form of the E-Poetry Festival and Conference, organized by the State University of New York's Electronic Poetry Center, being celebrated in Latin America for the first time in 2015.

Definitions and Terminology: Bracketing the New in New Media Poetry

Attentive readers will note that I started to put the word "new" in parentheses during the course of the last two paragraphs in reference to "media poetry." Arguably, despite Kac's use of the term "new media poetry" to refer to this kind of poetry, the technologies that he and his peers were experimenting with in the early 1980s are hardly something that we would consider as "new" or part of "new media" today. Lev Manovich defines this as the confluence of all forms of media with computing technologies for their generation, storage, circulation, and consumption, identifiable by the principles of numerical representation, modularity, automation, variability, and transcoding, this last understood as the significant influence exerted by the "computer's ontology, epistemology and pragmatics" on "the cultural layer of new media: its organization, its emerging genres, its contents" and vice versa.[2] Thus, following Kac's own arguments put forth in the second edition of his anthology entitled simply *Media Poetry* (Kac, 7), for the purposes of this chapter, I propose to bracket the "new" of "new media" since, while I will be focusing predominantly on very late twentieth and twenty-first century works that are indeed intrinsically bound up with what we currently call "new media," the adjective "new" is far too ephemeral in its relationship to technology to be really helpful in the long term.

But if "new" is unhelpful as a qualifier, why not ditch the term "new media," with or without parentheses, and agree to refer to this kind of poetry by another name? The terms "digital poetry," "electronic poetry," and its abbreviated form "e-poetry" circulate interchangeably, although careful users do sometimes distinguish between artefacts created with and for electronic (but analog) as opposed to digital technologies, for example those created for reading via a VHS player versus those created for reading via a computer, with or without internet connection. Sometimes the difference in use of these terms has more to do with a focus on the apparatus used for

---

[2] Lev Manovich, *The Language of New Media* (Cambridge, MA; MIT Press, 2001), 46.

display (electronic poetry) versus a concern for the base technologies on which such poetry is built (digital poetry).[3] Arguably, in a (Latin) American context and *pace* Kac, these terms are far more frequently used than "new media poetry."[4] But to grasp why "(new) media poetry" might be a preferable term, we need to start by understanding what any of these terms might mean. The most frequently defined is "digital poetry."

Given the increasingly blurred boundaries between different art forms, digital *poetry* is perhaps best identified following Talan Memmott's minimalist definition: the requirements can only be "that the object in question be 'digital,' mediated through digital technology, and that it be called 'poetry' by its author or by a critical reader."[5] We can therefore consider some of Giselle Beiguelman's work to be poetry rather than art simply because she defines it as "nomadic poetry."[6] If we shift emphasis away from whether this kind of cultural production qualifies as poetry to focus on the impact of the "digital" modifier, digital poetry may be defined as poetry that is "actively formed" by digitality and where the poet should evidence "thinking through the new medium."[7] An "embedded aesthetics"[8] born of the focus on making and on process, and for the reader, of the requirement to actively participate in the work's (re)creation and meaning-making, should be the result. Expanding to embrace other definitions by Peter Shillingburg and Christopher Funkhouser, Flores goes on to argue that "we can define the digital poem as one that distinctively uses digital media in the creation, production, or reception performances of the poem."[9] The flip side of this definition of "born-digital" poetry is that, as Stephanie Strickland has argued

---

[3] Osvaldo Cleger, "La creación ciberliteraria: definición, perfil y carta de navegación para orientarse en un campo emergente," *Letras Hispanas* 11 (2015): 264. Terms such as "computer poetry," "cyberpoetry," or "techno-poetry" also exist, although their usage is rather less frequent. "Cyber" as a prefix is very much a relic of the 1990s and the early 2000s though it has been used to particularly productive effect in Espen J. Aarseth's work on "ergodic" literature; see *Cybertext: Perspectives on Ergodic Literature* (Baltimore, MD: Johns Hopkins University Press, 1997).

[4] The anthology, *New Media Poetics: Context, Technotexts, and Theories*, ed. Adelaide Morris and Thomas Swiss (Cambridge, MA: MIT University Press, 2006) is a notable and helpful exception.

[5] Talan Memmott, "Beyond Taxonomy: Digital Poetics and the Problem of Reading," in *New Media Poetics: Contexts, Technotexts, and Theories*, ed. Adelaide Morris and Thomas Swiss (Cambridge, MA: MIT Press, 2006), 293.

[6] Giselle Beiguelman, "Nomadic Poems," in Kac, *Media Poetry*, 97–103.

[7] Katherine Hayles and Loss Pequeño Glazier respectively, qtd in Leonardo Flores, "Digital Poetry," in *The Johns Hopkins Guide to Digital Media*, ed. Marie-Laure Ryan, Lori Emerson and Benjamin J. Robertson (Baltimore, MD: The Johns Hopkins University Press, 2014), 155.

[8] Faye Ginsburg, "Embedded Aesthetics: Creating a Discursive Space for Indigenous Media," *Cultural Anthropology* 9.3 (1994): 365–82.

[9] Flores, in Ryan, Emerson and Robertson, *Digital Media*, 156.

in the wider context of e-literature, "If it could possibly be printed out, it isn't e-lit."[10] Thus poetry that circulates on any amount of data storage devices or via individual poets' blogs, is not digital poetry if we can just as easily read it from a piece of paper with no loss of meaning or overall reading experience. This is just a case of very simple "remediation"[11] that does not engage in a reconsideration of the nature of the work of art as it changes from one medium to another.[12]

What my overarching use of the term "(new) media poetry" offers is a palimpsestic reading of "digital" poetry in a broader historical, social and material context that allows us to consider works of (new) media poetry that led up to "digital poetry" proper and even works on paper that exist in "dialogue" with technological inventions/new media; that is, works of "pre-historic digital poetry,"[13] and relevant works of pre/nondigital poetry "(todavía) *in print*,"[14] as well as those works of poetry that really exceed the limitations of new media/digital poetry, moving beyond the exclusivity of the "digital" and "new media platforms" to evermore hybrid forms of multi-media poetry that pertain to what we might term the current "post-digital moment." At this juncture, we might as well resume using the term media poetry ...

Medium–Message–Media: Of all literary genres, poetry is arguably the one which is most sensitive to, and self-aware about, its medium. Where the novel or the play may seduce us into a "willing suspension of disbelief" as we cease to perceive the medium of its delivery, poetry rarely does so, not even when in

---

[10] Stephanie Strickland, "Born Digital: A Poet in the Forefront of the Field Explore What Is – and Is Not – Electronic Literature," *Poetry Foundation* (2010), www.poetryfoundation.org/article/182942.

[11] Jay David Bolter and Richard Grusin, *Remediation: Understanding New Media* (Cambridge, MA: MIT Press, 1999).

[12] As a new media alternative to the distribution of sheets of handwritten, later mimeographed, later photocopied poems, blogs such as the Argentine *Las afinidades electivas/Las elecciones afectivas* or the Mexican *Poesía virtual* have arguably proven to be a fantastic means of increasing the audience for poetic works of all sorts.

[13] Christopher Thompson Funkhouser, *Prehistoric Digital Poetry: An Archaeology of Forms, 1959–1995* (Tuscaloosa, AL: University of Alabama Press, 2007).

[14] See Luis Correa-Díaz, "La poesía cibernética latinoamericana (todavía) *in print*: un recorrido desde los años 50 y 60 hasta finales de la primera década del 2000," *New Readings* 13 (2013): 57–73. There have been several useful genealogies of digital poetry, see Funkhouser, *Prehistoric Digital Poetry*, and his subsequent *New Directions in Digital Poetry* (New York, NY: Continuum, 2012); and Flores, in Ryan, Emerson, and Robertson, *Digital Media*). Funkhouser's 2007 study of "prehistoric digital poetry" is particularly useful in so far as it makes a compelling case for the fact that all the key features of "digital poetry" proper (i.e. *new media* poetry) are no more than logical extensions of practices that were developed in the period from the development of the first computers to the popularization of the internet (1959–1995). Digital poetry proper dates from 1995 onwards.

conversational mode. Thus, where artists seek to create poetry to "think through the new medium," we may expect to find this same characteristic once more – a heightened awareness of the medium itself. Such poetry is "hypermediatized" (Bolter and Grusin, *Remediation*); it seeks to draw our attention to what it has to say about the medium it is created in/for; to draw our attention to the limits of these new paradigms and to stretch them where possible. As such it is generally more conceptual and experiential than it is "thematic," and it moves well beyond the paradigm of lyric poetry and the perspective of a singular lyrical subject.[15] Such works often seek to expose the principles of new media as enumerated by Manovich – numerical representation, modularity, automation, variability, and transcoding – making us aware of the political choices that underpin them.

But the medium is not the only message in this kind of poetry. So while we may not find too much evidence of the *topoi* of traditional Latin American lyric poetry – romantic love, the suffering lyrical self, or the Latin American natural environment – there are some thematic common threads to be discerned. One theme is, of course, the hugely important role played by the media, including new media, in contemporary life. As Jill Kuhnheim notes, one of the goals of "electronic poetry" may precisely be "to confront the propagandistic use of language by the mass media."[16] Another recurrent theme coalesces around posthumanist concerns and the figure of the cyborg. While this theme can be developed in many different ways, there is often a sense that there are distinctively Latin American interests at play here as the hybrid figure of the cyborg – part human-part machine – is reclaimed as a revitalization of the discourse of *mestizaje* where Latin Americans are most adept at such combinations and, cocking a snook at typical assumptions made about Latin American technocultural belatedness, are most suited to survival under "techno-human conditions,"[17] becoming a pathogenic force to be reckoned with.

Latin American (New) Media Poetry: Origins and Intertextual Relationships

To continue with my determination to bracket the "new" of "new media poetry," writing poetry, or other forms of literature, that seeks to exploit the

---

[15] Loss Pequeño Glazier, *Digital Poetics: The Making of E-poetries* (Tuscaloosa, AL: University of Alabama Press, 2001), 53.

[16] Jill Kuhnheim, *Spanish American Poetry at the End of the Twentieth Century: Textual Disruptions* (Austin, TX: University of Texas Press, 2004), 12.

[17] Chela Sandoval, "New Sciences: Cyborg Feminism and the Methodology of the Oppressed," in *Cybersexualities: A Reader on Feminist Theory, Cyborgs and Cyberspace*, ed. Jenny Wolmark (Edinburgh: Edinburgh University Press, 1999), 248.

expressive capabilities of new technologies as and when they occur is nothing new – poets have always done this, in Latin America as elsewhere. The focus on newness in "new media" therefore perhaps runs the risk of exaggerating the value of such poetry and a more considered appreciation is required of its relationship to works, movements and aesthetic currents that predate its emergence. That said, the following exploration of precursors in no way seeks to deny the originality of (new) media poetry – it simply tries to offer the reader a few *points de repère* in what is otherwise very unfamiliar territory to readers of traditionally printed poetry.

Funkhouser argues that while, in the diverse field that is (prehistoric) digital poetry, influences may be many and varied, "The aesthetics of digital poetry are an extension of modernist techniques [...] Yet on a theoretical level these works are in many ways typical of the postmodern condition of the text" (Funkhouser, *Prehistoric Digital Poetry*, 3). That is to say, we can easily identify precursors and sources of inspiration from the Symbolist poet Stéphane Mallarmé's "Un Coup de Dés" (1897) for interactive digital poetry; from the "collage techniques" of Surrealism, Dadaism, and poets such as Ezra Pound and T.S. Eliot through to the combinatory games of the Ouvroir de Littérature Potentielle (Oulipo) movement for generative digital poetry; from Guillaume Apollinaire's *Calligrammes* (1918) through the 1950s Brazilian (Neo-)Concrete Poetry movement for visual, sound, and performance poetry in its new digital incarnations; and from the Fluxus movement for multimedia digital poetry. Nevertheless, digital poetry still very much responds to our contemporary "condition" in its refusal to offer stable messages and totalizing impulses, and in its demand that the reader participate actively in the meaning-making process of the work lest it cease to exist. Indeed, the use of the term "reader" is dismissed by many as insufficient for the role that he or she must play in the "experience" or "event" that is a new media poem.[18]

Of all the precursors listed above, the single most frequently cited influence, particularly in a Latin American context, has to be that of the Brazilian *concretistas* and *neo-concretistas* and their experiments in visual, sound and performance poetry; not only the Noigandres group – brothers Haroldo and Augusto de Campos (b. 1929 and b. 1931, respectively), and Décio Pignatari (1927–2012), and others – but also the *neo-concretistas* Wlademir Dias-Pino (b.1927) and Ferreira Gullar (1930–2016). As Angélica Huízar notes of Concretism's relevance for digital poetry, "The form of Concrete poetry

---

[18] See, for example, Rui Torres's discussion of the concept of the "wreader" (Torres, "Digital Poetry and Collaborative Wreadings of Literary Texts," 2004, telepoesis.net/papers/dpoetry.pdf).

lends itself to this new medium precisely because its original aim was to accentuate the flexibility of the written word: the "verbivocovisual" components of poetic language."[19] Augusto de Campos himself embraced the advent of new technologies enthusiastically as offering possibilities that enabled him to creatively remediate earlier works. He transferred his earlier poems such as "cidadecitycité" (1963) – originally published as a very long word on folded paper – first in 1975 to an audio recording contained on machine-readable punch cards, then, in 1991 to a CD-recording of its performance, and finally in the late 1990s to a Macromedia Flash version to be circulated on his website. Huízar goes as far as to argue that the potential for multimedia performances offered by software tools such as Flash "revitalizes the precepts of the Brazilian concrete avant-garde of the 1950s" (Huizar, 176) and even has the possibility of offering improvements to those original works. Other Latin American poets of predigital generations whose incursions into digital poetry are clearly influenced by their relationship to Concretism include Uruguayan poet Clemente Padín (b. 1939). Younger poets such as the Argentines Fabio Doctorovich (b. 1961) and Ladislao Pablo Györi, and the Brazilians Arnaldo Antunes (b. 1960) and André Vallias (b. 1963) can also trace points of influence back to the original Concrete and Neo-Concrete poets and have made the trajectory in their work from predigital visual, sound and performance poetry to digital experimental works and beyond.[20] Many of them have, like Augusto de Campos, also reworked their poems to fit the changing digital technologies available to them.

Nonetheless, the very earliest exponents of what we might term (new) media poetry in Latin America are really contemporaneous with, and part of, Neo-Concretism rather than derived from it: Albertus Marques (Brazil, 1930–2005) created what he called a "Poema elétrico" in 1961 that required the "reader" to press a button for the word "FIM" to appear on a screen only to disappear the moment the button was released.[21] In 1966 Omar Gancedo (Argentina, b. 1937) published a series of poems called *IBM* that comprised a set of 3 IBM punch cards that each had a poem encoded in the perforations on the card and then the text of that poem

[19] Angélica J. Huízar, *Beyond the Page: Latin American Poetry from the Calligramme to the Virtual* (Palo Alto, CA: Academica Press, 2008), 158.

[20] For more on the relationship of the work of some of these poets to Concretism and variants see Eduardo Ledesma, "Literatura digital, concretismo y vanguardia histórica en Brasil: ¿Qué tiene de viejo lo nuevo?" *Arizona Journal of Hispanic Cultural Studies* 14 (2010): 261–80.

[21] Albertus Marques, "Poesia neoconcreta no objeto poema elétrico," in *Projeto construtivo brasileiro na arte: 1950–1962*, ed. Aracy Amaral (Rio de Janeiro: Museu de Arte Moderna, 1977), 156.

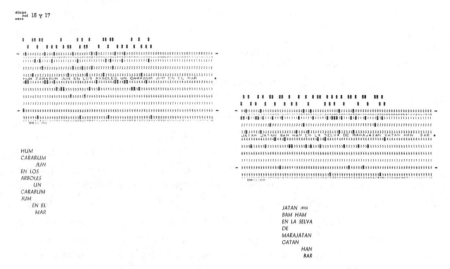

Fig. 1: Omar Gancedo, "IBM" (1966). First published in the art journal *Diagonal Cero*, 20 (La Plata, 1966).

printed across it.[22] Here there is a clear determination to work with electronic and digital technologies that is not evident in the better known Concrete poetry of the same era.

In terms of the influence of other currents of poetry and significant names in the field, particularly within Latin America, the intertextual references embedded in digital poetry speak loud and clear of the relationships between old and new forms of poetry – Latin American (new) media poetry is just as strongly intertextual as it is "hypermediatized" and both aspects combine to provide much of its attachment to that form of "literature" that we call poetry. At one extreme, some poets "limit themselves" to highly creative rewritings of older works via data visualization techniques – see, for example, the version of *The Iliad* (2012) by Santiago Ortiz (Colombia, b. 1975). At the other we have the playful approach of Benjamín Moreno Ortiz (Mexico, b. 1980) whose *Concretoons: poesía digital* (2010) is a series of explicit tributes in new media to other key (usually) Latin American poets such as Octavio Paz, Nicanor Parra, Jorge Luis Borges, and so on.[23] A new media writer/artist such as Belén Gache (Spain-Argentina, b. 1960) also produces works that rely heavily on

[22] Claudia Kozak, in Luis Correa-Díaz, ed., Dossier: "Poesía digital latinoamericana: muestrario crítico y creativo," *Ærea: Revista Hispanoamericana de Poesía*, 10 (2016): 131–32.
[23] Huízar, in Correa-Díaz, "Poesía digital latinoamericana," 142–44.

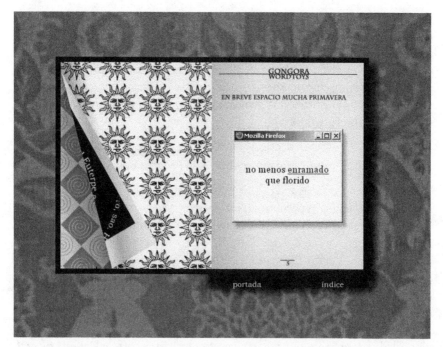

Fig. 2: Belén Gache, "En breve espacio mucha primavera," *Góngora Wordtoys* (2011).

intertextuality, particularly with Baroque poet Luis de Góngora, as well as Miguel de Cervantes and Jorge Luis Borges, in her *Góngora Wordtoys* (2011), thus aligning her work very clearly with the Neo-Baroque current in contemporary Latin American poetry.

Gache's use of Góngora is particularly complex. Each poem in *Góngora Wordtoys* is a deliberate remixing or "mash-up" of Góngora's *Soledades* (1613) that does not seek to reveal the meaning of Góngora's works but to explore how the principles that underpin his pushing at the limits of traditional poetry on a printed page can transfer to the new media poet's experimental toolkit such that "hyperbaton has become animated spirals; catachresis is now hotlinking."[24] However, this drawing of parallels between Baroque literary experimentation and the language of new media does not just evidence the continuity of poetic innovation through from the Baroque to (new) media poetry. Instead, as Taylor argues, Gache's work simultaneously makes us aware of the limitations of new technologies themselves, for example via hypertextual links that offer a

[24] Claire Taylor, "Re-Mixing the Baroque: Belén Gache's *Góngora Wordtoys*," *Bulletin of Hispanic Studies* (forthcoming).

single chain of lexia rather than forking paths to explore, thereby questioning the more utopianist discourses that circulate vaunting the novelty and limitless possibilities of new media. So as much as Gache cleverly remediates Góngora, she also challenges her own medium in parallel to the way that Góngora challenged the rules of classical poetry. This subversive, resistant approach is a frequent feature of Latin American works of electronic literature.[25]

A Bestiary of Latin American (New) Media Poetic Forms

There are many different types of (new) media poetry: generative, visual, kinetic, multimedia, hypertextual, interactive, and so on. This section offers a brief overview of some of these subgenres in a Latin American context. A formalist approach,[26] as I shall argue, is not necessarily the best way to approach such works, but it does offer some sense of the wide variety of different works that have been created under the rubric of (new) media poetry. We should start by mentioning those works that are quite traditionally "printable" but that explicitly dialogue with the subject of digital technologies and/or cybernetics in their subject matter, and that do not necessarily cease being written as digital poetry takes off. Selections of such poetry have been gathered together in anthologies such as Loaiza Largo's *Poca tinta: antología de ciberpoesía* (2012) or in scholarly articles on the form. (Correa-Díaz, "La poesía cibernética latinoamericana (todavía) *in print*") Examples of this "poesía cibernética latinoamericana (todavía) *in print*" include "¡Oh hada cibernética!" (1961, 1962) by Carlos Germán Belli (Peru, b. 1927), the collection *Playstation* (2009) by Cristina Perri Rossi (Uruguay, b. 1941), the "performance poem" *Tech-illa Sunrise (.txt dot con Sangrita)* (2001) by Rafael Lozano-Hemmer (Mexico, b. 1967) and Guillermo Gómez-Peña (Mexico, b. 1955), and the bilingual Spanish/English collection *Cosmological Me* (2010) by Luis Correa-Díaz (Chile, b. 1961).

Posthumanist concerns are clearly thematized in many of the above works. Here, the "lyric subject" is either cyborg himself and/or intimidated/seduced by the figure of the cyborg-as-muse. Correa-Díaz's *Cosmological Me* includes the free-verse poem "i, the worst of all cyborgs,"[27] which skilfully combines references to the work of Sor Juana Inés de la Cruz and to María Luisa

---

25 See Thea Pitman, "El arraigo de la cibercultura: un análisis comparativo de las obras hipertextuales de Doménico Chiappe y Blas Valdez," *Arizona Journal of Hispanic Cultural Studies* 14 (2010): 217–34, for other examples.
26 See, for example that taken by Flores, in "Digital Poetry."
27 Luis Correa-Díaz, *Cosmological Me: EPs*, trans. Heather Cleary Wolfgang (Buenos Aires: El Fin de la Noche, 2010), 32–33.

Bemberg's biopic of the poet's life (*Yo, la peor de todas* [1990]), with Donna Haraway's "famous battle-cry": "I'd rather be a cyborg than a goddess,"[28] and with cybercultural texts by Andy Clark (*Natural-Born Cyborgs* [2003]) and Kevin Warwick (*I, Cyborg* [2002]), in order to explore love in an age of cyborgs and virtual reality projections. Lozano-Hemmer and Gómez-Peña's much ree-dited prose and free-verse "performance poem" *Tech-illa Sunrise (.txt dot con Sangrita)* functions as a manifesto advocating a viral counterattack by Mexican *mestizo* cyborgs and "techno-cannibals" on tacitly white, Anglophone cyber-space that very much parallels his even better known manifesto "The Virtual Barrio @ the Other Frontier; or the Chicano Interneta" (1995–97).[29]

Moving on, there are also examples of poets whose work spans tradi-tional print and (new) media formats in ways that are more complex than simply using a CD-Rom or a blog to distribute one's work more widely. *Árbol veloz* (1998) by Luis Bravo (Uruguay, b. 1957) was distributed as a single-authored book together with a CD-Rom that focused on a selection of the original poems and where, with the help of twenty other artists, Bravo sought to explore more fully the new opportunities for expression offered by the new medium of the CD-Rom.[30] Working in reverse, *Plagio del afecto* (2003–2005) by Carlos Cociña (Chile, b. 1950) is a poetry collection that was originally created on his website and derived from materials found online and then published in book form in 2010.[31]

One final form of poetry that more often pertains to the field of nondigital poetry than it does to that of digital poetry proper is "code" poetry (Funkhouser, *Prehistoric Digital Poetry*, 8); that is to say, this kind of experimental poetry draws on computation for its inspiration but does not necessarily require a computer and its screen for its display. Drawing on Alan Sondheim's concept of "codework," such poetry portrays "the computer stirring into the text" (qtd. in Funkhouser, *Prehistoric Digital Poetry*, 258) as the languages of text encoding and/or of programming (ASCII, Unix, C++)

[28] Donna Haraway, "A Cyborg Manifesto: Science, Technology, and Socialist-Feminism in the Late Twentieth Century," in *Simians, Cyborgs, and Women: The Reinvention of Nature* (London: Free Association Books, 1991), 181.
[29] The poem was probably inspired by the 1991 Tequila computer virus that was the first multipartite virus to spread globally (Gustavo Romano, "Tequila," *Cyberzoo*, www.cyberzoo.org/cast/tour10.htm). For more on *Tech-illa Sunrise*, see Pitman, in Correa-Díaz, "Poesía digital latinoamericana," 135–38.
[30] For more on *Árbol veloz*, see Kuhnheim, *Spanish American Poetry*, 158–63, and María Rosa Olivera-Williams, "La nueva vanguardia, tecnología y Árbol veloz de Luis Bravo," *Arizona Journal of Hispanic Cultural Studies* 14 (2010): 349–60.
[31] For more on Cociña, see Carolina Gainza, "Hackear la cultura: poéticas del plagio en la poesía de Carlos Cociña," *Revista 404* (2015), editorial.centroculturadigital.mx/es/publicacion/hackear-la-cultura-poeticas-del-plagio-en-la-poesia-de-carlos-cocina.html; and Megumi Andrade Kobayashi, in Correa-Díaz, "Poesía digital latinoamericana," 121–23.

are included as part of the stanzas of a poem written to a greater or lesser extent in otherwise recognizable human languages.

Funkhouser traces the concepts underpinning the "code" poem directly back to the Brazilian Concrete poets, citing Luiz Angelo Pinto and Décio Pignatari's 1964 *Poemas códigos* as the original code poems.[32] Nevertheless, a crucial difference lies in the refusal of more recent writers of "code" poetry to offer a key to the code with the implication being that there is no one truth that underlies the code: all languages are codes and their meaning is equally questionable. Computer coding, as used by poets, is frequently dysfunctional rather than a source of absolute commands. It does not just "aestheticize" code or negate poetry through technification, but in fact is a highly political move since, as Mark Marino and other Digital Humanists have argued, "code is ideology, yet an ideology that is doubly hidden by our illiteracy and by the very screens on which its output delights and distracts."[33]

Examples of code poetry in a Latin American context include most notably Mexican artist Laura Balboa's (b. 1979) "you CODE me" (2009) – also written "you C O D E me" – a project available online as a PDF to print out or, in a different variant, as a Flash book, and which proposes to try to reinscribe human communication and interactions in the semantics of code by writing nonexecutable HTML code that humans therefore have to decode for themselves. She also moves between Spanish and English in the work, thus challenging the centrality of English as the language that interfaces most directly with computer code.[34] Other artists whose work is associated with code poetry, or codework more generally conceived, include Brazilians André Vallias (*The Verse*, 1991) and Giselle Beiguelman (*//**Code_UP*, 2004), Cuban Antonio Mendoza (*Subculture.com*, 2003), and the live coding performances of Mexican Mitzi Olvera.[35]

---

[32] Funkhouser, *Prehistoric Digital Poetry*, 263; see also Charles Perrone, *Seven Faces: Brazilian Poetry since Modernism* (Durham, NC: Duke University Press, 1996), 54. According to Kac, Pignatari was here simplifying Dias-Pino's slightly earlier poetry and, therefore, Dias-Pino is the true father of the "code poem" (personal interview with author, April 4, 2017).

[33] Mark C. Marino, "Critical Code Studies," *Electronic Book Review*, December 4, 2006, www.electronicbookreview.com/thread/electropoetics/codology.

[34] Eduardo Ledesma, "The Poetics and Politics of Computer Code in Latin America: Codework, Code Art, and Live Coding," *Revista de Estudios Hispánicos*, 49.1 (2015): 94–95.

[35] For more on Beiguelman, Mendoza, and Olvera, see Ledesma, "The Poetics and Politics of Computer Code." For more on Vallias, see Funkhouser, *Prehistoric Digital Poetry*, 261–63.

Fig. 3: Ana María Uribe, "Deseo – Desejo – Desire" (2002) – 3 screengrabs.

Moving on to the subgenres of digital/new media poetry proper, visual poetry has a long history, as we have seen already. However, it has had a new lease of life with the facilities offered by (increasingly) Graphical User Interfaces. What new technologies have most notably added to visual poetry is movement and kinetic poetry is the result. One of the most engaging exponents of visual and kinetic poetry in a Latin American context is Ana María Uribe (Argentina, 1944–2004) who moved from creating what she called "tipoemas" focusing on typescript and layout in the 1960s to what she called "anipoemas" or animated poems from the 1990s onwards. In one set of three "anipoemas" entitled "Deseo – Desejo – Desire: 3 anipoemas eróticos" (2002), for example, the letters of each word perform a kind of dance, with musical accompaniment, to illustrate the word's meaning.

Clearly, with the introduction of movement and music, we are now starting to move into the realm of digital multimedia poetry; that is to say, poetry that exploits all the different media that may be presented in digital format including video, digital art, animation, and so on. This kind of poetry is also frequently referred to as "Flash poetry" with reference to the preeminent software package that has been used for its creation thus far. The videopoem *Atame: a angústia do precário* (2005) by Wilton Luiz de Azevedo (Brazil, 1958–2016) is a good example of his extensive work in the field of what he terms "interpoesia" (interactive hypermedia poetry). The work is 50 minutes long and comprises a series of poems about love, passion, memory and perception in our technologically-mediated times – quite unusual topics in the field of new media poetry. A woman's voice reads the poems, accompanied by piano and violin background music. Parts of the text appear in different formats on the screen itself, interrupting a flickering, gaudily retouched video of a lone woman as she sits on a sofa or moves around her apartment. All of this combines to create a trancelike and melancholic atmosphere.

Fig. 4: Wilton Luiz de Azevedo, ATAME; A ANGUSTIA DO PRECARIO (2005) – 2 screengrabs – Azevedo: text and images; Fernanda Nardi: monologue; Rita Varlesi: video and performance

A logical step on from multimedia poetry is that of interactive, video game or virtual reality poetry, a form of new media poetry that is not all pre-scripted by the poet but that requires active engagement on the part of the reader to exist. Here the structure of hypertext is significant in its offering of multiple different options to move from one "window" to another via hyperlinks; indeed, some forms of this subgenre are sometimes referred to as hypertext poetry. It should be noted that the purportedly limitless possibilities of hypertext extend only as far as the poet is willing to include links[36] and some interactive poetry may really offer no more than the illusion of

[36] See Aarseth's *Cybertext* for a critique of the hype about hypertext.

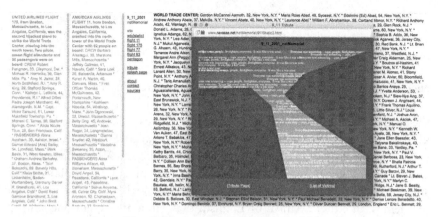

Fig. 5: Eduardo Navas, *9_11_2001_netMemorial* (2002).

choice, as in Gache's *Góngora Wordtoys*. However, other examples of interactive poetry allow "readers" to contribute their own materials to the poet's original poem.

Good examples of this kind of poetry include *9_11_2001_netMemorial* (2002) by Salvadorean artist Eduardo Navas that commemorates the dead of 9/11 by projecting jerkily moving headlines concerning the event onto a field delimited by a basic outline image of the Twin Towers and which also allows users to input selected headlines or submit their own brief personal statements and thereby adapt the animation for themselves. *Palavrador* (2006) – a "poetic cyberworld built in 3D" – directed by Chico Marinho (Brazil, b. 1958) and made in a team with Alckmar Luiz dos Santos (Brazil, b. 1959) and others, offers an immersive experience where several of Marinho's poems that seek to explore the balance in human beings between "eros" and "caos" appear as "flocks" of words with flapping wings that the "user" can explore at will as he or she stumbles through a labyrinthine virtual environment. Santos and Marinho have also collaborated on the game poetry project *Liberdade* (2013); and much of the work in the 1990s of Argentine poets Ladislao Pablo Györi in the field of "virtual reality poetry,"[37] and Fabio Doctorovich in that of hypertext poetry,[38] also fall under this rubric.

And finally, one of the most distinctive forms of new media poetry is generative poetry where the poet's input is not centered on the polishing of self-expression but on the programming of algorithms that then draw forth

---

[37] Ladislao Pablo Györi, "Criterios para una poesía virtual," *Dimensão: Revista Internacional de Poesía*, 15.24 (1995), www.altamiracave.com/criterio.htm.

[38] Clemente Padín, "La poesía interactiva de Fabio Doctorovich," *Escáner Cultural*, 4.37 (2002), www.escaner.cl/escaner37/acorreo.html.

material from specified corpora, most often these days from the internet itself, hence the related terms internet or net poetry. The best of such poems may then be presented to their readers, as selected by the poet, much as Dadaist ready-mades or the result of Surrealist-inspired "chance encounters." Alternatively they may be generated in real time for the reader, possibly depending on some amount of reader input in terms of the specification of parameters for the poem. An excellent example of this kind of work is *Migraciones* (2005) by Leonardo Solaas (Argentina, b. 1971) where the *Quixote* as stored in the Biblioteca Virtual Miguel de Cervantes is "generated" in swirls of text that mix with similar swirls stemming from the BBC World News service, together with an audio of phonemes, in either Spanish or English, that "migrate" from one source text to the other, offering mesmerizing patterns, hybridizations, and incongruous juxtapositions. According to Claudia Kozak, although we might simply appreciate this as a highly aestheticized version of nonsense "verse," evidencing an almost total distrust of languages' potential to carry meaning, the "migrations" of phonemes might also cause us to think of the colonial histories of both languages and their contemporary geopolitical relationships, or to consider how the infamous misinterpretations of text in the *Quixote* might provoke us to view the purportedly factual text of the news with rather more suspicion.[39] Other significant examples of generative poetry include some of the work of poet/programmer Eugenio Tisselli (Mexico, b. 1972) who uses his *MIDIPoet* (2003–) software to generate visual/kinetic poems, and some of that of Colombian poet/programmer Santiago Ortiz whose *Bacterias argentinas* (2004), for example, is a generative digital poetic work that simulates a neoliberal "ecosystem" where bacteria-words eat each other, grow fat or die out, following preprogrammed algorithms and reader interventions.

Of course, already evident in some of the descriptions above, many poetic works do not fit neatly within one subgenre or another. Each poet draws on a repertoire of ever more sophisticated and diverse software tools to create artefacts that best express his or her intentions with little regard for defining works as pertaining to one form or another. Furthermore, it has always been the case that such works are often more than just something that can be viewed on a computer. Since the inception of this kind of poetic practice in Latin America in the 1980s, these works have often been integrated as parts of physical installations that require curation in gallery spaces in order to be

[39] Claudia Kozak, "Out of Bounds: Searching Deviated Literature in Audiovisual Electronic Environments," paper given at Electronic Literature Organization annual conference: "Chercher le texte," September 23–28, 2013, Paris, 4–5, conference.eliterature.org/sites/default/files/papers/Out%20of%20Bounds_0.pdf.

appreciated, or they are designed for display around the urban environment as tactical media interventions in public space. And now, despite the fact that the internet has become the most evident place for this kind of poetry to circulate, poets are not content to just create work with and for this most comprehensive platform but continue to push against the boundaries and limitations of the internet itself. The result is that we need, as Kac argued, to speak once again of media poetry, rather than new media poetry, as our attention is redirected to the hybrid, transmedial nature of much of this kind of work.

Examples of this kind of hybrid poetry can be found in the field of digital sound and performance poetry where a poet (or poets) typically recite their work while supporting the performance through elements of live coding, electronic music, the display of accompanying digital multimedia content projected onto walls or screens, the use of tools for voice distortion, and so on.[40] Another excellent example is the *IP Poetry Project* (2004–) by Argentine poet/programmer Gustavo Romano (b. 1958). This project has been exhibited as an installation at various international venues over the last decade and also has an online version. As an installation, it consists of four "robots": these are screens showing the same man's mouth as he recites phonemes, sometimes presented as part of something that looks like a bass amplifier with carrying handle, thus providing a body for the mouth, other times as a thin screen with an awning. A further master-robot or MC-bot can be asked to search the internet to find phrases beginning with words suggested by the "user." The structure of each poem can be determined by selecting various criteria to specify a refrain and aspects of its choral structure; nevertheless, each time it is played the material is drawn afresh from the internet, so every recital of a poem with given specifications will be different. The four bots are fed this data and prompted to recite it using prerecorded phonemes. This they do with typically robotic lack of intonation, but the poems are nonetheless comprehensible. The idea is that members of the public can "commission" the bots to perform a poem to their own specification and, if deemed "good" by Romano, such a poem may be kept as part of the poetry collection, or the bots can be set to recite poems that others have asked them to generate previously. Belén Gache, Romano's partner, has contributed several poems to the online version and she has also used the software to generate her own *Manifiestos Robots* (2009), a series of poems that seek to explore the rhetoric of political discourse as captured via the internet. Furthermore, the concept is essentially at the base of her *Radikal Karaoke* (2011) project where audiences can perform political speeches based on found materials online, together

---

[40] See, for example, the work of the Chilean/Uruguayan Orquesta de Poetas (2011–).

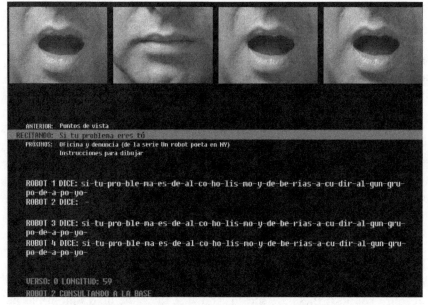

Fig. 6: Gustavo Romano, *IP Poetry Project* (2004–), online version.

with sound and visual effects that the performer can choose in order to augment the impact of his or her speech.[41]

New Architectures of Language

Back in the late 1990s, many Latin American cultural critics worried that there was "no Latin American *language* in which to express our specific content in that global hall of mirrors that is the Internet";[42] that the "semiotic and aesthetic limits" of the Spanish language – or Portuguese, or Indo-American languages, for that matter – would not withstand the "expansion of communications subordinated to commercial criteria";[43] that the internet marginalized reading and spelt the end for "Literature" in the region;[44] and that such

---

[41] For more on Romano, see Scott Weintraub, "Autopoiesis y robopoética en el IP Poetry Project de Gustavo Romano," in Poesía y poéticas digitales / electrónicas / tecnos / new-media en América Latina: definiciones y exploraciones, ed. Luis Correa-Díaz and Scott Weintraub (Bogotá: Editorial Universidad Central, 2016), 166–84.

[42] Raúl Trejo Delarbre, "La Internet in América Latina," in *Las industrias culturales en la integración latinoamericana*, ed. Néstor García Canclini and Carlos Juan Moneta (Mexico City: Grijalbo, 1999), 330; original emphasis.

[43] Néstor García Canclini, *La globalización imaginada* (Buenos Aires: Paidós, 1999), 161.

[44] Carlos Monsiváis, "Del rancho a Internet," *Letra Internacional*, 4.53 (1997), 13.

literary experimentation as was emerging in the field of hypertext was little more than unreadable "avant-garde pyrotechnics."[45] Even in 2006, Joseba Gabilondo was, rather contentiously, claiming that Spanish was destined to be "a language studied and learnt *on* the web, but not a language *of* the web [...] a technological object, not a tool of the internet,"[46] and that Spanish speakers would "remain passive/receptive users, rather than creative/productive agents, of the internet for the foreseeable future" (Gabilondo, 114). Yet rather more optimistically, others have advocated that digital technologies and the internet are creating "a new qualitative episteme" that promotes "an entirely new play of interfaces, new architectures of language,"[47] and that Latin Americans need to seize the opportunity to "invent, identify and define [their] own principles of technological design,"[48] so that they have their own languages in which to express themselves, not just on the surface of the screen, but in the depths of programming and software design. (New) media poetry, for all the pyrotechnics, arguably attempts to make some headway in this regard. And proof of the growing visibility of Latin American (new) media poetry is the inclusion of a significant number of these works in the canon-forming *Electronic Literature Collection*, Volume 3 (2016).[49]

Most critics of digital poetry agree that it has not produced any recognizable masterpieces as yet. Indeed, such an ambition is difficult to even conceive in a field where there are few if any definitive versions of these works, where most works are not designed to sustain stable interpretation, and where many poets develop and remediate their works over periods of ten, fifteen, even twenty years. Furthermore, digital poets generally conceive of themselves as improvisers, meddlers, technocultural magpies. In order to evaluate this kind of poetry we may, however, also need to change the way we as critics approach it, borrowing techniques developed by Digital Humanists such as Franco Moretti's "distant reading" (2013), combined with data visualization techniques, to supplement our tried and tested "close reading"

[45] Carlos Jáuregui, "Writing Communities on the Internet: Textual Authority and Territorialization," in *Latin American Literature and Mass Media*, ed. Edmundo Paz-Soldán and Debra A. Castillo (New York, NY: Garland, 2001), 289.
[46] Joseba Gabilondo, "Spanish, Second Language of the Internet? The Hispanic Web, Subaltern-Hybrid Cultures, and the Neo-liberal Lettered City," *Revista Canadiense de Estudios Hispánicos* 31:1 (2006): 114; original emphasis.
[47] Jesús Martín-Barbero, "Art/Communication/Technicity at Century's End," trans. Hugh O'Donnell, in *Cultural Politics in Latin America*, ed. Anny Brooksbank Jones and Ronaldo Munck (Basingstoke: Macmillan, 2000), 69.
[48] Rocío Rueda Ortiz, "Apropiación social de las tecnologías de la información: ciberciudadanías emergentes," *América Latina en movimiento*, November 28, 2005, www.movimientos.org/foro_comunicacion/show_text.php3%3Fkey%3D5930.
[49] *Electronic Literature Collection*, Vol. 3, ed. Stephanie Boluk, Leonardo Flores, Jacob Garbe, and Anastasia Salter, 2016, collection.eliterature.org/3/.

Fig. 7: Thea Pitman, "Poesía obra digital," generated with www.wordclouds.com/, 18 January 2016, based on the manuscript for Luis Correa-Díaz, ed., "Poesía digital y/o electrónica latinoamericana: un muestrario," *Revista Ærea* (2016).

techniques and situated approaches.[50] It may also be more appropriate to present such research in formats other than the traditional book chapter with

---

[50] Reading (new) media poetry from the perspective of science and technology studies would be another fruitful approach. See, for example, Scott Weintraub, "Autopoiesis y robopoética en el *IP Poetry Project* de Gustavo Romano."

screengrabs. To that end, as an alternative to reading a traditional chapter, readers may like to use the following tag cloud, generated (with permission) from the text of Luis Correa-Díaz *et al.*'s most recent dossier, "Poesía digital y/o electrónica latinoamericana: un muestrario," in order to grasp the subject in a more visual, poetic way altogether.[51]

---

[51] I would like to express my gratitude to Luis Correa-Díaz, Scott Weintraub, and Eduardo Kac for their helpful comments on this chapter.

18

VALENTINO GIANUZZI

English Translations

To the memory of Michael Smith
(1942–2014)

Despite earlier efforts, it wasn't until the 1940s that Anglophone writers showed a sustained interest in knowing, disseminating, and translating the poetry of their Latin American counterparts. Although the cultural trans-American network charted for part of the nineteenth century clearly attests for an interaction between intellectuals from both Americas, the role played by the translation of Spanish poems into English was still relatively small, and its impact on U.S. poetry, limited. As Kirsten Silva Gruesz has stated, despite some noteworthy translations "a Latin American cultural presence [...] would continue to be ignored in the North for the rest of the century."[1] *Modernismo*, Latin America's dominant turn-of-the-century poetry style, produced a considerable amount of literary scholarship in English, partly due to the academic institutionalization of contemporary Latin American culture as a subject of study, yet seemed also to have had a narrow influence in the realm of translation.[2] In the earlier half of the twentieth century, more than through translations of a single author, poetry was disseminated via anthologies that served as historical surveys.[3] Thus, neither José Martí nor Rubén Darío, poets who would become the proclaimed role models for later Latin American poets,

---

[1] Kirsten Silva Gruesz, *Ambassadors of Culture: The Transamerican Origins of Latino Writing* (Princeton, NJ: Princeton University Press, 2001), 71. Among the most famous early efforts were those of William Cullen Bryant, who translated (and co-translated) poems by the Cuban poet José María Heredia y Heredia. For more information on translations and imitations during the nineteenth century, see Gruesz's book, especially chapters 2 and 3.

[2] For a list of early publications in English about Latin America, including poetry anthologies and literary magazines, see Pedro Henríquez Ureña, *Historia cultural y literaria de la América Hispánica* (Madrid: Verbum, 2007), 259–61.

[3] These included Alice Stone Blackwell's *Some Spanish American Poets* (Philadelphia, PA: University of Pennsylvania Press, 1929; 2nd edition, 1937), and G. Dundas Craig's *The Modernist Trend in Spanish American Poetry: A Collection of Representative Poems of the Modernist Movement and the Reaction, Translated into English Verse with a Commentary* (Berkeley, CA: University of California Press, 1934).

were championed in the English-speaking world with the same vigor as later poets would be.[4]

One anthology from the early forties stands out for bringing contemporary Latin American poetry not only to the attention of a broader public, but also, and more importantly, to that of poet-translators who would further disseminate and incorporate it substantially into their own tradition. Dudley Fitts's omnibus *Anthology of Contemporary Latin American Poetry* (1942) was significant mainly because of its sheer scope: ninety-five poets from eighteen Spanish-speaking countries, plus Brazil, Haiti, and Puerto Rico, and a roster of sixteen translators. Funded by Nelson Rockefeller's Office for the Coordinator of Inter-American Affairs (although such sponsorship is not acknowledged in the book itself), the anthology was produced within the institutional support for Inter-American relations that, during the forties and under the shelter of Roosevelt's Good Neighbor policy, attempted to act as a means of cultural diplomacy in an increasingly politically polarized global context.[5] The publishing house that brought out the book, James Laughlin's New Directions, would soon become one of the most prestigious independent publishers in the United States, and it would stay close to the spirit of that seminal anthology by remaining as one of the main outlets for Latin American poetry in translation throughout the twentieth century. Laughlin had been Fitts's student at Choate School in Wellingford, Connecticut, and Fitts had introduced the young would-be-publisher to the work of modern poets – Eliot, Joyce, Pound, Stein, Williams – whose spirit would become the backdrop for New Directions's focus on innovative writing.[6] Yet the anthology was to embrace a rather conservative approach to translation. Dudley Fitts embarked on the task of translating and assembling the material for his bilingual anthology with a fixed aim in mind: instead of composing "a new poem in English," he believed that since the original Spanish appeared *en face*, his team of translators should merely provide an aid for the educated

---

[4] Thomas Walsh and Salomón de la Selva's brief *Eleven Poems of Rubén Darío* (New York, NY: Putnam's, 1916) did not have a major repercussion. Modern editions of Darío include Lysander Kemp's *Selected Poems of Rubén Darío* (Austin, TX: University of Texas Press, 1965), Alberto Acereda and Will Derusha's *Selected Poems of Rubén Darío* (Lewisburg, PA: Bucknell University Press, 2001) and *Songs of Life and Hope* (Duke, NC: Duke University Press, 2004), as well as a *Selected Writings*, edited by Ilan Stavans (Harmondsworth: Penguin, 2005).

[5] See Harris Feinsod, "Fluent Mundo: Inter-American Poetry, 1939–1973" (PhD Diss., Stanford University, 2011), 26, 37–45. As he explains, one of the conditions for funding was that the anthology should include at least one poet for each Latin American nation (44).

[6] For Fitts and Laughlin's relationship, see Ian S. MacNiven, *Literchoor is My Beat: The Life of James Laughlin, Publisher of New Directions* (New York, NY: Farrar, Straus and Giroux, 2014), 28, 33–35.

reader. Partly apologetic, he stated that this method "meant the sacrifice of sonal and metrical effects in the interest of a greater literal fidelity," and then confessed: "Our versions are not poetry, except accidentally." Additionally, this process of translation also influenced the selection of poems, so that more experimental works, such as parts of Huidobro's *Altazor*, albeit described as "a poem of enormous importance in many ways," were not selected.[7] The anthology is a good example of this early period of translation of Latin American poetry in which, as Cohen has summarized for the case of Neruda, translators "were more interested in the original Spanish than in their English versions of it."[8] Fitts's book was to be, overall, informative, and didactic, in keeping with the diplomatic aims of its official sponsor.

The following year, H. R. Hays, a poet who had collaborated with Fitts, published a more selective anthology of his own. Under the title *12 Spanish American Poets* (1943) he brought together his own translations of, among others, López Velarde, Huidobro, Borges, Carrera Andrade, Gorostiza, Pablo de Rokha, Nicolas Guillén, Neruda, and Vallejo. Although moving away from Fitts's literalism, Hays also attempted to remain as close as possible to the originals, yet paying more attention to their imagistic and aural properties, as he tried "to render the images faithfully and to preserve in every case the character of the original meter and to add nothing of his own."[9] In contrast to Fitts's, Hays's anthology was appreciated by later translators – such as Robert Bly and James Wright – as not only informative, but also as the work of a real poet. In a 1979 letter, for example, Wright noted Hays's importance as a pioneer, highlighting also his poetic talent, which enabled him "to create translations that are at once accurate render-ings and also themselves original poems in the American language."[10] Even more importantly, Hays's reading of Latin American poetry would also coincide with and perhaps even inform the approach of later translators.

---

[7] Dudley Fitts (ed.), *Anthology of Contemporary Latin American Poetry* (New York, NY: New Directions, 1942), xv, xvii. Although a couple of Huidobro's novels were translated into English during his lifetime, *Altazor* would not appear in English until Eliot Weinberger's translation (Minneapolis, MN: Graywolf Press, 1988). David M. Guss's edition of his *Selected Poems* (New York, NY: New Directions, 1981) remain the most extensive survey of his work in English.

[8] Jonathan Cohen, "Neruda in English: the Controversy Over Translation Poetics," *The Missouri Review* 6.3 (2011): 176.

[9] *The Selected Poems of H.R. Hays, with Essays on Translation*, ed. Sandy McIntosh (Bloomington, IN: XLibris, 2000), 185.

[10] *A Wild Perfection: The Selected Letters of James Wright*, ed. Anne Wright and Saundra Rose Maley (Middletown, CT: Wesleyan University Press, 2005), 543. Bly also indicated Hays' groundbreaking role when stating that he "is to the translator of South American poetry as Madame Curie is to the x-ray"; from the dust jacket blurb in Hays' *12 Spanish American Poets* (Boston, MA: Beacon Press, 1972).

Despite noting its multiplicity, Hays described Latin American poetry as "abundant with imagery, sacrificing formal discipline at times to robustness, perfection of finish to spontaneity."[11] He thus highlighted several of the aspects that would later be associated with the work of Vallejo and Neruda specially – illogical metaphors, relative artlessness, virility – and which stood in contrast to the qualities he attributed to contemporary American poetry. Looking back on his own role as a precursor, Hays saw that his own time had not been ripe for a proper reception of this kind of poetry in translation, since the influence of poets such as W.H. Auden "had a deadening effect on the appreciation of anything which resembled romantic feeling or spontaneous expression. We had to wait for a new local revolution, a new romanticism."[12] For him, a more supportive time for translators had been the fifties and sixties, when Latin American poetry started to be taken as an alternative to the Anglo-American poetic tradition revered by the New Criticism; facing formalism and impersonality, Vallejo and Neruda wrote a poetry that was perceived as more plastic, dependent on striking images and a personal, Romantic outlook. Their names would soon crop up alongside that of influential European poets (Lorca, Hernández, Rilke) whose work was also regarded as a nurturing element to the alleged academicized, artificial American verse. The Cuban Revolution, the 1960s countercultural movement, coupled with American cultural diplomacy and its infrastructural support all came together to make the 1960s a propitious time for translations.[13]

Thanks in part to these anthologies, Vallejo and Neruda saw their names foregrounded, and their work would come to be regarded as the most representative from Spanish America. Aside from multiple appearances in magazines, several volumes of both poets' work appeared in translation between the 1950s and 1970s.[14] César Vallejo, who had died in 1938, became

---

[11] *The Selected Poems of H.R. Hays, with Essays on Translation*, 185.

[12] H. R. Hays, "On Vallejo and Neruda: Another Look," *The American Poetry Review* 3.2 (1974): 31. In the same article, Hays also blames industrialization and capitalism for the artificial nature of American poetry, though not avoiding a certain exoticization of Latin America: "Our colleagues of the South remain closer to the jungle, the snowtopped peaks, the untamed rivers and the pampas than we. It appears we suffer from the castrating effect of our packaged civilization and even our emotions are in danger of being wrapped in cellophane."

[13] For an assessment of several case studies of institutional support for Latin American literature since the 1950s, see Deborah Cohn, *The Latin American Literary Boom and U.S. Nationalism During the Cold War* (Nashville, TN: Vanderbilt University Press, 2012).

[14] For an extensive list of English translations of Neruda, see Jason Wilson, *A Companion to Pablo Neruda* (Woodbridge: Tamesis, 2008), appendix 3; for a list of Vallejo's, see *César Vallejo, The Complete Poems* (Exeter: Shearsman, 2012), 759–61.

renowned for his mixture of experimentalism, nativism, and politically committed poetry; the more multifaceted Neruda, on the other hand, lived until 1973 and benefited from the publicity beset on the Latin American "Boom" writers, with which he was at times associated, as well as from his Nobel Prize. According to Cramer, one can identify two main strands of influence which Neruda's poetry had on American poets: "That which seeks expression through 'deep' or irrational imagery, and that which finds an important link between poetry and social protest."[15] It is thus not surprising that many of the most significant American translators of Vallejo and Neruda have been those whose own work has been associated with the label "deep image": James Wright, Robert Bly, W.S. Merwin. Their work marks the "great shift" in translation approach that Cohen dates around the mid-1950s, when "translating Neruda [and, one could add, Vallejo] became part of their own efforts to revitalize American poetry."[16] No longer just a means of information and a faithful guide to a Spanish original, translated poems were also to be an integral part of the writer's poetics, so that forging a translation became also an act of personal creation and a form of literary apprenticeship.[17] In keeping with this view, even the poets' limited knowledge of the source language did not act as deterrent to their task and, as Cohen has remarked for Neruda translators, they often had to rely on "people fluent in both Spanish and English to check the accuracy of their translations."[18] It was thanks to the work of these poets, which enacted a creative act of reading and reshaping of the source text, that the definitive crossover of Vallejo and Neruda's poetry into Anglophone literature took place.

Although parallel efforts to translate the work of other poets – Nicolás Guillén, Jorge Carrera Andrade, and later Nicanor Parra, Gabriela Mistral, and Jorge Luis Borges – had also began in the 1950s, the number of translators devoted to them was never comparable to that of Vallejo and Neruda.[19]

[15] Mark Jonathan Cramer, "Neruda and Vallejo in Contemporary United States Poetry," PhD Diss., University of Illinois at Urbana-Champaign, 1976, 6.

[16] Jonathan Cohen, "Neruda in English," 179.

[17] The most extreme case must be that of Clayton Eshleman, for whom translating Vallejo was a struggle which was a matter of his "becoming or failing to become a poet"; see "Introduction," in César Vallejo, The Complete Posthumous Poetry (Berkeley, CA: University of California Press, 1978), xxix.

[18] Cohen, "Neruda in English," 180. Cohen notes how, for example, Bly relied on suggestions by Hardie St. Martin for translating Neruda; for his 1978 Vallejo translation, Eshleman worked alongside Spanish scholar José Rubia Barcia.

[19] Langston Hughes's co-translation of Nicolás Guillén's poetry, published as Cuba Libre (1948) must be mentioned as an early translation involving a noted American poet with a rather different cultural project in mind. For a detailed discussion of Hughes's translation, see Vera M. Kutzinski, "Havana Vernaculars: The Cuba Libre Project," in The Worlds of

The exception was the work of Octavio Paz, the third Latin American poet who would ignite analogous attention in translators. Paz, who had himself edited an *Anthology of Mexican Poetry* (1958), with translations by Samuel Beckett, saw his first translated volumes appear in the early 1960s; they were the work of American poet Muriel Rukeyser: *Sun Stone* (1962) and *Selected Poems of Octavio Paz* (1963). By the 1970s the names of Paz's translators came to include such important poets as Denise Levertov, Charles Tomlinson, Paul Blackburn, Eliot Weinberger, Elizabeth Bishop, and Mark Strand. Most valued in Paz's work was its surreal texture and its non-Western themes (pre-Columbian and Asian); yet unlike Vallejo's and Neruda's, his poetry was not perceived as artless nor as particularly political, which perhaps meant an appeal to a wider range of American poet-translators, form conservative to radical.

Across the Atlantic, the publication of Latin American poetry in translation beyond literary magazines was less significant and took place sometime later than in the U.S., doubtless because of the limited readership interested in the region but also because of the limited infrastructural support. Early publications include J.M. Cohen's *Latin American Writing Today* (1967), E. Caracciolo-Trejo's *Penguin Book of Latin American Verse* (1971, with plain prose translations), a Vallejo volume for the Penguin Poets series (translated by Gordon Brotherston and Ed Dorn), and several translations of Neruda. Nonetheless, the availability of Latin American poetry still relied generally on original American translations or on joint transatlantic ventures, such as Neruda's 500-page *Selected Poems* published in New York and London in 1970, the first major and extensive translation of a modern Latin American poet in English. Later publishers of original translations and reprints of American editions include Carcanet (Paz, Homero Aridjis, Dulce María Loynaz), Salt (Eugenio Montejo, Ida Vitale, Marco Antonio Campos, Eduardo Chirinos), and Shearsman Books, whose translation catalogue has a noticeable bias for contemporary poetry from Latin America (Gloria Gervitz, Elsa Cross, Pura López-Colomé, Eduardo Milán, José Kozer). In the U.S. independent labels (New Directions, White Pine, Copper Canyon) and university presses (Texas, Wesleyan, California, Indiana) have kept the names of Latin American poets in their catalogues, making available to contemporary readers the important poetry of José Emilio Pacheco and Raúl Zurita, among many others. But along with the broadening of the list of Latin American poets, is the tendency in recent years to offer comprehensive, all-encompassing editions of the work of the canonical three names: Ilan

Langston Hughes: Modernism and Translation in the Americas (Ithaca, NY: Cornell University Press, 2012), 132–83.

Stavan's editions of Neruda (*The Poetry of Pablo Neruda*, 2005; *All the Odes*, 2014), Eshleman's Vallejo (*The Complete Poetry*, 2007), and Eliot Weinberger's most recent edition of Paz (*The Poems of Octavio Paz*, 2012); a similar endeavor in the UK is Michael Smith's and my own *The Complete Poems of César Vallejo* (2012).[20] Thus, just as it has proven difficult for the reader of the Latin American novel in translation to get past the names of the Boom writers, it has proven quite difficult in poetry to go beyond the Vallejo-Neruda-Paz triumvirate.

Perhaps more recent anthologies may trigger a much needed revisionism, igniting, like Fitts's and Hays's work more than half a century before, a renewed interest of Anglophone poets and translators for their Latin American contemporaries, and for lesser known names. These names could be found in Cecilia Vicuña's and Ernesto Livón Grossman's *The Oxford Book of Latin American Poetry* (2009) or Mónica de la Torre's and Michael Wiegers's *Reversible Monuments: Contemporary Mexican Poetry* (Copper Canyon Press, 2002), both of which include translations from indigenous languages and from the work of less notorious poets.[21] In recent times the poetry of Alejandra Pizarnik has also drawn the attention of U.S. publishers (Ugly Duckling Press and New Directions). These examples attest to the firm presence of contemporary Latin America poetry in English translation for the current century.

---

[20] The tendency has also meant a broadening of the range of their works available, as can be seen in the translations of the often overlooked late poetry of Neruda (several volumes translated by William O'Daly and published by Copper Canyon Press) and the *Selected Writings of César Vallejo*, ed. Joseph Mulligan, (Middletown, CT: Wesleyan University Press, 2015).

[21] Other later inclusive anthologies that have continued the example set by Fitts, include Emir Rodríguez-Monegal's and Thomas Colchie's *Borzoi Anthology of Latin American Literature* (New York, NY: Knopf, 1977), 2 vols; Stephen Tapscott's *Twentieth-Century Latin American Poetry* (Austin, TX: University of Texas Press, 1996); and Ilan Stavans's *The FSG Book of Twentieth Century Latin American Poetry* (New York, NY: Farrar, Straus and Giroux, 2011). On the other hand, *An Anthology of Twentieth-Century Brazilian Poetry* (Middletown, CT: Wesleyan University Press, 1972), co-edited by Elizabeth Bishop, must be mentioned as the most important gathering of translations from the Portuguese.

GUIDE TO FURTHER READING

For anthologies of Latin American poetry, see Antonio R. de la Campa and Raquel Chang-Rodríguez's *Poesía hispanoamericana colonial; antología* (Madrid: Editorial Alhambra, 1985), for the Spanish American colonial; complemented by Alfonso Méndez Plancarte (ed.), *Poetas novohispanos*, 3 vols (Mexico City: UNAM, 1942–1945); and Martha Lilia Tenorio (ed.), *Poesía novohispana: antología*, 2 vols (Mexico City: El Colegio de México/Fundación para las Letras Mexicanas, 2010). For Brazilian colonial poetry consult Péricles Eugênio da Silva Ramos, *Poesia barroca. Antologia* (São Paulo: Melhoramentos, 1967). Manuel Bandeira's *Antologia dos poetas brasileiros: fase romântica* (Rio do Janeiro: Editôra Nova Fronteira, 1996) offers a good selection of Brazilian Romantic poets. For *modernismo* consult Gordon Brotherston's *Spanish American Poets: A Critical Anthology* (2nd ed., Bristol: Bristol Classical Press, 1995) as a first step, alongside Ivan Schulman and Evelyn Picón Garfield's *Poesía modernista hispanoamericana y española (Antología)* (Madrid: Taurus, 1986). For early twentieth-century poetry, see Giovanni Pontiero's *An Anthology of Brazilian Modernist Poetry* (London: Pergamon, 1969). For later twentieth-century poetry, see Stefan Baciu's *Antología de la poesía latinoamericana, 1950–1970* (Albany, NY: State University of New York, 1974) along with José Olivio Jiménez's *Antología de la poesía hispanoamericana contemporánea: 1914–1987* (Madrid: Alianza: 1988), and, for more recent poets, see Miguel Ángel Zapata's *Nueva poesía latinoamericana* (Mexico City: UNAM, 1999). As for Amerindian verse, Carlos Montemayor and Donald Frischmann's three-volume collection of anthologies of contemporary Mexican indigenous language writers, *Words of the True Peoples/Palabras de los Seres Verdaderos: Anthology of Contemporary Mexican Indigenous-Language Writers/Antología de Escritores Actuales en Lenguas Indígenas de México* (Austin, TX: University of Texas Press, 2004, 2005, 2007) offers an excellent multilingual selection of poetry. Both Allison Hedge Coke's anthology *Sing: Poetry from the Indigenous Americas* (Tucson, AZ: University of Arizona Press, 2011) and *Collar de historias y lunas: antología de poesía de mujeres indígenas de América Latina*, ed. Jennie Carrasco Molina (2011; scribd), offer multilingual selections of contemporary poetry written in various Latin American indigenous languages. Also of interest are the anthology of Guaraní poetry *Ñe epoty aty: Voces de poetas en guaraní*, edited by Natalia Krivoshein de Canese and Feliciano Acosta Alcaraz (Asunción: Servilibro, 2005), and the bilingual anthology of poetry written by Mapuche women (*Küme Dungun/Küme Wirin*, 2011). Contemporary authors writing in indigenous languages of Latin American and who have published collections of poetry in their mother tongues include many poets writing in Mayan K'iche' languages (Humberto Ak'ab'al, Feliciano Sánchez Chan, Briceida Cuevas Cob and Isaac Esaú Carrillo Can), the Shuar Chicham poet María Clara Shurupi (Ecuador), Aymaran poets Clemente Mamani, Elvira Espejo Ayca, Mauro Alwa, and Diether Flores (Bolivia), as well as Mapudungún language poets such as Elicura Chichualiaf, David Aniñir, Leonel Lienlaf, and Viviana Ayilef (Chile and Argentina).

There are also some good Spanish-English bilingual anthologies, including Dudley Fitts's *Anthology of Contemporary Latin American Poetry* (Norfolk, CO: A New Directions Book, 1947); E. Caracciolo-Trejo's *The Penguin Book of Latin American Verse* (Harmondsworth: Penguin, 1971); Stephen Tapscott's *Twentieth-Century Latin American Poetry* (Austin, TX: University of Texas Press, 1996); Ludwig Zeller's *The Invisible Presence: Sixteen Poets of Spanish America 1925–1995* (Oakville, ON: Mosaic, 1996); Cecilia Vicuña and Ernesto Livon-Grosman's *The Oxford Book of Latin American Poetry* (Oxford: Oxford University Press, 2009); and Ilan Stavans's *The FSG Book of Twentieth-Century Poetry* (New York, NY: Farrar, Straus and Giroux, 2011). *An Anthology of Twentieth-Century Brazilian Poetry* (Middletown, CT: Wesleyan University Press, 1972), co-edited by Elizabeth Bishop, is excellent. For discussion of these latter works, see Chapter 18 of this study.

For the background on colonial poetry, the following are recommended: John H. Elliott, *The Old World and the New, 1492–1650* (Cambridge: Cambridge University Press, 1970); Roberto González Echevarría and Enrique Pupo-Walker (eds.), *The Cambridge History of Latin American Literature*, 3 vols (Cambridge: Cambridge University Press, 1996); Rolena Adorno, *Colonial Latin American Literature: A Very Short Introduction* (Oxford/New York: Oxford University Press, 2011); Stephen Greenblatt, *Marvelous Possessions: The Wonder of the New World* (Chicago, IL: The University of Chicago Press, 1991); Karl Kohut and Sonia V. Rose (eds.), *La formación de la cultura virreinal*, 3 vols (Frankfurt/Madrid: Vervuert/Iberoamericana, 2000–2006); James Lockhart and Stuart B. Schwartz, *Early Latin America: A History of Colonial Spanish America and Brazil* (Cambridge: Cambridge University Press, 1983); Stephanie Merrim, *The Spectacular City, Mexico, and Colonial Hispanic Literary Culture* (Austin, TX: University of Texas Press, 2010); Walter D. Mignolo, *The Darker Side of the Renaissance: Literacy, Territoriality and Colonization* (Ann Arbor, MI: University of Michigan Press, 2003); Raquel Chang-Rodríguez, *"Aquí, ninfas del sur, venid ligeras": voces poéticas virreinales* (Madrid/Frankfurt: Iberoamericana/Vervuert, 2008); Roland Greene, *Unrequited Conquests: Love and Empire in the Colonial Americas* (Chicago, IL: University of Chicago Press, 1999); and Ángel Rama, *La ciudad letrada* (Hanover: Ediciones del Norte, 1984). For studies of individual writers, see Georgina Sabat de Rivers, *Estudios de literatura hispanoamericana: Sor Juana Inés de la Cruz y otros poetas barrocos de la colonia* (Barcelona: PPU, 1992). Also worth consulting are Óscar Coello, *Los inicios de la poesía castellana en el Perú* (Lima: Pontificia Universidad Católica del Perú, 1999); Matthew Restall and Kris Lane, *Latin America in Colonial Times* (Cambridge: Cambridge University Press, 2011); and Jorge Téllez, *Poéticas del Nuevo Mundo: articulación del pensamiento poético en América colonial: siglos XVI, XVII y XVIII* (Mexico City: Siglo XXI, 2012).

With regard to the nineteenth century, an excellent overview is provided by Octavio Paz, *Los hijos del limo: Del romanticismo a la vanguardia* (Barcelona: Seix Barral, 1998). See also Emilio Carrilla's *El romanticismo en la América Hispánica*, 2 vols (Madrid: Gredos, 1967); Gwen Kirkpatrick, "Romantic Poetry in Latin America," in *Romantic Poetry*, ed. Angela Esterhammer (Philadelphia, PA: Johns Benjamins Publishing Company, 2002), 410–16; and Oscar Rivera-Rodas, *La poesía hispanoamericana del siglo XIX (Del romanticismo al modernismo)* (Madrid: Editorial Alhambra, 1988). For Spanish American *modernismo*, see Gerard Aching, *The Politics of Spanish American modernismo by Exquisite Design* (Cambridge, MA: Harvard University Press, 1999) and Gwen Kirkpatrick's *The Dissonant Legacy of Modernismo* (Berkeley, CA: University of California Press, 1989). For an excellent study of Darío's work, see Ángel Rama's *Rubén Darío y el modernismo* (Caracas: Biblioteca de la Universidad Central de Venezuela, 1970). Since the *modernistas* experimented so much with rhyme schemes, Tomás Navarro Tomás's *Métrica española: reseña histórica y descriptiva* (Madrid: Guadarrama, 1972) should be consulted; also helpful is Antonio Quilis's *Métrica española* (Barcelona: Ariel, 1989). There is some excellent discussion of the postmodernist poets, including Agustini, in Emir Rodríguez Monegal's *Sexo y poesía en el 900 uruguay* (Montevideo: Alfa, 1969) and Cathy L. Jrade, *Delmira Agustini, Sexual Seduction, and Vampiric Conquest* (New Haven, CT: Yale University Press, 2012).

For analysis of the avant-garde, see Jorge Schwartz, *Vanguardia y cosmopolitismo en la década del veinte: Oliverio Girondo y Oswald de Andrade* (Rosario: Beatriz Viterbo Editora, 1993); the same author's *Fervor das vanguardas: arte e literatura na América Latina* (São Paulo: Companhia das Letras, 2013); Vicky Unruh, *Latin American Vanguards: The Art of Contentious Encounters* (Berkeley, CA: The University of California Press, 1994); and Fernando Rosenberg, *The Avant-Garde and Geopolitics in Latin America* (Pittsburgh, PA: University of Pittsburgh Press, 2006). In addition, see the introductory essays by Jorge Schwartz, "Introducción," in *Las vanguardias latinoamericanas: textos programáticos y críticos*, ed. Jorge Schwartz (Mexico City: Fondo de Cultura Económica, 2002), 33–94; and Mari Carmen Ramírez, "A Highly Topical Utopia: Some Outstanding Features of the Avant-Garde in Latin America," in *Inverted Utopias: Avant-Garde Art in Latin America*, ed. Mari Carmen Ramírez and Héctor Olea (New Haven, CT: Yale University Press, 2004), 1–15. For the historical avant-gardes in Brazil, see Maria Eugenia Boaventura Boaventura, *A vanguarda antropofágica* (São Paulo: Editora Ática, 1985); K. David Jackson, "Literature of the São Paulo Week of Modern Art," in *Texas Papers on Latin America* (Austin, TX: Institute of Latin American Studies, University of Texas at Austin, 1987); and Charles A. Perrone, *Brazil, Lyric, and the Americas* (Gainesville, FL: University Press of Florida, 2010), and the same author's *Seven Faces: Brazilian Poetry Since Modernism* (Durham, NC: Duke University Press, 1996); Gonzalo Aguilar, *Poesía concreta brasileña: Las vanguardias en la encrucijada modernista* (Rosario: Beatriz Viterbo, 2003); and Adam Joseph Shellhorse, *Anti-Literature: The Politics and Limits of Representation in Modern Brazil and Argentina* (Pittsburgh: University of Pittsburgh Press, 2017). For an overview of the avant-garde in Spain and Spanish America, see Stephen Hart, "The Avant-Garde in Spain and Spanish America," in *The Hispanic Connection: Spanish, Catalan and Spanish-American Poetry from "modernism" to the Spanish Civil War* (Lampeter: The Edwin Mellen Press, 1990), 41–66; and Hugo J. Verani, "The Vanguardia and its

Implications," *The Cambridge History of Latin American Literature*, ed. Pupo-Walker and González Echeverría, 1996), II, 114–37. Essential studies on conversational poetry are Carmen Alemany Bay, *Poética coloquial hispanoamericana* (Alicante: Universidad Publicaciones, 1997); Rosa Sarabia, *Poetas de la poesía hispanoamericana hablada* (London: Tamesis, 1997) and Roberto Fernández Retamar's "Antipoesía y poesía conversacional en Hispanoamérica," in *Para una teoría de la poesía hispanoamericana y otras aproximaciones* (Havana: Casa de las Américas, 1975), 111–26.

For an excellent overview of the interplay between literature and culture from the colonial period to the present, see *A Companion to Latin American Literature and Culture*, ed. Sara Castro-Klaren (Oxford: Wiley-Blackwell, 2008). The one main overview of Latin American poetry is the now classic study by Gordon Brotherston, *Latin American Poetry: Origins and Presence* (Cambridge: Cambridge University Press, 1975); essential reading. For excellent overview studies of twentieth-century poetry, see Mike Gonzalez and David Treece, *The Gallery of Voices: Twentieth-Century Poetry of Latin America* (London: Verso, 1992); William Rowe, *Poets of Contemporary Latin America: History and the Inner Life* (Oxford: Oxford University Press, 2000); Jill Kuhnheim, *Spanish American Poetry at the End of the Twentieth Century: Textual Disruptions* (Austin, TX: University of Texas Press, 2004); and Donald Shaw, *Beyond the Vanguard: Spanish American Poetry after 1950* (London: Tamesis, 2008). For very helpful introductory essays on individual poets, especially poets of the latter half of the twentieth century, the reader is referred to the separate entries in Verity Smith's *Encyclopedia of Latin American Literature* (London: Dearborn, 1997), and to the essays in *Twentieth Century Spanish American Literature to 1960*, ed. David William Foster and Daniel Altamiranda (New York, NY: Garland Publishing, 1997).

For a good introduction to some of the issues relating to the themes, theorization and visibility of women's writing, including poetry, the reader is referred to L.P. Condé and S.M. Hart (eds.), *Feminist Readings on Spanish and Latin American Literature* (Lampeter: Edwin Mellen, 1991), Debra Castillo's *Talking Back: Toward a Latin American Feminist Literary Criticism* (Ithaca, NY: Cornell University Press, 1992); Anny Brooksbank Jones and Catherine Davies (eds.), *Latin American Women's Writing: Feminist Readings in Theory and Crisis* (Oxford: Oxford University Press, 1997); and Martha Lorena Rub's *Politically Writing Women in Hispanic Literature: The Feminist Tradition in Contemporary Latin American and U.S. Latina Writers* (Bloomington, IN: Xlibris, 2011). Crucial, foundational works on LGBTQ Hispanic literature are David William Foster's *Gay and Lesbian Themes in Latin American Writing* (Austin, TX: Texas University Press, 1991); and *¿Entiendes? Queer Readings, Hispanic Writings*, ed. Emilie L. Bergmann and Paul Julian Smith (Durham, NC: Duke University Press, 1995), the latter of which contains some excellent essays on LGBT poets; Ben Sifuentes-Jáuregui's *Transvestism, Masculinity, and Latin American Literature: Genders Share Flesh* (New York, NY: Palgrave, 2002); and Lourdes Torres and Inmaculada Pertusa (eds.), *Tortilleras: Hispanic and U.S. Latina Lesbian Expression* (Philadelphia, PA: Temple University Press, 2003), which provides some important context. For a detailed overview of Mexico's pre-Colombian literary traditions, see Miguel León-Portilla, *Las literaturas precolombinas de México* (Mexico City: Pomarca, 1964). Jean Franco, "Some Reflections on Contemporary Writing in the Indigenous

Languages of America," *Comparative American Studies* 3.4 (2005): 455–69, gives a brief overview of the trajectories of several indigenous Latin American literary traditions, with particular attention to contemporary Zapotec poetry. For the backdrop to Afro-Hispanic literature the reader is advised to consult Vera M. Kutzinski, "Afro-Hispanic American Literature," in *The Cambridge History of Latin American Literature*, ed. Pupo-Walker and González Echeverría, II, 164–94, as well as Richard Jackson's *The Black Image in Latin American Literature* (Albuquerque, NM: University of New Mexico Press, 1976), and by the same author, *Black Writers and the Hispanic Canon* (Boston, MA: Twayne, 1997). Carlota Caulfield and Darién J. Davis (eds.), *A Companion to US Latino Literatures* (Woodbridge: Tamesis, 2006), provides an excellent survey of Latino literature and some important context on Latino/a poetry. Also important are Rafael Pérez-Torres, *Movements in Chicano Poetry: Against Myths, Against Margins* (New York, NY: Cambridge University Press, 1995); and Michael Dowdy, *Broken Souths: Latina/o Poetic Responses to Neoliberalism and Globalization* (Tucson, AZ: University of Arizona, 2013). The best available anthology of Media poetry is Eduardo Kac's *Media Poetry: An International Anthology* (Bristol: Intellect, 2007). For some excellent cultural context on electronic poetry, see Jill Kuhnheim, *Spanish American Poetry at the End of the Twentieth Century: Textual Disruptions* (Austin, TX: University of Texas Press, 2004). In similar fashion, for contemporary media and digital poetry in Brazil and Spanish America, see Alessandra Santos, *Arnaldo Canibal Antunes* (São Paulo: nVersos, 2013); and Eduardo Ledesma, *Radical Poetry: Aesthetics, Politics, Technology, and the Ibero-American Avant-Gardes, 1900–2015* (Albany: State University of New York Press, 2016).

SELECT BIBLIOGRAPHY

Aching, Gerard. *The Politics of Spanish American* modernismo *by Exquisite Design*. Cambridge, MA: Harvard University Press, 1999.

Adams, Clementina R. *Common Threads: Themes in Afro-Hispanic Women's Literature*. Miami, FL: Ediciones Universal, 1998.

Adorno, Rolena. *Colonial Latin American Literature: A Very Short Introduction*. Oxford/New York: Oxford University Press, 2011.

Aguilar, Gonzalo. *Poesía concreta brasileña: las vanguardias en la encrucijada modernista*. Rosario: Beatriz Viterbo, 2003.

Alemany Bay, Carmen. "Para una revisión de la poesía conversacional." *Alma mater*, 13–14 (1997): 49–55.

Poética coloquial hispanoamericana. Alicante: Universidad Publicaciones, 1997.

Anka Ninawaman, Ch'aska Eugenia. *Poesía en Quechua: Chaskaschay*. Quito: Abya Yala, 2004.

Baciu, Stefan. *Antología de la poesía latinoamericana, 1950–1970*. Albany, NY: State University of New York, 1974.

Bandeira, Manuel. *Antologia dos poetas brasileiros: fase romântica*. Rio de Janeiro: Editôra Nova Fronteira, 1996.

Bergmann, Emilie L., and Paul Julian Smith, ed. *¿Entiendes? Queer Readings, Hispanic Writings*. Durham, NC: Duke University Press, 1995.

Bishop, Elizabeth, and Emanuel Brasil, ed. *An Anthology of Twentieth-Century Brazilian Poetry*. Middletown, CT: Wesleyan University Press, 1972.

Boaventura, Maria Eugenia. *A vanguarda antropofágica*. São Paulo: Editora Ática, 1985.

Bollig, Ben. *Néstor Perlongher: The Poetic Search for an Argentine Marginal Voice*. Cardiff: University of Wales Press, 2008.

Brooksbank Jones, Anny, and Catherine Davies, ed. *Latin American Women's Writing: Feminist Readings in Theory and Crisis*. Oxford: Oxford University Press, 1997.

Brotherston, Gordon. *Latin American Poetry: Origins and Presence*. Cambridge: Cambridge University Press, 1975.

Spanish American Poets: A Critical Anthology, 2nd ed. Bristol: Bristol Classical Press, 1995.

Cáceres Romero, Adolfo. *Poesía Quechua del Tawantinsuyu*. Buenos Aires: Ediciones del Sol, 2009.

Camacho Ríos, Gladys. *Phuyup Yawar Waqaynin*. Cochabamba, Editorial Kipus, 2013.

Campa, Antonio R. de la, and Raquel Chang-Rodríguez, ed. *Poesía hispanoamericana colonial; antología*. Madrid: Editorial Alhambra, 1985.

Caracciolo-Trejo, E., ed. *The Penguin Book of Latin American Verse*. Harmondsworth: Penguin, 1971.

Carrera, Arturo, ed. *Monstruos. Antología de la joven poesía argentina*. Buenos Aires: Fondo de cultura económica argentina, 2001.

Carrilla, Emilio. *El romanticismo en la América Hispánica*, 2 vols. Madrid: Gredos, 1967.

Castillo, Debra. *Talking Back: Toward a Latin American Feminist Literary Criticism*. Ithaca, NY: Cornell University Press, 1992.

Castro-Klaren, Sara, ed. *A Companion to Latin American Literature and Culture*. Oxford: Wiley-Blackwell, 2008.

Caulfield, Carlota, and Darién J. Davis, ed. *A Companion to US Latino Literatures*. Woodbridge: Tamesis, 2006.

Chang-Rodríguez, Raquel, ed. *"Aquí, ninfas del sur, venid ligeras": voces poéticas virreinales*. Madrid/Frankfurt: Iberoamericana/Vervuert, 2008.

Clüver, Claus. "The 'Ruptura' Proclaimed by Brazil's Self-Styled 'Vanguardas' of the Fifties." *Neo-Avant-Garde*. Ed. David Hopkins. Amsterdam: Rodopi, 2006. 161–96.

Coello, Óscar. *Los inicios de la poesía castellana en el Perú*. Lima: Pontificia Universidad Católica del Perú, 1999.

Condé, L.P., and S.M. Hart, ed. *Feminist Readings on Spanish and Latin American Literature*. Lampeter: Edwin Mellen, 1991.

Crow, Mary, ed. *Woman Who Has Sprouted Wings: Poems by Contemporary Latin American Women Poets*, 2nd ed. Pittsburgh, PA: The Latin American Literary Review Press, 1988.

Debicki, Andrew P. *Poetas hispanoamericanos contemporáneos. Punto de vista, perspectiva, experiencia*. Madrid: Editorial Gredos, 1976.

DeCosta-Willis, Miriam. "Afra-Hispanic Writers and Feminist Discourse." In *Women in African and the African Diaspora: A Reader*, edited by Rosalyn Terborg-Penn and Andrea Benton, 247–61. Rushing. Washington, DC: Howard University Press, 1996.

Dowdy, Michael. *Broken Souths: Latina/o Poetic Responses to Neoliberalism and Globalization*. Tucson, AZ: University of Arizona, 2013.

Echavarren, Roberto, ed. *Medusario. Muestra de poesía latinoamericana*. Mexico City: Fondo de Cultura Económica, 1996.

ed. *Indios de espíritu. Muestra de poesía del Cono Sur*. Buenos Aires: La Flauta Mágica, 2013.

Elliott, John H. *The Old World and the New, 1492–1650*. Cambridge: Cambridge University Press, 1970.

Enjuto Rangel, Cecilia. *Cities in Ruins: The Politics of Modern Poetics*. West Lafayette, IN: Purdue University Press. Purdue Studies in Romance Literatures, 2010.

Epps, Brad. "Virtual Sexuality: Lesbianismo, Loss, and Delivrance in Carme Riera's 'Te deix, amor, la mar com a penyora.'" In *¿Entiendes?, ¿Entiendes? Queer Readings, Hispanic Writings*, edited by Emilie Bergmann and Paul Julian Smith, 318–45. Durham, NC: Duke University Press, 1995.

Facioli, Valentim, and Antonio Carlos Olivieri, ed. *Antologia de Poesia Brasileira. Romantismo*. Sao Paulo: Editora Ática, 1985.

Fernández Retamar, Roberto. "Antipoesía y poesía conversacional en Hispanoamérica." In *Para una teoría de la poesía hispanoamericana y otras aproximaciones*, 111–26. Havana: Casa de las Américas, 1975.

Fitts, Dudley. *Anthology of Contemporary Latin American Poetry*. Norfolk, CO: A New Directions Book, 1947.

Foster, David William. *Gay and Lesbian Themes in Latin American Writing*. Austin, TX: Texas University Press, 1991.

Foster, David William, and Daniel Altamiranda, ed. *Twentieth Century Spanish American Literature to 1960*. New York, NY: Garland Publishing, 1997.

Franco, Jean. "Some Reflections on Contemporary Writing in the Indigenous Languages of America." *Comparative American Studies* 3.4 (2005): 455–69.

Gonzalez, Mike, and David Treece, ed. *The Gallery of Voices: Twentieth-Century Poetry of Latin America*. London: Verso, 1992.

González, Yanko, and Pedro Araya, ed. *ZurDos. Última poesía latinoamericana. Antología*. Madrid: Bartleby, 2005.

González Echevarría, Roberto, and Enrique Pupo-Walker, ed. *The Cambridge History of Latin American Literature*, 3 vols. Cambridge: Cambridge University Press, 1996.

Greenblatt, Stephen. *Marvelous Possessions: The Wonder of the New World*. Chicago, IL: The University of Chicago Press, 1991.

Greene, Roland, *Unrequited Conquests: Love and Empire in the Colonial Americas*. Chicago, IL: University of Chicago Press, 1999.

Guerrero, Gustavo, ed. *Cuerpo plural. Antología de la poesía hispanoamericana contemporánea*. Madrid/Buenos Aires/Valencia: Pre-textos/Instituto Cervantes, 2010.

Harrison, Regina. *Signs, Songs, and Memory in the Andes: Translating Quechua Language and Culture*. Austin, TX: University of Texas Press, 1989.

Hart, Stephen M. "The Avant-Garde in Spain and Spanish America." In *The Hispanic Connection: Spanish, Catalan and Spanish-American "modernism" to the Spanish Civil War*, 41–66. Lampeter: The Edwin Mellen Press, 1990.

"Is Women's Writing in Spanish America Gender-Specific?" *MLN* 110.2 (1995): 335–52.

"The Twilight of the Idols in Modernism's 1922." In *Modernisms and Modernities: Studies in Honour of Donald L. Shaw*, edited by Susan Carvalho, 175–99. Newark, DE: Juan de la Cuesta, 2006.

"Latin American Poetry." In *A Companion to Latin American Literature and Culture*, edited by Sara Castro-Klaren, 426–41. Oxford: Wiley-Blackwell, 2008.

César Vallejo: una biografía literaria. Lima: Cátedra Vallejo, 2014.

Hedge Coke, Allison. *Sing: Poetry from the Indigenous Americas*. Tucson, AZ: University of Arizona Press, 2011.

Huízar, Angélica J. *Beyond the Page: Latin American Poetry from the Calligramme to the Virtual*. Palo Alto, CA: Academica Press, 2008.

Jackson, K. David. "Literature of the São Paulo Week of Modern Art." In *Texas Papers on Latin America*, 1–16. Austin, TX: Institute of Latin American Studies, University of Texas at Austin, 1987.

Jackson, Richard. *The Black Image in Latin American Literature*. Albuquerque, NM: University of New Mexico Press, 1976.

Black Writers in Latin America. Albuquerque, NM: University of New Mexico Press, 1979.

Black Literature and Humanism in Latin America. Athens, GA: University of Georgia Press, 1988.

Black Writers and the Hispanic Canon. Boston, MA: Twayne, 1997.

Jáuregui, Carlos. "Writing Communities on the Internet: Textual Authority and Territorialization." In *Latin American Literature and Mass Media*, edited by Paz-Soldán, Edmundo and Debra A. Castillo, 288–300. New York, NY: Garland, 2001.

Jiménez, José Olivio. *Antología de la poesía hispanoamericana contemporánea: 1914–1987*. Madrid: Alianza, 1988.

Jrade, Cathy J. *Delmira Agustini, Sexual Seduction, and Vampiric Conquest*. New Haven, CT: Yale University Press, 2012.

Jrade, Cathy L. *Modernismo, Modernity and the Development of Spanish American Literature*. Austin, TX: University of Texas Press, 1998.

Kac, Eduardo, ed. *Media Poetry: An International Anthology*, 2nd revised edn. Bristol: Intellect, 2007.

Kesselman, Violeta, Ana Mazzoni, and Damián Selci, ed. *La tendencia materialista. Antología crítica de la poesía de los 90*. Buenos Aires: Paradiso, 2012.

Kirkpatrick, Gwen. *The Dissonant Legacy of Modernismo. Lugones, Herrera y Reissig, and the Voices of Modern Spanish American Poetry*. Berkeley, CA: University of California Press, 1989.

"Romantic Poetry in Latin America." In *Romantic Poetry*, edited by Angela Esterhammer, 410–16. Philadelphia, PA: John Benjamins Publishing Company, 2002.

Kohut Karl, and Sonia V. Rose, ed. *La formación de la cultura virreinal*, 3 vols. Frankfurt/Madrid: Vervuert/Iberoamericana, 2000–2006.

Krivoshein de Canese, Natalia, and Feliciano Acosta Alcaraz, ed. *Ñe epoty aty: Voces de poetas en guaraní*. Asunción: Servilibro, 2005.

Krögel, Alison. *Food, Power, and Resistance in the Andes: Exploring Quechua Verbal and Visual Narratives*. Lanham, MD: Lexington Books, 2011.

"The Dawn of Our Lives," *Kilkakunawarmikuna*: The Rising Voices of Kichwa Women Poets in Ecuador. *Latin American Indian Literatures Journal* 30.1 (2017).

Kuhnheim, Jill. *Spanish American Poetry at the End of the Twentieth Century: Textual Disruptions*. Austin, TX: University of Texas Press, 2004.

Kutzinski, Vera M. "Afro-Hispanic American Literature." In *The Cambridge History of Latin American Literature*, Pupo-Walker and González Echeverría, II, 164–94. Cambridge: Cambridge University Press, 1996.

Ledesma, Eduardo. *Radical Poetry: Aesthetics, Politics, Technology, and the Ibero-American Avant-Gardes, 1900–2015*. Albany: State University of New York Press, 2016.

León-Portilla, Miguel. *Las literaturas precolombinas de México*. Mexico City: Pomarca, 1964.

Lilia Tenorio, Marta, ed. *Poesía novohispana: antología*, 2 vols. Mexico City: El Colegio de México/Fundación para las Letras Mexicanas, 2010.

Lockhart James, and Stuart B. Schwartz, *Early Latin America: A History of Colonial Spanish America and Brazil*. Cambridge: Cambridge University Press, 1983.

Luz, Guilherme Amaral. "O canto de Proteu ou a corte na colônia em *Prosopopéia* (1601), de Bento Teixeira." *Tempo* 13.25 (2008): 193–215.

Malvaceda E. "Ñakari: Formas culturales de sufrimiento tras la violencia política en el Perú," *Revista IIPSI* 13.2 (2010): 130.

Masiello, Francine. *Lenguaje e Ideología: Las escuelas argentinas de vanguardia.* Buenos Aires: Hachette, 1986.

Mazzotti, José Antonio. "Bilingualism, Quechua Poetry, and Migratory Fragmentations in Present-Day Peru." In *Bilingual Games: Some Literary Investigations*, edited by Doris Sommers, 97–120. New York, NY: Palgrave Macmillan, 2003.

Meem, Deborah T., Michelle A. Gibson, and Jonathan Alexander, ed. *Finding Out: An Introduction to LGBT Studies.* London: Sage, 2009.

Méndez Plancarte, Alfonso, ed. *Poetas novohispanos*, 3 vols. Mexico City: UNAM, 1942–1945.

Merrim, Stephanie. *The Spectacular City, Mexico, and Colonial Hispanic Literary Culture.* Austin, TX: University of Texas Press, 2010.

Mignolo, Walter D. *The Darker Side of the Renaissance: Literacy, Territoriality and Colonization.* Ann Arbor, MI: University of Michigan Press, 2003.

Montemayor, Carlos, and Donald Frischmann, ed. *Words of the True Peoples/ Palabras de los Seres Verdaderos: Anthology of Contemporary Mexican Indigenous-Language Writers/Antología de Escritores Actuales en Lenguas Indígenas de México.* Austin, TX: University of Texas Press, 2004, 2005, 2007.

Nachon, Andi, ed. *Poetas argentinas (1961–1980).* Buenos Aires: Del Dock, 2007.

Navarro Tomás, Tomás. *Métrica española: reseña histórica y descriptiva.* Madrid: Guadarrama, 1972.

Negroni, María, ed. *La maldad de escribir: 9 poetas latinoamericanas del siglo XX.* Montblanc, Tarragona: Igitur, 2003.

Nicholson, Melanie. *Surrealism in Latin American Literature: Searching for Breton's Ghost.* New York: Palgrave Macmillan, 2013

Ninamango Mallqui, Eduardo. *Pukutay/Tormenta.* Lima: Tarea, Centro de Publicaciones Educativas, 1982.

Noriega Bernuy, Julio E. *Poesía quechua escrita en el Perú: Antología.* Lima: CEP, 1993.

Pichka harawikuna: Five Quechua Poets, An anthology, translated by Maureen Ahern. New York, NY: Americas Society, Latin American Literary Review Press, 1998.

Poesía quechua en Bolivia. Lima: Pakarina Ediciones, 2016.

Ojeda, Martha. *Nicomedes Santa Cruz: Ecos de Africa en Perú.* London: Tamesis, 2003.

Ortega, Julio, ed. *El turno y la transición. Antología de la poesía latinoamericana del siglo XXI.* Mexico City: Siglo XXI, 2001.

Padín, Clemente, and Karl Young. *La poesía experimental latinoamericana.* Colmenar Viejo, Spain: Información y producciones, 2000.

Paz, Octavio. *Los hijos del limo: Del romanticismo a la vanguardia.* Barcelona: Seix Barral, 1998.

Pérez-Torres, Rafael. *Movements in Chicano Poetry: Against Myths, Against Margins.* New York, NY: Cambridge University Press, 1995.

Perrone, Charles A. *Seven Faces: Brazilian Poetry Since Modernism.* Durham, NC: Duke University Press, 1996.

Brazil, Lyric, and the Americas. Gainesville, FL: University Press of Florida, 2010.

Pitman, Thea. "El arraigo de la cibercultura: un análisis comparativo de las obras hipertextuales de Doménico Chiappe y Blas Valdez." *Arizona Journal of Hispanic Cultural Studies* 14 (2010): 217–34.

Pontiero, Giovanni, ed. *An Anthology of Brazilian Modernist Poetry.* London: Pergamon, 1969.

"Brazilian Poetry from Modernism to the 1990s." In *Cambridge History of Latin American Literature*, edited by Pupo-Walker and González Echeverría, 247–67. Cambridge: Cambridge University Press, 1996.

Price, Rachel. *The Object of the Atlantic: Concrete Aesthetics in Cuba, Brazil, and Spain, 1868–1968.* Evanston: Northwestern University Press, 2014.

Puccini, Dario, and Saúl Yurkievich. *Historia de la cultura literaria en Hispanoamérica I.* México D.F.: Fondo de Cultura Económica, 2010.

Quilis, Antonio. *Métrica española.* Barcelona: Ariel, 1989.

Rama, Ángel. *Rubén Darío y el modernismo.* Caracas: Biblioteca de la Universidad Central de Venezuela, 1970.

La ciudad letrada. Hanover: Ediciones del Norte, 1984.

Ramírez, Mari Carmen. "A Highly Topical Utopia: Some Outstanding Features of the Avant-Garde in Latin America." In *Inverted Utopias: Avant-Garde Art in Latin America*, edited by Mari Carmen Ramírez and Héctor Olea, 1–15. New Haven, CT: Yale University Press, 2004.

Restall, Matthew, and Kris Lane. *Latin America in Colonial Times.* Cambridge: Cambridge University Press, 2011.

Rivera-Rodas, Óscar. *La poesía hispanoamericana del siglo XIX. (Del romanticismo al modernismo.* Madrid: Editorial Alhambra, 1988.

Rodríguez Monegal, Emir. *Sexo y poesía en el 900 uruguayo.* Montevideo: Alfa, 1969.

Rosenberg, Fernando. *The Avant-Garde and Geopolitics in Latin America.* Pittsburgh, PA: University of Pittsburgh Press, 2006.

"Cultural Theory and Avant-Gardes: Mariátegui, Mário de Andrade, Oswald de Andrade, Pagú, Tarsila do Amaral, César Vallejo." In *A Companion to Latin American Literature and Culture*, edited by Sara Castro-Klaren, 410–25. Oxford: Wiley-Blackwell, 2008.

Rowe, William. *Poets of Contemporary Latin America: History and the Inner Life.* Oxford: Oxford University Press, 2000.

"Latin American Poetry." In *The Cambridge Companion to Modern Latin American Culture*, edited by John King, 136–70. Cambridge: Cambridge University Press, 2004.

Rub, Martha Lorena. *Politically Writing Women in Hispanic Literature: The Feminist Tradition in Contemporary Latin American and U.S. Latina Writer.* Bloomington, IN: Xlibris, 2011.

Sabat de Rivers, Georgina. *Estudios de literatura hispanoamericana: Sor Juana Inés de la Cruz y otros poetas barrocos de la colonia.* Barcelona: PPU, 1992.

Santos, Alessandra. *Arnaldo Canibal Antunes.* São Paulo: nVersos, 2013.

Sarabia, Rosa. *Poetas de la poesía hispanoamericana hablada.* London: Tamesis, 1997.

Schulman, Ivan A., and Evelyn Picón Garfield, ed. *Poesía modernista hispanoamericana y española (Antología).* Madrid: Taurus, 1986.

Schwartz, Jorge. *Vanguardia y cosmopolitismo en la década del veinte: Oliverio Girondo y Oswald de Andrade*. Rosario: Beatriz Viterbo Editora, 1993.
"Introducción." In *Las vanguardias latinoamericanas: textos programáticos y críticos*, edited by Jorge Schwartz, 33–94. Mexico City: Fondo de Cultura Económica, 2002.
Fervor das vanguardas: arte e literatura na América Latina. São Paulo: Companhia das Letras, 2013.
Sefamí, Jacobo. *Contemporary Spanish American Poets: A Bibliography of Primary and Secondary Sources*. New York, NY: Greenwood Press, 1992.
Shaw, Bradley A. *Latin American Literature in English Translation: An Annotated Bibliography*. New York, NY: New York University Press, 1976.
Shaw, Donald. *Beyond the Vanguard: Spanish American Poetry after 1950*. London: Tamesis, 2008.
Shellhorse, Adam Joseph. "Subversions of the Sensible: The Poetics of Antropofagia in Brazilian Concrete Poetry." *Revista Hispánica Moderna* 68.2 (2015): 165–90.
Anti-Literature: The Politics and Limits of Representation in Modern Brazil and Argentina. Pittsburgh, PA: The University of Pittsburgh Press, 2017.
Sifuentes-Jáuregui, Ben. *Transvestism, Masculinity, and Latin American Literature: Genders Share Flesh*. New York, NY: Palgrave, 2002.
Silva Ramos, Péricles Eugênio da, ed. *Poesia barroca. Antologia*. São Paulo: Melhoramentos, 1967.
Smith, Verity, ed. *Encyclopedia of Latin American Literature*. London: Dearborn, 1997.
Stavans, Ilan, ed. *The FSG Book of Twentieth-Century Poetry*. New York, NY: Farrar, Straus and Giroux, 2011.
Tapscott, Stephen, ed. *Twentieth-Century Latin American Poetry*. Austin, TX: University of Texas Press, 1996.
Téllez, Jorge. *Poéticas del Nuevo Mundo: articulación del pensamiento poético en América colonial: siglos XVI, XVII y XVIII*. Mexico City: Siglo XXI, 2012.
Torre, Guillermo de. *Literaturas europeas de vanguardia*. Madrid: Rafael Caro Raggio, 1925.
Torres, Lourdes, and Inmaculada Pertusa, ed. *Tortilleras: Hispanic and U.S. Latina Lesbian Expression*. Philadelphia, PA: Temple University Press, 2003.
Unruh, Vicky. *Latin American Vanguards: The Art of Contentious Encounters*. Berkeley, CA: The University of California Press, 1994.
Verani, Hugo J. "The Vanguardia and its Implications." In *The Cambridge History of Latin American Literature*, edited by Pupo-Walker and González Echeverría, II, 114–37. Cambridge: Cambridge University Press, 1996.
Vicuña, Cecilia, and Ernesto Livon-Grosman, ed. *The Oxford Book of Latin American Poetry*. Oxford: Oxford University Press, 2009.
Wilson, Jason. *An A to Z of Modern Latin American Literature in English Translation*. London: Institute of Latin American Studies, 1989.
Zapata, Miguel Ángel, ed. *Nueva poesía latinoamericana*. Mexico City: UNAM, 1999.
Zeller, Ludwig, ed. *The Invisible Presence: Sixteen Poets of Spanish America 1925–1995*. Oakville, ON: Mosaic, 1996.

URL Bibliography

Las afinidades electivas/Las elecciones afectivas (c.2013–). laseleccionesafectivas .blogspot.co.uk.

Azevedo, Wilton Luiz de. *Atame: a angustia do precário* (2005). www.youtube.com/ watch?v=jJIDnonv3Ag.

Balboa, Laura. *"you CODE me."* (2009). youcode.me.

Beiguelman, Giselle.//**Code_UP* (2004). container.zkm.de/code_up/web/english/ index.htm.

Bravo, Luis ("+ 20 artistas"). *Árbol veloz (poemas 1990–1998). Book with CD-Rom* (Montevideo: Trilce, 1998). Partially available online from the *Virtual Poetry Project* at ojs.gc.cuny.edu/index.php/VPP/issue/view/99/showToc.

Cociña, Carlos. *Plagio del afecto* (2003–05). www.poesiacero.cl/plagiodelafecto .html.

Gache, Belén. *Manifiestos Robots* (2009). findelmundo.com.ar/belengache/manifies tosrobot.htm.

  Góngora Wordtoys (Madrid: Sociedad Lunar, 2011). http://belengache.net/gongor awordtoys/gongorawordtoys.html.

  Radikal Karaoke (2011). belengache.net/rk.

Lozano-Hemmer, Rafael and Guillermo Gómez-Peña. *Tech-illa Sunrise (.txt dot con Sangrita)* (2001). www.pochanostra.com/antes/jazz_pocha2/mainpages/tech illa.htm.

Marinho, Chico, dir. *Palavrador* (2006). collection.eliterature.org/2/works/marin ho_palavrador/palavrador.mp4.

Mendoza, Antonio. *Subculture.com* (2003).subculture.com.

Moreno Ortiz, Benjamín R. *Concretoons: poesía digital* (2010). www.concretoons .net84.net.

Navas, Eduardo. *9_11_2001_netMemorial* (2002). www.navasse.net/netMemorial/ 911Static.html.

Orquesta de Poetas (2011). www.orquestadepoetas.cl. All videos available from www.orquestadepoetas.cl/videos.

Ortiz, Santiago. *Bacterias argentinas* (2004). moebio.com/santiago/bacterias.

  The Iliad (2012). moebio.com/iliad.

Poesía virtual (2001–). www.poesiavirtual.com.

Romano, Gustavo. *The IP Poetry Project* (2006). ip-poetry.findelmundo.com.ar.

Santos, Alkmar Luiz dos, and Chico Marinho, dirs. *Liberdade* (2013). Downloadable from collection.eliterature.org/3/work.html?work=liberdade.

Solaas, Leonardo. *Migraciones* (2005). Available online at solaas.com.ar/migra ciones/migraciones.htm from 2006–2014. A filmed version of the full 'poem' is now available at ancien-nt2.aegirnt2.uqam.ca/repertoire/migraciones/media.

Tisselli, Eugenio. *MIDIPoet* (2003). www.motorhueso.net/midipeng/index.htm.

Uribe, Ana María. *Tipoemas y anipoemas* (c. 1967–2002). www.vispo.com/uribe/ index.html.

Vallias, André. *The Verse* (1991). www.andrevallias.com/theverse/theverse.htm.

INDEX

Cambridge Companions to ...

AUTHORS